2003

THE EURODOLLAR FUTURES AND OPTIONS HANDBOOK

Other Titles in the Irwin Library of Investment and Finance

Convertible Securities
by John P. Calamos

Pricing and Managing Exotic and Hybrid Options
by Vineer Bhansali

Risk Management and Financial Derivatives
by Satyajit Das

Valuing Intangible Assets
by Robert F. Reilly and Robert P. Schweihs

Managing Financial Risk
by Charles W. Smithson

High-Yield Bonds
by Theodore Barnhill, William Maxwell, and Mark Shenkman

Valuing Small Business and Professional Practices, 3rd edition
by Shannon Pratt, Robert F. Reilly, and Robert P. Schweihs

Implementing Credit Derivatives
by Israel Nelken

The Handbook of Credit Derivatives
By Jack Clark Francis, Joyce Frost, and J. Gregg Whittaker

The Handbook of Advanced Business Valuation
by Robert F. Reilly and Robert P. Schweihs

Global Investment Risk Management
by Ezra Zask

Active Portfolio Management, 2nd edition
by Richard Grinold and Ronald Kahn

The Hedge Fund Handbook
by Stefano Lavinio

Pricing, Hedging, and Trading Exotic Options
by Israel Nelken

Equity Management
by Bruce Jacobs and Kenneth Levy

Quantitative Business Valuation
by Jay B. Abrams

Asset Allocation, 2nd edition
by Roger Gibson

Valuing a Business, 4th edition
by Shannon Pratt, Robert F. Reilly, and Robert P. Schweihs

The Complete Arbitrage Deskbook
by Stephane Reverre

THE EURODOLLAR FUTURES AND OPTIONS HANDBOOK

GALEN BURGHARDT
Director of Research, Carr Futures
Adjunct Professor of Finance,
University of Chicago Graduate School of Business

McGraw-Hill

New York Chicago San Francisco Lisbon London
Madrid Mexico City Milan New Delhi
San Juan Seoul Singapore
Sydney Toronto

The McGraw-Hill Companies

Library of Congress Cataloging-in-Publication Data

Burghardt, Galen.
The eurodollar futures and options handbook / by Galen Burghardt.
p. cm.
ISBN 0-07-141855-5 (hardcover : alk. paper)
1. Eurodollar market. 2. Futures—United States. 3. Options.
(Finance)—United States. I. Title.
HG3897.B87 2003
332.4'5—dc21

2003000686

3 4 5 6 7 8 9 0 AGM/AGM 0 9 8 7 6 5 4 3

ISBN 0-07-141855-5

This book is printed on recycled, acid-free paper containing a minimum of 50% recycled de-inked fiber.

CONTENTS

List of Exhibits xix
List of Examples xxxi
List of Equations xxxiii
List of Contributors xxxv
Foreword xxxix

PART ONE

THE EMERGENCE OF THE EURODOLLAR MARKET

Chapter 1

The Emergence of the Eurodollar Market 3

The Revolution in Finance 3
The Futures Revolution 5
Key Money Market Developments 6
Why Eurodollars? 9
Eurodollar Futures 11
The Death of CD Futures and the Birth of Eurodollar Futures 16
The Market for Interest Rate Derivatives at the Beginning of the 21st Century 17
Exchange-Traded Money Market Futures and OTC Interest Rate Swaps 18
Options on Futures, Forward Rates, and Swaps 19
Markets around the World 20

PART TWO

BUILDING BLOCKS: EURODOLLAR FUTURES

Chapter 2

The Eurodollar Time Deposit 23

Maturities and Settlement 23
Quotes 25
LIBOR and LIBID 25
Interest Calculations 25

Chapter 3

The Eurodollar Futures Contract 29

Contract Specifications 30
Contract Unit 30
Price Quote 30
Tick Size 30
Minimum Fluctuation 30
Listed Contract Months 30
Contract Month Symbols 32
Color-Coded Grid 32
Expiring versus Lead Contract 33
Trading Hours and Mutual Offset 34
Final Settlement Price 34
Last Trading Day 35
Value Dates 36
Additional Trading Facilities 36
Initial and Maintenance Performance Bonds 37
Volume and Open Interest 38
Other 3-Month Money Market Futures Contracts 39

Chapter 4

Forward and Futures Interest Rates 43

Deriving a Forward Rate from Two Term Deposit Rates 44
Locking an Effective Forward Lending Rate Using Eurodollar Futures 49
Important Differences between Forward and Futures Markets 53
Determining the Fair Value of a Eurodollar Futures Contract 54
Richness and Cheapness 57
Forward Rates Are Break-Even Rates 59
Yield Curve Trades 63
Finding the Forward Term Deposit Curve Implied by Today's Futures Rates 65

Chapter 5

Hedging with Eurodollar Futures 69

The Tool Is a Eurodollar Futures Contract 70

Basic Hedge Algebra 70

Deriving Present and Forward Values from Eurodollar Futures Rates 71

Calculating a Forward Value (Terminal Wealth) 72

Calculating a Zero-Coupon Bond Price (Present Value) 72

Hedging or Replicating Forward Cash Flows 74

Forward Valuing the Gain or Loss on the Eurodollar Futures Contract 75

Present Valuing the Gain or Loss on a Floater 77

Hedging or Replicating Present Values of Cash Flows 78

Calculating the Price of a Zero-Coupon Bond 78

Calculating the Present Value of a Basis Point 78

Finding the Hedge for a Zero-Coupon Bond 80

Faster Hedge Ratio Calculations with Calculus 80

Pricing and Hedging a Coupon-Bearing Bond 82

Managing Hedge Ratios 85

As Rates Rise or Fall 85

As Time Passes 86

Practical Considerations in Real Hedges 87

The Stub Period 88

Date and Term Mismatches 91

Whole Contracts 93

Credit Spreads 93

Variable Credit Spreads 93

Chapter 6

Pricing and Hedging a Swap with Eurodollar Futures 95

Fixed/Floating Interest Rate Swaps 96

Notional Principal Amount 96

Cash Flows in Arrears 97

Periodicity 97

Spot and Forward-Starting Swaps 98

Day-Count Conventions and Swap Yields 98

Approaches to Pricing and Hedging Interest Rate Swaps 100
Cash Flow Approach 101
Hypothetical Security Approach 101
Pricing a Swap Using the Cash Flow Method 101
Hedging a Swap Using the Cash Flow Method 106
Primary Effects 107
Secondary Effects 109
Calculating Hedge Ratios 109
Hedge Ratios Are Dynamic 111
Pricing a Swap Using the Hypothetical Securities Method 111
Hedging a Swap Using the Hypothetical Securities Method 112
Floating Rate Liability 112
Fixed Rate Asset 113
Find the Hedge Ratios 114
Pricing and Hedging Off-the-Market Swaps 116
Convexity Differences between Forward and Futures Rates 117
Comparing Three Yield Curves: Forward, Zero Coupon, and Par Coupon 125
The Difference between Money Market Rates and Bond Yields 127

PART THREE

EURODOLLAR FUTURES APPLICATIONS

Convexity Bias (Chapters 7 through 10) 131
Term TED Spreads (Chapters 11 and 12) 132
Hedging and Trading with Eurodollar Stacks, Packs, and Bundles (Chapter 13) 133
Hedging Extension Risk in Callable Agency Notes (Chapter 14) 133
Opportunities in the S&P Calendar Roll (Chapter 15) 134
Trading the Turn (Chapters 16 and 17) 134

Chapter 7

The Convexity Bias in Eurodollar Futures 135
Galen Burghardt and William Hoskins
Research note originally released September 16, 1994

Synopsis 135
Introduction 137

Interest Rate Swaps and Eurodollar Futures 137
A Forward Swap 138
The Value of a Basis Point 140
Eurodollar Futures 140
Reconciling the Difference in Cash Flow Dates 141
Hedging the Forward Swap with Eurodollar Futures 142
The Other Source of Interest Rate Risk in the Forward Swap 143
Interaction between the Two Sources of Risk 143
Trading the Hedge 147
How Much Is the Convexity Bias Worth? 147
How Correlated Are the Rates? 148
Estimating the Value of the Convexity Bias 149
Calculating the Value of the Bias 150
Reconciling the Difference between a Swap and a Eurodollar Futures Contract 152
How One Would Pay for the Advantage 153
Translating the Advantage into Basis Points 154
A Workable Rule of Thumb 154
Applying the Rule of Thumb 155
The Importance of Time to Contract Expiration 158
The Cumulative Effect of All This Drift 159
How Sensitive Are the Estimates to the Assumptions? 160
Practical Considerations in Applying the Rule 166
The Importance of the Bias for Pricing Term Swaps 166
Biases in Forward Swap Rates 168
The Market's Experience with the Convexity Bias 169
Now What? 170
Running a Receive Fixed, Pay Floating Swap Book 170
Marking a Swap Book to Market 170
Volatility Arbitrage 171
Evaluating Term TED Spreads 171

APPENDIX A

Deriving the Rule of Thumb 172

APPENDIX B

Calculating Eurodollar Strip Rates and Implied Swap Rates 175

Chapter 8

Convexity Bias Report Card 179
Galen Burghardt, William Hoskins, and Niels Johnson
Research note originally released April 15, 1997

What Is the Convexity Bias? 179
How Have We Done? 180
Convexity Bias Greeks 181
Convexity Bias Delta 181
Convexity Bias Vega 183
Convexity Bias Theta 183

Chapter 9

New Convexity Bias Series 185
Galen Burghardt and Lianyan Liu
Research note originally released February 1, 2002

Chapter 10

Convexity Bias: An Update 189

Chapter 11

Measuring and Trading Term TED Spreads 195
Galen Burghardt, William Hoskins, and Susan Kirshner
Research note originally released July 26, 1995

Synopsis 195
TED Spreads 196
Simple TED Spreads 197
Term TED Spreads 198
Two Kinds of Term TED Spreads 199
Unweighted Eurodollar Strip Yields versus Treasury Yields 199
Weighted Eurodollar Strip Yields versus Treasury Yields 200
Implied Eurodollar Yield versus Treasury Yield 200
Fixed Basis Point Spread to Eurodollar Futures Rates 201
How Do These Rates Compare? 201
How Directional Is the Spread? 204
Trading the Spreads 206
Hedge Ratios 207

What to Do with the Stub 209
Overnight Financing 209
Term Financing 209
Carry and Convergence 210
Convexity 211
Forward Term TED Spreads 211
Term TED Spreads and Swap Spreads 212

APPENDIX

Complete Operating Instructions for Calculating Term TED Spreads and Hedge Ratios 216

Chapter 12

TED Spreads: An Update 243

Chapter 13

Hedging and Trading with Eurodollar Stacks, Packs, and Bundles 249
Galen Burghardt, George Panos, and Fred Sturm
Research note originally released December 15, 1999

Synopsis 249
Three Objectives 250
How Good Are Stack, Pack, and Bundle Hedges? 250
Curve-Augmented TED Spreads? 251
Hedging and Trading with Eurodollar Stacks, Packs, and Bundles 251
Basics: Dates, Names, Packs, Bundles, and Quotes 252
Contract Colors 252
Packs and Bundles 254
Quote Practices 1: Ticks 257
Quote Practices 2: Use Price Level for Individual Contracts 258
Quote Practices 3: Use Price Changes for Packs and Bundles 259
Unpacking Packs, Unbundling Bundles 260
Hedging with Stacks, Packs, and Bundles 263
What Happens to the Correlations? 264
Best Pack Proxies for Key Treasury Maturities 267
Horizon Matters 268
The Dangers of Decorrelation 269

Scaling Your Hedges to Reduce Hedge Error 271
Trading Curve TEDs 272
Calculating the Hybrid Spread 274
Looking for Opportunities 277

Chapter 14

Hedging Extension and Compression Risk in Callable Agency Notes 281
Galen Burghardt and William Hoskins
Research note originally released March 24, 1995

Synopsis 281
Introduction 282
What Is the Exposure in a Callable Agency Issue? 284
Extension and Compression Risk 285
A Packaged Deal 285
What Is the Package Worth? 285
What Is the Risk Exposure? 286
Structuring a Hedge 286
The Option Is Tougher 286
Focus on Delta Hedging 287
Synthetic Forward Notes 288
Different Deltas 290
Example of Hedging a 10-Year, 8.5 Percent Coupon Note, Callable in 5 Years 291
Step 1: Find the Price of the Forward Note 292
Step 2: Find the Embedded Option's Delta 295
Step 3: Calculate Spot Market Hedge Ratios 297
Step 4: Calculate Futures Hedge Ratios 297
Step 5: Adjust the Hedge as Interest Rates Change 298
The Costs and Risks of Delta Hedging 299
Risks in the Hedge 300
The Yield Spread between Agencies and Treasurys 301
What If There Is Little or No Call Protection? 303
Sometimes Strips of Eurodollar Futures Provide Better Hedges 306
Netting Positions 307
Adjusting the Hedges 308

Chapter 15

Opportunities in the S&P 500 Calendar Roll 311

Galen Burghardt and George Panos
Research note originally released June 7, 1999

Synopsis 311
Save 15 Basis Points per Year on the Roll 311
Eliminate Interest Rate Risk in the Roll 313
Earn Superior Money Market Returns 313
The Value of the Calendar Spread 313
Fair Value of the Spread 314
Implied Financing Rate 314
How the Calendar Spread Has Behaved 316
What Is Your Exposure to Interest Rates? 317
Handling Rate Exposure in the Roll 317
Hedging against Interest Rate Risk 320
Cash Management and Portfolio Replication 320

Chapter 16

Trading the Turn: 1993 323

Galen Burghardt, Mike Bagatti, and Kevin Ferry
Research note originally released October 25, 1993

Synopsis 323
What Is "the Turn"? 325
Two-Day Turns 325
Three-Day Turns 325
Four-Day Turns 325
Rate Behavior around the Turn 326
Effects on Eurodollar and LIBOR Futures Prices 328
Rule of Thumb for a 4-Day Turn 330
Rule of Thumb for a 3-Day Turn 330
Rule of Thumb for a 2-Day Turn 331
Implied Turn Rates 332
Implications for Futures Spreads 333
December LED Spread 333
December/January LIBOR Spread 333

December/March Eurodollar Spread 334
December TED Spread 334
Effect of the Turn on LIBOR and Eurodollar Volatilities 335
Theoretical Turn Volatility Premiums 338
So What? 338
The Risks in the Trade 341

Chapter 17

The Turn: An Update 343

Hedging the Stub 343

PART FOUR

BUILDING BLOCKS: EURODOLLAR OPTIONS

Chapter 18

The Eurodollar Option Contract 351

Option Expirations and Underlying Futures 351
Standard Quarterly Options 352
Serial Options 352
Mid-curve Options 352
Five-Year Bundle Options 355
Option Contract Specifications 355
Contract Unit 355
Price Quote 355
Tick Size 357
Minimum Fluctuation 357
Strike Price Increments 357
Listed Contract Months 358
Contract Type and Month Symbols 359
Sample Option Quotes 360
Trading Hours 360
Last Trading Day 360
Exercise of Option 360
Assignment 362

Chapter 19

Price, Volatility, and Risk Parameter Conventions 363

Pricing Options on Futures 363
Option Price (Market) 365
Volatility 365
Relative Rate Volatility 366
Rate (Basis Point) Volatility 368
Period Volatility 368
Implied Volatility 370
Risk Parameters 371
Delta 372
Gamma 372
Vega 372
Theta 373
Rho 373
Intrinsic and Time Value 374

Chapter 20

Caps, Floors, and Eurodollar Options 375

Chapter 21

Structure and Patterns of Eurodollar Rate Volatility 381

Historical, Implied, Realized, and Break-Even Volatilities 381
Term Structure of Eurodollar Rate Volatility 386
Volatility Calendar Spread Trade 389
Yield Curve Trade 389
Maturity Structure of Volatility (Volatility Cones) 390
Volatility Skews 393
Implied Rate Distributions 395

Chapter 22

Practical Considerations 399

Early Exercise 399
Cash Settlement and Exercise 400

PART FIVE

EURODOLLAR OPTION APPLICATIONS

Trading with Serial and Mid-curve Eurodollar Options (Chapters 23 and 24) 403

What Happens to Eurodollar Volatility when Rates Fall? (Chapters 25 and 26) 404

Hedging Convexity Bias (Chapter 27) 404

Chapter 23

Trading with Serial and Mid-curve Eurodollar Options 405

Galen Burghardt and Scott Lyden

Research note originally released June 22, 1998

Synopsis 405

Eurodollar Strategy Triangle 406

FOMC and Other Volatility Trades 407

Spreads against OTC Treasury Options 407

LIFFE Joins the Crowd 407

The Full Constellation of Eurodollar Options 407

Standard Quarterly Options 408

Serial Options 408

Mid-curve Options 408

Serial 1-Year Mid-curve Options 409

The Beauty of This Design 409

The Eurodollar Strategy Triangle 410

June/Short June (A Yield Curve Spread) 410

Short June/Red June (A Time Decay Spread) 413

March/Red June (A Volatility Curve Spread) 415

Different Volatility Horizons 417

Mid-curve Options versus OTC Treasury Options 419

Eurodollar/Treasury Volatility Spread Trading 419

How Do You Compare the Volatilities? 421

How Do You Construct the Trades? 424

Some Things to Keep in Mind 424

LIFFE's Options 425

Chapter 24

Serial and Mid-curve Options: An Update 427

Chapter 25

What Happens to Eurodollar Volatility When Rates Fall? 429
Galen Burghardt, George Panos, and Eric Zhang
Research note originally released October 18, 2001

Background 429
Was Volatility Rich or Cheap? 430
Volatility and Rate Levels 430
Why Relative Rate Volatility? 432
What Is the Evidence? 432
Is it the Fed? 433
Practical Consequences 434

Chapter 26

Eurodollar Volatility: An Update 437

Chapter 27

Hedging Convexity Bias 441
Galen Burghardt and George Panos
Research note originally released August 2, 2001

Synopsis 441
- *The Challenges 441*
- *Overcoming the Challenges 442*

Hedging a 4-Year Swap/Eurodollar Position 442
- *Gamma 442*
- *Vega 444*
- *Eurodollar Options 445*
- *Gamma Mismatch? 450*
- *The Choice? 450*
- *Robustness? 450*

GLOSSARY 453

INDEX 463

LIST OF EXHIBITS

PART ONE

THE EMERGENCE OF THE EURODOLLAR MARKET

Chapter 1

The Emergence of the Eurodollar Market

Exhibit 1.1 Milestones in the Development of the Dollar Money Markets 7

Exhibit 1.2 Inflation and 3-Month Treasury Bill Yields (1960 through May 2002) 9

Exhibit 1.3 Growth of the Eurodollar Market: Eurodollars Outstanding (Year-End 1973 through 2001) 10

Exhibit 1.4 CD Futures Volume versus Eurodollar/CD Futures Rate Spread 12

Exhibit 1.5 The Spread between 3-Month CD and Treasury Bill Rates (June 1964 through June 2002) 13

Exhibit 1.6 Average Daily Trading Volume for 3-Month Treasury Bill, Certificate of Deposit, and Eurodollar Futures (1976 through 2001) 15

Exhibit 1.7 Global Interest Rate Swaps Outstanding (Converted to U.S. Dollars) 18

Exhibit 1.8 Global versus U.S. Interest Rate Swaps Outstanding (Converted to U.S. Dollars) 19

Exhibit 1.9 Exchanges That Trade Money Market Futures 20

PART TWO

BUILDING BLOCKS: EURODOLLAR FUTURES

Chapter 2

The Eurodollar Time Deposit

Exhibit 2.1 Eurodollar Deposit Rates (Monday, June 17, 2002) 24

Chapter 3

The Eurodollar Futures Contract

Exhibit 3.1 Eurodollar Futures Contract Specifications 31

Exhibit 3.2 Contract Month Symbols 33

Exhibit 3.3 Bloomberg EDSF Function (Prices for June 17, 2002) 34

Exhibit 3.4 Contract Year Color Grid (As of June 12, 2002) 35

Exhibit 3.5 How Eurodollar Futures Work 37
Exhibit 3.6 Eurodollar Futures Volume and Open Interest (1982 through June 2002) 38
Exhibit 3.7 Bond and Eurodollar Futures Open Interest by Contract (Year-End 2001) 39
Exhibit 3.8 Other 3-Month Money Market Futures Contract Specifications 40

Chapter 4

Forward and Futures Interest Rates

Exhibit 4.1 Eurodollar Futures Prices and Rates (June 17, 2002) 45
Exhibit 4.2 Eurodollar Deposit Rates (Monday, June 17, 2002) 48
Exhibit 4.3 Key Differences between Forward and Futures Markets 52
Exhibit 4.4 Are Futures Rich or Cheap? (June 17, 2002) 58
Exhibit 4.5 Is Term LIBOR Rich or Cheap? (June 17, 2002) 59
Exhibit 4.6 Return by Contract for Simple Buy and Hold Strategies (Mean of Return, Standard Deviation of Return, Sharpe Ratio) 64
Exhibit 4.7 Eurodollar Futures Prices and Rates (Monday, June 17, 2002) 67
Exhibit 4.8 Spot and Forward-Starting Term Rates (June 17, 2002) 67

Chapter 5

Hedging with Eurodollar Futures

Exhibit 5.1 Terminal Wealths and Zero-Coupon Bond Prices (June 17, 2002) 73
Exhibit 5.2 Effect of Rate Changes on the Value of the $100 Million 1-Year Zero 79
Exhibit 5.3 Pricing a 2-Year, 5% Coupon Bond (June 17, 2002) 83
Exhibit 5.4 Number of Eurodollar Futures Needed to Hedge $1 Million Par Amount Zero (June 17, 2002) 84
Number of Eurodollar Futures Needed to Hedge $100 Million Par Amount 5% Semiannual Coupon Bond (June 17, 2002) 84
Exhibit 5.5 Number of Eurodollar Futures Needed to Hedge the Cost of Borrowing $100 Million for 91 Days (June 17, 2002) 86
Exhibit 5.6 Constructing Terminal Wealths and Zero Prices Using a Stub Rate (Trade Date = Thursday, July 18, 2002) (Value Date for Stub Rate = Monday, July 22, 2002) 89

Exhibit 5.7 Correlation between Weekly Changes in Lead Eurodollar Futures Rates and Spot LIBOR (January 1997 through July 2002) 90

Exhibit 5.8 Interpolating Terminal Wealths (July 18, 2002) 92

Chapter 6

Pricing and Hedging a Swap with Eurodollar Futures

Exhibit 6.1 1-Year Fixed/Floating Interest Rate Swap with Quarterly Payments 102

Exhibit 6.2 Eurodollar Futures Prices, Terminal Wealths, and Zero-Coupon Bond Prices (June 17, 2002) 103

Exhibit 6.3 Eurodollar Futures Rates vs. Swap Fixed Rate (June 17, 2002) 104

Exhibit 6.4 Net Cash Flows and Present Values for a 1-Year Receive Fixed/Pay Floating Interest Rate Swap (Fixed Rate = 2.40670876%) 105

Exhibit 6.5 Hedging the Swap's Cash Flows (June 17, 2002) 108

Exhibit 6.6 Swap Hedge Based on the Cash Flow Method Effect of a 1-Basis-Point Increase in Each Futures Rate (June 17, 2002) 110

Exhibit 6.7 Swap Hedge Based on the Hypothetical Securities Method Effect of a 1-Basis-Point Increase in Each Futures Rate (June 17, 2002) 115

Exhibit 6.8 Hedge for Below-the-Market Swap (0.4067%) Effect of a 1-Basis-Point Increase in Each Futures Rate (June 17, 2002) 118

Hedge for Above-the-Market Swap (4.4067%) Effect of a 1-Basis-Point Increase in Each Futures Rate (June 17, 2002) 119

Exhibit 6.9 Convexity Characteristics of a Non-Callable Bond 120

Exhibit 6.10 Estimating the Convexity Bias between Futures and Forward Rates (June 17, 2002) 121

Exhibit 6.11 Eurodollar Futures and Swap Convexity Bias (June 17, 2002) 122

Exhibit 6.12 Convexity Bias by Futures Contract and Swap Maturity (June 17, 2002) 124

Exhibit 6.13 Three Yield Curves: Futures, Zero Coupon, and Par Coupon (June 17, 2002) 126

Exhibit 6.14 Three Yield Curves: Futures, Zero Coupon, and Par Coupon (June 17, 2002) 128

PART THREE

EURODOLLAR FUTURES APPLICATIONS

Chapter 7

The Convexity Bias in Eurodollar Futures

Exhibit 7.1	Convexity Bias (June 13, 1994) 136
Exhibit 7.2	Structure of Eurodollar Futures Rates (June 13, 1994) 139
Exhibit 7.3	Cash Consequences of a Change in a Forward Rate 141
Exhibit 7.4	Swap and Eurodollar Futures P/Ls 145
Exhibit 7.5	The Convexity Difference between Swaps and Eurodollar Futures 146
Exhibit 7.6	Net P/Ls for a Receive Fixed/Pay Floating Swap Hedged with Short Eurodollar Futures 148
Exhibit 7.7	Changes in 5-Year Term Rates versus Changes in the 4-3/4 Year Futures Rate In Basis Points (Weekly Interval, 7/10/92 through 7/1/94) 149
Exhibit 7.8	Hedge P/L for a 3-Month Swap 1-3/4 Years Forward (Weekly Gains per Futures Contract, 1/5/90 through 7/1/94) 151
Exhibit 7.9	Hedge P/L for a 3-Month Swap 4-3/4 Years Forward (Weekly Gains per Futures Contract, 7/10/92 through 7/1/94) 152
Exhibit 7.10	Calculating the Value of the Convexity Bias 156
Exhibit 7.11	Standard Deviation of Eurodollar Futures Rate Changes (Annualized) 160
Exhibit 7.12	Standard Deviation of Term Yield Changes 161
Exhibit 7.13	Correlation of Eurodollar Rates and Term Rates 161
Exhibit 7.14	Eurodollar and Swap Convexity Bias (June 13, 1994) 163
	Convexity Adjusted Swap Yields 164
Exhibit 7.15	Convexity Bias in Forward Swaps (bp) 168
Exhibit 7.16	Spreads between Market and Implied Swap Yields 169

Chapter 8

Convexity Bias Report Card

Exhibit 8.1	Eurodollar/Swap Convexity Adjustments (Theoretical vs. Market) 180
Exhibit 8.2	Eurodollar Convexity Bias Greeks (April 14, 1997) 182
Exhibit 8.3	Convexity Bias Greeks for Swaps (April 14, 1997) 183

Chapter 9

New Convexity Bias Series

Exhibit 9.1 Eurodollar Futures Rates (January 4, 2001, and January 4, 2002) 186

Eurodollar Futures Implied Volatilities (January 4, 2001, and January 4, 2002) 186

Exhibit 9.2 Convexity Bias Values for 5-Year Swaps (January 26, 1996, through December 31, 2001) 187

Convexity Bias Values for 10-Year Swaps (January 26, 1996, through December 31, 2001) 187

Chapter 10

Convexity Bias: An Update

Exhibit 10.1 Daily Zero to Ten 190

Chapter 11

Measuring and Trading Term TED Spreads

Exhibit 11.1 History of the TED Spread, 1970–1995 (3-Month LIBOR Less 3-Month Treasury Bill Rate) 197

Exhibit 11.2 2-Year Term TED 198

Exhibit 11.3 Term TED Spreads (June 5, 1995) 202

Exhibit 11.4 5-Year Term TED Spreads (September 1993 through May 1995) 202

Exhibit 11.5 Effect of Yield Curve Slope on the Difference between Unweighted and Weighted TED Spreads (5-Year) 203

Exhibit 11.6 2-Year TED Spread versus 2-Year Note Yield (1989 through 1995) 205

Exhibit 11.7 Change in 2-Year Term TED Spread versus Change in 2-Year Treasury Yield (Monthly Intervals, May 1989 through May 1995) 206

Exhibit 11.8 Eurodollar Futures Hedge Ratios for a 2-Year Term TED ($100 Million of the 6-1/8s of 5/31/97) 207

Exhibit 11.9 Forward Term TED Spreads (Implied Eurodollar/Treasury Spreads for June 5, 1995) 212

Exhibit 11.10 2-Year versus 5-Year Term TED Spreads 213

2×5 Forward Term TED 213

Exhibit 11.11 Eurodollar Hedge for a 2×5 Term TED Spread (June 5, 1995) 214

Exhibit 11.12 Components of the Term TED Spread (June 5, 1995) 215

Exhibit 11.13 Parsing the 5-Year Term TED Spread (Basis Points) 216
Exhibit 11.A1 Terminal Wealths and Discount Factors (June 5, 1995) 218
Exhibit 11.A2 Time Line 1: Calculating a Spot Stub Rate 220
Exhibit 11.A3 Time Line 2: Calculating a Discount Factor for a Particular Cash Flow 221
Exhibit 11.A4 Interpolating Terminal Wealths 223
Exhibit 11.A5 Time Line 3: Tracking the Cash Flows on a Treasury Note 225
Exhibit 11.A6 TED Spread: Eurodollar Strip Rate versus Treasury Yield 227
Exhibit 11.A7 TED Spread: Implied Eurodollar Yield versus Treasury Yield 229
Exhibit 11.A8 TED Spread: Fixed Spread to Eurodollar Rates 231
Exhibit 11.A9 Forward Term TED Spread 233
Exhibit 11.A10 Hedge Ratios for TED Spread Trades ($100 Million of the 6-1/8s of 5/31/97) (Trade June 5, 1995, Settle June 6, 1995) 237
Exhibit 11.A11 Hedge Ratios: Fixed Spread against Eurodollar Rates 239

Chapter 12

TED Spreads: An Update

Exhibit 12.1 2-Year Note TED Spreads (Plus Forward TEDs to September 18, 2002) (September 10, 2002) 244
Exhibit 12.2 TED Spreads (Plus Forward TEDs to December 18, 2002) (September 10, 2002) 246

Chapter 13

Hedging and Trading with Eurodollar Stacks, Packs, and Bundles

Exhibit 13.1 Treasury Note Correlations with ED Packs (June 1994 to June 1999) 250
Exhibit 13.2 Eurodollar Hedges for a 2-Year Note (5-1/2s of 7/31/01 as of August 4, 1999) 251
Exhibit 13.3 Eurodollar Futures Contract Rates (Closing Levels, August 4, 1999) 253
Exhibit 13.4 Contracts by Color (August 4, 1999) 254
Exhibit 13.5 The Menu of Eurodollar Bundles 256

Exhibit 13.6 Best Pack and Bundle Hedges (2-Year Note, 5-Year Note, and 10-Year Note) 265
Exhibit 13.7 Best Single Contract, Pack, and Bundle Hedges 266
Exhibit 13.8 Treasury Note Correlations with Eurodollar Packs (Daily Price Changes, June 1994 to June 1999) 267
Exhibit 13.9 Hedge Horizon and Best Hedges 268
Exhibit 13.10 Short-Term versus Long-Term Correlation between Price Changes in 5-Year Treasurys and First White 5-Year Bundle (Daily, June 14, 1994 to June 14, 1999) 269
Exhibit 13.11 The Consequences of Decorrelation: Errors from DV01-Hedging OTR 5-Year Treasury Note with First White 5-Year Bundle (Daily, June 14, 1994 to June 14, 1999) 270
Exhibit 13.12 Volatility of Daily Changes in ED Contract Rates and Term TED Yields (Standard Deviations, Mid-1994 to Mid-1999) 272
Exhibit 13.13 Scaled Hedges for a 2-Year Treasury Note (5-5/8s of 9/30/01 as of October 27, 1999, Daily Standard Deviation = $227,618) 273
Exhibit 13.14 Deconstructing a Curve TED Spread 274
Exhibit 13.15 The Curve Trade Implied by a Red Pack Hedge for a 2-Year Treasury Note 275
Exhibit 13.16 Calculating the Curve Spread 276
Exhibit 13.17 Curve Exposure 277
Exhibit 13.18 Generic Eurodollar Curve Spreads 278
Exhibit 13.19 Augmenting a 2-Year TED Spread 279

Chapter 14

Hedging Extension and Compression Risk in Callable Agency Notes

Exhibit 14.1 Callable Agency Yield Spread over 10-Year Treasury (Yield Spread in Basis Points) 282
Exhibit 14.2 Structure of a Callable Agency Security (10-Year Note That Cannot Be Called During the First 5 Years of Its Life) 283
Exhibit 14.3 Standard Maturities and Call Features 283
Exhibit 14.4 Components of Risk in a Callable Note (10-Year Note, Callable in 5 Years) 286
Exhibit 14.5 Constructing a Synthetic Forward Note 289
Exhibit 14.6 Alternative Hedges for a 10-Year Note Callable in 5 Years (Call Option's Delta = 0.5) 289
Exhibit 14.7 Delta Hedges for $10 Million of a Callable Agency Note (10-Year Maturity, Callable in 5 Years) 291

Exhibit 14.8 How to Price a Forward Note 292
Exhibit 14.9 Callable Agency Hedge: 10-Year Callable in 5 (Trade January 20, 1995, Settlement January 30, 1995) 293
Exhibit 14.10 Callable Agency Yield Spread over 10-Year Treasury (8.5 Percent Coupon, 10-Year Callable in 5) (Yield Spread in Basis Points) 302
Exhibit 14.11 Value of American Option versus European Options 304
Exhibit 14.12 European Call Option Values (No Call Protection) 305
Exhibit 14.13 European Call Option Values (5 Years of Call Protection) 306
Exhibit 14.14 Hedging with Eurodollar Futures (3-Year Callable Note with 2 Years of Call Protection) 307
Exhibit 14.15 Hedging with Eurodollar Futures (3-Year Callable Note with No Call Protection) 309

Chapter 15

Opportunities in the S&P 500 Calendar Roll

Exhibit 15.1 Average S&P 500 Futures Calendar Spreads (First Deferred – Lead) versus Business Days to Lead Contract Expiry (1Q 1996 through 4Q 1998)
Actual Calendar Spread (Index Points)
Actual Less Theoretical Spread (Index Points)
Implied Financing Rate Less Lead ED Rate (bps) 312
Exhibit 15.2 Implied Financing Rate Less Lead ED Rate (1988–1998) 315
Exhibit 15.3 Daily Changes in the Lead ED Futures Rate 318
Exhibit 15.4 Target Fed Funds Rate 318
Exhibit 15.5 Lead ED Futures Rate Less Target Fed Funds Rate (bps) 319

Chapter 16

Trading the Turn: 1993

Exhibit 16.1 LIBOR Futures Calendar Spread (December 1992/January 1993) 324
Exhibit 16.2 Time Line for the 1993 Turn 326
Exhibit 16.3 Fed Funds Behavior around Year-End 327
Exhibit 16.4 How the Turn Fits In 328
Exhibit 16.5 Effect of Turn Rate on the Fair Values of Dec '93 LIBOR and Eurodollar Futures Prices (3-Day Turn) 331
Exhibit 16.6 Implied 1-Month Forward Deposit Rates (September 13, 1993) 332
Exhibit 16.7 LIBOR Futures Calendar Spread (December 1992/January 1993) 335

Exhibit 16.8 LIBOR Futures Calendar Spread (December 1993/January 1994) 336
Exhibit 16.9 Add-on Turn Volatility Premium (3 percent Forward Rate) 337
Exhibit 16.10 Add-on Turn Volatility Premium (6 percent Forward Rate) 337
Exhibit 16.11 LED Volatility Spreads (December 1991 Contracts) 339
Exhibit 16.12 LED Volatility Spreads (December 1992 Contracts) 340
Exhibit 16.13 LED Volatility Spreads (December 1993 Contracts) 341

Chapter 17

The Turn: An Update

Exhibit 17.1 Eurodollar and LIBOR Turn Report 344
Exhibit 17.2 Stub Hedges (Using CBOT Fed Funds Futures) 347

PART FOUR

BUILDING BLOCKS: EURODOLLAR OPTIONS

Chapter 18

The Eurodollar Option Contract

Exhibit 18.1 Grid of Available Options (June 17, 2002, Close of Trading) 353
Exhibit 18.2 Eurodollar Option Contract Specifications 356
Exhibit 18.3 Number of Standard, Serial, Mid-curve, and Bundle Option Contracts 358
Exhibit 18.4 Option Type Symbols 359
Exhibit 18.5 Contract Month Symbols 359
Exhibit 18.6 October '02 1-Year Mid-curve Option Prices 361

Chapter 19

Price, Volatility, and Risk Parameter Conventions

Exhibit 19.1 Pricing Sep '02 Eurodollar Options (Closing Values, June 17, 2002) (Futures = 97.895; Discounting Interest Rate = 1.879%) 364
Exhibit 19.2 Option Pricing Model (Assumed Volatility → Theoretical Price) 365
Exhibit 19.3 Distribution of Rate Changes 366

Exhibit 19.4 Option Pricing Model (Market Price → Implied Volatility) 370

Exhibit 19.5 Summary of Risk Parameters 371

Application of Risk Parameters (For Small Changes in Market Conditions) 371

Chapter 20

Caps, Floors, and Eurodollar Options

Exhibit 20.1 Cap and Eurodollar Put; Floor and Eurodollar Call 376

Exhibit 20.2 Rate Setting on a 2-Year Cap 376

Exhibit 20.3 An Interest Rate Cap Is Like a Eurodollar Put (Put Strike Price = 100 − Cap Rate) 377

Exhibit 20.4 Comparing Eurodollar Puts to an Interest Rate Cap (June 17, 2002) 378

Chapter 21

Structure and Patterns of Eurodollar Rate Volatility

Exhibit 21.1 Summary: Historical, Implied, Realized, and Break-Even Volatilities 382

Exhibit 21.2 Implied versus Historical Eurodollar Volatility (Lead Contract, 1984 through 2002) 383

Exhibit 21.3 Break-Even Volatility 385

Exhibit 21.4 Normalized Historical Eurodollar Basis Point Volatility (1994 through 2002) 387

Normalized Historical Eurodollar Relative Rate Volatility (1994 through 2002) 387

Exhibit 21.5 Basis Point Implied Volatilities for At-the-Money Call Options (June 17, 2002) 388

Exhibit 21.6 Volatility Cones and Histograms (Sep '02 and Dec '02 Quarterly Eurodollar Options) (June 17, 2002) 391

Exhibit 21.7 Volatility Cones and Histograms (Sep '02 and Dec '02 1-Year Mid-curve Eurodollar Options) (June 17, 2002) 392

Exhibit 21.8 Implied Volatilities—Sep '02 Quarterly Eurodollar Options (June 17, 2002) (Sep '02 Futures = 97.895) 394

Exhibit 21.9 Implied Volatility Skew—Sep '02 Quarterly Eurodollar Options (June 17, 2002) (Sep '02 Futures = 97.895) 395

Exhibit 21.10 Implied Distribution of Futures Rates from Market Option Prices (Sep '02 Futures = 97.895) (June 17, 2002) 396

PART FIVE

EURODOLLAR OPTION APPLICATIONS

Chapter 23

Trading with Serial and Mid-curve Eurodollar Options

Exhibit 23.1 Quarterly, Serial, and Mid-curve Eurodollar Options 406

Exhibit 23.2 Vega, Gamma, and Theta (At-the-Money Call) 409

Exhibit 23.3 Risk Parameters of a Curve Steepener (Long 94.375 June '98 Call, Short 94.25 "Short June" '98 Call) 411

Exhibit 23.4 A Curve-Steepening Trade with Eurodollar Options (Long 94.375 June '98 Call, Short 94.25 "Short June" '98 Call) 412

Exhibit 23.5 P/L of a Curve-Steepening Trade at Expiration (Long 94.375 June '98 Call, Short 94.25 "Short June" '98 Call) 413

Exhibit 23.6 P/L for a Delta-Neutral Time Decay Spread 415

Exhibit 23.7 90-Day Historical Eurodollar Volatility (A Cross-sectional View) 416

Exhibit 23.8 Term Structure of Implied Eurodollar Volatility 417

Exhibit 23.9 Timeline of FOMC Meetings 418

Exhibit 23.10 First Eurodollar Rate (Dependent) against OTR 2-Year Treasury Yield (Independent) (April 26, 1996–March 25, 1998; $R^2 = 0.52$) 420

Exhibit 23.11 Fifth Eurodollar Rate (Dependent) against OTR 2-Year Treasury Yield (Independent) (April 26, 1996–March 25, 1998; $R^2 = 0.94$) 421

Exhibit 23.12 TED Spread 422

Exhibit 23.13 Yields of U.S. 5-Year Notes and 5th Eurodollar since June '94 422

Exhibit 23.14 Yield Spread between 5-Year Notes and 5th Eurodollar since June '94 (In Basis Points) 423

Chapter 25

What Happens to Eurodollar Volatility when Rates Fall?

Exhibit 25.1 Key Rate Levels versus Dec '01 Implied Rate Volatility (September 10, 2001, to October 4, 2001) 430

Exhibit 25.2 Eurodollar Volatility Cones (2-Year History as of Close of Business October 4, 2001) 431

Exhibit 25.3 Eurodollar Rate Levels and Basis Point Volatilities (1983 to October 4, 2001) 433

Exhibit 25.4 Eurodollar Rate Levels and Basis Point Volatilities (December 6, 1990, to October 4, 2001) 434

Exhibit 25.5 Relative and Basis Point Rate Volatilities (January through October 2001) 435

Chapter 26

Eurodollar Volatility: An Update

Exhibit 26.1 Volatility Cones and Return Distributions (2-Year History as of September 10, 2002) 438

Chapter 27

Hedging Convexity Bias

Exhibit 27.1 Net Swap/Eurodollar P/L ($100MM 4-Year Receive Fixed Swap/Short Eurodollar Futures Strip) 443

Change in Net DV01 (With Respect to Changes in Eurodollar Futures Rates) 443

Exhibit 27.2 Convexity Bias Value and Vega 444

Exhibit 27.3 Options on Eurodollar Futures (August 1, 2001) 445

Exhibit 27.4 Option and Swap Characteristics (August 1, 2001) 446

Exhibit 27.5 Second Red, Fourth Short, and Second Green Eurodollar Rates As Proxies for a 4-Year Term Rate (Weekly Changes, 1/24/97–6/30/01) 447

Exhibit 27.6 Second Red Eurodollar Implied Volatility As Proxy for Term Swaption Implied Volatility 448

Exhibit 27.7 Second Red, Fourth Short, and Second Green Eurodollar Implied Volatilities As Proxies for Term Swaption Implied Volatility (Weekly Changes, 9/25/98–7/13/01) 449

LIST OF EXAMPLES

PART TWO

BUILDING BLOCKS: EURODOLLAR FUTURES

Chapter 2

The Eurodollar Time Deposit

Example 2.1 Calculate Interest on a 1-Month Eurodollar Deposit 26

Example 2.2 Calculate Interest on a 2-Year Eurodollar Deposit 27

Chapter 4

Forward and Futures Interest Rates

Example 4.1 Find a 3-Month Rate 6 Months Forward 46

Example 4.2 Find a 3-Month Rate 6 Months Forward (Revisited) 49

Example 4.3 Lock the Forward Lending Rate 50

Example 4.4 Compare Forward versus Futures Cash Flows 53

Example 4.5 Calculate the Fair Value of a Eurodollar Futures Contract 55

Example 4.6 Track Date Mismatches between the Cash and Futures Markets 56

Example 4.7 Evaluate the Performance of a "Positive Carry" Trade 59

Example 4.8 Present Value the Cash Flows from Example 4.7 62

Example 4.9 Replicate the Positive Carry Trade with Futures 63

Example 4.10 Find a Forward-Starting Term Deposit Curve 66

Chapter 5

Hedging with Eurodollar Futures

Example 5.1 Convert a Floating Rate Liability into a Fixed Rate Liability 74

Example 5.2 Find the Hedge Amount through Forward Valuing 76

Example 5.3 Find the Hedge Amount through Present Valuing 77

Example 5.4 Price a Coupon Bond 82

Chapter 6

Pricing and Hedging a Swap with Eurodollar Futures

Example 6.1 Swap Basics: An IMM Swap 99

LIST OF EQUATIONS

PART TWO

BUILDING BLOCKS: EURODOLLAR FUTURES

Chapter 2

The Eurodollar Time Deposit

Equation 2.1 Interest on a Eurodollar Term Deposit 26

Chapter 4

Forward and Futures Interest Rates

Equation 4.1 Combine a Short Rate with a Forward Rate to Get a Long Rate 47

Equation 4.2 Calculate a Forward Rate from Long and Short Deposit Rates 48

Chapter 5

Hedging with Eurodollar Futures

Equation 5.1 Hedge Ratio 71

Equation 5.2 Hedge Ratio for Forward Values 71

Equation 5.3 Hedge Ratio for Present Values 71

Equation 5.4 Calculate Terminal Wealth Using Futures Rates 72

Equation 5.5 Calculate the Zero-Coupon Bond Price (Using Terminal Wealth) 74

Equation 5.6 Calculate the Zero-Coupon Bond Price (Using Spot and Futures Rates) 81

Equation 5.7 Calculate a Hedge Ratio Using Calculus 81

Chapter 6

Pricing and Hedging a Swap with Eurodollar Futures

Equation 6.1 Find the 1-Year Swap Net Present Value Using the Cash Flow Method 106

Equation 6.2 Find the Change in the 1-Year Swap NPV Given a Change in Futures 107

Equation 6.3 Find the Eurodollar Futures Hedge Ratios for the Swap 111

PART FOUR

BUILDING BLOCKS: EURODOLLAR OPTIONS

Chapter 19

Price, Volatility, and Risk Parameter Conventions

Equation 19.1 One-Day Relative Rate Change 367
Equation 19.2 Annualized Volatility 367
Equation 19.3 One-Day Rate Change 368
Equation 19.4 Calculate Period Standard Deviations from Annualized Volatility 369
Equation 19.5 Basis Point Volatility over Time Period t 370

Chapter 21

Structure and Patterns of Eurodollar Rate Volatility

Equation 21.1 Calculate Period Standard Deviations from Annualized Volatility 384
Equation 21.2 The Relationship between Gamma, Theta, and Realized Volatility 386

LIST OF CONTRIBUTORS

Mike Bagatti is Vice President for Carr Futures where he heads the Eurodollar options desk on the floor of the CME. Before joining Carr Futures, he served in the same capacity with Dean Witter Institutional Futures and Discount Corporation of New York Futures.

Terry Belton is Managing Director and head of U.S. fixed income strategy at J.P. Morgan. He also serves as global head of derivatives strategy. He was formerly Director of Research for Discount Corporation of New York Futures, a Senior Economist at Freddie Mac, and an Economist at the Federal Reserve Board in Washington, D.C. Terry is also Adjunct Professor at the University of Chicago and is co-author of *The Treasury Bond Basis* (McGraw-Hill, 1994) and *Eurodollar Futures and Options: Controlling Money Market Risk* (McGraw-Hill, 1991). Terry received a Ph.D. in economics from the University of Michigan in 1983.

Galen Burghardt is Senior Vice President and Director of Research for Carr Futures. He is also Adjunct Professor of Finance at the University of Chicago Graduate School of Business. His research career includes stints with Dean Witter Institutional Futures, Discount Corporation of New York Futures, the Chicago Mercantile Exchange, and the Research Division of the Federal Reserve Board. He holds a B.S. and Ph.D. in economics from the University of Washington. He is the lead author of *The Treasury Bond Basis* (McGraw-Hill, 1994) and *Eurodollar Futures and Options: Controlling Money Market Risk* (McGraw-Hill, 1991).

Kevin Ferry is Vice President and a futures broker for Commerzbank Futures and was First Vice President at Carr Futures when he contributed to the research in this book. He holds a B.A. in economics from John Carroll University.

William Hoskins, Ph.D., is the Director of Fixed Income Research at Mellon Capital Management. His research focuses on enhancing bond portfolio returns by combining rich-cheap valuation models with futures and options to control risk. His experience in fixed income markets includes research positions with Dean Witter Institutional Futures and Barclays Global Investors. He received his doctorate in finance from the University of Chicago.

Niels Johnson is a Fixed Income Research Officer and Principal at Barclays Global Investors currently developing active credit selection strategies for pension and hedge funds. Niels began his career in fixed income research at Merrill Lynch in 1990 later working at Barra and Nomura. He had the great privilege of working for and learning from Galen Burghardt at Dean Witter for several years.

Susan Kirshner is a Director of Business Development at Ritchie Capital Management. She was Vice President with Dean Witter Institutional Futures when she assisted with the research notes incorporated in this book. Since that time she has worked with OTC instruments and risk management issues at the Bank of Montreal and Arthur Andersen. She received her M.B.A. in finance and marketing from Northwestern University's Kellogg Graduate School of Management and a B.S. in computer science engineering from the University of Illinois.

Morton Lane is President of Lane Financial, LLC, a broker-dealer engaged in consulting and transaction activity in securitization and reinsurance. Prior to starting his own firm in reinsurance risk management, Morton held leadership positions in financial futures and options at Bear Stearns and Discount Corporation of New York Futures, among others. Morton is a prominent speaker and writer on insurance and securitization. In 1999 he was awarded the Reinsurance Broking Initiative of the Year by The Review and in 2001 he was awarded the Charles A. Hachemeister Prize by the Casualty Actuarial Society for his work on pricing. In 2002 he produced *Alternative Risk Strategies*, an edited volume about insurance securitization, and has co-authored two books, *The Treasury Bond Basis* (Probus, 1989) and *Eurodollar Futures and Options: Controlling Money Market Risk* (McGraw-Hill, 1991). Morton earned his B.Soc.Sc. from Birmingham University, and his Ph.D. in mathematics, business administration and computer science from the University of Texas at Austin.

Lianyan Liu is Quantitative Financial Analyst with Carr Futures. He holds a B.S. in nuclear physics from Fudan University in Shanghai, China, and a Ph.D. in nuclear engineering from North

Carolina State University. Before joining Carr, he did research on radiation transport modeling and its application in oil exploration, and radiotherapy physics.

Geoffrey Luce is currently Director and Manager of the Merrill Lynch Eurodollar desk at the Chicago Mercantile Exchange. He has been brokering Eurodollar futures and options for the past 14 years. His contributions to this volume were made when he was part of the brokerage team at Discount Corporation of New York Futures and where he was co-author of *Eurodollar Futures and Options: Controlling Money Market Risk* (McGraw-Hill, 1991). Prior to coming to the floor, he received an M.B.A. from the University of Chicago and an M.Sc. from the London School of Economics.

Scott Lyden was a Vice President at Carr Futures when he performed the research reported in this book. After leaving Carr, he worked on topics in credit risk and corporate bond portfolio management at Barclays Global Investors and ran a quantitative market-neutral equity hedge fund. Lyden holds undergraduate and graduate degrees in economics from the University of Chicago. He is currently taking some time off to play competitive badminton.

Rick McVey is Chief Executive Officer and founder of MarketAxess Corporation. Before founding MarketAxess, Rick was Managing Director and head of Fixed Income Sales at J.P. Morgan where he managed the institutional distribution of corporate, government, mortgage backed, asset backed, structured product and derivative sales to investors. From 1992 to 1996, Rick led J.P. Morgan's North America futures and options group. His contributions to this volume were made while he was with Discount Corporation of New York Futures, where he began his securities career and where he was co-author of *Eurodollar Futures and Options: Managing Money Market Risk* (McGraw-Hill, 1991). He holds an M.B.A. from Indiana University and a B.A. in finance from Miami (Ohio) University.

George Panos is Vice President/Research for Carr Futures, where he conducts courses on futures and options and offers risk management services to clients. Before entering the futures brokerage industry, he brokered bonds, clerked stock at the Chicago Board Options Exchange, and worked on new contract development at the Chicago Board of Trade. He holds a B.S. in business from the University of Illinois at Chicago and an M.B.A. from DePaul University.

Frederick Sturm is Senior Economist at the Chicago Board of Trade, where he designs futures and options contracts. Besides having served in the Research Department of Carr Futures, he was formerly Director of Futures and Options Research for Fuji Securities Inc. and First Vice President of Research for Kleinwort Benson Government Securities. He holds an M.A. and M.Phil. in economics from Columbia University.

Eric Zhang is Quantitative Financial Analyst with Carr Futures. He earned his Ph.D. in physics from the University of Illinois at Chicago and his B.S. from the National Defense University of Science and Technology in China. He is currently an M.B.A. student in the Graduate School of Business at the University of Chicago.

FOREWORD

At a recent conference, I remarked that I felt a little like the Forrest Gump of interest rate futures. One accident after another has placed me in the company of people who have been innovative thinkers and doers in the futures business, and it has been my good fortune that many of them have been willing to work with me. I have, as a result, accumulated a long string of debts to people and would like to take this opportunity to acknowledge them.

First, I would like to express my thanks to Rick Kilcollin, who was a colleague of mine at the Federal Reserve Board in Washington and who, when he became Chief Economist at the Chicago Mercantile Exchange, freed me from a life of bureaucratic strife and brought me to Chicago in 1983. Rick worked with Fred Arditti on the design of the Eurodollar futures contract, and it was through my association with the Exchange membership and work on various Exchange committees that I began to get an appreciation of what this market was all about.

Once in Chicago, I jumped ship in 1986 to work for Morton Lane at Discount Corporation of New York Futures, and it is to Morton that I may well owe the greatest debt. Morton is insatiably curious about the way the world works and believes passionately that research and education provide the most solid foundations for building customer relationships. He also assembled one of the finest futures brokerage teams ever in the history of the business, and he expected all of his senior sales people to be able to think and teach. As a result of his commitment to research and his genius in recruiting, we were able to write and publish the original *Eurodollar Futures and Options* with Probus in 1991. My coauthors on that volume were Terry Belton, Morton Lane, Geoff Luce, and Rick McVey, each of whom brought a host of insights to our understanding of Eurodollar futures and options.

All that remains of the original volume appears here in chapter 1, which recounts the history of the Eurodollar cash and derivatives markets. But the influence of my original coauthors pervades everything. Terry taught me how to solve problems. Morton lived and breathed the markets as they developed. Geoff was the original designer of what we called the "Short End" money market report (which has morphed into the "Daily Zero to Ten" report that you will find later in this book). Rick taught me the practical difference between one-sided arbitrage (shopping for the best price) and two-sided arbitrage (using the bank's balance sheet) and which was more important for keeping cash and futures rates in line with one another.

Soon after the publication of *Eurodollar Futures and Options,* Discount Corporation of New York Futures was sold to Dean Witter, where we became Dean Witter Institutional Futures. It was here that I was able to embark on a string of research projects that produced several of the chapters that make up this book. The really serious work was done at Dean Witter, largely because we were able to hire Bill Hoskins out of the Ph.D. program at the University of Chicago. Bill is one of those living, breathing whizzes who can combine theoretical insight and understanding with views of the world that traders understand.

Perhaps the high point of my career in Eurodollar futures was my work with Bill Hoskins on the value of the convexity bias in (or, as Bill would argue, not in) Eurodollar futures. A lot of people claimed to know something about convexity, and Terry Belton and I had even written a piece called "The Financing Bias in Eurodollar Futures" that covered the same ground in 1989. Even so, it was Bill's particular insight that allowed us to present the problem the way we have in "The Convexity Bias in Eurodollar Futures" (see chapter 7). He combined his theoretical understanding of convexity with the way a trader would think about the problem, and it was this combination that made the research so accessible to the market. Bill also provided the key thinking behind "Measuring and Trading Term TED Spreads" in chapter 11 and "Hedging Extension and Compression Risk in Callable Agency Notes" in chapter 14. I still call him whenever I need help with whatever thorny problem I am wrestling with at the time.

I have learned from and been helped by several other colleagues in research. These include: Niels Johnson, who personifies positive gamma and whose programs still run; Lianyan Liu, who is a blindingly fast thinker and problem solver; Scott Lyden, who brought great insight to our understanding of Eurodollar options; George Panos, who, more than anyone I have known, loves to tackle pricing and hedging questions and has been invaluable in keeping our research grounded in the problems that vex our clients; Fred Sturm, who has a marvelous turn of mind and a visual way with data that is a wonder to behold; and Eric Zhang, who is another blindingly fast thinker and problem solver. I have learned, too, from my colleagues in sales as well. Both Mike Bagatti and Kevin Ferry found themselves pulled into research projects on Eurodollar options and the year-end turn, and I am in debt to them both.

I would like to thank several others for the help they have provided over the years. Jeff Johnson (Carr Futures) has been tireless and faithful in working with data, charts, publication issues, and general all-around work. Steve Youngren (Chicago Mercantile Exchange) was a colleague of mine in research when I arrived there in 1983. He was then and is now part of the corporate memory of the Exchange and is still just as generous with his time and energies as he was then. Celeste Pretzel (Carr Futures) and Sandy Gartler (Carr Futures) helped us with some thorny desktop publishing questions. And Sean Doyle and Sandy Sloane (both of Bank of America) have always been willing to answer questions about the real workings of the swap market.

I have a special affection for the Chicago Mercantile Exchange, and I am happy to say that they seem to have an affectionate regard for me as well. In June 2002 I spoke with Peter Barker, Vice President of Interest Rate Marketing at the CME, about this project and asked him if they could support it. His immediate answer was yes, and at his urging, the CME's support was both generous and immediate. It is my good fortune to know such people and that my friends at the Merc think enough of this work that they were willing to publish the book jointly with McGraw-Hill.

I am grateful, too, for my position at Carr Futures, where I have been director of research for the past six years. Never in my wildest dreams could I have imagined a working life like the one I have now; it has given me the freedom and flexibility to undertake projects like this book. I have enjoyed the complete support of my colleagues, both in research and in sales, and it is only through their support that I have ever been able to get anything done at all.

And last, I would like to thank Susan Kirshner. Susan's contributions are everywhere. She joined me at Discount Futures in 1986 and was a colleague of mine in research for more than ten years. She helped with the original research notes. She wrote code.

She helped teach our classes. She is a co-author of two of the papers that appear in this volume. She prepared the two chapters on contract specifications and the glossary. And it is only because of her extraordinary ability and commitment to this project that *The Eurodollar Futures and Options Handbook* has seen the light of day. Our objective in this book was to create a volume that would combine basic tools with research applications and that would allow us to include our collected research on Eurodollar futures in a single volume. And while the idea was a simple one, its execution was not. Through sheer force of intellect, will, and hard work, Susan has pulled together the separate pieces and imposed a beautiful sense of cohesion and flow on the whole thing. One could not ask for more.

I hope that you enjoy the fruits of our labor.

Galen Burghardt
Chicago
April 2003

PART ONE

The Emergence of the Eurodollar Market

It was my good fortune in 1983 to be hired by Rick Kilcollin, who was Chief Economist at the Chicago Mercantile Exchange and one of the designers of the Eurodollar futures contract. I later went to work for Morton Lane at Discount Corporation of New York Futures. Morton was doing pioneering work in the money markets. Prior to Discount, he had spent time in the investments group at the World Bank and had gained expertise in the swap market.

I arrived in Chicago just about the time Eurodollar futures began to take off. I spent much of my time working with people who not only knew where we had been but who had a remarkable vision about where the world of applied finance might be going. The history of Eurodollar futures that you will find in this section is the collective work of those who were there at the creation and those who had a lot to do with making these contracts a success.

CHAPTER 1

The Emergence of the Eurodollar Market

Galen Burghardt, Terry Belton, Morton Lane, Geoffrey Luce, and Rick McVey

The Eurodollar market—the market for dollar-denominated deposits outside of the United States—is perhaps the largest and most liquid of the world's short-term dollar markets. At the same time, swaps based on the London Interbank Offered Rate (LIBOR) and Eurodollar futures, together with their option counterparts, are without question the most liquid and actively traded money market derivatives. For that matter, the LIBOR-based swap market has become so large and liquid that swap rates have largely displaced government bonds as the standard of value against which fixed income instruments are compared.

Our purpose in this chapter is to provide a thumbnail history of where these markets came from and how they got to be as big as they are.

THE REVOLUTION IN FINANCE

The 1970s, 1980s, and 1990s witnessed a complete transformation in the world of banking and finance. Before 1970, banks did business by accepting short-term deposits at low regulated rates and then offering longer-term business and personal loans at higher rates.

Then came the 1970s and inflation, which forced the banking system to realize two things. First, the high interest rates produced by inflation forced cash out of the regulated deposit market and led to the creation of an active, unregulated money market. If banks were to compete for cash, the shackles of deposit regulation would have to be removed, and in time they were. Second, the steep inversion of the yield curve, which was most extreme during Paul Volcker's first two years as Chairman of the Federal Reserve in 1979 and 1980, forced the banks to face up to the yield curve risk that went with the old model of banking. By the 1980s, cash had become a traded commodity, and banks knew that they had to find ways to manage their interest rate risk.

At the same time, the finance profession was hard at work fanning the flames of revolution. The intellectual offsprings of Markowitz, Modigliani, and Miller produced a great outpouring of new ideas that led to the trading of options on exchanges, the stripping of Treasury bonds into their individual parts, the worldwide integration of money markets, and the market for interest rate derivatives.

Two innovations in applied finance matter most for the readers of this book. First was the idea that each cash flow associated with a coupon-bearing bond not only could, but should, be treated as a zero-coupon bond. This insight allowed financial engineers to look at any given bond as simply a collection of zeros, each of which could be valued separately and consistently. Second was the idea that one could trade the price of a commodity without trading the commodity itself. This insight allowed the market to focus in on price or interest rate risk and to develop interest rate derivatives—swaps, forward rate agreements, and futures on bank deposit rates and government bonds. It was interest rate derivatives that finally allowed bankers to understand their interest rate risk and to manage it cheaply and effectively.

Zero-coupon bonds and interest rate derivatives really took hold in the 1980s, as people learned how to strip the coupons from U.S. Treasury bonds and to reassemble them, and how to unbundle and repackage residential mortgages in the form of mortgage-backed securities.

By the time the 1990s arrived, most of the real thinking and innovation was in place for the revolution in banking and finance to take complete hold. The 1990s were a time of growth, expansion, and consolidation for the interest rate derivatives market. Interest rate swaps in the over-the-counter market and Eurodollar futures in the exchange-traded market grew by leaps and bounds. Moreover, swaps and bank deposit rate futures spread to every major money market in the world. At this writing, swap rates have muscled their way into the center of the fixed income world and have become the interest rates against which nearly all yields are compared. It is now standard practice for every well-run bank to state its interest rate exposure in terms of 3-month Eurodollar futures equivalents.

THE FUTURES REVOLUTION

Such a complete transformation of the world of banking and finance would not have been possible without futures in general and Eurodollar futures in particular.

The futures market pioneered the idea that one could trade the price separately from the commodity itself. Economists have argued for years that a commodity possesses several useful characteristics, only one of which is its price. And once one could trade the price without actually buying or selling the commodity, the costs of hedging and speculating dropped like a stone. The futures market also pioneered a set of risk management practices that have slowly taken hold in other parts of the financial world. The ideas of requiring collateral to guaranty performance, marking positions to market every day, and settling up gains and losses in cash on a regular basis have had a wonderfully tonic effect on risk managers outside of the futures world.

The idea of financial futures took hold in the early 1970s. Although futures had been traded on a wide range of metals and agricultural commodities since the middle of the 19th century in this country, and had a history reaching back several centuries in other parts of the world, the idea of trading futures contracts on things like foreign currencies and interest rates at first struck people as outrageous.

By the early 1980s, however, we were able to trade futures contracts on foreign currencies, stock indexes, government bonds, and Eurodollar bank deposit rates. Of these, perhaps the most important was the Eurodollar contract, without which the interest rate swap market would never have gotten off the ground and grown the way it has. Eurodollar futures are the financial building blocks of the swap market. They provide the rates from which swaps can be priced, and they provide the tools that dealers need to hedge them.

KEY MONEY MARKET DEVELOPMENTS

The Eurodollar market now dominates trading in private short-term money market instruments. This was not always so. For almost two decades, until the early 1980s, certificates of deposit (CDs) issued by U.S. banks played this role.

The seeds of the money market revolution were planted in 1961 when Citibank (then First National City Bank of New York) issued the first CD. This was followed in 1966 with the issuance of the first Eurodollar CD. (See Exhibit 1.1 for a summary of key money market developments.)

The importance of the CD was that it could be traded. Until CDs came along, bank deposits were a sticky kind of liability or asset (depending on whether you were the bank or the depositor). CDs, however, could be bought and sold just like Treasury bills. As a result, banks and depositors could change the shapes of their respective balance sheets at will. The value that depositors placed on the right to trade CDs was reflected in a lower yield than was paid on conventional term deposits.

CD issuance exploded in the 1970s because of the combined forces of inflation and the ceilings placed on bank deposit rates by the Federal Reserve's Regulation Q. Exhibit 1.2 shows the effect of rising inflation on short-term interest rates. The upper limits on the rates banks could pay put banks at a competitive disadvantage in the market for funds.

Large CDs were finally freed from deposit rate regulation, and gave banks a way out. Money market funds became a conduit for placing large CDs in the hands of people who otherwise would have held their liquid assets at banks. Rising inflation throughout the 1970s kept forcing interest rates up, and CDs became a major force in U.S. money markets.

The beginning of the end of the CD market's explosive growth came in 1982. For one thing, the Federal Reserve took a big step in removing regulations from bank deposits by creating money market deposit accounts in December 1982. These new accounts meant that people could get competitive interest rates

EXHIBIT 1.1

Milestones in the Development of the Dollar Money Markets

Year	Event
1961	The first certificate of deposit (CD) is issued by Citibank (then First National City Bank of New York).
1966	The first Eurodollar CD is issued.
1970	The Federal Reserve eliminates interest rate ceilings on large CDs with maturities of less than 3 months.
1972	The first money market fund is created. The Chicago Mercantile Exchange (CME) lists the first financial futures (foreign currencies).
1973	The Federal Reserve eliminates interest rate ceilings on large CDs with maturities past 3 months.
1976	Milton Friedman rings the opening bell for the first money market futures contract, the CME's 3-month Treasury bill futures.
1977	The Chicago Board of Trade (CBOT) lists a 90-day commercial paper contract, which fails.
1978	Money market fund balances reach $10 billion. The CME lists a 1-year Treasury bill futures contract.
1979	Paul Volcker, the Federal Reserve Board Chairman, undertakes his "monetarist experiment," which ushers in a period of extraordinary interest rate volatility and financial turmoil. The CBOT lists a 30-day commercial paper contract, which also fails.
1980	Bank short-term interest rates reach 20 percent after a 10-percentage-point free fall.
1981	The CME, the CBOT, and the New York Futures Exchange all list 3-month CD futures. Citibank arranges the first interest rate swap. The CME lists futures on 3-month Eurodollar time deposit rates.

EXHIBIT 1.1

Continued

Year	Event
1982	The U.S. CD market is rocked by a series of bank problems, including Continental Illinois' withdrawal from the CD market because of its financial woes, and Chase's encounter with Drysdale over defaults in the Treasury repo market. The Federal Reserve effectively deregulates bank deposit rates by creating money market deposit accounts, thereby reducing the demand through money market funds for large CDs. The London International Financial Futures Exchange (LIFFE; now the London International Financial Futures and Options Exchange) lists Eurodollar futures.
1984	The Singapore International Monetary Exchange (SIMEX; now the Singapore Exchange, SGX) lists Eurodollar futures that are directly fungible with the CME's Eurodollar contracts through a system of mutual offset.
1985	The CME lists options on Eurodollar futures.
1989	The CME adds year 4 to Eurodollar futures.
1992	The CME adds year 5 to Eurodollar futures. Eurodollar futures and options begin trading on GLOBEX, the CME's electronic trading system.
1993	The CME adds years 6 through 10 to Eurodollar futures. Mid-curve options begin trading.
1994	The CME introduces bundles as a trading vehicle.
1995	The CME adds packs.
1997	The CME switches from its own survey to the British Bankers' Association (BBA) survey to settle Eurodollar futures.
1998	Options on bundles begin trading.
2002	The CME lists the 7th and 8th quarterly option expirations, thereby extending the original life of an option to 2 years from 18 months.

directly from banks rather than indirectly through money market funds.

For another, the banks that issued CDs were running into serious financial problems that greatly affected the world's per-

EXHIBIT 1.2

Inflation and 3-Month Treasury Bill Yields
1960 through May 2002

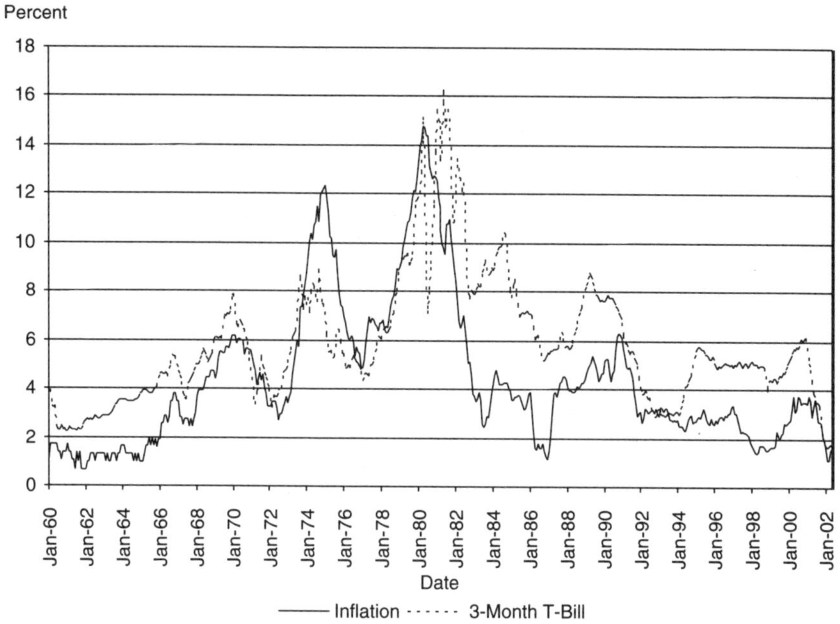

ception of banks' creditworthiness. Continental Illinois, for example, faced huge loan losses on its Mexican debt portfolio and had to withdraw from the domestic CD market in the summer of 1982. Chase Manhattan encountered defaults in the Treasury repo market through its dealings with Drysdale. Until these problems surfaced, the CDs of the top ten U.S. banks had been bought and sold as if they were part of a nearly homogeneous, high-quality pool. Continental's and Chase's problems made it clear that not all CDs were the same, and the secondary market for CDs lost much of its liquidity as a result.

The combined effect of the new money market deposit accounts and the credit problems of various large banks was a huge reduction in the demand for CDs.

WHY EURODOLLARS?

At the same time, the Eurodollar market was moving from strength to strength. As shown in Exhibit 1.3, the Eurodollar mar-

EXHIBIT 1.3

Growth of the Eurodollar Market: Eurodollars Outstanding*
Year-End 1973 through 2001

Year	Eurodollars ($ billions)
1973	182
1974	218
1975	267
1976	328
1977	310
1978	398
1979	509
1980	638
1981	769
1982	806
1983	1,121
1984	1,363
1985	1,254
1986	1,750
1987	2,049
1988	2,268
1989	2,637
1990	2,877
1991	2,807
1992	2,809
1993	2,615
1994	2,891
1995	3,046
1996	3,259
1997	3,897
1998	3,932
1999	3,957
2000	4,512
2001	4,911

* End-of-period dollar liabilities of banks outside the U.S. for countries reporting to the BIS.

Source: Bank for International Settlements.

ket continued to grow even after 1982 when the CD market began to shrink.

The Eurodollar market owes its early success to a variety of forces:

- Eurodollar deposits were always unregulated and therefore were a competitive source of funds during the years before the interest rate ceilings on domestic deposits were lifted by the Federal Reserve.
- Eurodollar deposits were a cheaper source of funds to the extent they were free of reserve requirements and deposit insurance assessments.
- The dollar was becoming the currency of choice for a great number of the world's trade and asset transactions.
- The Soviet Union's international trade dealings required them to hold substantial dollar deposits, but they were unwilling to hold them in banks in the United States.

Reasons for the continued success of the Eurodollar market throughout the 1980s are less clear, but three things stand out.

First, the Eurodollar market escaped the worst of the problems of creditworthiness that had such a depressing effect on the U.S. CD market. Second, money markets were almost completely integrated by the middle of the 1980s, so that banks were nearly indifferent between borrowing domestically or borrowing abroad. This point is illustrated clearly in Exhibit 1.4, which shows that the difference between Eurodollar deposit rates and CD rates was nearly constant by the beginning of 1986. The difference between the two rates represented nothing more than the cost of reserve requirements and deposit insurance. Third, interest rate derivatives such as swaps and caps appeared in the early 1980s and proved to be very successful financial instruments.

EURODOLLAR FUTURES

The Eurodollar futures contract, which today is the most widely traded money market contract in the world, was the product of considerable experimentation. The key events leading up to the listing of the Eurodollar contract are summarized in Exhibit 1.1. To begin, the CME listed futures contracts on foreign currencies

EXHIBIT 1.4

CD Futures Volume versus Eurodollar/CD Futures Rate Spread

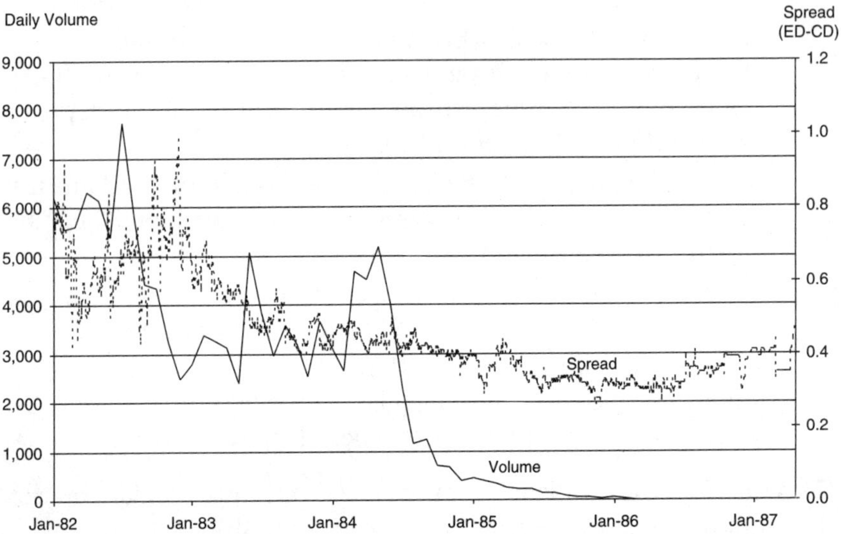

Lead series switches on first day of contract month.
Daily volume is the average over each month for lead contract.

Source: Chicago Mercantile Exchange.

in 1972. These were the first financial futures ever traded. Then, in 1976, the CME listed futures on 3-month Treasury bills. These were the first money market futures ever traded.

The Treasury bill contract proved successful, and the Chicago exchanges as well as the newly formed New York Futures Exchange (NYFE) began to look elsewhere for new products. As shown in Exhibit 1.5, the events surrounding the financial upheavals of 1973 and 1974 proved just how volatile the spread between private money market instruments and Treasury bills could be. In the face of this much volatility in the private money market credit spread, Treasury bill futures could be a very bad hedge for private short-term liabilities.

From this, the futures exchanges concluded that the world could use a futures contract on private short-term obligations. The first effort was the Chicago Board of Trade's (CBOT) contract on 90-day commercial paper, which was listed in 1977. This contract failed, largely because 90-day commercial paper was not a suffi-

EXHIBIT 1.5

The Spread between 3-Month CD and Treasury Bill Rates
June 1964 through June 2002

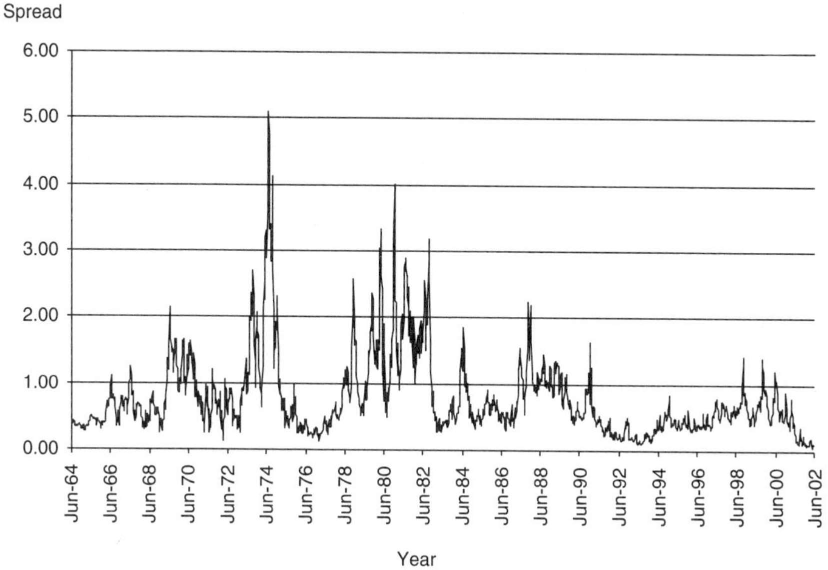

ciently homogeneous commodity. The credit risks behind the individual issuers, especially in light of the problems created by Chrysler's brush with bankruptcy, loomed much too large in people's minds for them to take the contract seriously. The CBOT's second effort, a 30-day commercial paper contract, also failed.

The exchanges turned next to the domestic CD and Eurodollar markets, which had been growing rapidly since 1972. The CME's records show that its Interest Rate Committee was working on the details of both a domestic CD and a Eurodollar contract as early as July 1979, which predates the onset of Volcker's monetary experiment.

By the spring of 1980, the CBOT, the CME, and the NYFE had all filed their respective applications. They did not get approval until the next year, and in July 1981, all three CD contracts were listed for trading.

Technically, the NYFE's contract was listed first. Of the three, however, the CME's prevailed and began its short but comparatively active trading life, which is charted in Exhibit 1.6. The race does not always go to the swift!

All three exchanges also had been working on various forms of a Eurodollar futures contract, which posed interesting design challenges. The biggest of these challenges was answering the question of delivery. Eurodollar CDs were a tradable commodity, but they represented a comparatively small slice of the Eurodollar market. Even so, the CBOT filed for approval but never listed a contract based on the delivery of Euro CDs.

Eurodollar time deposits, on the other hand, made up a large part of the Eurodollar market but were not negotiable. The CME originally proposed a time deposit contract that would be settled by the short opening a time deposit on behalf of the long. This approach had the advantage of preserving delivery integrity, but it was cumbersome, and the idea of cash settlement was floated.

At the time, there was no such thing as a cash-settled futures contract. Once the CME was satisfied that the cash settlement procedures would not be subject to manipulation, they filed a Eurodollar contract on that basis, as did the NYFE. Because the idea of cash settlement was breaking new ground, the Commodity Futures Trading Commission's deliberations on the concept required considerable time. Their approval when it came, however, was revolutionary and paved the way for stock index futures as well.

Although Eurodollar futures took longer to gain regulatory approval, the end result was a contract that was rooted in a large, liquid, and growing market that was designed to be insulated from the dangers posed by heterogeneous bank credits.

The device that protected the Eurodollar contract from the forces that brought the CD contract down was cash settlement. Initially, the final settlement price on the last day of trading for a Eurodollar contract was determined by the CME, which conducted a poll of banks in London. The CME's survey had two important features:

- The CME asked each bank its perception of the rate at which banks in London were willing to lend to other prime quality banks. The CME avoided in this question asking a bank the rate at which it was lending to any other particular bank.

EXHIBIT 1.6

Average Daily Trading Volume for 3-Month Treasury Bill, Certificate of Deposit, and Eurodollar Futures
1976 through 2001

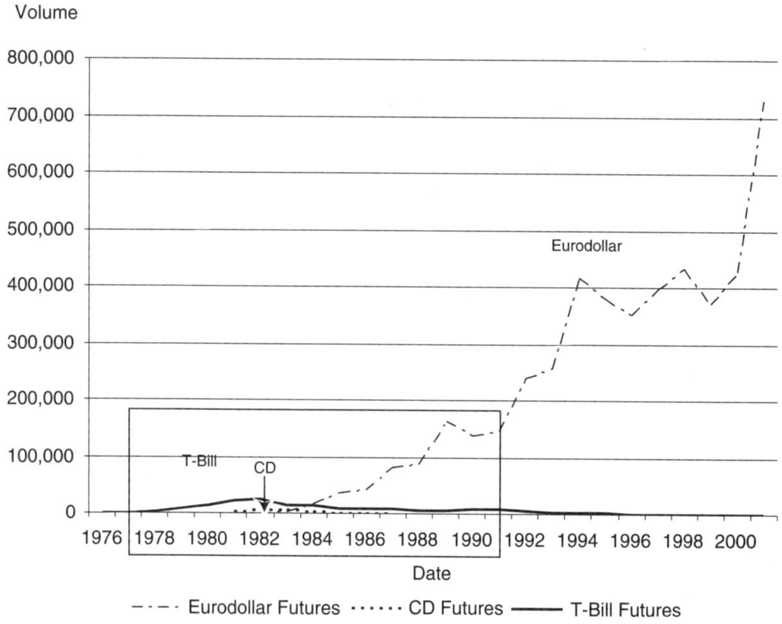

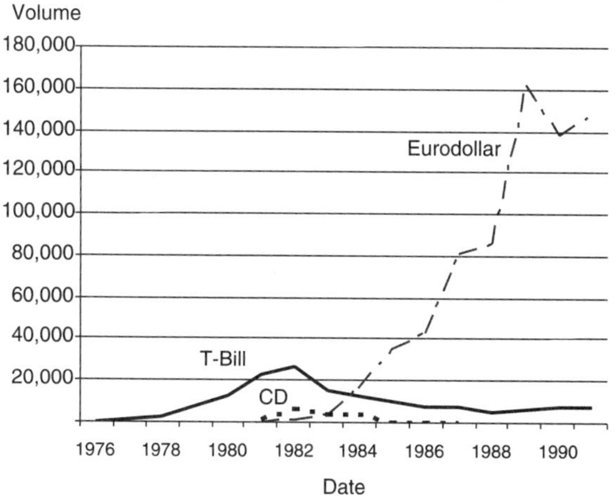

- The CME threw out high and low responses and calculated the final settlement price using the middle quotes.

The effect of the first of these features was that the survey skirted the problem of individual bank credits. The intended effect of the second was to insulate the final settlement price from capricious manipulation. A bank that misrepresented the market outrageously would have no effect on the final outcome. As a result, the banks polled in the CME's survey likely responded truthfully, although it would be naïve to suppose that their responses never reflected their positions in the cash and futures markets.[1]

THE DEATH OF CD FUTURES AND THE BIRTH OF EURODOLLAR FUTURES

The big turning point in the lives of these two contracts came in 1982, which was also a watershed for their respective cash markets. The depressing effect on the CD market of deposit deregulation and the financial difficulties of banks such as Continental Illinois and Chase Manhattan were felt as well in the CD futures market. The banks' credit problems also unsettled the market for the CD futures contract by clouding the picture about what would be deliverable.

For some time, the CDs of the top ten banks had been traded almost as if they were a homogeneous commodity. When Continental withdrew from the domestic CD market in 1982 and other banks began to feel the effects of financial stress, the upper tier of the CD market began to lose its homogeneity. Traders became more acutely aware of whose CDs were offered by other traders and how much of any one bank's CDs were on their books.

1. Today, the Eurodollar futures final settlement price is based on a survey conducted by the British Bankers' Association of 16 reference banks in London. The banks are asked at what rate they could borrow U.S. dollars for a 3-month term. The responses are placed in rank order, and then the middle two quartiles are arithmetically averaged. The final settlement price is 100 minus this average rate, rounded to 4 decimal places.

This concern about credit quality spilled over into the CD futures markets, where traders began to worry about just which bank's CDs they would receive if they took delivery. The price of a futures contract that involves the delivery of an actual commodity is driven by the price of the commodity in the eligible set that is cheapest to deliver. Traders became cautious about trading CD futures because there was so much uncertainty both about what and how cheap the cheapest to deliver might be.

At about the same time, as shown in Exhibit 1.4, the integration of world money markets was stabilizing the spread between U.S. and Eurodollar CD rates. From the standpoint of futures traders, this stabilization of the spread meant that Eurodollar and CD futures were becoming nearly perfect financial substitutes for one another. The only differences came down to issues such as liquidity and deliverable supply. Given the headaches caused by the uncertain quality of deliverable supply for the CD contract, traders began to favor Eurodollar futures.

The results of these various developments are summarized in Exhibit 1.6. CD futures trading had peaked by early 1983. By 1984, Eurodollar futures trading had caught up with and passed trading in CD futures. By 1985, Eurodollar futures were more actively traded than 3-month Treasury bill futures and have been so ever since. By 1986, CD futures were dead, although the CME did not officially bury the contract until 1987.

THE MARKET FOR INTEREST RATE DERIVATIVES AT THE BEGINNING OF THE 21ST CENTURY

At this writing, in 2002, the interest rate derivatives market is highly developed and quite complete. There are exchange-traded money market futures for the wholesale market and over-the-counter swaps for the retail corporate market. There are options on futures, interest rate caps, and options on swaps (swaptions). And one can find these instruments in every major financial market in the world. The growth of the markets has been explosive. Exhibit 1.7, for example, shows the global growth of swaps outstanding from 1987 through 2001. Exhibit 1.8 displays the growth of U.S. versus global swaps from 1998 through 2001.

EXHIBIT 1.7

Global Interest Rate Swaps Outstanding
Converted to U.S. Dollars

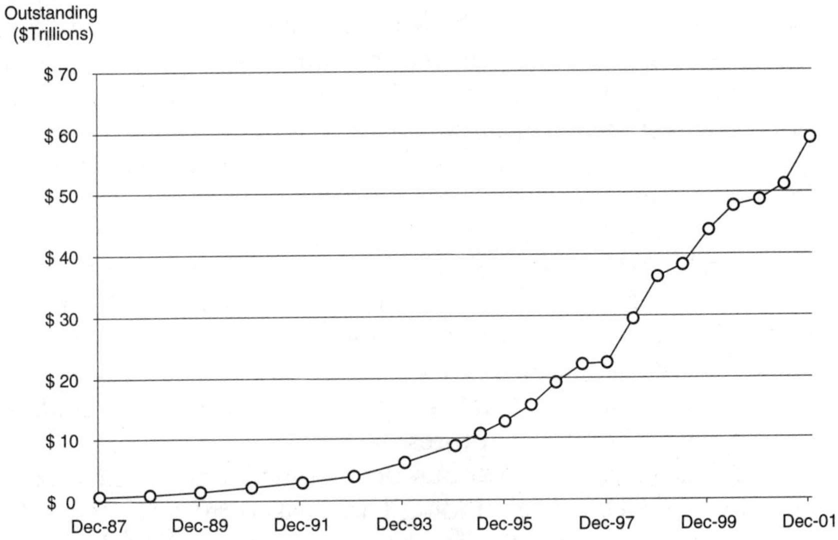

Exchange-Traded Money Market Futures and OTC Interest Rate Swaps

The exchange-traded and over-the-counter (OTC) interest rate markets go hand in hand but appeal to very different markets. Eurodollar futures are for the wholesale financial market—the dealers who price and hedge interest rate swaps and the banks whose business it is to serve as conduits for cash and to manage their exposure to the yield curve with considerable finesse. Eurodollar futures are great at what they do but require their users to settle gains and losses daily in cash; to be able to deal with yield curve approximations; to understand the subtleties of forward, zero-coupon, and coupon yield curves; and to appreciate the importance of convexity in understanding rate relationships between competing interest rate products.

The OTC swap market is best designed for retail corporate users because they transact less frequently and work under a different set of accounting, regulation, and tax standards. For corporate treasurers, the cash flows are less frequent and more pre-

EXHIBIT 1.8

Global versus U.S. Interest Rate Swaps Outstanding
Converted to U.S. Dollars

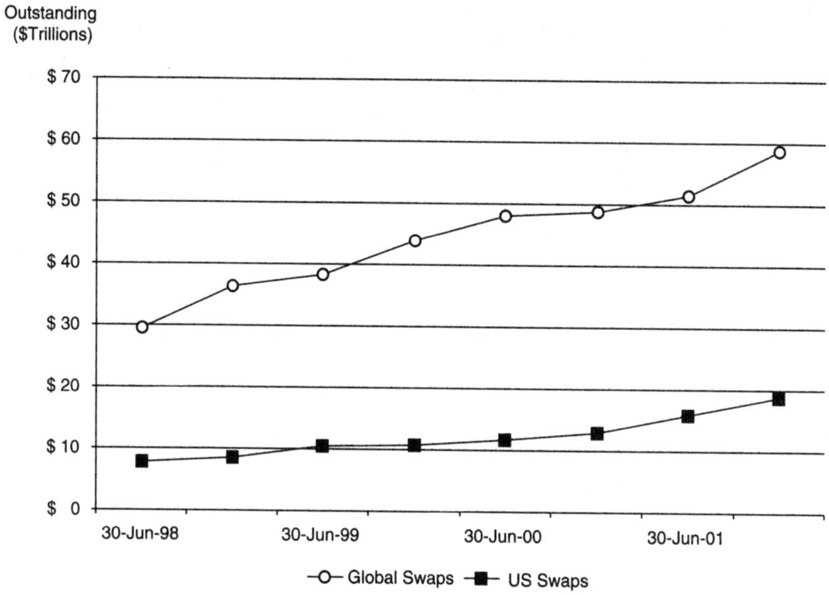

dictable. And the collateral requirements often are less onerous. Using swaps correctly does require a solid appreciation of credit risk, counterparty risk, and balance sheet issues that tend not to be a problem in the futures market.

Options on Futures, Forward Rates, and Swaps

In the market for options on futures, exchanges provide a rich and varied set of possible instruments. These include the standard quarterly options for which the option and the underlying futures contract expire on the same day, and the serial and mid-curve options for which the options expire before the underlying futures contract. The over-the-counter market offers two basic choices: caps, which represent a sequence of options on forward rates, and swaptions, which represent single options on a term swap rate, which in turn represents a combined sequence of forward rates.

EXHIBIT 1.9

Exchanges That Trade Money Market Futures

Exchange	Money Market Contract
BM&F (Brazilian Mercantile & Futures Exchange)	1-day interbank deposit
CME (Chicago Mercantile Exchange)	3-month Eurodollar
CBOT (Chicago Board of Trade)	30-day Fed funds
HKEx (Hong Kong Futures Exchange)	3-month HIBOR
KOFEX (Korea Futures Exchange)	3-month CD
LIFFE (London International Financial Futures and Options Exchange/ Euronext)	3-month Euribor 3-month Sterling 3-month Euro Swiss franc
Montréal Exchange	3-month Canadian bankers' acceptance 30-day overnight repo rate
SFE (Sydney Futures Exchange)	Australian 90-day bank bill New Zealand 90-day bank bill
SGX (Singapore Exchange)	3-month Eurodollar 3-month Euroyen
TIFFE (Tokyo International Financial Futures Exchange)	3-month Euroyen

Markets around the World

If we take the presence of an exchange-traded money market futures contract as evidence of an active interest rate derivatives market, we can conclude that all of the world's major money markets are covered. Exhibit 1.9 provides a list of exchanges on which one can trade money market futures and options. The list shows how widely accepted interest rate derivatives trading has become.

PART TWO

Building Blocks: Eurodollar Futures

The Eurodollar time deposit market has become the linchpin of the private credit market for dollar-denominated transactions. Maturities in this market extend out as far as 10 years. At the same time, one of the major thrusts of financial innovation has been to separate conventional financial products into their basic components. This is evident, for example, in the creation of many zero-coupon bonds by the stripping of coupons from conventional Treasury bonds. We also find investors breaking up the yield curve into segments. The result is a mix-and-match world in which a borrower or lender can have just about any kind of liability or asset imaginable.

In part because of the extraordinary success of the 3-month Eurodollar futures contract, the 3-month Eurodollar time deposit has become one of the basic building blocks of the short end of the yield curve.

The purpose of these chapters is to provide what you need to know about the Eurodollar time deposit market and to show how Eurodollar futures fit in. In particular, we will explain what Eurodollar futures are, how they are priced, and how they can be used to hedge the cost of funds.

CHAPTER 2

The Eurodollar Time Deposit

A Eurodollar time deposit is nothing more than a dollar deposit with a bank or bank branch outside of the United States or with an international banking facility (IBF) located in the United States. The world's center for Eurodollar trading is London, but there are active Eurodollar markets in other parts of the world as well.

In this chapter, we cover various aspects of the Eurodollar time deposit market, including:

- Maturities and settlement
- Quotes
- LIBOR and LIBID
- Interest rate calculations

MATURITIES AND SETTLEMENT

Exhibit 2.1 shows the bid and ask rates for Eurodollar time deposits with maturities ranging from overnight to 10 years. The rates begin with two 1-day term deposits: overnight (O/N) and tomorrow next (T/N). Each represents a 1-day term, but the overnight rate settles today and the tomorrow next rate settles tomorrow. A spot/next rate, not shown here but available for trading, represents a 1-day rate that settles 2 days from now.

EXHIBIT 2.1

Eurodollar Deposit Rates
Monday, June 17, 2002

Term	Bid	Ask
O/N (Overnight)	1.760	1.880
T/N (Tomorrow next)	1.750	1.870
1 week	1.720	1.840
2 week	1.780	1.800
3 week	1.780	1.800
1 month	1.780	1.810
2 month	1.780	1.820
3 month	1.800	1.830
4 month	1.830	1.860
5 month	1.850	1.880
6 month	1.850	1.970
7 month	1.950	1.980
8 month	2.010	2.040
9 month	2.090	2.120
10 month	2.160	2.190
11 month	2.250	2.280
12 month	2.255	2.375
2 year	3.295	3.355
3 year	3.890	3.950
4 year	4.285	4.345
5 year	4.575	4.635
6 year	4.805	4.865
7 year	4.995	5.055
8 year	5.140	5.200
9 year	5.270	5.330
10 year	5.370	5.430

Data source: Bloomberg. Visit www.Bloomberg.com.

The next basic maturities are 1, 2, and 3 weeks. Beyond this, the standard maturities range from 1 month to 12 months in single-month increments. Maturities then fall every year out to 10 years. Any other maturity can be negotiated. The settlement period is 2 London business days for all deposit maturities, with the exception of overnight and tomorrow next deposits.

QUOTES

Eurodollar deposits are add-on as opposed to discount instruments. Consequently, a $1 million Eurodollar transaction requires the initial transfer of $1 million, while a $1 million Treasury bill transaction requires an initial transfer of something less than $1 million.

Interest rates for Eurodollar deposits are money market yields quoted in percentage points and fractions of percentage points. The Eurodollar deposit market uses the ACT/360 day count convention to calculate interest.

LIBOR AND LIBID

In practice, the rate at which a London bank is willing to lend dollars is known as LIBOR, which is an acronym for London Interbank Offered Rate. The rate at which a London bank is willing to borrow is referred to by the less well known LIBID, or London Interbank Bid Rate. For example, as shown in Exhibit 2.1, 1-month Eurodollars were offered at 1.81 percent (LIBOR) and bid at 1.78 percent (LIBID) as of June 17, 2002. That is, the quoting bank was willing to lend dollars for 1 month to a prime credit at 1.81 percent and to accept anyone's deposit at 1.78 percent for a spread of 3 basis points.

INTEREST CALCULATIONS

For deposits with maturities less than or equal to 1 year, interest is paid at maturity. For deposits with maturities past 1 year, interest is paid on each anniversary and at maturity. For example, interest on a Eurodollar deposit with 1 year or less to maturity would be calculated as shown in Equation 2.1.

EQUATION 2.1

Interest on a Eurodollar Term Deposit

$$Interest = Deposit\left[Rate\frac{Days}{360}\right]$$

where

Deposit is the dollar amount
Rate is the quoted rate
Days is the actual number of days in the deposit term

Days/360 represents the fraction of a year based on the ACT/360 day count convention. The U.S. dollar, Euro (€), Japanese yen, and Swiss franc money markets all use the ACT/360 day count convention. The British pound and Canadian dollar money markets use the ACT/365 convention. For these currencies, the fraction of a year in Equation 2.1 would be Days/365.

Interest on a time deposit with more than 1 year to maturity would be calculated in stages. On each anniversary, the interest paid out on the deposit would be calculated as shown in Equation 2.1, with "Days" equal to the actual number of days between anniversary dates. The final interest calculation for any remaining partial year is done just as it would be for a deposit with less than 1 year to maturity, using the actual number of days remaining in the deposit's life.

EXAMPLE 2.1

CALCULATE INTEREST ON A 1-MONTH EURODOLLAR DEPOSIT

Calculate interest on a 1-month deposit as of Monday, June 17, 2002, with 1-month LIBID at 1.780%.

By Eurodollar money market convention, the settlement date is 2 London business days later, on Wednesday, June 19. Maturity for this 1-month deposit is on Friday, July 19. There are 30 days in the deposit period (from June 19 to July 19). Interest on each $1 million of this 1-month deposit is:

EXAMPLE 2.1 Continued

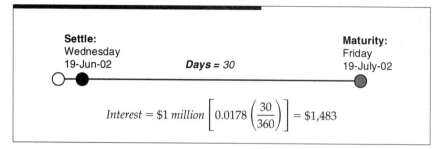

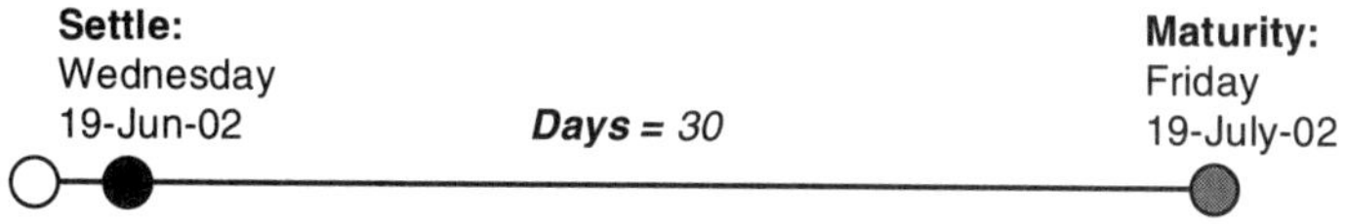

$$Interest = \$1\ million\left[0.0178\left(\frac{30}{360}\right)\right] = \$1{,}483$$

EXAMPLE 2.2

CALCULATE INTEREST ON A 2-YEAR EURODOLLAR DEPOSIT

Calculate interest on a 2-year deposit as of Monday, June 17, 2002, with 2-year LIBID at 3.295%.

The deposit settlement date is June 19, 2002. The first interest payment will be paid on Thursday, June 19, 2003. The second and final payment falls 2 years later on June 19, 2004, but this is a Saturday, so maturity of the deposit gets moved to Monday, June 21, 2004.

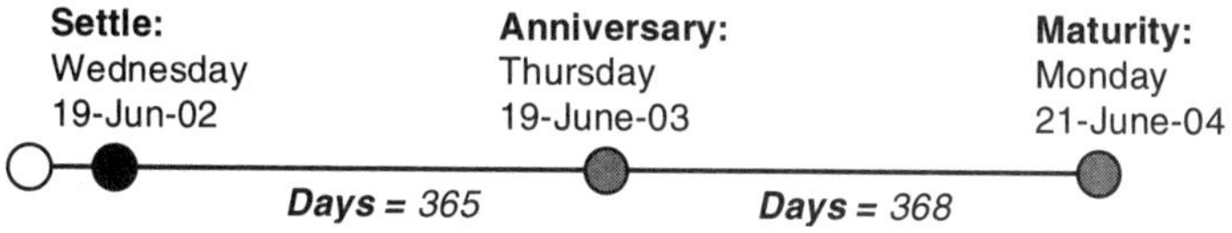

There are 365 days in the first interest period. The interest on a $1 million deposit is:

$$Interest_{19Jun03} = \$1\ million\left[0.03295\left(\frac{365}{360}\right)\right] = \$33{,}408$$

The second interest payment covers the 368-day period between June 19, 2003 and June 21, 2004. The interest is:

$$Interest_{21Jun04} = \$1\ million\left[0.03295\left(\frac{368}{360}\right)\right] = \$33{,}682$$

CHAPTER 3

The Eurodollar Futures Contract

Eurodollar futures contracts were first listed by the Chicago Mercantile Exchange (a.k.a. CME or "Merc") in December 1981. They were followed in 1982 by the London International Financial Futures Exchange (now the London International Financial Futures and Options Exchange, LIFFE) and in 1984 by the Singapore International Monetary Exchange (SIMEX; now the Singapore Exchange, SGX).[1]

Today, only the CME and SGX are major players in Eurodollar futures. The contract is traded via open outcry at the CME and SGX and electronically via the CME's GLOBEX system. With the exception of trading hours, the contracts traded at the CME and SGX are identical.

The purpose of this chapter is to introduce Eurodollar futures by covering:

- Contract specifications
- Performance bonds
- Volume and open interest

1. All three of these contracts were based on 3-month LIBOR. In 1989, the Tokyo International Financial Futures Exchange (TIFFE) listed a 3-month Eurodollar contract that settled to TIBOR, the offered rate in Tokyo.

We also highlight several non-dollar 3-month money market futures.

CONTRACT SPECIFICATIONS[2]

The Eurodollar futures contract specifications are described below and summarized in Exhibit 3.1.

Contract Unit

The contract unit is $1,000,000 3-month Eurodollar time deposits.

Price Quote

Bids and offers are quoted in terms of the IMM (International Monetary Market) index, or 100.00 minus the yield on an annual basis for a 360-day year. For example, a deposit rate of 3.25 will be quoted as 96.75 [= 100.00 − 3.25].

Tick Size

The basic tick size is 0.01 (or 1 basis point, often represented by bp). The dollar value of a tick is $25, which accords with the change in the value of a 90-day $1,000,000 instrument.

Minimum Fluctuation

The nearest expiring contract month trades in quarter ticks or 0.0025 ($6.25). The minimum price fluctuation for all other contracts is a half tick or 0.005 ($12.50).

Listed Contract Months

Each Eurodollar futures contract represents a 3-month deposit rate beginning some time in the future. Eurodollar futures contracts trade out 10 years in the quarterly cycle and have expirations in

2. The contract specifications were taken from the CME Rulebook as of June 4, 2002. Please visit the CME's website at www.cme.com for the most recent information.

EXHIBIT 3.1

Eurodollar Futures Contract Specifications

Contract unit		Eurodollar time deposit having a principal value of $1,000,000 with a 3-month maturity
Price quote		100 − annualized futures interest rate
Tick size		0.01 (1 basis point)
Tick value		$25
Minimum fluctuation	CME Floor	*Regular*: 0.01 = $25.00 *Half tick*: 0.005 = $12.50 for all months except nearest expiring *Quarter tick*: 0.0025 = $6.25 for nearest expiring month
	CME GLOBEX	*Regular*: 0.01 = $25.00 *Half tick*: 0.005 = $12.50
	SGX	*Regular*: 0.01 = $25.00 *Half tick*: 0.005 = $12.50 for all months except nearest expiring *Quarter tick*: 0.0025 = $6.25 for nearest expiring month
Price limits	CME Floor	None
	CME GLOBEX	2.00 index points above or below the reference regular trading hour price
	SGX	None
Listed contract months		40 months in the March, June, September, December quarterly cycle and the 4 nearest serial contract months
Trading hours	CME Floor	Monday through Friday: 7:20 a.m.–2:00 p.m. CST
	CME GLOBEX	Monday through Thursday: 4:30 p.m.–4:00 p.m. CST the following day Sunday: 5:30 p.m.–4:00 p.m. CST the following day
	SGX	Monday through Friday: 7:45 a.m.–7:00 p.m. local time (5:45 p.m. the previous day–5:00 a.m. Chicago time)

[illegible]	Cash settled
[illegible]	100 − BBAISR
[illegible] trading [illegible] day	11:00 a.m. London time (usually 5:00 a.m. Chicago time) on the second London bank business day before the third Wednesday of the contract month
Delivery day	Delivery shall be cash settled on the third Wednesday of the contract month
Additional trading facilities	Packs and bundles

March, June, September, and December. Four serial contracts with expirations outside of the quarterly cycle also trade. Serial contract months include January, February, April, May, July, August, October, and November. For example, during June, the 44 listed contracts include the 40 quarterly contracts plus the 4 serial contracts in July, August, October and November.

Contract Month Symbols

Each Eurodollar futures contract is identified by its month and year. The futures market has created symbols to represent each month (see Exhibit 3.2).

For example, the contract that expires in September 2003 is often represented as EDU3, where ED represents Eurodollar futures, U represents September, and 3 represents the last digit of the year. Bloomberg makes use of the contract month symbols in its EDSF function, which displays Eurodollar futures prices for each of the 40 quarterly expirations. (Exhibit 3.3 shows the first EDSF screen, with 14 Eurodollar futures contracts.)

Color-Coded Grid

With 10 years of contracts, the market has also come up with creative ways to indicate groups of contracts. The CME defines ex-

EXHIBIT 3.2

Contract Month Symbols

Month	Symbol
January	F
February	G
March	H
April	J
May	K
June	M
July	N
August	Q
September	U
October	V
November	X
December	Z

piration years in terms of a color-coded grid, with 4 quarterly cycle contract expirations per color (see Exhibit 3.4). For example, the first 4 quarterly contracts make up the "whites." As of June 12, 2002, this would be the June 2002, September 2002, December 2002, and March 2003 contracts. The next 4 quarterly contracts make up the "reds." The next 4 contracts make up the "greens" and so on.

This color-coded grid also allows traders to describe a specific part of the yield curve. For example, the "third red," as shown in Exhibit 3.4, represents a 3-month deposit rate between 1-1/2 to 1-3/4 years in the future, depending on how soon the lead contract expires.

Expiring versus Lead Contract

Market terminology can be confusing at times. For example, people often use the phrases "expiring contract" and "lead contract" interchangeably. This is not correct. The expiring contract is the one that is nearest to futures expiration. The lead contract is the most active contract and is designated as the lead contract by its location on the floor of the exchange. The expiring contract and the lead contract may or may not be the same.

EXHIBIT 3.3

Bloomberg EDSF Function
Prices for June 17, 2002

GRAB Index EDSF
PRICES AS OF CLOSE: Mon 6/17 Enter 0 <Page> for today's prices.

IMM EURODOLLAR SYNTHETIC FORWARD RATES

	Date	Days	IMM	Last	Rate	6-Mo	1-Yr	2-Yr	5-Yr	7-Yr	10-Yr
Spot strip		1	Front	98.1477	1.8523	1.996	2.403	3.377	4.755	5.264	5.799
1)	6/19/02	91	EDM2	98.1212s	1.8788	1.997	2.405	3.374	4.758	5.264	5.800
2)	9/18/02	91	EDU2	97.8950s	2.1050	2.307	2.852	3.763	4.976	5.440	
3)	12/18/02	91	EDZ2	97.5050s	2.4950	2.785	3.368	4.145	5.187	5.609	
4)	3/19/03	91	EDH3	96.9450s	3.0550	3.359	3.882	4.498	5.384	5.767	
5)	6/18/03	91	EDM3	96.3650s	3.6350	3.896	4.311	4.790	5.553	5.904	
6)	9/17/03	91	EDU3	95.8800s	4.1200	4.331	4.643	5.026	5.697	6.022	
7)	12/17/03	91	EDZ3	95.5050s	4.4950	4.634	4.892	5.206	5.818	6.123	
8)	3/17/04	91	EDH4	95.2800s	4.7200	4.849	5.088	5.353	5.926	6.214	
9)	6/16/04	91	EDM4	95.0800s	4.9200	5.032	5.245	5.484	6.022		
10)	9/15/04	91	EDU4	94.9200s	5.0800	5.199	5.384	5.598			
11)	12/15/04	91	EDZ4	94.7500s	5.2500	5.323	5.502	5.701			
12)	3/16/05	91	EDH5	94.6750s	5.3250	5.420	5.604	5.799			
13)	6/15/05	98	EDM5	94.5650s	5.4350	5.525	5.712	5.892			
14)	9/21/05	91	EDU5	94.4600s	5.5400	5.643	5.811	5.986			

Exchanges: IMM,SMX
FRA and Bond yld:
Daytype ACT/ACT
Frequency S

Start	End	days	years	Front	stub	Back	stub	Bond yield	m-mkt yield ACT/360
7/11/02	7/11/03	365	1.00	1.88%	69 days	3.62%	23 days	2.537	2.516
7/11/02	7/11/03	365	1.00	1.88%	69 days	3.62%	23 days	2.537	2.516
7/11/02	7/11/03	365	1.00	1.88%	69 days	3.62%	23 days	2.537	2.516
7/11/02	7/11/03	365	1.00	1.88%	69 days	3.62%	23 days	2.537	2.516
7/11/02	7/11/03	365	1.00	1.88%	69 days	3.62%	23 days	2.537	2.516

Trading Hours and Mutual Offset

Since 1984, the Chicago Mercantile Exchange and the Singapore Exchange have used a mutual offset system (MOS) to create a trade linkage between the two exchanges. The mutual offset system allows a trade executed at the CME to be transferred to SGX or a trade executed at SGX to be transferred to the CME. This offset is possible because the Eurodollar futures contracts on the two exchanges are fungible.

Final Settlement Price

The Eurodollar futures contract is cash settled to a final settlement price that is tied to spot 3-month LIBOR. The final settlement price is 100 minus the British Bankers' Association Interest Settlement Rate (BBAISR) for 3-month Eurodollar interbank time deposits,

EXHIBIT 3.4

Contract Year Color Grid
As of June 12, 2002

Year	Expiration Year	First	Second	Third	Fourth
1	White	Jun '02	Sep '02	Dec '02	Mar '03
2	Red	Jun '03	Sep '03	Dec '03	Mar '04
3	Green	Jun '04	Sep '04	Dec '04	Mar '05
4	Blue	Jun '05	Sep '05	Dec '05	Mar '06
5	Gold	Jun '06	Sep '06	Dec '06	Mar '07
6	Purple	Jun '07	Sep '07	Dec '07	Mar '08
7	Orange	Jun '08	Sep '08	Dec '08	Mar '09
8	Pink	Jun '09	Sep '09	Dec '09	Mar '10
9	Silver	Jun '10	Sep '10	Dec '10	Mar '11
10	Copper	Jun '11	Sep '11	Dec '11	Mar '12

rounded to the nearest 1/10,000th of a percentage point, on the second London bank business day immediately preceding the third Wednesday of the contract month.

In order to calculate the BBAISR, the British Bankers' Association selects 16 reference banks, all of whom are major participants in the London Eurodollar market, and asks them to provide rates at which they could borrow U.S. dollars through the interbank market. The quotes are rank ordered and the middle two quartiles are arithmetically averaged for the fixing. The fixing is conducted at 11 a.m. London time.

Last Trading Day

The Eurodollar futures contract terminates trading at 11:00 a.m. London time on the second London bank business day immediately preceding the third Wednesday of the contract month. This is 5:00 a.m. Chicago time, except when daylight savings time is in effect in either, but not both, London or Chicago.

From a practical perspective, the last day of trading *on the CME floor* is the third business day immediately preceding the third Wednesday of the contract month. Barring holidays, this is the Friday preceding expiration. The contract is last traded *on GLOBEX* at 11:00 a.m. London time (usually 5:00 a.m. Chicago time) on the day of Eurodollar futures expiration.

Value Dates

The value dates for Eurodollar futures fall 2 London business days after contract expiration. This is because the contract is settled to 3-month LIBOR, which has a 2-day settlement period. Eurodollar futures value dates always fall on the third Wednesday of the contract month.

Additional Trading Facilities

Market participants often want to execute a series of Eurodollar futures contracts in order to target specific segments of the yield curve. Rather than execute each contract month individually and incur execution risk, packs and bundles can be used to execute all of the desired contract months in a single transaction.

Packs are the simultaneous purchase or sale of an equally weighted, consecutive series of 4 Eurodollar futures, quoted on an average net change basis from the previous day's close. All packs trade in quarter ticks.

Bundles also involve the simultaneous purchase or sale of a consecutive series of Eurodollar futures contracts, but bundles have maturities of 1, 2, 3, 4, 5, 6, 7, 8, 9, and 10 years. The first contract in a bundle is generally the first quarterly contract. An exception to this is the 5-year forward bundle, which covers years 5 through 10 of the Eurodollar futures strip. All bundles trade in quarter ticks.

"Rolling" packs and bundles allow market participants to execute packs and bundles with "non-standard" start dates. Consequently, market players can trade packs and bundles that start with any quarterly contract. For additional information on packs and bundles, see "Hedging and Trading with Eurodollar Stacks, Packs, and Bundles," chapter 13.

INITIAL AND MAINTENANCE PERFORMANCE BONDS

The financial integrity of a futures exchange is ensured by its clearing house. The clearing house is responsible for settling trading accounts, clearing trades, collecting and maintaining performance bond funds, requiring delivery, and reporting trade data. Clearing firms stand between the customers and the clearing house. A customer who wishes to trade Eurodollar futures, or any other futures for that matter, is required to deposit funds known as initial performance bond (or initial margin) with his or her clearing firm.

On a daily basis, the customer's position is marked to market and gains or losses are posted to the customer's performance bond account. If the customer's funds drop below the maintenance performance bond level, the clearing firm will demand additional funds from the customer to bring the level back to the initial performance bond amount. This call for additional funds is known as a performance bond call (previously, a margin call). Exhibit 3.5 shows a summary of how Eurodollar futures work.

EXHIBIT 3.5

How Eurodollar Futures Work

- The Eurodollar futures price is equal to 100 minus the futures rate where the futures rate is expressed in percentage points.
- Each tick, or 0.01, is worth $25.
- The expiring month contract trades in quarter ticks (0.0025); all other contract months trade in half ticks (0.005).
- A decrease of 1 basis point in the futures rate increases the futures price by 1 basis point, which produces a $25 gain for the long and a corresponding $25 loss for the short.
- Gains and losses are settled daily. Money is taken from the accounts of those with losses and paid through the clearing house to the accounts of those with gains.
- Eurodollar futures are cash settled to 3-month LIBOR upon contract expiration. The final settlement price of the Eurodollar futures contract is 100 minus the British Bankers' Association Interest Settlement Rate for 3-month Eurodollar interbank time deposits.

VOLUME AND OPEN INTEREST

The growth of trading and open interest in Eurodollar futures at the CME is chronicled in Exhibit 3.6. What began as a contract trading in the shadows of Treasury bill and CD futures has grown to gigantic proportions. At this writing (June 2002), open interest in all contract months combined was over 4.5 million. At $1 million notional amount per contract, this translates into open positions on the books of traders and hedgers that are the equivalent of more than 4.5 trillion of 3-month deposits. This is big money.

Part of the reason for the success of the contract is illustrated in Exhibit 3.7, which compares the open interest across contract months in Eurodollar and Treasury bond futures. Nearly all of the open interest in bond futures is concentrated in the first 2 months. In contrast, there is substantial open interest in back-month Eurodollar futures.

Eurodollar futures differ from bond futures in one other key respect. The ratio of daily trading volume to open interest in bond futures is often more than one-to-one. In contrast, the ratio of daily trading volume to open interest in Eurodollar futures is much

EXHIBIT 3.6

Eurodollar Futures Volume and Open Interest
1982 through June 2002

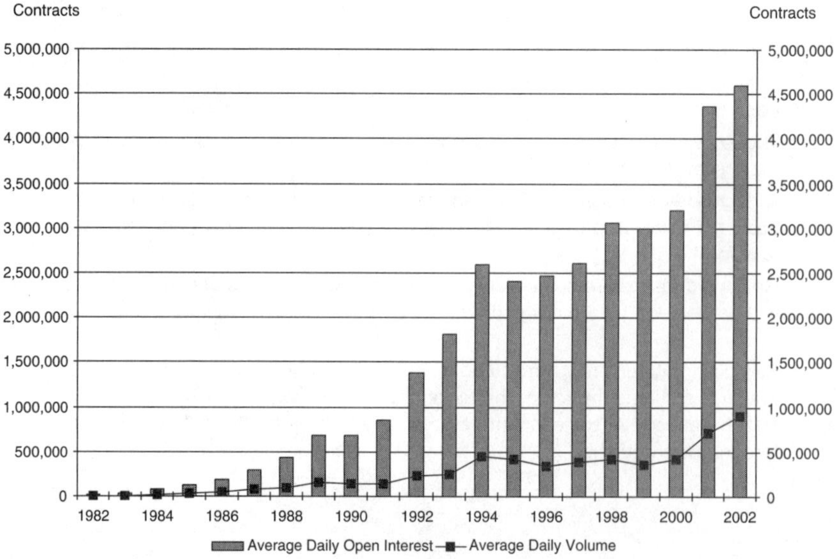

EXHIBIT 3.7

Bond and Eurodollar* Futures Open Interest by Contract
Year-End 2001

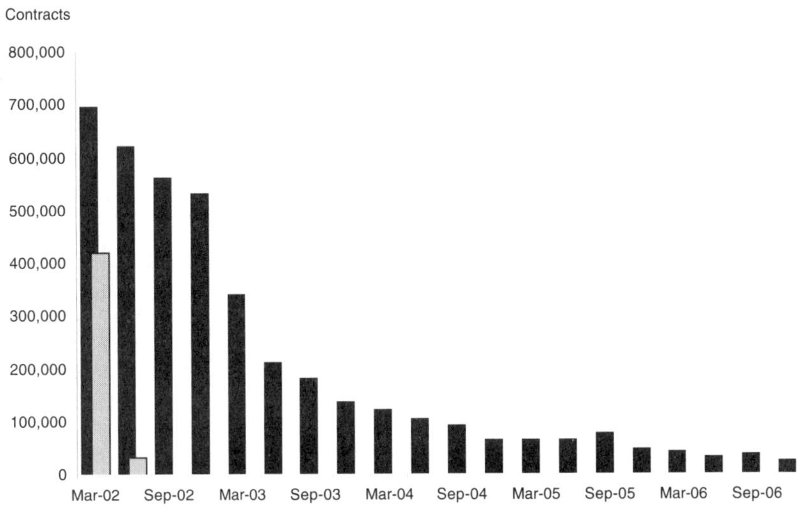

*First 20 quarterly contracts

lower, around one-to-five. Stated differently, the open interest in bonds turns over once a day on average. The open interest in Eurodollars turns over only once a week.

What this suggests is that Eurodollar futures are a hedger's contract, while Treasury bond futures are much more akin to a trader's contract. This fits what we already know about Eurodollar futures. The growth in the contract has been driven by the flexibility it affords in shaping and hedging interest rate exposure at the short end of the yield curve. It is no accident that the market for back-month Eurodollar futures has kept pace with the burgeoning interest rate swap market.

OTHER 3-MONTH MONEY MARKET FUTURES CONTRACTS

The success of the CME's Eurodollar futures contract led other exchanges to create 3-month deposit futures. There were PIBOR futures on French deposit rates; Euro lira futures on Italian deposit

EXHIBIT 3.8

Other 3-Month Money Market Futures Contract Specifications

	Euribor	Short Sterling	Euroyen
Exchange	LIFFE	LIFFE	TIFFE
Trading type	Electronic	Electronic	Electronic
Contract unit	€1,000,000	£500,000	¥100,000,000
Price quote	100 − annualized futures interest rate	100 − annualized futures interest rate	100 − annualized futures interest rate
Tick size and value	0.005 (€12.50)	0.01 (£12.50)	0.005 (¥1,250)
Listed contract months	March, June, September, December, and 2 serial months, such that 22 delivery months are available	March, June, September, December, and 2 serial months, such that 22 delivery months are available	March, June, September, and December, listed on a 3-year cycle
Trading hours	07:00–18:00	07:30–18:00	09:00–11:30 12:30–15:30 15:40–18:00
Settlement	Cash settled	Cash settled	Cash settled
Final settlement price	100 − EBF Euribor Based on the European Bankers Federation's Euribor Offered Rate (EBF Euribor) for 3-month Euro deposits at 11:00 Brussels time (10:00 London time) on the last trading day	100 − BBA LIBOR Based on the British Bankers' Association London Interbank Offered Rate (BBA LIBOR) for 3-month sterling deposits at 11:00 on the last trading day	100 − ZENGINKYO TIBOR
Last trading day	10:00—two business days prior to the third Wednesday of the delivery month	11:00—third Wednesday of the delivery month	11:00—two business days prior to the third Wednesday of the delivery month
Delivery day	First business day after the last trading day	First business day after the last trading day	First business day after the last trading day

rates; EuroDM futures on German deposit rates; and MIBOR futures on Spanish rates. With the introduction of the Euro (€) as the currency of the European Economic and Monetary Union, these money market contracts were superseded by Euribor futures. Other active 3-month deposit futures include Short Sterling futures on British deposit rates and Euroyen futures on Japanese rates. Exhibit 3.8 shows the contract specifications for some of these actively traded contracts.

CHAPTER 4

Forward and Futures Interest Rates

People who work with interest rates encounter three fundamental kinds of yield curves. One is a zero-coupon curve that represents the yields used to value single cash flows, which are known as zero-coupon bonds. The second is a coupon yield curve that represents the yields—typically internal rates of return—that are used to value bonds that carry periodic coupons in addition to a final principal amount. The third is a forward rate curve that can be used to compare the value of cash between any two dates. Of the three, the forward rate is the most basic and is the curve from which both the zero-coupon and coupon yield curves can be derived. The forward rate curve contains the building blocks that financial engineers use to construct and price any fixed income product. Throughout the chapters in this book, we will have opportunities to work with all three curves and to understand the relationships between them.[1]

Eurodollar futures are the exchange-traded equivalent of forward borrowing and lending arrangements. In this role,

1. Excellent discussions of the relationships between these three yield curves can be found in John C. Hull's *Options, Futures, and Other Derivatives*, 5th ed. (Upper Saddle River, NJ: Prentice Hall, 2003) and in Antti Ilmanen's "Overview of Forward Rate Analysis, Understanding the Yield Curve: Part 1," Salomon Brothers, May 1995.

Eurodollar futures provide two things. First, a Eurodollar futures contract's price, when subtracted from 100, provides an indication of what the forward rate is for the period covered by that particular contract. Second, a Eurodollar futures contract is a tool for locking in synthetically a forward borrowing or lending rate. And, because futures contracts have quarterly expirations going out a full 10 years, we can use them to see the structure of 3-month forward interest rates for a 10-year horizon. Eurodollar futures also can be used to either hedge or construct synthetically any fixed income instrument whose cash flows fall within that 10-year span. Exhibit 4.1 shows Eurodollar futures prices and rates for each of the 40 quarterly contracts on June 17, 2002.

The purpose of this chapter is to lay out the relationship between term and forward deposit rates, explain why Eurodollar futures can be treated like forward rate contracts, and explore some of the uses of forward rates. In particular, in this chapter, you will learn how to:

- Calculate a forward rate from term deposit rates
- Lock in the effective rate on a forward investment using Eurodollar futures
- Determine the fair value of a Eurodollar futures contract
- Calculate richness/cheapness of a futures contract
- Find the break-even conditions for a trade in which you borrow short and lend long
- Find the term deposit curve implied by today's futures rates

DERIVING A FORWARD RATE FROM TWO TERM DEPOSIT RATES

Suppose you want to lend money for 9 months and know what your total interest income will be at the end of the period. In practice, there are many ways you can do this. For example, you can lend the money at a 9-month term rate that you know today. Or you can lend the money at a 6-month term rate that you know today, and then roll the money plus interest into a 3-month rate.

EXHIBIT 4.1

Eurodollar Futures Prices
June 17, 2002

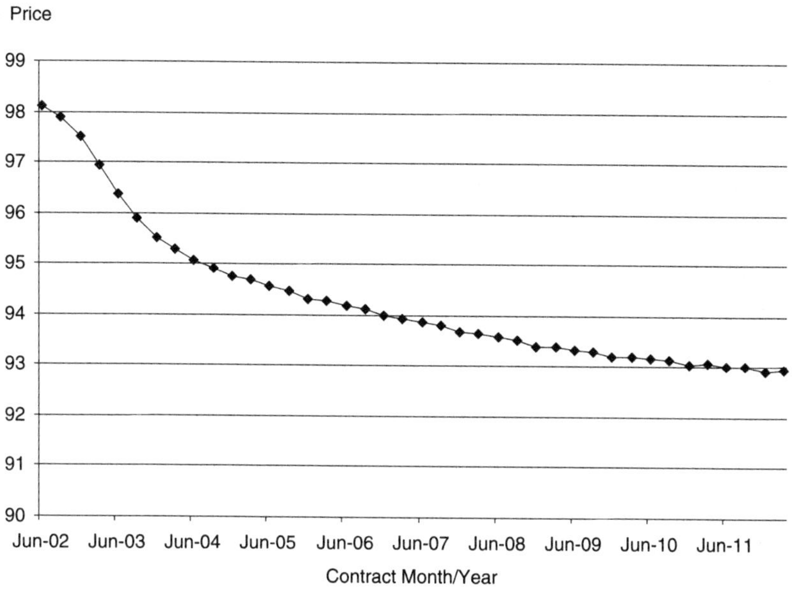

Eurodollar Futures Rates
June 17, 2002

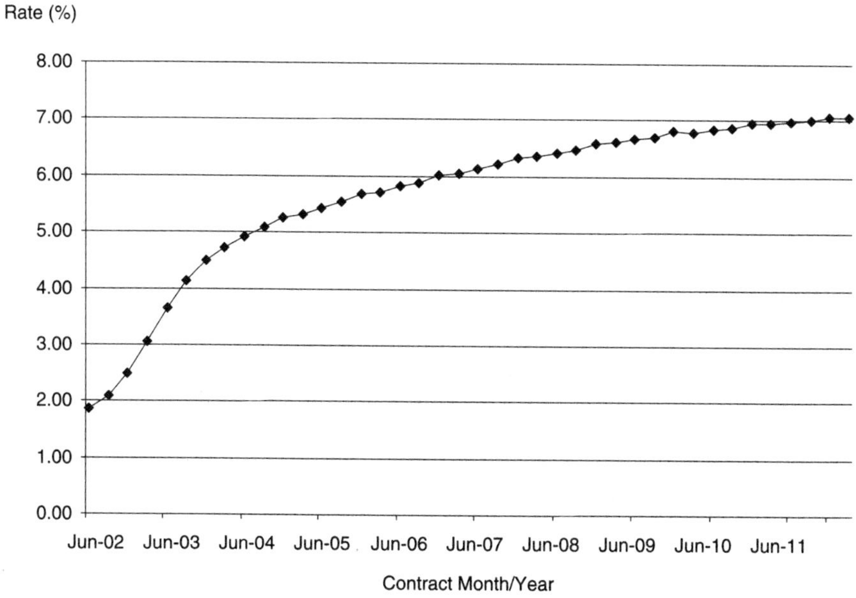

For you to be indifferent between these two scenarios, you would want to lock in the 3-month rate that will start in 6 months. This rate is the forward rate. The fair value of this forward rate is the value that makes you indifferent between investing at a 9-month term rate versus investing at a 6-month term rate and then reinvesting at the 3-month forward rate.

EXAMPLE 4.1

FIND A 3-MONTH RATE 6 MONTHS FORWARD

A bank wants to lend $1,000,000 for 9 months. It considers two alternatives: 1) lend at the 9-month term rate and 2) lend at the 6-month term rate, and then reinvest the loan plus interest for 3 months.

Using the Eurodollar term deposit rate schedule in Exhibit 4.2, on Monday, June 17, 2002, suppose that this bank can lend for 9 months at a rate of 2.12% and for 6 months at 1.97%. At what rate would the bank need to reinvest the money 6 months from now for it to be indifferent between these two lending scenarios?

Scenario 1: Lend $1,000,000 for 9 months at 2.12% on Monday, June 17, 2002. The loan settles on June 19, 2002 and matures 9 months later on March 19, 2003. For each dollar lent by the bank, the total amount it will receive on March 19, 2003 is:

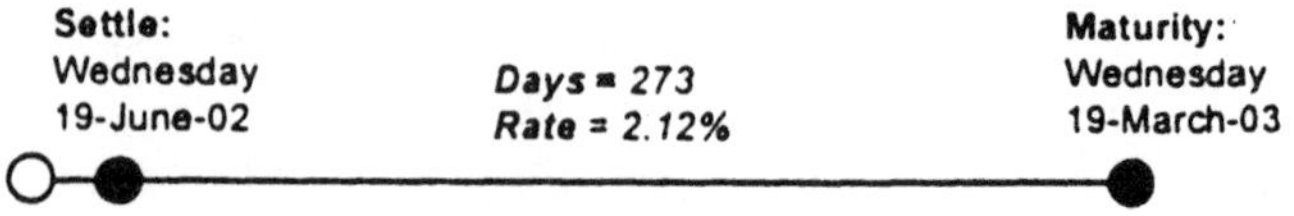

$$Value_{19Mar03} = \$1\left[1 + 0.0212\left(\frac{273}{360}\right)\right] = \$1.0161$$

Scenario 2: Lend $1,000,000 for 6 months at 1.97% on Monday, June 17, 2002. This loan should mature on Thursday, December 19, but to match the Eurodollar futures value date, we move the maturity to December 18.[2] Reinvest the loan plus interest through March 19, 2003.

2. Here, we modify the maturity dates of the cash market to exactly match Eurodollar futures value dates, which fall on the third Wednesday of the contract month.

EXAMPLE 4.1 Continued

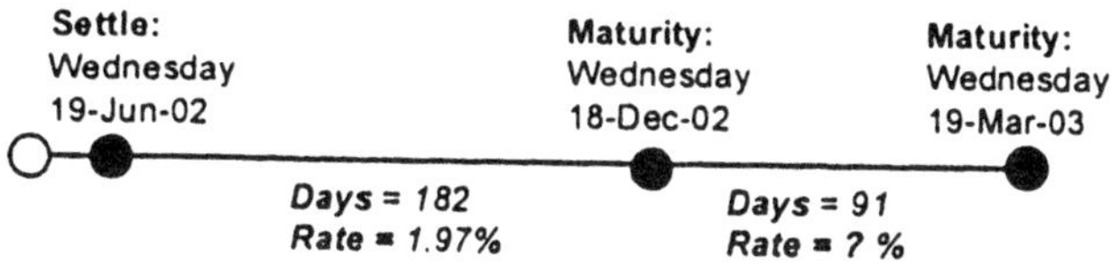

After 182 days, the total amount received for each dollar lent is:

$$Value_{18Dec02} = \$1\left[1 + 0.0197\left(\frac{182}{360}\right)\right] = \$1.0100$$

This value is then reinvested for the remaining 91 days, but at what rate? The fair value of this forward rate will make the income produced by Scenario 2 equal to the income produced by Scenario 1.

Income Scenario 2 Income Scenario 1

$$Value_{19Mar03} = \underbrace{\$1.0100\left[1 + Rate_{Forward}\frac{91}{360}\right]}_{\text{Income Scenario 2}} = \underbrace{\$1.0161}_{\text{Income Scenario 1}}$$

We can then solve for the 3-month rate 6 months forward.

$$\left[\frac{\$1.0161}{\$1.0100} - 1\right]\frac{360}{91} = Rate_{Forward} = 0.0239 = 2.39\%$$

We have effectively calculated a forward-starting 3-month rate (from December 18, 2002, through March 19, 2003) using only term deposit rates.

Two generalized equations prove very useful in solving for forward rates using spot deposit rates. Equation 4.1 shows how to combine a short rate with a forward rate to get a long rate. We can then rearrange Equation 4.1 to solve for the forward rate using the short-term and long-term deposit rates (see Equation 4.2).

EQUATION 4.1

Combine a Short Rate with a Forward Rate to Get a Long Rate

$$\$1\left[1 + R_S\left(\frac{D_S}{360}\right)\right]\left[1 + R_F\left(\frac{D_F}{360}\right)\right] = \$1\left[1 + R_L\left(\frac{D_L}{360}\right)\right]$$

EXHIBIT 4.2

Eurodollar Deposit Rates
Monday, June 17, 2002

Term	Bid	Ask
Overnight	1.760	1.880
Tomorrow next	1.750	1.870
1 week	1.720	1.840
2 week	1.780	1.800
3 week	1.780	1.800
1 month	1.780	1.810
2 month	1.780	1.820
3 month	1.800	1.830
4 month	1.830	1.860
5 month	1.850	1.880
6 month	1.850	1.970
7 month	1.950	1.980
8 month	2.010	2.040
9 month	2.090	2.120
10 month	2.160	2.190
11 month	2.250	2.280
12 month	2.255	2.375

Data source: Bloomberg. Visit www.Bloomberg.com.

EQUATION 4.2

Calculate a Forward Rate from Long and Short Deposit Rates

$$R_F = \left\{ \frac{\left[1 + R_L\left(\frac{D_L}{360}\right)\right]}{\left[1 + R_S\left(\frac{D_S}{360}\right)\right]} - 1 \right\} \frac{360}{D_F}$$

where

R_L is the long-term deposit rate
R_S is the short-term deposit rate

R_F is the forward deposit rate
D_L is the number of days in the long term
D_S is the number of days in the short term
D_F is the number of days in the forward term

EXAMPLE 4.2

FIND A 3-MONTH RATE 6 MONTHS FORWARD (REVISITED)

Calculate a 3-month rate 6 months forward, given the following term deposit rates:

6-month term deposit: 1.97% for 182 days
9-month term deposit: 2.12% for 273 days

The forward 3-month rate covers a 91-day period [= 273 − 182]. Use Equation 4.2 to solve for the forward rate.

$$R_F = \left\{ \frac{\left[1 + 0.0212\left(\frac{273}{360}\right)\right]}{\left[1 + 0.0197\left(\frac{182}{360}\right)\right]} - 1 \right\} \frac{360}{91} = 2.40\%$$

Interim rounding in Example 4.1 accounts for the 1-basis-point difference between the two answers.

LOCKING AN EFFECTIVE FORWARD LENDING RATE USING EURODOLLAR FUTURES

You can use Eurodollar futures to lend or borrow synthetically. In particular, if you combine a long Eurodollar futures contract with a plan to lend money at whatever the market lending rate proves to be when you reach the expiration of the futures contract, the result will look very much like what you would earn on a forward investment at a known forward rate. Similarly, if you combine a short Eurodollar position with a plan to borrow at whatever the market borrowing rate proves to be when you reach futures expiration, the result will be very much like borrowing in the forward market at a known forward rate.

EXAMPLE 4.3

LOCK THE FORWARD LENDING RATE

On June 17, 2002, a bank wants to lock in a lending rate on a $10,000,000 3-month loan that will be issued 6 months from now. The lender can either:

1. *Lend $10,000,000 at a forward rate of 2.40% or*
2. *Buy 10 December 2002 Eurodollar futures contracts at 97.60 [= 100 − 2.40] and lend at the prevailing market rate at futures expiration.*

The 91-day loan period runs from December 18, 2002, through March 19, 2003 (futures value dates).

Scenario 1: Lock in a forward lending rate of 2.40% on June 17.

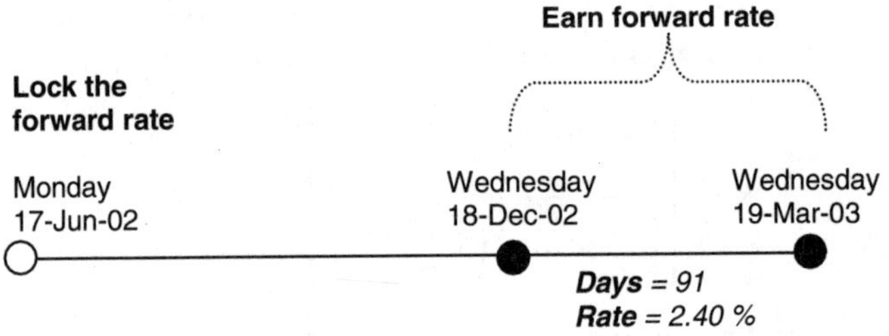

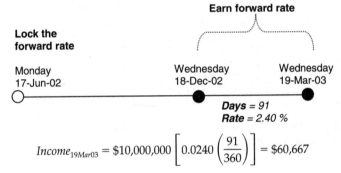

$$Income_{19Mar03} = \$10{,}000{,}000\left[0.0240\left(\frac{91}{360}\right)\right] = \$60{,}667$$

Scenario 2: Buy 10 of the December 2002 Eurodollar futures contract at 97.60, then issue the 91-day loan at the prevailing market rate on December 16, 2002.[3]

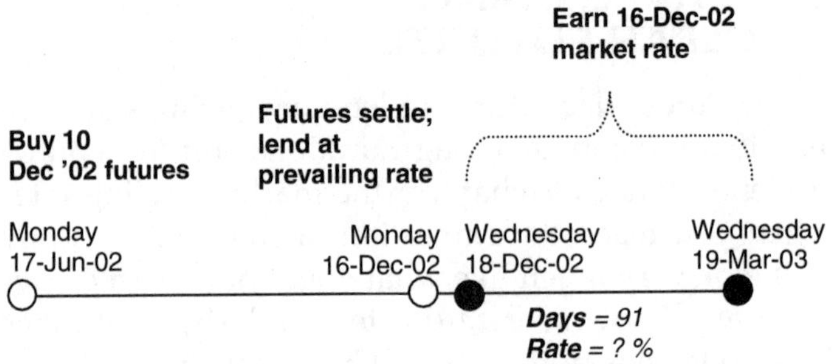

3. We sold one contract for each $1 million of the cash transaction, but more precise hedging methodology is discussed in "Hedging with Eurodollar Futures," chapter 5.

EXAMPLE 4.3 Continued

Look at three rate scenarios on December 16, 2002:

a) 3-month LIBOR = 2.40%
December 2002 futures = 97.60 [= 100 − 2.40]
Lender neither pays nor receives variation margin
Lend at 2.40% for 91 days (value date December 18, 2002)

$$\textit{Futures income}_{16Dec02} = 10\,[97.60 - 97.60]\,\$2500$$

$$= \$0$$

$$\textit{Loan income}_{19Mar03} = \$10{,}000{,}000\left[0.0240\left(\frac{91}{360}\right)\right]$$

$$= \$60{,}667$$

$$\textit{Total income}_{19Mar03} = \$60{,}667$$

b) 3-month LIBOR = 2.50%
December 2002 futures = 97.50 [= 100 − 2.50]
Lender pays variation margin
Lend at 2.50% for 91 days

$$\textit{Futures income}_{16Dec02} = 10\,[97.50 - 97.60]\,\$2500$$

$$= -\$2{,}500$$

$$\textit{Loan income}_{19Mar03} = \$9{,}997{,}500\left[0.0250\left(\frac{91}{360}\right)\right]$$

$$= \$63{,}179$$

$$\textit{Total income}_{19Mar03} = \$60{,}679$$

c) 3-month LIBOR = 2.30%
December 2002 futures = 97.70 [= 100 − 2.30]
Lender receives variation margin
Lend at 2.30% for 91 days

$$\textit{Futures income}_{16Dec02} = 10\,[97.70 - 97.60]\,\$2500$$

$$= \$2{,}500$$

$$\textit{Loan income}_{19Mar03} = \$10{,}002{,}500\left[0.0230\left(\frac{91}{360}\right)\right]$$

$$= \$58{,}153$$

$$\textit{Total income}_{19Mar03} = \$60{,}653$$

EXAMPLE 4.3 Continued

By combining a long futures position with a loan issuance at prevailing market rates upon futures expiration, you can make the overall returns immune to changes in interest rates. Under the three rate outcomes in Scenario 2, the returns were just about identical to when we "locked" the forward rate at 2.40%.

Note that buying futures does not fix the rate at which you lend forward. Rather, futures "lock" the rate by compensating you for changes in the market rate: when rates rise (and prices fall), the loss in the long futures is offset by the increase in loan income; when rates fall (and prices rise), the gain in the long futures is offset by the smaller loan income.

EXHIBIT 4.3

Key Differences between Forward and Futures Markets

	Forward Markets	Futures Markets
Cash flows	Cash changes hands only on the forward date.	Gains and losses are settled daily in the form of variation margin payments.
Security deposits	Security deposits are rarely required.	Security deposits in the form of initial and maintenance performance bonds (margins) are standard.
Offsets of longs and shorts	Purchases and sales, even with the same trading partner, remain on the books as open long and short positions.	Purchases and sales (as long as they are cleared through the same broker) offset one another.
Credit exposure	You face the credit risk of each trading partner.	You face the credit risk only of the clearing house and the clearing member.
Settlement dates	Settlement dates can be set to suit the trading partners.	Expirations are standard.

IMPORTANT DIFFERENCES BETWEEN FORWARD AND FUTURES MARKETS

The key differences between borrowing or lending forward and selling or buying Eurodollar futures are these. First, with futures, you must settle all gains and losses on the contracts every day, while with forwards, you carry a sequence of unrealized gains or losses on your forward position until the contract comes due. Second, with futures, you do not know the spread between LIBOR and the rate at which you will borrow or lend until the time comes to actually borrow or lend. For additional differences between forward and futures markets, see Exhibit 4.3.

EXAMPLE 4.4

COMPARE FORWARD VERSUS FUTURES CASH FLOWS

Illustrate the cash flows for the two scenarios in Example 4.3.

Scenario 1: Lock the forward lending rate at 2.40% on June 17.

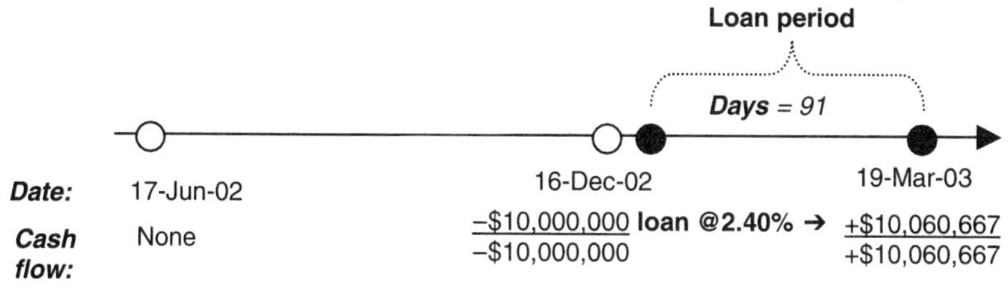

Scenario 2: Buy futures on June 17 and lend at the prevailing market rate on December 16.

a) LIBOR = 2.40%

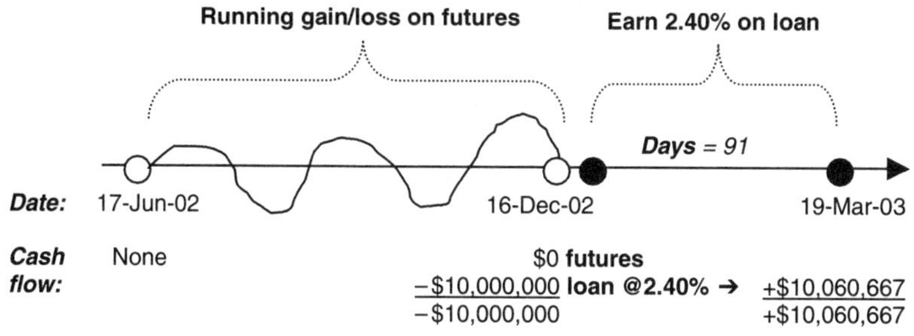

EXAMPLE 4.4 Continued

b) LIBOR = 2.50%

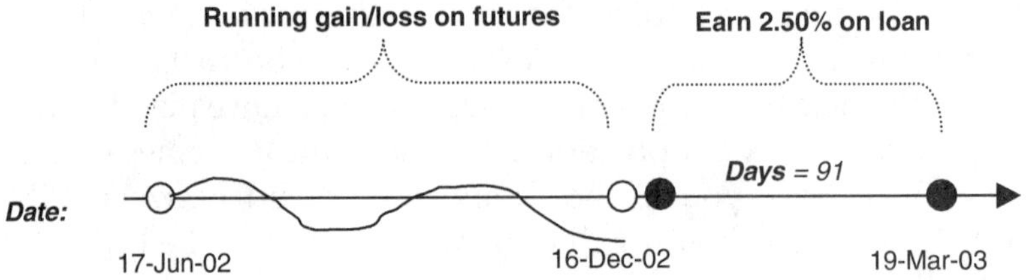

Cash flow: None

−$2,500 **futures**	
−$9,997,500 **loan @2.50%** →	+$10,060,679
−$10,000,000	+$10,060,679

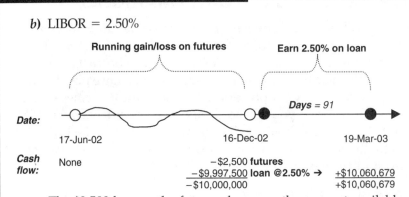

The $2,500 loss on the futures decreases the amount available to loan, but this is offset by the ability to issue the loan at a higher rate.

c) LIBOR = 2.30%

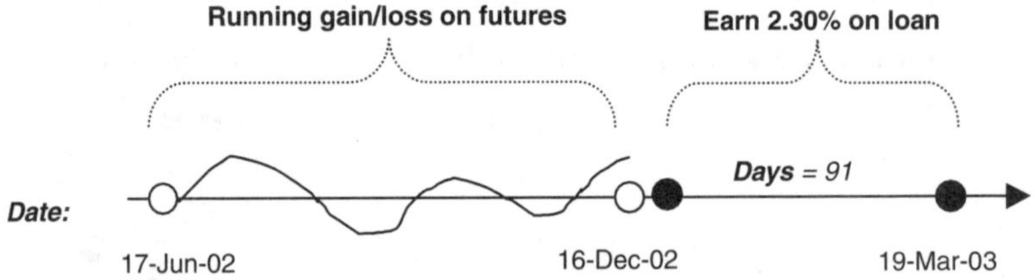

Cash flow: None

+$2,500 **futures**	
−$10,002,500 **loan @2.30%** →	+$10,060,653
−$10,000,000	+$10,060,653

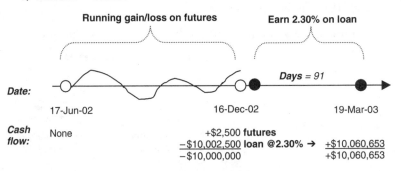

The gain from the futures allows the bank to loan an extra $2,500, but this larger loan is offset by a lower interest rate.

In all three cases, when the bank bought futures and then lent at market rates upon futures expiration, it was able to effectively replicate the cash flows of the locked forward lending.

DETERMINING THE FAIR VALUE OF A EURODOLLAR FUTURES CONTRACT

Once you know that a Eurodollar futures contract can be used to borrow or lend forward synthetically at 3-month LIBOR (plus or minus an appropriate spread), it follows that the fair value of a Eurodollar futures contract's price is simply 100 less the fair forward value of 3-month LIBOR for the period covered by the contract.

When calculating the fair value of a futures contract's price, three practical things govern what you do. The first is that the contract settles at expiration to 100 less the value of 3-month LIBOR. As a result, when calculating forward rates, we work with rates on the offered or ask side of the term deposit curve. The second is that the value dates for the rates used to settle the contract have the usual lag of 2 London business days. As a result, the value date for a rate used to settle a contract on Monday would be the following Wednesday, barring any bank holidays. The third is that the term covered by the cash market rate used to settle the contract may be longer or shorter than the period covered by the futures contract.

EXAMPLE 4.5

CALCULATE THE FAIR VALUE OF A EURODOLLAR FUTURES CONTRACT

Use the market data for term deposit rates in Exhibit 4.2 to calculate the fair value of the December 2002 Eurodollar futures contract.

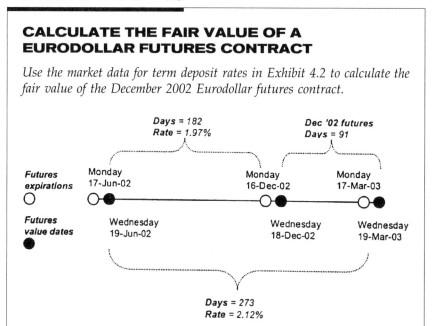

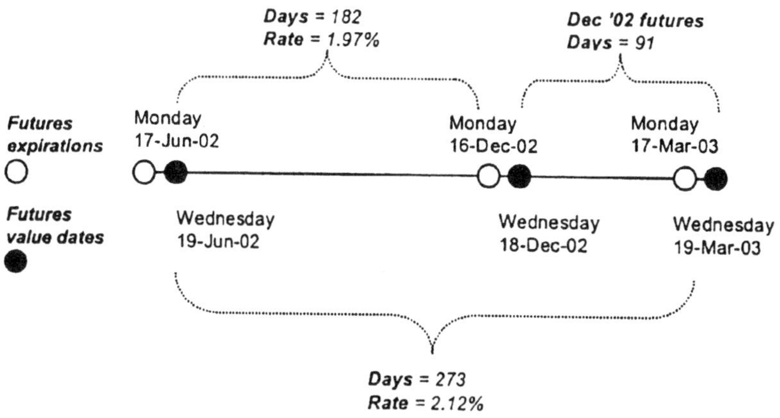

EXAMPLE 4.5 Continued

Use term deposit rates and Equation 4.2 to solve for the forward rate.

$$Rate_{Forward} = \left\{ \frac{\left[1 + 0.0212\left(\frac{273}{360}\right)\right]}{\left[1 + 0.0197\left(\frac{182}{360}\right)\right]} - 1 \right\} \frac{360}{91}$$

$$= 0.0240 = 2.40\%$$

We convert this forward rate to a futures price by subtracting it from 100. So, the fair value of the December 2002 futures contract is 97.60 [= 100 − 2.40].

The fair value calculation obscures date mismatches between the cash LIBOR and futures markets. We highlight some differences below.

EXAMPLE 4.6

TRACK DATE MISMATCHES BETWEEN THE CASH AND FUTURES MARKETS[4]

What date mismatches occurred during the calculation of the fair value of the December 2002 Eurodollar futures contract on June 17, 2002?

Futures Value Dates

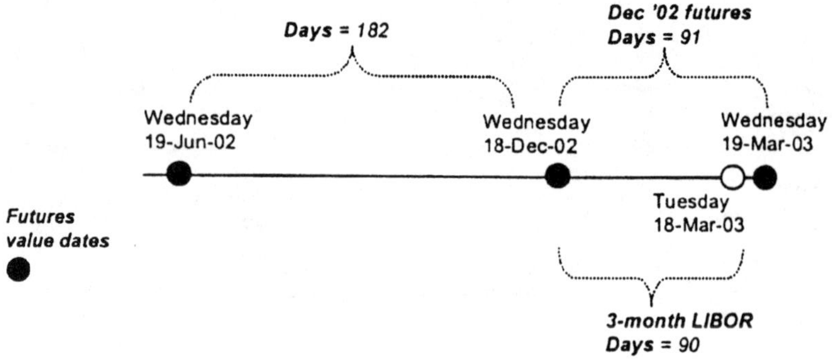

4. We discuss how to account for value date mismatches between the LIBOR term deposit market and the Eurodollar futures market in chapters 5 and 11.

E X A M P L E 4.6 Continued

a) Futures market convention is to count the days covered by a futures contract as the days between futures value dates. The December 2002 futures rate, for example, covers the period from Wednesday, December 18, 2002, through Wednesday, March 19, 2003. This 91-day forward period is used in the fair value calculations.

b) The December 2002 futures contract settles to 3-month LIBOR whose value date is Wednesday, December 18, 2002, and whose maturity date is Tuesday, March 18, 2003. This 90-day period is shorter than that covered in the fair value calculation.

c) The forward fair value calculation used 6-month and 9-month LIBOR. The value date for these two deposits was Wednesday, June 19, 2002. The respective maturity dates were Thursday, December 19, 2002, and Wednesday, March 19, 2003. The 6-month maturity date falls 1 day after the futures value date of December 18.

Cash Market Dates

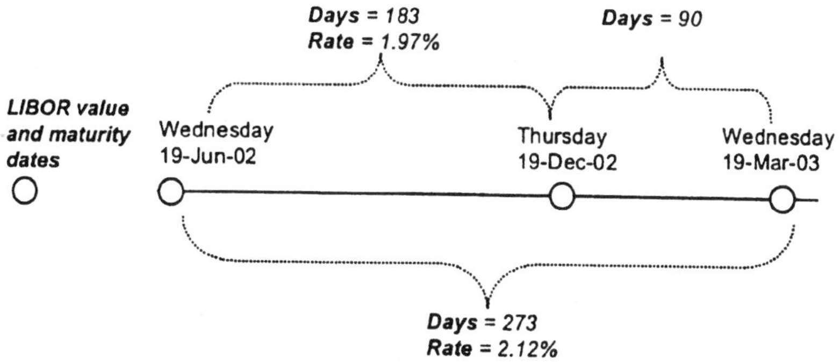

As date mismatches go, the differences are small, and you would not be far wrong if you used 2.40% as the fair value of the forward 3-month LIBOR to which the futures contract settled.

RICHNESS AND CHEAPNESS

We have calculated the fair forward values of 3-month LIBOR for the first three Eurodollar contracts using the offered term deposit rates provided in Exhibit 4.2. Subtracting these rates from 100

EXHIBIT 4.4

Are Futures Rich or Cheap?
June 17, 2002

Contract Month	Fair Values: Forward Rate	Fair Values: Futures Price	Market Futures Price	Futures Rich/Cheap?
Sep '02	2.100%	97.900	97.895	cheap 0.005
Dec '02	2.396%	97.604	97.505	cheap 0.099
Mar '03	3.090%	96.910	96.945	rich 0.035

results in the fair futures contract prices shown in Exhibit 4.4. Market futures prices are listed next to the fair prices, and a comparison of the two provides a measure of contract richness or cheapness. For example, the market price of the Sep '02 contract on June 17, 2002, was 97.895, which was a scant 0.005 below the contract's fair value. This contract was then trading 0.005 cheap to fair value. The Dec '02 contract was cheaper, at 0.099 below fair value, while the Mar '03 contract was trading 0.035 (or 3.5 ticks) rich.

In this example, the relative richness or cheapness of the futures contract is reckoned using the term deposit market as the standard of value. In many ways, since the Eurodollar futures market is considered rightly to be the more liquid and competitive of the two markets, it might make more sense to value the richness or cheapness of the term deposit market relative to the Eurodollar futures market.

To do this, one can calculate the term deposit rates implied by Eurodollar futures rates. This is what we have done in Exhibit 4.5, where we find that the market value of 6-month LIBOR was 1.970 percent, which was 0.002 less than the term deposit rate of 1.972 percent implied by the futures market. The 9-month term deposit rate was 3.5 basis points below its "fair" value, while the 12-month deposit rate was 1.7 basis points below its fair value.

EXHIBIT 4.5

Is Term LIBOR Rich or Cheap?
June 17, 2002

Contract Month	Market Futures Price	Implied Rate	Term	Term LIBOR Rates: Implied	Term LIBOR Rates: Market	Term LIBOR Rich/Cheap?
Sep '02	97.895	2.1050	6 months	1.972	1.970	cheap 0.002
Dec '02	97.505	2.4950	9 months	2.155	2.120	cheap 0.035
Mar '03	96.945	3.0550	12 months	2.392	2.375	cheap 0.017

FORWARD RATES ARE BREAK-EVEN RATES

A forward rate is the rate at which a yield curve trade will break even. The fact that forward rates are break-even rates is perhaps one of the most powerful practical applications of forward rates.

To see this, consider a standard "positive carry" trade in which a bank borrows money for 3 months and lends it for 6 months.

EXAMPLE 4.7

EVALUATE THE PERFORMANCE OF A "POSITIVE CARRY" TRADE

On June 17, 2002, a bank is able to borrow $100,000,000 for 3 months at 1.83% and lend $100,000,000 for 6 months at 1.97%. Because the bank earns 1.97% on its 6-month asset and pays 1.83% on its 3-month liability, it is said to have positive carry.

How will this trade perform if 3 months from now, the 3-month rate:

1. *Remains at 1.83%?*
2. *Goes to 2.10%, which is the forward rate implied by today's term deposit rates?*

EXAMPLE 4.7 Continued

Yield Curves for Roll-Down and Break-Even Scenarios

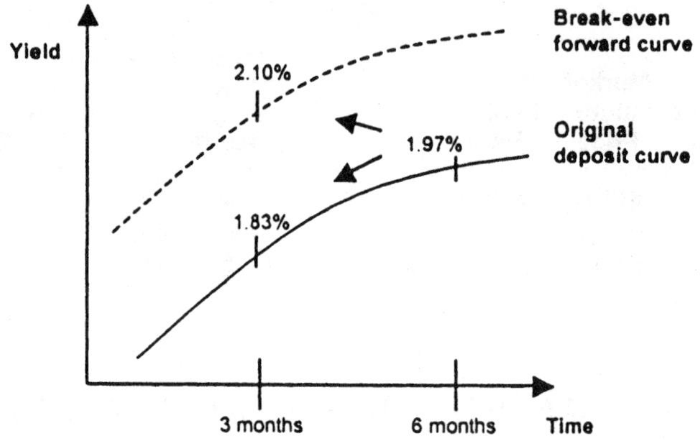

1. The 3-month rate 3 months from now is 1.83%

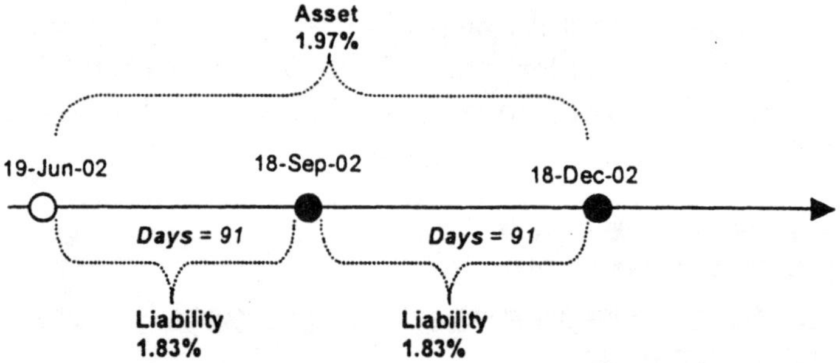

$$Asset_{18Dec02} = \$100{,}000{,}000\left[1 + 0.0197\left(\frac{182}{360}\right)\right] = \$100{,}995{,}944$$

$$Liability_{18Dec02} = \$100{,}000{,}000\left[1 + 0.0183\left(\frac{91}{360}\right)\right]\left[1 + 0.0183\left(\frac{91}{360}\right)\right]$$

$$= \$100{,}927{,}306$$

$$Income_{18Dec02} = \$100{,}995{,}944 - \$100{,}927{,}306 = \$68{,}638$$

The banker would make $68,638 if the 3-month rate is 1.83% 3 months from now.

EXAMPLE 4.7 Continued

2. The 3-month rate 3 months from now is 2.10%

$$Asset_{18Dec02} = \$100{,}000{,}000\left[1 + 0.0197\left(\frac{182}{360}\right)\right] = \$100{,}995{,}944$$

$$Liability_{18Dec02} = \$100{,}000{,}000\left[1 + 0.0183\left(\frac{91}{360}\right)\right]\left[1 + 0.0210\left(\frac{91}{360}\right)\right]$$

$$= \$100{,}995{,}872$$

$$Income_{18Dec02} = \$100{,}995{,}944 - \$100{,}995{,}872 = \$72$$

The banker just about breaks even if the 3-month rate 3 months from now is 2.10%.

The refinancing rate at which a trade like this breaks even is the fair value of the forward rate at the beginning of the trade.

Since we know that borrowing short term and lending long term is like being long a forward asset, we know that we should be able to reproduce the gains on this trade by buying an appropriate number of the right Eurodollar contract. In this example, rather than borrowing for 3 months and lending for 6, we can simply buy the Sep '02 futures contract. To compare the results of the two approaches, we need to compare what the two approaches make on the same day. With the Sep '02 futures contract, we will know what we have made when the contract expires on September 16, 2002 (value date of September 18). We need, then, a way to find what we have made on the cash and carry trade on that day.

To do this, we need to rearrange the information we used to reckon the gain or loss in December to find the present value of our gain or loss as of September. That is, if we divide the December values of the asset and liability by [1 + Sep LIBOR(Days/360)], we can compare the present value of the long-term asset with the September value of the original 3-month liability. Notice in Example 4.8 that if we do this, we find that the net value of our position would be \$68,322, which, as it happens, is simply the present value of the \$68,638 that was our net gain in December. That is, \$68,322 = \$68,638/[1 + 0.0183(91/360)].

EXAMPLE 4.8

PRESENT VALUE THE CASH FLOWS FROM EXAMPLE 4.7

Evaluate the asset and liability from Example 4.7 on September 18, rather than December 18.

To present value the cash flows to September 18, divide the maturity value on December 18 by the invested value of \$1 from September 18 to December 18.

1. The 3-month rate in September is 1.83%

$$Asset_{18Sep02} = \frac{\$100{,}000{,}000\left[1 + 0.0197\left(\frac{182}{360}\right)\right]}{\left[1 + 0.0183\left(\frac{91}{360}\right)\right]}$$

$$= \$100{,}530{,}905$$

$$Liability_{18Sep02} = \frac{\$100{,}000{,}000\left[1 + 0.0183\left(\frac{91}{360}\right)\right]\left[1 + 0.0183\left(\frac{91}{360}\right)\right]}{\left[1 + 0.0183\left(\frac{91}{360}\right)\right]}$$

$$= \$100{,}462{,}583$$

$$Income_{18Sep02} = \$100{,}530{,}905 - \$100{,}462{,}583 = \$68{,}322$$

The banker would make \$68,322 as of September 18.

2. The 3-month rate in September is 2.10%

$$Asset_{18Sep02} = \frac{\$100{,}000{,}000\left[1 + 0.0197\left(\frac{182}{360}\right)\right]}{\left[1 + 0.0210\left(\frac{91}{360}\right)\right]} = \$100{,}462{,}655$$

$$Liability_{18Sep02} = \frac{\$100{,}000{,}000\left[1 + 0.0183\left(\frac{91}{360}\right)\right]\left[1 + 0.0210\left(\frac{91}{360}\right)\right]}{\left[1 + 0.0210\left(\frac{91}{360}\right)\right]}$$

$$= \$100{,}462{,}583$$

$$Income_{18Sep02} = \$100{,}462{,}655 - \$100{,}462{,}583 = \$72$$

The banker just about breaks even.

Now we are ready to show how a positive carry trade can be replicated with futures.

EXAMPLE 4.9

REPLICATE THE POSITIVE CARRY TRADE WITH FUTURES

Borrowing for 3 months at 1.83% and lending for 6 months at 1.97% on June 17, 2002, is akin to buying September 2002 Eurodollar futures at a fair value of 97.90 [= 100 − 2.10].

How would the futures position perform 3 months later on September 16 (its expiration date) if:

1. *The 3-month rate comes in at 1.83%?*
2. *Futures settle at their fair value of 2.10%?*

On June 17:

Buy 101 September 2002 futures at 97.90[5]

On September 16:

1. 3-month LIBOR = 1.83%

$$\textit{September 2002 futures} = 98.17\ [= 100 - 1.83]$$

$$\textit{Gain} = 101\ [98.17 - 97.90]\ \$2500 = \$68{,}175$$

2. 3-month LIBOR = 2.10%

$$\textit{September 2002 futures} = 97.90\ [= 100 - 2.10]$$

$$\textit{Gain} = 101\ [97.90 - 97.90]\ \$2500 = \$0$$

The futures trade comes very close to matching the cash trade in Example 4.8 under the two interest rate scenarios. The cash trade income was $68,322 when the 3-month rate starting in 3 months was 1.83%. At a rate of 2.10%, the income was $72.

YIELD CURVE TRADES

The fact that Eurodollar futures replicate a carry trade provides further insight into the risks and rewards of borrowing short and lending long. Exhibit 4.6 shows the results of simple roll trades in

5. We discuss hedge ratios in "Hedging with Eurodollar Futures," chapter 5.

EXHIBIT 4.6

Return by Contract for Simple Buy and Hold Strategies

Mean of Return

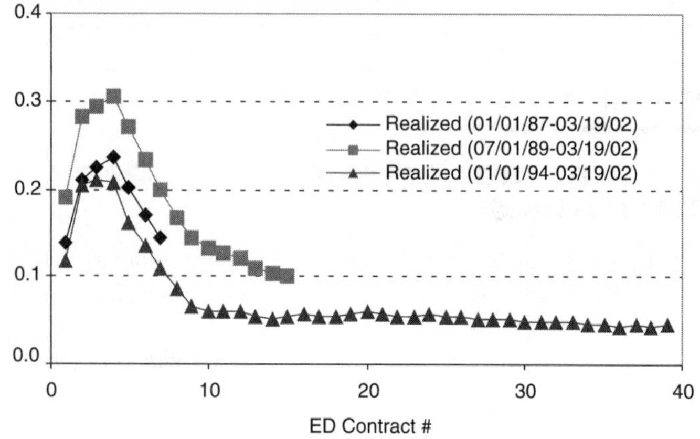

Standard Deviation of Return

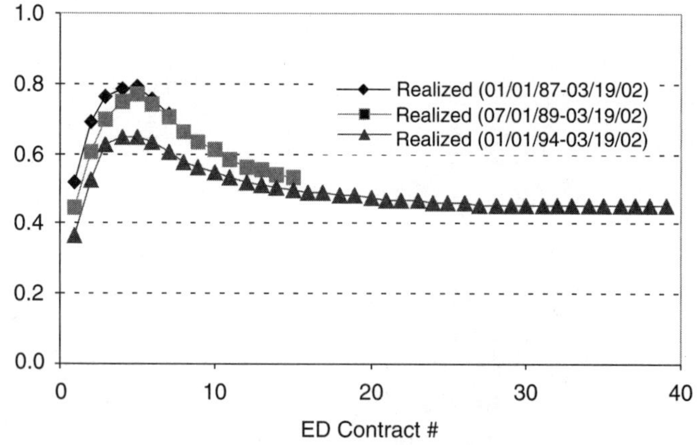

Sharpe Ratio

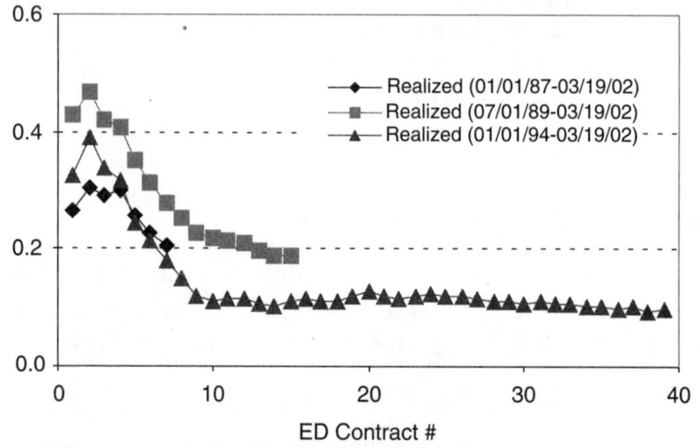

which one buys a Eurodollar contract, holds it for 3 months, and then "rolls" the position into the next contract month. For example, you might buy the contract that is next to expire when it has 3 months to expiration, hold it to expiration, and then replace it with the next contract. On June 17, 2002, this would entail first buying the Sep '02 contract, holding it until it expires, and then replacing it on September 16 with the Dec '02 contract, and so forth. This sequence of trades would be like borrowing for 3 months, lending for 6, and then closing out the position every 3 months.

If, instead, we buy the Dec '02 contract and hold it until September and then replace it with the Mar '03 contract, and so on, we would be replicating the returns to borrowing money for 6 months, lending it for 9 months, and then closing out this position after 3 months.

FINDING THE FORWARD TERM DEPOSIT CURVE IMPLIED BY TODAY'S FUTURES RATES

Another handy application of forward (futures) rates is in the construction of forward-starting term deposit curves.

Forward-starting term deposit curves, like the one derived in Example 4.10, are useful in assessing yield curve trades. For example, Exhibit 4.8 shows two term deposit curves—one for today's spot market and one for the March 17, 2003, forward-starting date. The difference between the two is striking. For example, the 6-month deposit rate on June 17, 2002, was 1.97%. The March 17, 2003, value of the 6-month term rate 9 months forward was 3.359%. From this, we can conclude that any trade whose success depends on the value of the 6-month rate 9 months from now will break even at a rate of 3.359%, which is 139 basis points higher than today's spot 6-month rate.

EXAMPLE 4.10

FIND A FORWARD-STARTING TERM DEPOSIT CURVE

Use the futures market data on June 17, 2002, to find the forward-starting term deposit curve for March 19, 2003. See Exhibit 4.7 for futures prices and rates.

3-month rate: We know that the 3-month deposit for that date is 3.055%, which is simply the March '03 futures contract rate.

6-month rate: To find the 6-month term deposit rate, we chain together two forward rates—the March '03 and June '03 futures rates as follows:

$$\left[1 + Rate_{6\,mo}\frac{182}{360}\right] = \left[1 + 0.030550\left(\frac{91}{360}\right)\right]\left[1 + 0.036350\left(\frac{91}{360}\right)\right]$$

Solving for $Rate_{6\,mo}$, we find that the 6-month deposit rate for our March 19, 2003 forward curve is 3.359%.

9-month rate: The 9-month rate for our forward term deposit curve is 3.636%:

$$\left[1 + Rate_{9mo}\frac{273}{360}\right] =$$

$$\left[1 + 0.030550\left(\frac{91}{360}\right)\right]\left[1 + 0.036350\left(\frac{91}{360}\right)\right]\left[1 + 0.04120\left(\frac{91}{360}\right)\right]$$

Continuing this process, we find term deposit rates at 3-month intervals for maturities ranging from 3 to 24 months:

Term	Rate
3 month	3.055
6 month	3.359
9 month	3.636
12 month	3.882
15 month	4.086
18 month	4.268
21 month	4.431
24 month	4.585

EXHIBIT 4.7

Eurodollar Futures Prices and Rates
Monday, June 17, 2002

Contract	Mon/Yr	Price	Rate	Expiration Date	Days
EDM2	Jun '02	98.1212	1.8788	6/17/02	91
EDU2	Sept '02	97.895	2.1050	9/16/02	91
EDZ2	Dec '02	97.505	2.4950	12/16/02	91
EDH3	Mar '03	96.945	3.0550	3/17/03	91
EDM3	Jun '03	96.365	3.6350	6/16/03	91
EDU3	Sep '03	95.880	4.1200	9/15/03	91
EDZ3	Dec '03	95.505	4.4950	12/15/03	91
EDH4	Mar '04	95.280	4.7200	3/15/04	91
EDM4	Jun '04	95.080	4.9200	6/14/04	91
EDU4	Sep '04	94.920	5.0800	9/13/04	91
EDZ4	Dec '04	94.750	5.2500	12/13/04	91

EXHIBIT 4.8

Spot and Forward-Starting Term Rates
June 17, 2002

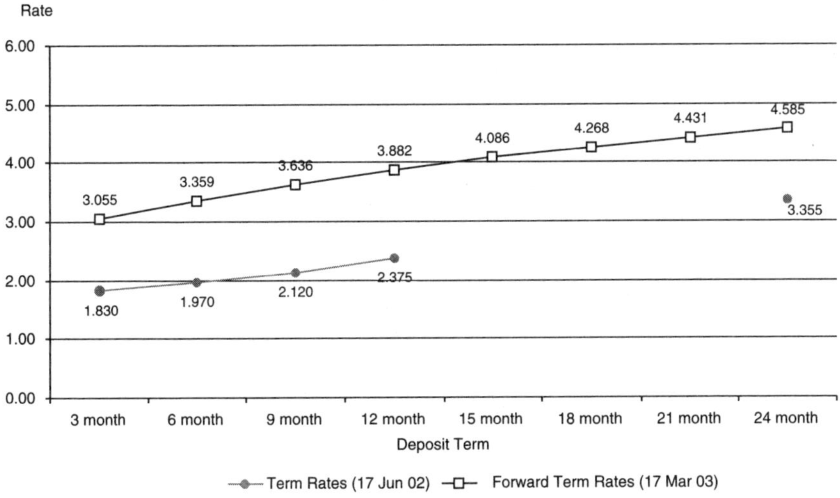

CHAPTER 5

Hedging with Eurodollar Futures

Hedging and replicating are two sides of the same coin. You may have this sense already, but you will find in this chapter that you can use a Eurodollar futures contract to convert a floating rate asset (or liability) into the equivalent of a fixed rate asset (or liability). Or you can convert a fixed rate asset into a floating rate asset.

In the one case—when you are converting a floating rate asset into a fixed rate asset—what you are really doing is hedging a forward cash flow. That is, you are fixing the amount of cash that will show up on some future date. Whether you think of this as cash flow hedging or as replicating future or forward cash flows is perfectly fine as long as your objective is clear.

In the other case—when you are turning a fixed rate asset into a floater—what you are really doing is fixing the present value of your position. And while protecting the present value of your position against changes in interest rates may sound more like hedging in the traditional sense, it is really only one way of thinking of it.

One thing is clear. If you hedge a forward cash flow, the present value of your position will vary with the level of interest rates. But if you hedge the present value of your position, your forward cash flows will vary with the level of interest rates. Thus, you can hedge cash flows, or you can hedge present values, but you cannot do both at the same time. Or what is the same thing, you can convert floating to fixed or fixed to floating, but not both at the same time.

Once we know what we want to do, the challenge is to do it correctly. The purpose of this chapter is to show how to reckon Eurodollar futures hedge ratios and how to manage the hedges over time.

In this chapter, we will work both with cash flow hedging and with present value hedging. In particular, we will show how to:

- Calculate zero-coupon bond prices from Eurodollar rates
- Convert a floating rate note into a fixed rate note
- Calculate the correct number of Eurodollar futures needed for a hedge
- Hedge the present value of a fixed rate instrument
- Manage a Eurodollar hedge over time
- Work with real-world complications

THE TOOL IS A EURODOLLAR FUTURES CONTRACT

Henry Ford's line about the customer being able to have a model T in any color he wanted as long as it was black is apt here. Our hedging tool is the Eurodollar futures contract. For hedging purposes, the contract has three important features that determine completely the way we have to use the tool. First, the value of the contract is determined by the value of a 3-month interest rate that spans the period covered by the contract (e.g., from March 19, 2003, to June 18, 2003, for the March '03 contract). Second, each basis point change in the underlying interest rate is worth $25. And third, because gains and losses on futures are settled every day in cash, the present value of the gain or loss is also $25.

BASIC HEDGE ALGEBRA

As a result of this structure, every hedging problem works the same way. We want a number of futures contracts whose change in value, for a given change in an underlying interest rate, will equal any change in the value of what we are trying to hedge or replicate. When using Eurodollar futures, we begin by isolating the effect of a change in the 3-month rate underlying a particular futures contract on what we want to hedge. We then divide this value by the change in the value of the Eurodollar futures contract. That is, once we have determined how much a change in any given Eurodollar futures rate will affect the value of our position, we calculate the hedge ratio as shown in Equation 5.1.

EQUATION 5.1

Hedge Ratio

$$\text{Hedge ratio} = \frac{\text{Change in the value of the position}}{\text{Change in the value of the futures}}$$

And, depending on whether the *change in the value of the position* is a forward value or a present value, the hedge ratio can be written, for a 1-basis-point change in the underlying 3-month futures rate, as shown in Equation 5.2 or Equation 5.3.

EQUATION 5.2

Hedge Ratio for Forward Values

$$\text{Hedge ratio} = \frac{\text{Change in the forward value of the position}}{\text{Forward value of } \$25}$$

EQUATION 5.3

Hedge Ratio for Present Values

$$\text{Hedge ratio} = \frac{\text{Change in the present value of the position}}{\$25}$$

The sign of the hedge ratio depends, of course, on whether you want to offset or replicate a change in value.

DERIVING PRESENT AND FORWARD VALUES FROM EURODOLLAR FUTURES RATES

Sooner or later, cash today must be translated into cash tomorrow, or cash tomorrow must be translated into cash today. Eurodollar futures not only allow us to do this, but provide us with information about the rates at which these conversions can be made.

Calculating a Forward Value (Terminal Wealth)

Consider Exhibit 5.1, which provides Eurodollar futures rates for all 40 contracts as of the expiration of the June '02 contract on June 17, 2002. The exhibit also shows the actual number of days between futures expirations for each contract. From these rates and days, we can determine how much $1, if invested at the sequence of Eurodollar rates implied by the futures contracts, would produce at the end of any given 3-month period. For example, $1 invested on June 17, 2002 (value date June 19, 2002) for 91 days would produce $1.0047 [= $1 × (1 + 0.018788 × (91/360))]. If this entire amount were rolled over at the next rate of 2.105% for the next 91 days, the result would be $1.0101 [= $1.0047 × (1 + 0.02105 × (91/360))], and so forth. The results of these calculations are shown in the column labeled *Terminal wealth*. Equation 5.4 shows the calculation of terminal wealth.

EQUATION 5.4

Calculate Terminal Wealth Using Futures Rates

$$Terminal\ wealth = \left[1 + Rate_1 \frac{Days_1}{360}\right] \times \cdots \times \left[1 + Rate_n \frac{Days_n}{360}\right]$$

where

Terminal wealth is the maturity value of $1
Rate is the interest rate for the spot or forward period
Days is the number of days in the interest rate period
n is the forward period

Calculating a Zero-Coupon Bond Price (Present Value)

The inverses of these terminal wealth values represent the prices of LIBOR-based zero-coupon bonds that mature on the respective dates (see Equation 5.5). For example, since $1 invested today would produce $1.0243 1 year from now, one need pay only

EXHIBIT 5.1

Terminal Wealths and Zero-Coupon Bond Prices
June 17, 2002

Contract	Mon/Yr	Eurodollar Rate	Expiration Date	Days	Terminal Wealth	Zero-Coupon Price
EDM2	Jun '02	1.8788	6/17/02	91	1.0047	0.9953
EDU2	Sep '02	2.1050	9/16/02	91	1.0101	0.9900
EDZ2	Dec '02	2.4950	12/16/02	91	1.0165	0.9838
EDH3	Mar '03	3.0550	3/17/03	91	1.0243	0.9763
EDM3	Jun '03	3.6350	6/16/03	91	1.0337	0.9674
EDU3	Sep '03	4.1200	9/15/03	91	1.0445	0.9574
EDZ3	Dec '03	4.4950	12/15/03	91	1.0564	0.9466
EDH4	Mar '04	4.7200	3/15/04	91	1.0690	0.9355
EDM4	Jun '04	4.9200	6/14/04	91	1.0823	0.9240
EDU4	Sep '04	5.0800	9/13/04	91	1.0962	0.9123
EDZ4	Dec '04	5.2500	12/13/04	91	1.1107	0.9003
EDH5	Mar '05	5.3250	3/14/05	91	1.1257	0.8884
EDM5	Jun '05	5.4350	6/13/05	98	1.1423	0.8754
EDU5	Sep '05	5.5400	9/19/05	91	1.1583	0.8633
EDZ5	Dec '05	5.6750	12/19/05	84	1.1736	0.8520
EDH6	Mar '06	5.7200	3/13/06	98	1.1919	0.8390
EDM6	Jun '06	5.8100	6/19/06	91	1.2094	0.8268
EDU6	Sep '06	5.8900	9/18/06	91	1.2274	0.8147
EDZ6	Dec '06	6.0200	12/18/06	91	1.2461	0.8025
EDH7	Mar '07	6.0600	3/19/07	91	1.2652	0.7904
EDM7	Jun '07	6.1350	6/18/07	91	1.2848	0.7783
EDU7	Sep '07	6.2100	9/17/07	91	1.3050	0.7663
EDZ7	Dec '07	6.3350	12/17/07	91	1.3259	0.7542
EDH8	Mar '08	6.3600	3/17/08	91	1.3472	0.7423
EDM8	Jun '08	6.4250	6/16/08	91	1.3691	0.7304
EDU8	Sep '08	6.4850	9/15/08	91	1.3915	0.7186
EDZ8	Dec '08	6.5950	12/15/08	91	1.4147	0.7069
EDH9	Mar '09	6.6050	3/16/09	91	1.4383	0.6952
EDM9	Jun '09	6.6600	6/15/09	91	1.4626	0.6837
EDU9	Sep '09	6.7100	9/14/09	91	1.4874	0.6723
EDZ9	Dec '09	6.8000	12/14/09	91	1.5129	0.6610
EDH0	Mar '10	6.7950	3/15/10	91	1.5389	0.6498
EDM0	Jun '10	6.8400	6/14/10	91	1.5655	0.6388
EDU0	Sep '10	6.8750	9/13/10	91	1.5927	0.6279
EDZ0	Dec '10	6.9550	12/13/10	91	1.6207	0.6170
EDH1	Mar '11	6.9400	3/14/11	91	1.6492	0.6064
EDM1	Jun '11	6.9750	6/13/11	98	1.6805	0.5951
EDU1	Sep '11	7.0050	9/19/11	91	1.7102	0.5847
EDZ1	Dec '11	7.0800	12/19/11	89	1.7402	0.5747
EDH2	Mar '12	7.0550	3/17/12	91	1.7712	0.5646

\$0.9763 [= 1/\$1.0243] for a bond that would pay \$1 dollar 1 year from now.

EQUATION 5.5

Calculate the Zero-Coupon Bond Price

$$\textit{Zero-coupon bond price}_m = \frac{1}{\textit{Terminal wealth}_m}$$

where

m is the number of days to maturity

HEDGING OR REPLICATING FORWARD CASH FLOWS

Much of the work in the world of applied finance is making certain amounts of money show up on certain days in the future. You have money today that must be converted into a different amount of money sometime later. With this in mind, consider the task of converting a 3-month floating rate liability, 9 months forward, into a fixed rate liability. That is, consider the problem of converting a floating rate note into a fixed rate note.

EXAMPLE 5.1

CONVERT A FLOATING RATE LIABILITY INTO A FIXED RATE LIABILITY

Suppose that on June 17, 2002, you commit to borrow \$1,000,000 on March 17, 2003, for 91 days. Under the terms of your agreement, you will pay whatever the value of 3-month LIBOR proves to be on March 17 plus or minus a fixed spread. For the sake of keeping things simple, assume the spread is zero.

Now suppose you want to convert your floating rate borrowing into the equivalent of fixed rate borrowing. To do this, you can sell the March '03 Eurodollar futures contract so that any increase in the rate you pay on your loan will be offset by gains in the value of your short Eurodollar position.

What are the cash flow consequences if the 3-month forward borrowing rate changes by 1 basis point?

E X A M P L E 5.1 Continued

Your source of risk in this example is the forward value of 3-month LIBOR from March 17, 2003, to June 16, 2003. If this rate rises 1 basis point, because there are 91 actual days in the 3-month borrowing period, your interest obligation on the loan will increase \$25.28 [= \$1,000,000 × 0.0001 × (91/360)]. If the interest rate were to fall by 1 basis point, your interest obligation would fall by \$25.28. In either case, the cash consequence of the rate change will be realized on June 16, 2003, which is 1 year from now.

The March '03 Eurodollar futures price will change in response to exactly the same rate. The big difference is that the change in the value of one March '03 Eurodollar contract will be \$25 for each basis point change in the underlying rate, and the \$25 will be paid or collected today. All futures gains or losses are realized today.

Cash Flow Effect of a 1-Basis-Point Increase in the 3-Month Forward Rate from March 17 through June 16, 2003

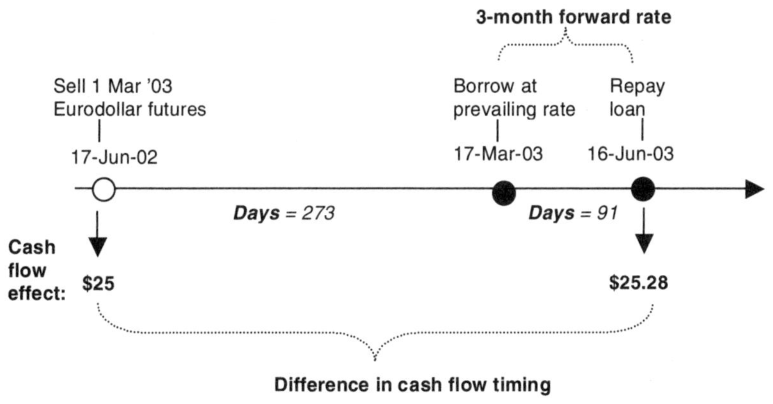

Forward Valuing the Gain or Loss on the Eurodollar Futures Contract

Suppose you are short 1 March '03 Eurodollar futures contract and that the March '03 rate rises 1 basis point. You have a \$25 gain today on your futures position and a \$25.28 loss 1 year from now on your floating rate loan. To know whether 1 Eurodollar futures contract is the right hedge for this position, you need to know whether \$25 today is more than you need, just enough, or less than you need to cover your \$25.28 loss 1 year hence.

EXAMPLE 5.2

FIND THE HEDGE AMOUNT THROUGH FORWARD VALUING

How many futures contracts do you need to hedge the \$1,000,000 forward borrowing in Example 5.1? In general, one contract per \$1,000,000 is not the right answer.

To answer this question, you need to know what \$25 today will produce 1 year from now if invested at a 1-year term rate. That is, if you can invest the \$25 for 364 days (from June 17, 2002, through June 16, 2003) at a term rate of $Rate_{364}$, you will have \$25 × (1 + $Rate_{364}$ (364/360)) when the interest on your loan is due. As a result, whether one Eurodollar contract is too much, just the right amount, or too little coverage depends on whether

$$\$25\left[1 + Rate_{364}\frac{364}{360}\right] \overset{?}{\gtreqless} \$25.28$$

The correct number of futures can be calculated as

$$Hedge\ ratio = \frac{\$25.28}{\$25\left[1 + Rate_{364}\frac{364}{360}\right]}$$

which can also be written as

$$Hedge\ ratio = \frac{\$25.28}{\$25\ TW_{364}}$$

where TW_{364} is the value to which \$1 would grow if invested at the sequence of Eurodollar rates shown in Exhibit 5.1. The numerator is the forward value of the rate change on your interest rate obligation and the denominator is the forward value of the \$25 that you would receive on a single futures contract. If the 1-year term deposit rate were 2.40%, the terminal wealth would be \$1.0243, and the forward value of \$25 would be \$25.61 [= \$25 × (1 + 0.0240 × (364/360))], which is more than the \$25.28 loss you need to offset. In fact, the correct hedge ratio would be

$$Hedge\ ratio = 0.987 = \frac{\$25.28}{\$25\left[1 + 0.0240\left(\frac{364}{360}\right)\right]} = \frac{\$25.28}{\$25.61}$$

EXAMPLE 5.2 Continued

which for a \$1 million obligation would necessarily round to 1 contract. For a \$100 million position, however, the hedge ratio would round to 99 contracts, which would be an improvement over the one contract per \$1 million approximation we used earlier.

Present Valuing the Gain or Loss on a Floater

The big advantage of approaching the hedging problem by forward valuing the \$25 per basis point on a Eurodollar futures contract is that it highlights the true hedging or replicating problem. Futures contracts either pay or take away cash on a daily basis. If you receive money, you must invest it until you need it. If you pay money, you must finance your payments until you have the cash to pay it off.

The big disadvantage of using forward values is that there are an infinite number of forward dates to handle.

EXAMPLE 5.3

FIND THE HEDGE AMOUNT THROUGH PRESENT VALUING

In Example 5.2, we found the Eurodollar futures hedge amount by forward valuing cash flows. Solve the hedge problem by present valuing cash flows.

As an analytical convenience, we can solve the hedge ratio problem by replacing the question

$$\$25\left[1 + Rate_{364}\frac{364}{360}\right] \overset{?}{\gtreqqless} \$25.28$$

with the question

$$\$25 \overset{?}{\gtreqqless} \frac{\$25.28}{\left[1 + Rate_{364}\frac{364}{360}\right]}$$

That is, we can divide both sides through by $(1 + Rate_{364}(364/360))$, which leaves us with present values on both sides. It is clear, though, that the solution to the hedge ratio will be the same.

The chief advantage of using present values rather than forward values is that there is a single present date, which is a great analytical simplification. The big drawback, of course, is that present values obscure the realities of forward cash flow management. So take your pick.

HEDGING OR REPLICATING PRESENT VALUES OF CASH FLOWS

If the forward cash flow is fixed, hedging becomes a problem of offsetting changes in the cash flow's present value. And if we do this, we will succeed in converting a fixed rate note into a floating rate note.

Calculating the Price of a Zero-Coupon Bond

Suppose you hold a $100,000,000 1-year zero-coupon bond issued by someone with LIBOR quality credit. Because the credit quality of the issue is the same as the credit quality implied by Eurodollar futures rates, the present value of this zero would be $100,000,000 times the price of a 1-year Eurodollar zero. From Exhibit 5.1, we find that this price is a function of four Eurodollar rates and can be written as

$$\frac{1}{\left(1 + R_{17Jun02}\frac{91}{360}\right)\left(1 + R_{16Sep02}\frac{91}{360}\right)\left(1 + R_{16Dec02}\frac{91}{360}\right)\left(1 + R_{17Mar03}\frac{91}{360}\right)}$$

Given rates of 1.8788%, 2.105%, 2.495%, and 3.055%, the price of a 1-year Eurodollar zero would be $0.9763, and the present value of your $100 million zero would be $97,630,000.

Calculating the Present Value of a Basis Point

Once you have determined the value of your zero-coupon bond, the next step is to determine how much the value of your bond will change if any of the four rates that determine the price of the zero change 1 basis point. The results of increasing and decreasing each of the four rates (while holding the other three fixed at their original values) are shown in Exhibit 5.2. In all cases, the zero-

EXHIBIT 5.2

Effect of Rate Changes on the Value of the $100 Million 1-Year Zero

Contract Month	*Zero-Coupon Price*			*Change in Position Value*			Eurodollar Hedge (Contracts)
	Original	Up 1 bp	Down 1 bp	Up 1 bp	Down 1 bp	Average	
Jun '02	0.9762617812	0.9762372207	0.9762863429	−2,456.05	2,456.17	2,456.11	−98.24
Sep '02	0.9762617812	0.9762372347	0.9762863289	−2,454.65	2,454.77	2,454.71	−98.19
Dec '02	0.9762617812	0.9762372587	0.9762863048	−2,452.25	2,452.37	2,452.31	−98.09
Mar '03	0.9762617812	0.9762372932	0.9762862704	−2,448.80	2,448.92	2,448.86	−97.95

coupon bond prices are calculated to 10 decimal places so that changes in the value of a $100 million zero-coupon bond could be determined to the nearest cent.

Consider, for example, a change in the Jun '02 rate. If this rate were to increase by 1 basis point, the price of the 1-year zero would fall from 0.9762617812 to 0.9762372207, a decrease of 0.0000245605, which would be worth $2,456.05 for a $100 million zero. If this same rate were to decrease by 1 basis point, we see that the zero price would increase to 0.9762863429, an increase of 0.0000245617, which would be worth $2,456.17. The difference in the size of the effect reflects what is known in fixed income markets as "positive convexity," which describes the fact that the bond's price will increase more as rates fall than it will decrease as rates rise.

Finding the Hedge for a Zero-Coupon Bond

When hedging the position, of course, you do not know which way rates will go, so you average the two results, which would produce an average change in position value of $2,456.11. To hedge this exposure, one would sell 98.24 [= $2,456.11/$25.00] of the Jun '02 contract to hedge a long position or buy 98.24 contracts to replicate the behavior of a long position.

The results for the other three contracts are very nearly the same. They differ from one another only because of the slight upward slope in the Eurodollar futures rate curve. Effects of a change in the Mar '03 rate are multiplied by a slightly smaller number (because the rates at the front of the curve are lower) than are the effects of changes in the Jun '02 rate (because the rates at the back of the curve are higher). If the four Eurodollar rates were identical, the resulting hedges would be identical, too.

Faster Hedge Ratio Calculations with Calculus

The advantage of reckoning the effects of rate changes up and down is that you can see the actual changes in position value. Because your hedges are averages of the effects of both increases and decreases in rates, however, you can find your hedge ratios faster, with less computing time, if you use calculus.

The price of any given zero-coupon bond is simply a function of a string of spot and Eurodollar futures rates, and the partial derivative of this function with respect to any one of those rates allows us to calculate hedge ratios quickly and accurately.

We begin with Equation 5.6, which shows the price of a zero that matures n quarters from now. We then use partial derivatives, as shown in Equation 5.7, to express the effect of a change in any one of the sequence of rates (e.g., the ith rate) on the zero's price.

EQUATION 5.6

Calculate the Zero-Coupon Bond Price

$$Z_n = \prod \left(\frac{1}{1 + Rate_i \dfrac{Days_i}{360}} \right), \quad (i = 1 \text{ to } n)$$

where

Z_n is the zero-coupon bond price at time n
$Rate_i$ is the interest rate for the spot or forward period i
$Days_i$ is the number of days in the interest rate period i
Π is the mathematical symbol for taking the product of the term that follows it over a specified range, in this case from 1 to n

EQUATION 5.7

Calculate a Hedge Ratio Using Calculus

$$\frac{\partial Z_n}{\partial Rate_i} = \frac{-0.0001 \dfrac{Days_i}{360}}{\left[1 + Rate_i \dfrac{Days_i}{360} \right]} Z_n$$

where

$\partial Z_n / \partial Rate_i$ is the change in the zero-coupon bond price given a change in the ith period rate

As long as we get the units right when we plug in the key values, this will give us what we need to calculate the correct hedge ratio. Consider a change in the June '02 rate on the price of the 1-year (4-quarter) zero in the example above. The original zero price is 0.9762617812, so the partial effect of a change in the June '02 rate would be

$$\frac{\partial Z_n}{\partial Rate_i} = \frac{-0.0001\left(\frac{91}{360}\right)}{\left[1+0.018788\left(\frac{91}{360}\right)\right]} \times 0.9762617812$$

$$= -0.00002456108$$

which, if multiplied by a $100,000,000 principal amount, would produce a total dollar effect of $2,456.11.

Pricing and Hedging a Coupon-Bearing Bond

Once you know how to price and hedge a zero-coupon bond, you will have no trouble pricing and hedging coupon bearing bonds, which are simply packages of zero-coupon bonds.

EXAMPLE 5.4

PRICE A COUPON BOND

Consider a 5% coupon bond that pays its coupon semiannually and that matures in 2 years. Price the bond by present valuing its cash flows, using the zero-coupon bond prices in Exhibit 5.1.

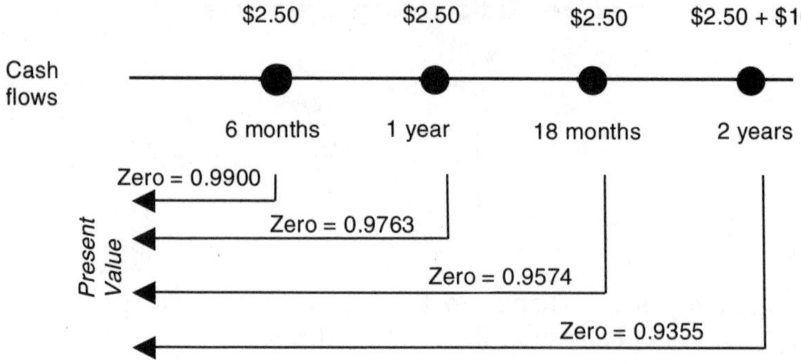

The cash flows associated with $100 par amount of the bond would be $2.50 at each 6-month interval plus $100 at the bond's maturity for a total cash flow on the last day of $102.50.

EXAMPLE 5.4 Continued

If we then use the Eurodollar zero prices from Exhibit 5.1, we find that the present value of the first coupon payment would be \$2.4750 [= \$2.50 × 0.9900], while the present value of the final coupon payment and principal would be \$95.8888 [= \$102.50 × 0.9355]. Adding up the four present values produces a total of \$103.1980 (see Exhibit 5.3). And, if this were a bond issued by LIBOR quality London banks, this total present value would be a good approximation of the bond's market price.

Finding the appropriate hedge for this bond requires nothing more than finding the correct hedges for each of the four cash flows and then adding them up. Using the hedge ratio formula derived in the previous section, we can calculate the number of Eurodollar futures needed to hedge \$1 million par amount of zeros with maturities of December 18, 2002, June 18, 2003, December 17, 2003, and June 16, 2004. The results of these calculations are shown in Exhibit 5.4.

For example, to hedge \$1 million of a zero that matures on December 18, 2002, we would have to sell 0.996 of the Jun '02 and Sep '02 contracts (see upper panel of Exhibit 5.4). As a result, to hedge the first coupon payment of \$2.5 million that arrives on

EXHIBIT 5.3

Pricing a 2-Year, 5% Coupon Bond
June 17, 2002

Payment			
Date	**Amount**	**Zero Price**	**Present Value**
12/18/2002	2.50	0.9900	2.4750
6/18/2003	2.50	0.9763	2.4408
12/17/2003	2.50	0.9574	2.3935
6/16/2004	102.50	0.9355	95.8888
		Total =	103.1980

EXHIBIT 5.4

Number of Eurodollar Futures Needed to Hedge $1 Million Par Amount Zero
June 17, 2002

	Zero Maturity			
Contract	**18-Dec-02**	**18-Jun-03**	**17-Dec-03**	**16-Jun-04**
Jun '02	0.99627	0.98244	0.96346	0.94141
Sep '02	0.99571	0.98188	0.96292	0.94087
Dec '02		0.98092	0.96197	0.93995
Mar '03		0.97954	0.96062	0.93863
Jun '03			0.95923	0.93727
Sep '03			0.95806	0.93613
Dec '03				0.93525
Mar '04				0.93473

Number of Eurodollar Futures Needed to Hedge $100 Million Par Amount 5% Semiannual Coupon Bond
June 17, 2002

	Cash Flow				
Contract	**18-Dec-02**	**18-Jun-03**	**17-Dec-03**	**16-Jun-04**	**Total**
Jun '02	2.49	2.46	2.41	96.49	103.85
Sep '02	2.49	2.45	2.41	96.44	103.79
Dec '02		2.45	2.40	96.34	101.20
Mar '03		2.45	2.40	96.21	101.06
Jun '03			2.40	96.07	98.47
Sep '03			2.40	95.95	98.35
Dec '03				95.86	95.86
Mar '04				95.81	95.81
Total	4.98	9.81	14.42	769.18	798.39

December 18, we would have to sell 2.49 of each (see lower panel of Exhibit 5.4). To hedge $1 million of a zero that matures on June 18, 2003, we would have to sell 0.982, 0.982, 0.981, and 0.980 of the Jun '02, Dec '02, Mar '03, and Jun '03 contracts respectively. To hedge the second semiannual coupon payment, then, we would have to sell 2.46, 2.45, 2.45, and 2.45 of each of these contracts. And so forth.

This example serves at least two useful purposes. First, it highlights the subtle but important effect of cash flow timing on hedge ratios. More distant cash flows require smaller hedge ratios because their present values are lower.

Second, it highlights an important feature of coupon-bearing bonds that might not otherwise be apparent. That is, the price of a coupon-bearing bond is relatively more sensitive to changes in near term forward rates than is the price of a zero-coupon bond with the same final maturity. A change in the Jun '02 or Sep '02 Eurodollar rates will affect the present value of four separate cash flows on a coupon-bearing bond, while a change in the Dec '03 or Mar '04 rates will affect the present value of only the final cash flow. With a zero, changes in these four contract rates would have nearly identical effects on the price because there is only one, final, cash flow. As a result, the Eurodollar hedge for a coupon-bearing bond will place greater weight on the nearby contract months (e.g., 103.85 of the June '02 contract) than on later contracts (e.g., 95.81 of the March '04 contract).

MANAGING HEDGE RATIOS

Eurodollar futures hedges are not static. We can see from the hedging problems we have solved in this chapter that our hedges will change as interest rates rise or fall and as time passes.

As Rates Rise or Fall

As interest rates fall, the prices of non-callable bonds become more sensitive to changes in interest rates while Eurodollar futures prices do not. As interest rates rise, non-callable bond prices become less sensitive to yield changes, while the present value of a basis point on a Eurodollar contract remains $25. Thus, Eurodollar hedge ratios for non-callable bonds will tend to increase as interest rates fall and to decrease as interest rates rise.

If you are hedging a long position in a non-callable bond (or are receiving fixed in an interest rate swap, which we consider in the next chapter), you will welcome these kinds of adjustments. Decreases in interest rates will require you to sell more Eurodollar futures, while increases in interest rates will require you to buy back some of your futures. Since these kinds of adjustments automatically prompt you to sell when prices have gone up and to buy when prices have gone down, you will find yourself making money on average with these adjustments. This advantage to being short Eurodollar futures when hedging bonds that possess positive convexity has important implications for the pricing of Eurodollar futures. The question of what this advantage is worth and the effect it has on Eurodollar futures prices is the subject of "The Convexity Bias in Eurodollar Futures," chapter 7.

As Time Passes

Because present values tend to rise with the passing of time, Eurodollar hedge ratios tend to rise as well. Consider the problem of converting a floating rate borrowing into a fixed rate borrowing.

EXHIBIT 5.5

Number of Eurodollar Futures Needed to Hedge the Cost of Borrowing $100 Million for 91 Days
June 17, 2002

Months Forward		Zero	*Basis Point Value*		Eurodollar
Takedown	**Maturity**	**Price***	**Nominal**	**Present**	**Hedge**
3	6	0.9900	2527.78	2502.52	100.1
6	9	0.9838	2527.78	2486.83	99.5
9	12	0.9763	2527.78	2467.78	98.7
12	15	0.9674	2527.78	2445.31	97.8
15	18	0.9574	2527.78	2420.10	96.8
18	21	0.9466	2527.78	2392.91	95.7
21	24	0.9355	2527.78	2364.70	94.6

*See Exhibit 5.1 for zero prices beginning with 12/16/02.

Exhibit 5.5 shows how many Eurodollar contracts are needed to convert a 3-month floater into a 3-month fixed rate note at forward horizons ranging from 3 to 21 months (and final loan maturities ranging from 6 to 24 months). In each case the nominal forward value of a basis point on the borrowing is $2,527.78 for a $100 million note with a 91-day maturity, but the present value of a basis point change in the borrowing rate is higher for nearer forward periods. For example, if you plan to initiate the forward borrowing in March 2003 (as the problem was originally cast), the loan would mature in June 2003, and the present value of the $2,527.78 nominal basis point value would be $2,467.78. To hedge this would require 98.7 contracts. On the other hand, if you plan to initiate the borrowing in March 2004 and pay it back in June 2004, the present value of the $2,257.78 would be $2,364.70, and the Eurodollar hedge would be 94.6 contracts.

An important implication of this result is that the number of futures needed to hedge a March 2003 forward borrowing would increase with the passing of time. In this example, you would have to add roughly 1 contract per quarter to your hedge. Such an effect is almost glacially slow, but in practice, the effect is large enough to make a difference if the book you are hedging is large enough. Banks that manage several hundreds of billions of dollars of assets and liabilities will find their hedge ratios changing every day.

While such day-to-day adjustments might seem to be a nuisance, the transaction economics of the futures industry is particularly well suited to this kind of fine tuning. For an active participant in the Eurodollar market, the cost of trading 1 contract is simply 1/100th the cost of trading 100 contracts. As a result, the hedger can make small adjustments to his position without incurring unduly large costs.

PRACTICAL CONSIDERATIONS IN REAL HEDGES

In any real hedging problem, you will come up against several gaps and misalignments. For one thing, you will find that you have exposure to a spot interest rate—called the stub rate—that spans the period from today until the first available Eurodollar futures expiration. For another, your own interest rate exposure almost certainly will not line up with the terms covered by Eurodollar futures. And for yet another, the rate at which you will borrow or lend will be done at what is now an unknown spread against LIBOR. All of which suggests that anyone who hedges with Eurodollar futures has to be willing to live with a certain amount of unhedgeable risk or to bring other hedging tools to bear.

The Stub Period

Every pricing and hedging problem with futures must deal with the stub period—the time that separates us from the first available Eurodollar futures contract expiration. In the examples so far in this chapter, we have assumed that the June '02 contract was still available for trading or hedging. As a practical matter, though, we will find ourselves with several days or weeks between us and the first available contract.

For example, when the June '02 contract expires, the next contract available in the quarterly contract cycle is the Sep '02 contract. When that happens, we find that the value of our position may depend on the 3-month rate from the middle of June until the middle of September, but that we have no obvious futures tool for dealing with the risk. Our stub period in this case would be 3 months long, and the stub rate would be a 3-month cash market rate.

The stub period shrinks with the passing of time, of course. By the middle of July, the stub period would have shrunk to 2 months, and the stub rate would be a 2-month cash rate. By the middle of August, our exposure would be to a 1-month cash rate.

The stub period poses two problems—one for pricing and one for hedging. The pricing problem is not especially difficult to solve. All we need, instead of a futures rate, is an appropriate term value for LIBOR with which we can begin the process of calculating terminal wealths and zero-coupon bond prices. In Exhibit 5.6, which reflects the market as of the close of business on Thursday, July 18, 2002, we found a cash stub rate of 1.8291 percent. The value date for any cash market transaction on Thursday would be the following Monday, July 22. With a value date of September 18 for the rate to which the Sep '02 futures contract will settle, this stub rate covered 58 actual days. As a result, terminal wealth for the end of the stub period was 1.0029 [= 1 + 0.018291 × (58/360)], which we assume can be rolled over at the rate of 1.87% that was implied by the price of the Sep '02 Eurodollar contract at the close of business on July 18.

The hedging problem posed by the stub rate is more difficult to solve. Changes in stub rates tend to exhibit a low correlation with changes in Eurodollar futures rates as shown in Exhibit 5.7.

This leaves the hedger with three choices. One is to leave the risk unhedged. Part of the reason for the low correlation between changes in stub rates and changes in the first Eurodollar contract rate is that Fed policy has a very powerful influence over short-term money markets. It is possible for 1-month and 2-month deposit rates to be very stable for long stretches of time. So it is possible for a well-informed hedger to take a considered risk and leave the exposure unhedged.

If the hedger wants to do something about the exposure, though, there are really just two choices. One is to effect a cash market transaction—for example, borrow cash for 58 days in this example at a term money market rate—or piece together a strip

EXHIBIT 5.6

Constructing Terminal Wealths and Zero Prices Using a Stub Rate
Trade Date = Thursday, July 18, 2002
Value Date for Stub Rate = Monday, July 22, 2002

Contract	Days	Rate	End of Period Terminal Wealth	Zero Price
Stub	58	1.8291	1.0029	0.99706
Sep '02	91	1.8700	1.0077	0.99237
Dec '02	91	2.0500	1.0129	0.98725
Mar '03	91	2.3200	1.0188	0.98150
Jun '03	91	2.7600	1.0260	0.97470
Sep '03	91	3.3200	1.0346	0.96659
Dec '03	91	3.8200	1.0446	0.95734
Mar '04	91	4.1700	1.0556	0.94736

EXHIBIT 5.7

Correlation between Weekly Changes in Lead Eurodollar Futures Rates and Spot LIBOR

January 1997 through July 2002

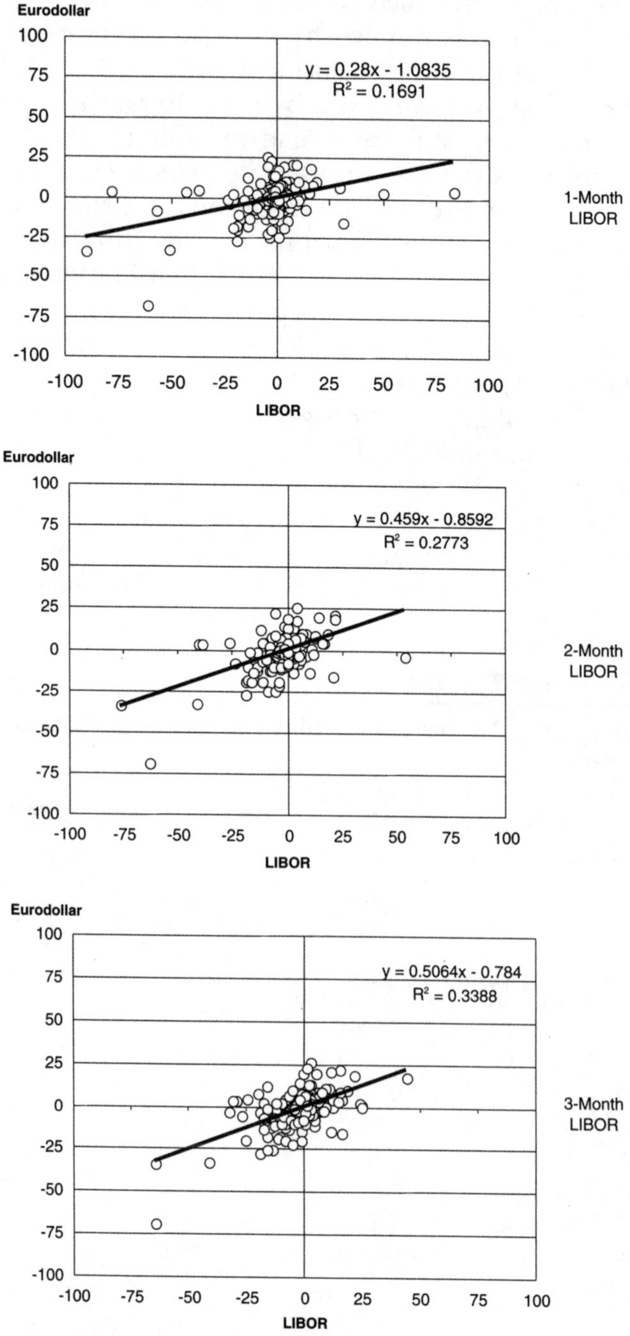

of Fed funds futures, which because of the way they settle, tend to provide excellent hedges for very short-term money market exposure.

Date and Term Mismatches

The interest rate that represents the source of your risk almost never will correspond exactly to the 3-month forward rate periods defined by the expirations of Eurodollar futures. The rate you care about typically will have a maturity other than 3 months, and the period spanned by your rate will begin and end on dates that do not line up with Eurodollar expirations.

Consider, for example, a problem in which the source of your risk is a 6-month rate that begins 1 month before the expiration of the Dec '02 contract and ends 2 months after the expiration of the March '03 contract. The links between this rate and the relevant Eurodollar futures rates is illustrated in Exhibit 5.8. In this exhibit, we show the terminal wealths that could be calculated from known stub and Eurodollar futures rates on July 18, 2002. We also show interpolated values of terminal wealths for the start and end dates of your 6-month period.

From these interpolated terminal wealths (TW), we can derive the implied forward rate we care about. The forward-starting 6-month rate is 2.10%.

$$TW_{15May03} = TW_{15Nov02}\left[1 + Rate_{Forward}\left(\frac{Days_{Forward}}{360}\right)\right]$$

$$1.0166 = 1.0060\left[1 + Rate_{Forward}\left(\frac{181}{360}\right)\right]$$

$$Rate_{Forward} = 2.10\%$$

The logical linkage, then, between changes in Eurodollar rates and changes in the rate that is the source of our risk, requires a reliable interpolation routine. For a wide range of hedging problems, we use linear interpolations of the natural logs of known terminals wealths. Just how this is done, along with pros and cons, is described in "Measuring and Trading Term TED Spreads," chapter 11.

EXHIBIT 5.8

Interpolating Terminal Wealths
July 18, 2002

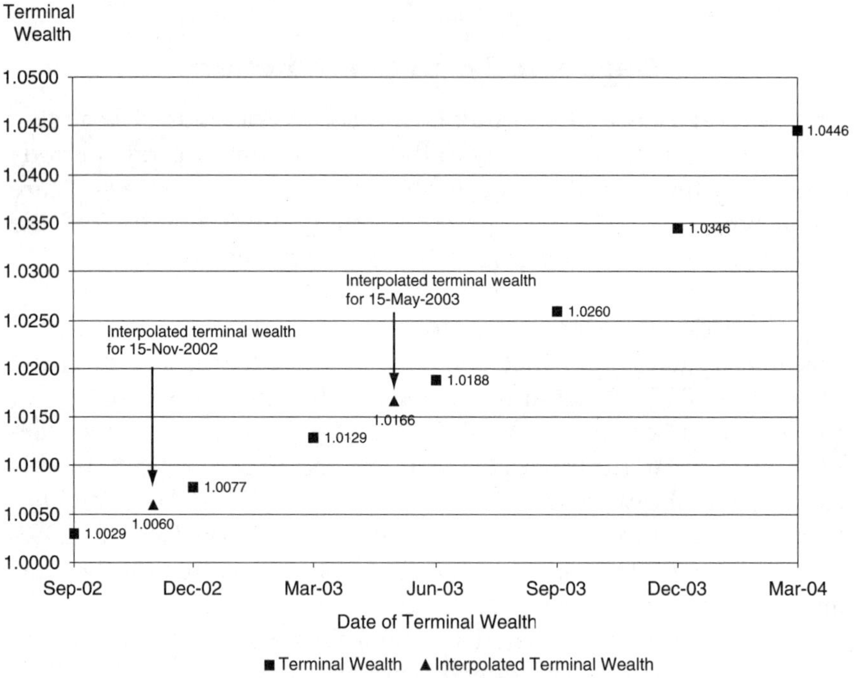

Contract	Start of Rate Period	End of Rate Period	Days	Rate	Terminal Wealth	Zero Coupon Price
Stub	7/22/02	9/18/02	58	1.8291	1.0029	0.99706
		11/15/02			1.0060	
Sep '02	9/18/02	12/18/02	91	1.8700	1.0077	0.99237
Dec '02	12/18/02	3/19/03	91	2.0500	1.0129	0.98725
		5/15/03			1.0166	
Mar '03	3/19/03	6/18/03	91	2.3200	1.0188	0.98150
Jun '03	6/18/03	9/17/03	91	2.7600	1.0260	0.97470
Sep '03	9/17/03	12/17/03	91	3.3200	1.0346	0.96659
Dec '03	12/17/03	3/17/04	91	3.8200	1.0446	0.95734
Mar '04	3/17/04	6/16/04	91	4.1700	1.0556	0.94736

Whole Contracts

In this chapter, we have shown several decimal places when reporting the results of hedge ratio calculations. The decimals are important because the effects of time and the level of interest rates can be subtle and hidden by rounding. At the same time, when you actually want to hedge something, you are constrained to transact in whole numbers of contracts. As a result, you must buy or sell either more or less than specified by the exact hedge ratio. To some extent, you can smooth things out by slightly underweighting one contract month and slightly overweighting a neighboring contract. Also, the whole contract problem becomes relatively less important as the size of the position you are hedging increases.

Credit Spreads

The U.S. Treasury has a better credit standing than do LIBOR quality banks. As a result, if you value a Treasury bond using Eurodollar zero prices, the present value produced by this approach would be lower than the bond's price. On the other hand, if we were valuing a junk bond, the present value produced by this approach would be higher than the bond's price.

If you plan to use futures to value or hedge bonds with credits that are either better or worse than the credit that underpins the LIBOR market, you need a way to determine the credit spread between the two markets. You also must be careful to work with the correct bond price when determining hedge ratios. Both of these problems are dealt with in detail in "Measuring and Trading Term TED Spreads," chapter 11. This chapter also contains a highly detailed technical appendix that covers problems of date mismatches and differences in day-count conventions that will be useful to anyone who has to do the coding for in-house computer programs.

Variable Credit Spreads

While the Eurodollar contract is tied to LIBOR, almost no one—with the exception of A1/P1 rated banks—actually borrows or lends at LIBOR. Almost all transactions will be done at a spread either above or below LIBOR, and the spread can vary, sometimes a lot. Changes in the spread are perhaps more important for borrowers than for lenders and a careful consideration of your own credit situation can play an important role in whether you decide to use Eurodollar futures to hedge. For example, if you have excellent credit but face the possibility of a worsening of your credit, you might well prefer to lock in your financing rates in the term financing market rather than borrowing at floating rates and using Eurodollar futures to cover your floating rate exposure. Eurodollar futures will protect you against changes in LIBOR but will afford no protection against a worsening of your own spread against LIBOR. In contrast, if your credit is already bad but may improve, you might better your financing costs by using futures to cover your variable rate exposure and leave yourself open to enjoying the benefit of a fall in your own financing rate relative to LIBOR.

CHAPTER 6

Pricing and Hedging a Swap with Eurodollar Futures

Interest rate swaps make up the lion's share of the over-the-counter interest rate derivatives market. They are extremely useful for both hedging and trading, are used extensively in corporate funding programs, and are rapidly becoming the core of fixed-income markets throughout the world. The market for interest rate swaps really began to open up in the early 1980s and quickly evolved to the point where most interest rate swaps use LIBOR as the basic reference rate.

The swap market is, in some sense, the end user or retail market for interest rate derivatives, while the Eurodollar futures market is the wholesale market where swap dealers get the raw material for pricing and hedging swaps. The purpose of this chapter is to provide a rudimentary introduction to fixed/floating interest rate swaps and to the relationship between swaps and Eurodollar futures. In this chapter, you will learn how to:

- Determine the size and timing of cash flows on a swap
- Price and hedge a swap using the cash flow method
- Price and hedge a swap using the hypothetical securities method
- Measure convexity differences between forward and futures rates

- Relate a swap yield curve to forward (futures) and zero-coupon yield curves

FIXED/FLOATING INTEREST RATE SWAPS

An interest rate swap is an agreement under which the two counterparties agree to exchange cash flows whose values are determined by the notional size of the swap and by the values of two interest rates. These two interest rates can be whatever rates the contracting parties choose. For example, swap counterparties could exchange cash flows based on commercial paper and Treasury bill rates. The most common swaps, however, are fixed/floating swaps in which the reference rate for the floating side is 3-month LIBOR. In such a swap, one counterparty agrees to receive payments based on a fixed rate that is established when the swap is transacted and to make payments based on a floating or variable rate that is set equal to 3-month LIBOR at key rate setting dates. The other counterparty does just the opposite.

To price or hedge an interest rate swap, you need to be able to determine the size and timing of all cash flows. To do this, you need to know:

- Notional principal amount
- Cash flows in arrears
- Periodicity
- Spot and forward-starting swaps
- Day-count conventions and swap yields

Notional Principal Amount

In principle, the cash flows on the interest rate swap could be replicated by borrowing and lending in the cash market. For example, the cash flows on the fixed/floating swap could be replicated by borrowing short term (say every 3 months) and lending long term (for the life of the swap). If you were replicating the cash flows on a \$100 million swap, you would actually borrow \$100 million and turn right around and lend \$100 million. Also, when the term of the swap is over, you would use the principal value of your asset to pay off the principal value of your liability.

With an interest rate swap, these principal amounts never change hands, so the opening and closing transactions are eliminated. Rather, a swap has what is known as a notional principal amount, which is used only to calculate hypothetical interest payments. For example, on a $100 million swap, you would apply the fixed and floating interest rates to $100 million. The resulting hypothetical interest payments are the swap's cash flows.

One consequence of this arrangement is that credit exposure in a swap is less than it is in the cash market. Rather than having to worry about the $100 million that someone owes you on your asset, you need worry only about the net present value of the swap, and then only if the net present value is positive and the other person owes you.

Cash Flows in Arrears

With most interest rate swaps, the hypothetical interest payments are paid and received just as they would be on real assets and liabilities—at the end of the interest calculation period. If you were to borrow money for 3 months, you would pay the interest on the loan at the end of the 3 months. And so it is with a swap. Cash flows occur at the end of the interest calculation period.

Periodicity

Fixed and floating cash flows can be done with any periodicity the two counterparties choose. The payments could be made monthly, quarterly, semiannually, or annually. The fixed and floating payments might have the same periodicity, in which case the cash flows are netted, or different periodicity. The floating rate reset dates have their own periodicity, which may or may not match the periodicity of the floating cash flows.

What constitutes the standard mix of fixed and floating payments varies over time, but at this writing, a very common mix is semiannual floating and fixed payments, with the floating rate tied to 3-month LIBOR compounded or to 6-month LIBOR.

Spot and Forward-Starting Swaps

With a spot swap, the initial net cash flow is defined when the trade is executed. For example, if you do a fixed/floating swap that starts today, you would determine both the fixed rate that will be used throughout the swap's entire life as well as the initial "floating" rate. As a result, you know when the swap is transacted exactly how much cash will change hands at the first cash flow date.

In contrast, a swap can start on a forward date. In this case, you might determine the fixed rate today, when the trade is done, and wait until the forward-starting date to determine the first of the floating rates. A common version of a forward-starting swap is an "IMM" swap, whose rate setting dates correspond exactly to the expiration dates for Eurodollar futures and whose cash flow dates correspond to futures value dates. By design, these swaps are especially easy to price and hedge because there are no date mismatches with the Eurodollar futures market.

Day-Count Conventions and Swap Yields

You also have your choice of day-count conventions for both legs of the swap. The most common would be an Actual/360 money market convention for the floating side and a 30/360 corporate convention for the fixed side. In practice, however, you can choose from:

- Actual/365 or Actual/Actual
- Actual/365 (Fixed)
- Actual/360
- 30/360 or Bond Basis
- 30E/360 or Eurobond Basis

for either the floating or the fixed side, and you can choose a different method for each side.

Swap yields describe the fixed side of the swap. In the dollar market, the usual convention is corporate—that is, semiannual 30/360—although the swap yield often is quoted in the same terms as the thing it is hedging. Therefore, if the swap is hedging a Treasury, its yield would be quoted using Treasury conventions.

If it is hedging a LIBOR-based loan, it might be quoted in money market terms.

In keeping with this, swap yields in other markets (e.g., Europe, the United Kingdom, and Canada) tend to be quoted using those markets' conventions.

EXAMPLE 6.1

SWAP BASICS:[1] AN IMM SWAP

Diagram the cash flows for the following 1-year fixed/floating IMM swap:

Notional amount = $100 million
Trade date = June 17, 2002
Maturity date = June 18, 2003
Fixed side
  Fixed rate = 2.41%
  Payment dates = Eurodollar futures value dates
  Day-count convention = Actual/360
Floating side
  Reset dates = Eurodollar futures expiration dates
  Payment dates = Eurodollar futures value dates
  Day-count convention = Actual/360
  Floating rate = 3-month LIBOR
  Spread over floating reference rate= 0 bp
  Floating rate for initial calculation = 1.8788%

For this IMM swap, the floating rate is reset on Eurodollar futures expiration dates. Payment occurs three months after the rate has been set. The first floating rate, for example, is set on the trade date, June 17. The actual cash flow occurs on September 18, the next futures value date. The swap payment is calculated by netting the fixed and floating rate payments:

$$\text{Payment} = \text{Notional amount}(\text{Fixed rate} - \text{Floating rate})\frac{\text{Days}}{360}$$

1. For a thorough explanation of swap conventions, please visit the website of International Swaps and Derivatives Association, Inc. (ISDA) at www.isda.org.

EXAMPLE 6.1 Continued

The first swap payment is:

$$Payment = \$100\ million(0.0241 - 0.018788)\frac{91}{360} = \$134{,}276$$

This first net cash flow of $134,276 is paid to the counterparty that receives fixed and pays floating. The remaining net cash flows are unknown at the time of the trade.

Swap trade date, June 17, 2002

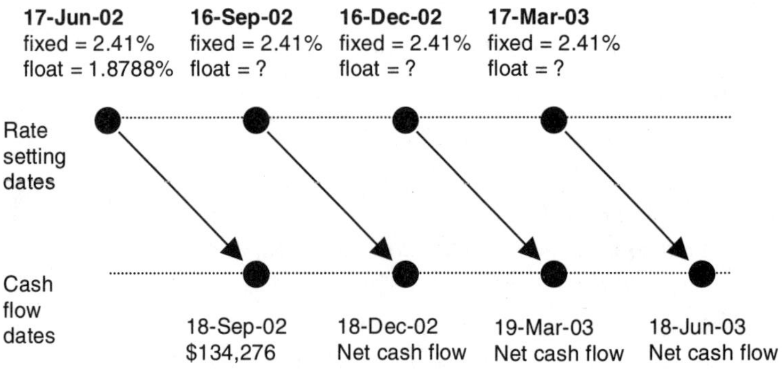

APPROACHES TO PRICING AND HEDGING INTEREST RATE SWAPS

The net cash flows on a fixed/floating swap are designed to mimic exactly the net cash flows that would be produced by combining fixed and floating rate assets and liabilities. For example, the person who receives fixed and pays floating on an interest rate swap could achieve the same thing by borrowing money at a variable rate and lending or investing the entire amount at a fixed rate. In such a transaction, the opening cash flows (i.e., the principal amounts) would offset one another exactly, so the initial net cash flow would be zero. Thereafter, net cash flows would reflect the values of the fixed and variable interest rates. And at the final maturity of the fixed rate asset, the principal amount would be used to pay off the principal amount on the floating rate loan.

With this in mind, you can tackle the problems of pricing and hedging a swap in either of two ways, both of which take you to the same answers.

Cash Flow Approach

With an interest rate swap, the principal amounts do not change hands—only the hypothetical interest payments. Because the initial net cash flow in the hypothetical trade described above is zero, you can solve the problem of pricing the swap by finding a fixed coupon that would produce a set of net cash flows whose present values sum to zero. Once you are in the swap, the variable cash flows on the floating side of the swap can be viewed as your source of risk, and you can hedge this risk by converting variable cash flows into fixed.

Hypothetical Security Approach

Because a swap is designed to mimic the cash flows on the trade described above, the swap can be valued as if it included the two hypothetical securities. On the trade date, both securities would trade at par because you are dealing at market rates. You already know the money market rate, so all that remains is to find the fixed coupon that would set the value of the hypothetical fixed rate note equal to par. Then, once you are in the swap, you can determine how sensitive the values of your hypothetical fixed and floating rate notes are to changes in Eurodollar rates and reckon your hedge ratios accordingly.

Of the two approaches, you are likely to find that the hypothetical security approach is both easier and more reliable than the cash flow method, which requires enormous attention to detail. As usual, the chief advantage of the cash flow approach is that it highlights the real financing issues involved in managing a hedge. The chief advantage of the hypothetical security approach is the simplicity afforded by working with present values.

PRICING A SWAP USING THE CASH FLOW METHOD

For the purposes of this exercise, you will receive fixed and pay floating on the very simple 1-year swap shown in Exhibit 6.1. Both fixed and floating payments are made quarterly (and so are netted) and fall on Eurodollar futures value dates. To simplify the upcoming analysis, fixed payments will be calculated using

EXHIBIT 6.1

1-Year Fixed/Floating Interest Rate Swap with Quarterly Payments

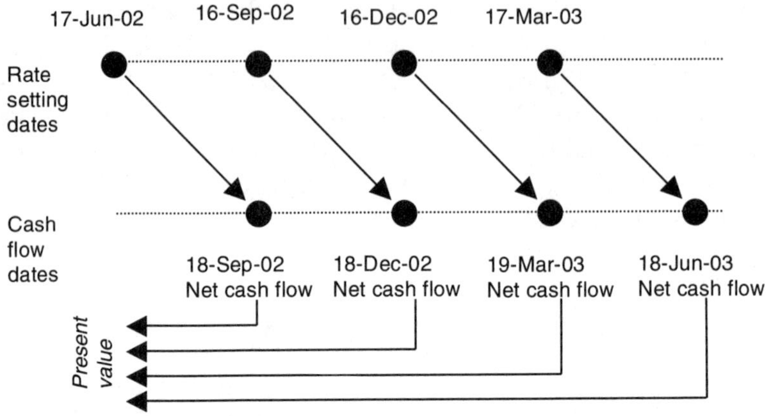

the fixed coupon and a fixed 90/360 day count fraction, while floating payments will be calculated using values of 3-month LIBOR together with an Actual/360 money market convention. And, although the fixed coupon on the swap does not depend on the swap's notional principal amount, we will work with a $100 million notional amount for the purpose of calculating hypothetical cash flows.

Everything you need to price and hedge this swap is provided by the Eurodollar futures market. First, the futures prices tell you the rates that you can lock in. Second, Eurodollar futures are the tools you, as a swap dealer, need to hedge any interest rate risk involved in taking one side or the other of the swap. As a dealer, you can agree to pay fixed and receive floating and offset your risk by buying Eurodollar futures. Or you can agree to receive fixed and pay floating and hedge your risk by selling Eurodollar futures. In either case, all you need to know is the fixed rate at which you can do the trade and break even.

Consider the market data for June 17, 2002, that are shown in Exhibit 6.2. To price a 1-year swap, we will use the first four Eurodollar futures rates, which are plotted in Exhibit 6.3. The Jun '02 contract price implied a 3-month rate of 1.8788%, which was also the spot value of 3-month LIBOR on that day. The Sep '02

EXHIBIT 6.2

Eurodollar Futures Prices, Terminal Wealths, and Zero-Coupon Bond Prices
June 17, 2002

Contract	Mon/Yr	Price	Rate	Expiration Date	Value Date	Days	Terminal Wealth	Zero-Coupon Price
EDM2	Jun '02	98.1212	1.8788	6/17/2002	6/19/2002	91	1.0047	0.9953
EDU2	Sep '02	97.895	2.1050	9/16/2002	9/18/2002	91	1.0101	0.9900
EDZ2	Dec '02	97.505	2.4950	12/16/2002	12/18/2002	91	1.0165	0.9838
EDH3	Mar '03	96.945	3.0550	3/17/2003	3/19/2003	91	1.0243	0.9763

contract implied a rate of 2.105%, the Dec '02 contract a rate of 2.495%, and the Mar '03 contract a rate of 3.055%. Given these rates, which can be locked in using their respective contracts, the problem of pricing the swap is to find a fixed rate that is somewhere in the middle of the pack.

On balance, if you use the right fixed rate for the swap, you should find that any positive net cash flows will just offset any negative net cash flows. More to the point, the present values of cash flows on the swap should net to zero. In this example, this condition will be met if you find the fixed coupon, C, for which:

$$\begin{aligned} &[C/4 - 0.018788\,(91/360)]Z_{18Sep02} \\ +\,&[C/4 - 0.021050\,(91/360)]Z_{18Dec02} \\ +\,&[C/4 - 0.024950\,(91/360)]Z_{19Mar03} \\ +\,&[C/4 - 0.030550\,(91/360)]Z_{18Jun03} \\ =\,&0 \end{aligned}$$

EXHIBIT 6.3

Eurodollar Futures Rates vs. Swap Fixed Rate
June 17, 2002

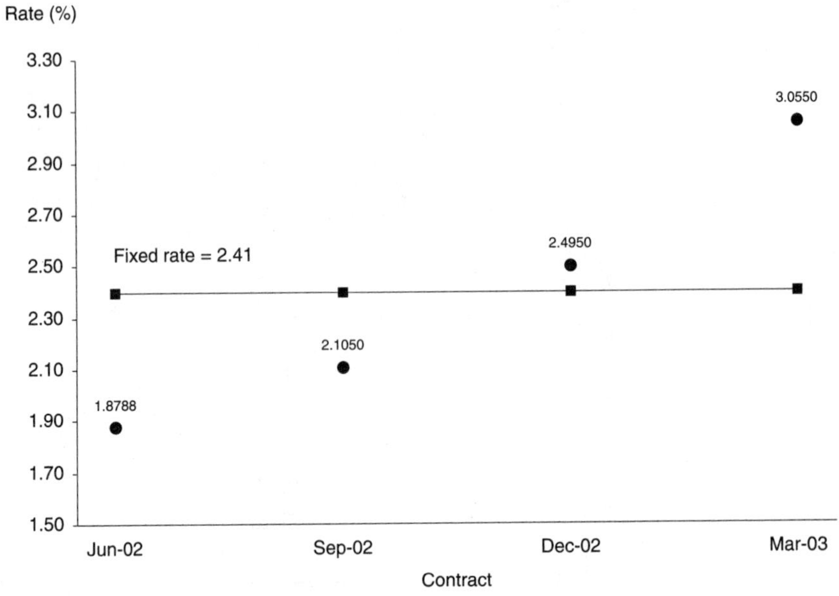

where the Z's represent the prices of Eurodollar zero-coupon bonds that mature on the four respective cash flow dates. These are available from Exhibit 6.2. Note that you use the price of a 3-month zero that matures on September 18 to value the first cash flow, the price of a 6-month zero that matures on December 18 to value the second cash flow, and so forth. If you plug the four zero prices into the equation, you can solve for $C = 2.40670876\%$ (see Exhibit 6.4).

Exhibits 6.3 and 6.4 provide the comfort you need to know that this solution is correct. First, you can see from the chart in Exhibit 6.3 that the rate looks reasonable. It is higher than the first two of the Eurodollar rates and lower than the last two. Second, as shown in Exhibit 6.4, if we use the fixed rate to calculate the fixed cash flows on a swap with a notional value of $100 million and use the four futures rates to calculate the so-called floating payments, we find that the present values of the net cash flows sum to 0.00.

In practice, you may find that the rate at which you do a swap is higher or lower than what you have solved for here. For one thing, you are unlikely ever to encounter this much precision. For another, in real market situations, you and your counterparty may well be using slightly different market data. For yet another, you will encounter the effects of bid/asked spreads and uncer-

EXHIBIT 6.4

Net Cash Flows and Present Values for a 1-Year Receive Fixed/Pay Floating Interest Rate Swap
Fixed Rate = 2.40670876%

Cash Flow Date	Cash Flows: Fixed	Cash Flows: Floating	Net Cash Flow	Zero Price	Present Value
9/18/02	601,677.19	474,918.89	126,758.30	0.9953	126,159.15
12/18/02	601,677.19	532,097.22	69,579.97	0.9900	68,884.55
3/19/03	601,677.19	630,680.56	(29,003.37)	0.9838	(28,533.54)
6/18/03	601,677.19	772,236.11	(170,558.92)	0.9763	(166,510.16)
				Total =	0.00

tainties about the costs of hedging a swap position. For all of these reasons and more, your objective in doing a swap is to obtain terms that are favorable to you. If at all possible, in other words, you would like the swap to be struck at a rate that produces a positive net present value for you.

HEDGING A SWAP USING THE CASH FLOW METHOD

To hedge a swap using the cash flow method, the best way to start is to write out the net present value (NPV) of the swap in terms of cash flows and zero-coupon bond prices. Equation 6.1 shows that our 1-year receive fixed/pay floating swap has four cash flows and four zero prices. Armed with this expression, we can proceed to determine just how much the net present value of the swap changes as we vary each of the four futures rates. This, in turn, will allow us to calculate the hedge ratio for each of our futures contracts.

EQUATION 6.1

Find the 1-Year Swap Net Present Value Using the Cash Flow Method

$$NPV(Swap) = CF_1Z_1 + CF_2Z_2 + CF_3Z_3 + CF_4Z_4$$

where

CF_i is the net cash flow for time i
Z_i is the zero bond price associated with time i

What we will find is that a change in each of the rates will have two effects. The first, and primary, effect is the outright cash flow effect. If we are receiving fixed and paying floating, any increase in a floating rate before its rate setting date will cost us money. Thus, we are exposed to increases in the Sep '02, Dec '02, and Mar '03 futures rates. We are not exposed to an increase in the Jun '02 futures rate since June 17, our trade date, marks the Jun '02 futures expiration and the rate setting date for our first cash flow.

The second, and secondary, effect is a sequence of present value effects. An increase in each of the rates will decrease the price of each zero-coupon bond that incorporates the rate. Note that even though the Jun '02 contract expires as of the swap trade date, we are still exposed to changes in spot LIBOR. As a result, an increase in spot LIBOR will decrease the prices of all four zero-coupon bond prices, while an increase in the Mar '03 rate will decrease only the price of the zero-coupon bond that matures on June 18, 2003.

The next step is to write out the partial derivatives (∂) to see how the swap's net present value is affected by a change in each futures rate. The results of this exercise are shown in Equation 6.2.

EQUATION 6.2

Find the Change in the 1-Year Swap NPV Given a Change in Futures

$$\frac{\partial NPV(Swap)}{\partial F_1} = Z_1\frac{\partial CF_1}{\partial F_1} + CF_1\frac{\partial Z_1}{\partial F_1} + CF_2\frac{\partial Z_2}{\partial F_1} + CF_3\frac{\partial Z_3}{\partial F_1} + CF_4\frac{\partial Z_4}{\partial F_1}$$

$$\frac{\partial NPV(Swap)}{\partial F_2} = Z_2\frac{\partial CF_2}{\partial F_2} + CF_2\frac{\partial Z_2}{\partial F_2} + CF_3\frac{\partial Z_3}{\partial F_2} + CF_4\frac{\partial Z_4}{\partial F_2}$$

$$\frac{\partial NPV(Swap)}{\partial F_3} = Z_3\frac{\partial CF_3}{\partial F_3} + CF_3\frac{\partial Z_3}{\partial F_3} + CF_4\frac{\partial Z_4}{\partial F_3}$$

$$\frac{\partial NPV(Swap)}{\partial F_4} = Z_4\frac{\partial CF_4}{\partial F_4} + CF_4\frac{\partial Z_4}{\partial F_4}$$

where

CF_i is the net cash flow for time i
Z_i is the zero bond price associated with time i
F_i is the futures rate for time i

Primary Effects

The first term in each of the four partial derivative equations represents the present value of the change in the floating cash flow given a change in the futures rate. The effect of a change in the rate on its associated cash flow is represented by $\partial CF_i/\partial F_i$, and the zero-coupon bond price we use to calculate the present value of the change is Z_i.

The schematic provided in Exhibit 6.5 illustrates these cash flow effects. Note, first, that when the deal is done, the first cash flow is set so that changes in spot LIBOR will have no effect on

EXHIBIT 6.5

Hedging the Swap's Cash Flows
June 17, 2002

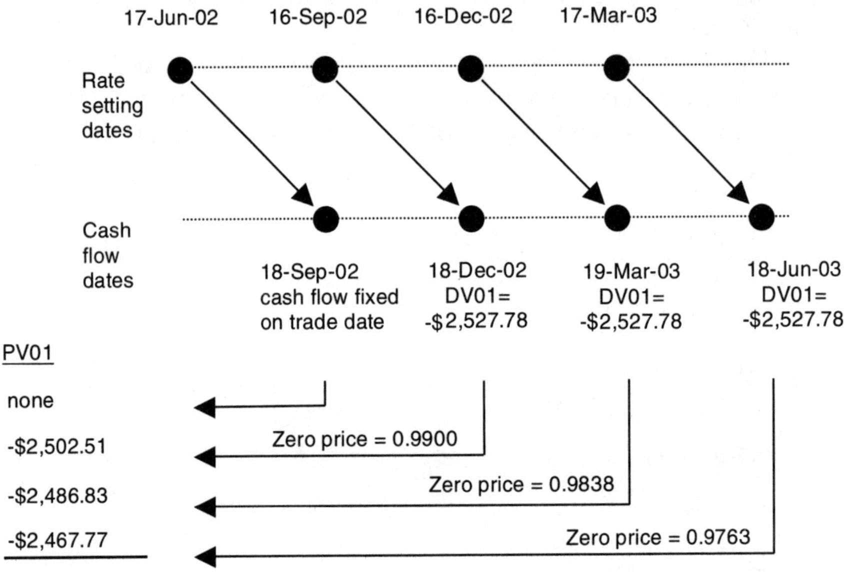

the cash flow that falls in September 2002. The values of the next three cash flows are still variable, however. And, given the assumptions we have used so far in this example, a 1-basis-point increase in any of these three rates will produce a loss of $2,527.78 [= $100,000,000 × 0.0001 × (91/360)] in its associated cash flow.

The time line presented in Exhibit 6.5 is very important for keeping the present values straight. For example, a change in the Sep '02 rate affects the swap's net cash flow on December 18, 2002, so we must use the price of a zero that matures on December 18 to determine the present value of the effect. A change in the Dec '02 rate will, in turn, affect the March 19, 2003 cash flow, so we need a March 19 zero to value that change. And finally, a change in the Mar '03 rate will affect the June 18, 2003 cash flow, so we need a June 18 zero to calculate the present value of that change.

We have, then, three variable cash flows, and, as shown in Exhibit 6.5, the present values of these effects depend on when they fall. The nominal or dollar value of a basis point (a.k.a. DV01) for each of the variable cash flows is a loss of $2,527.78, but the present value of a basis point (a.k.a. PV01) for each cash flow decreases with the length of the discounting horizon. The present value of the effect of a change in the Sep '02 rate, for example, is a loss of \$2,502.51 [= \$2,527.78 × 0.9900], while the present values of changes in the Dec '02 and Mar '03 rates are losses of \$2,486.83 [= \$2,527.78 × 0.9838] and \$2,467.77 [= \$2,527.78 × 0.9763] respectively.

Secondary Effects

To complete the hedge, the next step is to determine the sizes and signs of the present value effects. In Equation 6.2, the secondary effects of a change in each futures rate on the zero-coupon bond prices are represented by $\partial Z_i / \partial F_i$. A change in F_1, for example, affects the zero prices associated with each of the four cash flows.

For someone who is receiving fixed when the yield curve is upward sloping, the early cash flows will tend to be positive so that any decrease in the zero price used to calculate its present value will be a loss. On the other hand, the later cash flows will tend to be negative so that any decrease in present values will be a gain. The results of these calculations are shown in Exhibit 6.6.

Because we are working with the swap's net cash flows, these secondary present value effects are very small relative to the primary cash flow effects. A change in the Jun '02 rate (spot or stub LIBOR) on balance has no effect at all. The losses on the first two positive cash flows are exactly offset by the gains on the last two negative cash flows. A change in the Sep '02 rate, on the other hand, tends to offset very slightly the overriding cash flow effect. Taken together, these effects add to a gain of \$3.18, which reduces the effect of a change in that rate on the swap's net present value from \$2,502.51 to \$2,499.34.

Calculating Hedge Ratios

As usual, once you have done all the hard work of finding the present values of the effects of changes in the relevant futures rates, all that remains is to divide the results by \$25, as shown in Equation 6.3. The results of these calculations are shown in the bottom row of Exhibit 6.6.

EXHIBIT 6.6

Swap Hedge Based on the Cash Flow Method
Effect of a 1-Basis-Point Increase in Each Futures Rate
June 17, 2002

	Jun '02		***Sep '02***		***Dec '02***		***Mar '03***	
Cash Flow	**Primary Effect**	**Secondary Effect**	**Primary Effect**	**Secondary Effect**	**Primary Effect**	**Secondary Effect**	**Primary Effect**	**Secondary Effect**
First	0	−3.17	—	—	—	—	—	—
Second	—	−1.73	−2,502.51	−1.73	—	—	—	—
Third	—	0.72	—	0.72	−2,486.83	0.72	—	—
Fourth	—	4.19	—	4.19	—	4.18	−2,467.77	4.18
Net	**0.00**		**−2,499.34**		**−2,481.93**		**−2,463.60**	
Futures hedge	**0.00**		**−99.97**		**−99.28**		**−98.54**	

EQUATION 6.3

Find the Eurodollar Futures Hedge Ratios for the Swap

$$Hedge\ ratio_{F_i} = \frac{\dfrac{\partial NPV(Swap)}{\partial F_i}}{\$25}$$

where

F_i represents the *i*th futures contract.

Hedge Ratios Are Dynamic

Eurodollar hedge ratios are dynamic, of course, and vary with changes in the level of interest rates and with the passing of time. (The effects of interest rates and time show up in the zero price, which is used to calculate the PV01.) As a result, your hedge ratios will tend to rise if rates fall because the prices of the zeros you use will tend to rise. Also, your hedge ratios will tend to increase with the passing of time because the present values of the variable cash flows will tend to rise.

PRICING A SWAP USING THE HYPOTHETICAL SECURITIES METHOD

At the outset of this chapter, we noted that the purpose of a swap is to mimic the cash flows on transactions that could just as well be carried out in the cash market. In this case, instead of receiving fixed and paying floating on a $100 million notional swap, you could have borrowed $100 million at 3-month LIBOR on June 17, 2002, and used the proceeds to buy a $100 million fixed rate note that would pay its fixed coupon in quarterly installments. In such an arrangement, the 3-month borrowing would have to be rolled over as each leg matures and refinanced at whatever 3-month LIBOR happens to be at the time. At the end of one year, the fixed rate note would also pay back its original principal of $100 million, which you would use to pay off the principal amount of the fourth leg of your short-term financing.

If you approach the problem of pricing the swap this way (and this is far and away the most popular and reliable way to price a swap), all you need to do is find the fixed coupon, C, at which the price of the hypothetical note would equal par. In this particular case, this would be accomplished if:

$$\frac{C}{4}[Z_{18Sep02} + Z_{18Dec02} + Z_{19Mar03} + Z_{18Jun03}] + 100\,Z_{18Jun03} = 100$$

which can be rearranged as

$$C = \frac{400[1 - Z_{18Jun03}]}{[Z_{18Sep02} + Z_{18Dec02} + Z_{19Mar03} + Z_{18Jun03}]}$$

which also produces a solution of 2.40670876. Thus, the opening cash market trades that would begin to replicate the cash flows on the fixed/floating swap would be to borrow \$100 million on June 17 at a spot LIBOR rate of 1.8788 and invest the entire \$100 million in a 1-year note with a fixed coupon of 2.40670876. This way, the net initial cash flow would be zero (as it is with the swap) because the principal amounts offset each other perfectly. Thereafter, the net cash flows would be the difference between what you receive on the fixed rate note and what you pay on your floating rate financing. At final maturity, the principal amounts would offset again.

HEDGING A SWAP USING THE HYPOTHETICAL SECURITIES METHOD

Now we approach the problem of hedging the swap as if it were two hypothetical securities—a fixed rate asset financed with a floating rate liability. From the standpoint of someone with the position, the risk is not in the cash flows but in the values of the two securities. Of the two, the less risky is the floating rate liability, while the more risky is the fixed rate asset.

Floating Rate Liability

Consider the risks on June 17 once the two securities have been transacted. In the first place, you have a 3-month liability whose terminal value on September 18 will be

$$Liability = 100\left[1 + 0.018788\left(\frac{91}{360}\right)\right]$$

a value which is known today. At the instant the terms of the initial 3-month borrowing have been set, its present value can be represented as

$$PV(Liability) = 100\left[1 + 0.018788\left(\frac{91}{360}\right)\right]Z_{18Sep02}$$

where

$Z_{18Sep02}$ represents the variable value of a zero-coupon bond that matures on September 18 and whose price is

$$Z_{18Sep02} = \frac{1}{\left[1 + L\left(\frac{Days}{360}\right)\right]}$$

where

L represents the current (and variable) spot rate
$Days$ is the total number of days from now until September 18

In the middle of July, for example, L would represent a 2-month rate.

Fixed Rate Asset

The fixed rate asset represents four separate cash flows. The first three are straight coupon payments, each of which is worth $C/4$. The last is a combination of the final coupon payment and the bond's principal. The present value of this asset can be expressed as

$$PV(Asset) = \frac{C}{4}\left[Z_{18Sep02} + Z_{18Dec02} + Z_{19Mar03} + Z_{18Jun03}\right] + 100\,Z_{18Jun03}$$

which is the same expression we used to price the swap in the first place.

When the swap is viewed this way, all of the relevant cash flows are fixed and only the spot and futures rates can vary. Finding the correct hedge ratios is then simply a matter of determining the effect of a change in each of the component rates on the net present value of the swap.

Find the Hedge Ratios

Consider first the effect of varying the value of spot LIBOR, which may be referred to as the "stub" LIBOR rate. The change in the present value of the liability would be:

$$\frac{\partial PV(Liability)}{\partial L} = 100\left[1 + L^*\left(\frac{Days^*}{360}\right)\right]\frac{\partial Z_{18Sep02}}{\partial L}$$

where

L^* equals 0.018788 (fixed on trade date)
$Days^*$ equals 91 (fixed on trade date)
L represents the variable value of spot LIBOR
∂, borrowing from the calculus convention, represents a small change in whatever value follows it
Z is the zero-coupon bond price

The change in the present value of the asset would be

$$\frac{\partial PV(Asset)}{\partial L} = \frac{C}{4}\left[\frac{\partial Z_{18Sep02}}{\partial L} + \frac{\partial Z_{18Dec02}}{\partial L} + \frac{\partial Z_{19Mar03}}{\partial L} + \frac{\partial Z_{18Jun03}}{\partial L}\right] + 100\frac{\partial Z_{18Jun03}}{\partial L}$$

where

$$\frac{\partial Z}{\partial L} = \left[\frac{-Z\left(\frac{Days}{360}\right)}{1 + L\left(\frac{Days}{360}\right)}\right]$$

in which *Days* represents the actual number of days in the period covered by spot LIBOR. Taken together, the change in the net present value of the swap could be written as

$$\frac{\partial NPV(Swap)}{\partial L} = \frac{\partial PV(Asset)}{\partial L} - \frac{\partial PV(Liability)}{\partial L}$$

Once you have dealt with your exposure to changes in spot LIBOR, the rest of the hedging problem looks fairly easy. Changes in the Sep '02, Dec '02, and Mar '03 futures rates have no effect on the value of your short-term liability because they have no effect on the zero price used to value your liability. All that remains are effects on the value of your asset, which can be written as

$$\frac{\partial PV(Asset)}{\partial F_{Sep02}} = \frac{C}{4}\left[\frac{\partial Z_{18Dec02}}{\partial F_{Sep02}} + \frac{\partial Z_{19Mar03}}{\partial F_{Sep02}}\right] + \left[\frac{C}{4} + 100\right]\frac{\partial Z_{18Jun03}}{\partial F_{Sep02}}$$

$$\frac{\partial PV(Asset)}{\partial F_{Dec02}} = \frac{C}{4}\left[\frac{\partial Z_{19Mar03}}{\partial F_{Dec02}}\right] + \left[\frac{C}{4} + 100\right]\frac{\partial Z_{18Jun03}}{\partial F_{Dec02}}$$

$$\frac{\partial PV(Asset)}{\partial F_{Mar03}} = \left[\frac{C}{4} + 100\right]\frac{\partial Z_{18Jun03}}{\partial F_{Mar03}}$$

where the *Sep*02, *Dec*02, and *Mar*03 subscripts correspond to the futures contract month and year.

The results of calculating these expressions are shown in Exhibit 6.7.

Writing out the interest rate effects this way helps to highlight the fact that coupon-bearing notes are more sensitive to changes in nearby forward rates than they are to changes in more distant forward rates. A change in the Sep '02 rate, for example, affects the present value of three cash flows, while a change in the Dec '02 rate affects the present value of two cash flows, and a change in the Mar '03 rate affects the value of only one. As a result, when we solve for the hedge ratios, we find that we need fewer Dec '02 contracts than Sep '02 contracts, and we need still fewer Mar '03 contracts.

Note, too, that the results of calculating the hedge ratios this way are exactly the same as those we derived using the variable

EXHIBIT 6.7

Swap Hedge Based on the Hypothetical Securities Method

Effect of a 1-Basis-Point Increase in Each Futures Rate June 17, 2002

	Present Value of a Basis Point			
Rate	**Fixed (asset)**	**Floating (liability)**	**Difference**	**Eurodollar Hedge (contracts)**
Jun '02	−$2,515.83	−$2,515.83	$0.00	0.00
Sep '02	−2,499.34		−2,499.34	−99.97
Dec '02	−2,481.93		−2,481.93	−99.28
Mar '03	−2,463.60		−2,463.60	−98.54

cash flow approach. This is not an accident. Rather, it is because we took special care to express both hedging problems correctly and to keep track of all cash flow and present value effects in both problems.

This bears out a point made in the chapter on hedging with Eurodollar futures. That is, you can think of hedging as converting variable cash flows to fixed cash flows. Or you can think of hedging as converting variable present values to fixed present values. Either way, the two problems are really nothing more than two sides of the same coin and you should expect the answers to be the same.

PRICING AND HEDGING OFF-THE-MARKET SWAPS

So far in our analysis, we have dealt with swaps that are said to be on the market. These are swaps whose terms have been set at market and whose net present values are close to zero. Once the terms of a swap have been set, however, its value will rise or fall as the level of rates changes. And occasionally the fixed rate on a swap might be set above or below the current market level. In such cases, the net present value of the swap is not zero and the swap is said to be off the market.

Exhibit 6.8 shows how fixed coupons that are above or below the current market can affect the hedge for a swap. Consider, for example, a coupon of 0.4067 percent (0.004067), which is 2 percentage points below the market on June 17. If you are the counterparty who receives fixed, the swap is now a net liability; the swap's present value is negative. In such a case, an increase in any of the four spot or futures rates that affect the present value of cash flows on the swap will reduce the present value of this liability, which would be a gain to you. You can see this in the upper panel of the exhibit, where an increase in spot LIBOR, for example, increases the net present value of the swap by $49.63. Similarly, you can see that the losses produced by increases in the Sep '02, Dec '02, or Mar '03 rates are, on balance, smaller by roughly the same amount. As a result, the hedge would include a long position of 1.99 Eurodollar futures equivalent to hedge exposure to spot LIBOR and smaller short positions to hedge exposure to changes in each of the three futures rates. Overall, the total hedge would be net short approximately five fewer futures contracts.

Similarly, if you were to receive a fixed coupon of 4.4067 percent, which is 2 percentage points above the market, the swap would represent a net asset. Increases in any of the four rates would decrease the net present value of your position, and as a result, your exposure to changes in rates would be increased. You would now need to short the equivalent of 1.99 futures to hedge your exposure to a change in spot LIBOR, and you would need larger short positions to hedge your exposure to each of the futures rates.

CONVEXITY DIFFERENCES BETWEEN FORWARD AND FUTURES RATES

We have seen several times throughout this chapter and in earlier chapters that Eurodollar hedge ratios tend to rise as interest rates fall and fall as interest rates rise. This tendency stems from the fact that the present values of cash flows rise when rates fall and fall when rates rise. For students of fixed income markets, this tendency is known as "positive convexity," which describes the curvature in the relationship between the price of a non-callable bond and its yield as shown in Exhibit 6.9.

In contrast, Eurodollar futures have no convexity. The present value of a basis point is a fixed $25.00, which is entirely independent of the level of interest rates or the time to expiration of the Eurodollar futures contract.

The difference in convexity between non-callable fixed income instruments and Eurodollar futures is the source of dynamic hedge income for anyone who is long a non-callable bond or receiving fixed on a non-callable swap and who hedges the position by selling Eurodollar futures. For someone in the position, a decrease in rates increases the hedge ratio, which requires the hedger to sell more Eurodollar futures (and at a higher price). An increase in rates, on the other hand, decreases the hedge ratio, which requires the hedger to buy back Eurodollar futures (and at a lower price). Over time, as rates rise and fall at random, the hedger will pursue a dynamic hedging rule that involves selling futures as

EXHIBIT 6.8

Hedge for Below-the-Market Swap (0.4067%)
Effect of a 1-Basis-Point Increase in Each Futures Rate
June 17, 2002

	Jun '02/LIBOR		*Sep '02*		*Dec '02*		*Mar '03*	
Cash Flow	**Primary Effect**	**Secondary Effect**	**Primary Effect**	**Secondary Effect**	**Primary Effect**	**Secondary Effect**	**Primary Effect**	**Secondary Effect**
First	0	9.35	—	—	—	—	—	—
Second	—	10.72	−2,502.51	10.71	—	—	—	—
Third	—	13.09	—	13.09	−2,486.83	13.07	—	—
Fourth	—	16.47	—	16.46	—	16.44	−2,467.77	16.42
Net	49.63		−2,462.25		−2,457.31		−2,451.35	
Hedge	**1.99**		**−98.49**		**−98.29**		**−98.05**	

EXHIBIT 6.8

Hedge for Above-the-Market Swap (4.4067%)
Effect of a 1-Basis-Point Increase in Each Futures Rate
June 17, 2002

	Jun '02/LIBOR		*Sep '02*		*Dec '02*		*Mar '03*	
Cash Flow	**Primary Effect**	**Secondary Effect**	**Primary Effect**	**Secondary Effect**	**Primary Effect**	**Secondary Effect**	**Primary Effect**	**Secondary Effect**
First	0	−15.69	—	—	—	—	—	—
Second	—	−14.19	−2,502.51	−14.18	—	—	—	—
Third	—	−11.66	—	−11.65	−2,486.83	−11.64	—	—
Fourth	—	−8.09	—	−8.09	—	−8.08	−2,467.77	−8.07
Net	−49.63		−2,536.43		−2,506.55		−2,475.84	
Hedge	**−1.99**		**−101.46**		**−100.26**		**−99.03**	

EXHIBIT 6.9

Convexity Characteristics of a Non-Callable Bond

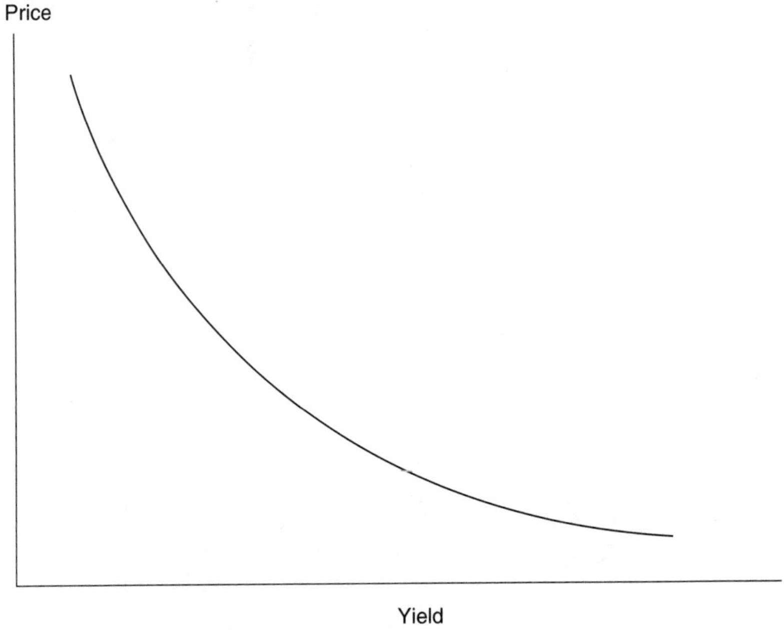

prices rise and buying futures as prices fall. The result is a trailing stream of hedging income that can be worth quite a lot if the process is allowed to run long enough.

The upshot of this difference between the positive convexity of non-callable fixed income instruments and the zero convexity one finds in Eurodollar futures is that futures rates must be higher than forward rates to compensate. That is, anyone who shorts Eurodollar futures must do so at a higher rate, and hence at a lower price, than the forward rate that determines the value of what one is hedging. Just how much this feature of Eurodollar futures is worth is detailed in chapters 7, 8, and 9, "The Convexity Bias in Eurodollar Futures," "Convexity Bias Report Card," and "New Convexity Bias Series," which show how the value of the bias is tied to interest rate volatility and time to futures expiration.

For the purposes of this chapter, however, it is enough to know that if we are using Eurodollar futures rates to price swaps, we must first adjust them downward to net out the value of the

EXHIBIT 6.10

Estimating the Convexity Bias between Futures and Forward Rates
June 17, 2002
Data as of 3:00 p.m. NY Close

Daily Zero to Ten

Convexity Bias Greeks

IMM EURODOLLAR FUTURES

Fut	Exp	Bias (bps)	1 bp Delta (bps)	1% Vega (bps)	1 day Theta (bps)
EDU2	9/16/02	0.0	0.000	0.000	0.000
EDZ2	12/16/02	0.2	0.002	0.010	−0.001
EDH3	3/17/03	0.6	0.004	0.027	−0.003
EDM3	6/16/03	1.1	0.006	0.057	−0.004
EDU3	9/15/03	1.7	0.009	0.098	−0.005
EDZ3	12/15/03	2.4	0.012	0.152	−0.006
EDH4	3/15/04	3.3	0.016	0.217	−0.008
EDM4	6/14/04	4.3	0.019	0.294	−0.009
EDU4	9/13/04	5.3	0.023	0.382	−0.010
EDZ4	12/13/04	6.4	0.027	0.477	−0.011
EDH5	3/14/05	7.6	0.031	0.580	−0.012
EDM5	6/13/05	8.8	0.035	0.691	−0.013
EDU5	9/19/05	10.0	0.039	0.809	−0.014
EDZ5	12/19/05	11.3	0.044	0.935	−0.015
EDH6	3/13/06	12.6	0.048	1.069	−0.016
EDM6	6/19/06	14.0	0.052	1.211	−0.17
EDU6	9/18/06	15.4	0.057	1.362	−0.018
EDZ6	12/18/06	16.9	0.062	1.524	−0.018
EDH7	3/19/07	18.6	0.067	1.697	−0.019
EDM7	6/18/07	20.3	0.072	1.881	−0.020
EDU7	9/17/07	22.2	0.078	2.076	−0.021
EDZ7	12/17/07	24.1	0.084	2.282	−0.022
EDH8	3/17/08	26.1	0.090	2.499	−0.023
EDM8	6/16/08	28.3	0.097	2.727	−0.024
EDU8	9/15/08	30.5	0.104	2.964	−0.025
EDZ8	12/15/08	32.7	0.110	3.208	−0.025
EDH9	3/16/09	35.0	0.117	3.459	−0.026
EDM9	6/15/09	37.3	0.124	3.718	−0.027
EDU9	9/14/09	39.7	0.131	3.983	−0.028
EDZ9	12/14/09	42.1	0.139	4.256	−0.029
EDH0	3/15/10	44.5	0.146	4.536	−0.030
EDM0	6/14/10	47.0	0.153	4.823	−0.030
EDU0	9/13/10	49.5	0.160	5.114	−0.031
EDZ0	12/13/10	51.8	0.167	5.404	−0.032
EDH1	3/14/11	54.1	0.174	5.693	−0.032
EDM1	6/13/11	56.2	0.181	5.982	−0.033
EDU1	9/19/11	58.3	0.187	6.271	−0.033
EDZ1	12/19/11	60.3	0.193	6.559	−0.033
EDH2	3/19/12	62.1	0.199	6.846	−0.033
EDM2	6/18/12	63.9	0.204	7.133	−0.033

SWAPS

Term	Est Bias (bps)	1 bp Delta (bps)	1% Vega (bps)	1 day Theta (bps)
2 yr	1.2	0.006	0.072	−0.003
3 yr	2.7	0.012	0.190	−0.006
4 yr	4.6	0.019	0.350	−0.008
5 yr	6.7	0.026	0.549	−0.010
7 yr	11.8	0.041	1.065	−0.013
10 yr	20.8	0.066	2.063	−0.017

SWAP RATE

Term	Rate
1 yr	2.39
2 yr	3.32
3 yr	3.90
4 yr	4.29
5 yr	4.58
6 yr	4.81
7 yr	5.00
8 yr	5.15
9 yr	5.28
10 yr	5.38

VOLATILITY

Term	Cap
1 yr	37.80
2 yr	33.50
3 yr	29.40
4 yr	27.10
5 yr	25.30
6 yr	
7 yr	22.90
8 yr	
9 yr	
10 yr	21.00

Source: Carr Futures.

EXHIBIT 6.11

Eurodollar Futures and Swap Convexity Bias
June 17, 2002

				Swap Rates				
Contract Month	**Futures Rate**	**Convexity Bias (bps)**	**Convexity Adjusted Futures Rates**	**Maturity**	**Raw**	**Adjusted**	**Difference (bps)**	**Market**
Jun '02	1.8788	0.0	1.8788					
Sep '02	2.105	0.0	2.105	Dec '02	2.019	2.019	0.0	
Dec '02	2.495	0.2	2.493	Mar '03	2.187	2.186	0.1	
Mar '03	**3.055**	**0.6**	**3.049**	**Jun '03**	**2.415**	**2.413**	**0.2**	**2.39**
Jun '03	3.635	1.1	3.624	Sep '03	2.665	2.661	0.4	
Sep '03	4.120	1.7	4.103	Dec '03	2.914	2.908	0.6	
Dec '03	4.495	2.4	4.471	Mar '04	3.143	3.134	0.9	
Mar '04	**4.720**	**3.3**	**4.687**	**Jun '04**	**3.343**	**3.332**	**1.2**	**3.32**
Jun '04	4.920	4.3	4.877	Sep '04	3.519	3.504	1.5	
Sep '04	5.080	5.3	5.027	Dec '04	3.677	3.658	1.9	
Dec '04	5.250	6.4	5.186	Mar '05	3.819	3.796	2.3	
Mar '05	**5.325**	**7.6**	**5.249**	**Jun '05**	**3.945**	**3.918**	**2.7**	**3.90**
Jun '05	5.435	8.8	5.347	Sep '05	4.088	4.056	3.2	
Sep '05	5.540	10.0	5.440	Dec '05	4.190	4.154	3.6	
Dec '05	5.675	11.3	5.562	Mar '06	4.259	4.219	4.0	
Mar '06	**5.720**	**12.6**	**5.594**	**Jun '06**	**4.374**	**4.328**	**4.6**	**4.29**
Jun '06	5.810	14.0	5.670	Sep '06	4.455	4.404	5.1	
Sep '06	5.890	15.4	5.736	Dec '06	4.532	4.476	5.6	
Dec '06	6.020	16.9	5.851	Mar '07	4.606	4.544	6.1	

EXHIBIT 6.11

Continued

Contract Month	Futures Rate	Convexity Bias (bps)	Convexity Adjusted Futures Rates	Swap Rates				
				Maturity	Raw	Adjusted	Difference (bps)	Market
Mar '07	**6.060**	**18.6**	**5.874**	**Jun '07**	**4.675**	**4.608**	**6.7**	**4.58**
Jun '07	6.135	20.3	5.932	Sep '07	4.739	4.667	7.3	
Sep '07	6.210	22.2	5.988	Dec '07	4.802	4.724	7.8	
Dec '07	6.335	24.1	6.094	Mar '08	4.863	4.778	8.4	
Mar '08	**6.360**	**26.1**	**6.099**	**Jun '08**	**4.920**	**4.830**	**9.1**	**4.81**
Jun '08	6.425	28.3	6.142	Sep '08	4.974	4.877	9.7	
Sep '08	6.485	30.5	6.180	Dec '08	5.027	4.923	10.4	
Dec '08	6.595	32.7	6.268	Mar '09	5.078	4.967	11.1	
Mar '09	**6.605**	**35.0**	**6.255**	**Jun '09**	**5.126**	**5.009**	**11.7**	**5.00**
Jun '09	6.660	37.3	6.287	Sep '09	5.172	5.047	12.5	
Sep '09	6.710	39.7	6.313	Dec '09	5.217	5.085	13.2	
Dec '09	6.800	42.1	6.379	Mar '10	5.260	5.121	13.9	
Mar '10	**6.795**	**44.5**	**6.350**	**Jun '10**	**5.301**	**5.155**	**14.7**	**5.15**
Jun '10	6.840	47.0	6.370	Sep '10	5.340	5.186	15.4	
Sep '10	6.875	49.5	6.380	Dec '10	5.378	5.216	16.2	
Dec '10	6.955	51.8	6.437	Mar '11	5.415	5.245	16.9	
Mar '11	**6.940**	**54.1**	**6.399**	**Jun '11**	**5.450**	**5.273**	**17.7**	**5.28**
Jun '11	6.975	56.2	6.413	Sep '11	5.494	5.308	18.5	
Sep '11	7.005	58.3	6.422	Dec '11	5.526	5.333	19.3	
Dec '11	7.080	60.3	6.477	Mar '12	5.554	5.354	20.0	
Mar '12	**7.055**	**62.1**	**6.434**	**Jun '12**	**5.584**	**5.376**	**20.8**	**5.38**

Source: Carr Futures.

EXHIBIT 6.12

Convexity Bias by Futures Contract and Swap Maturity
June 17, 2002

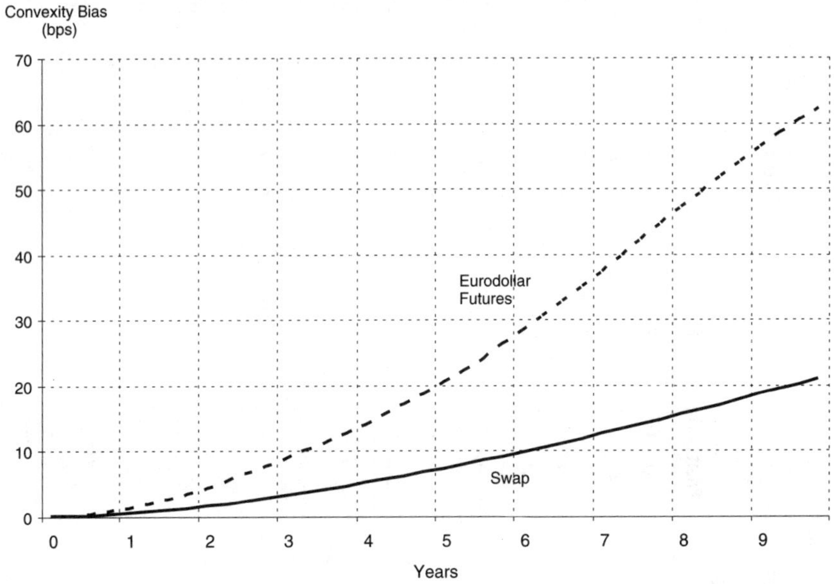

bias. Exhibit 6.10, which is excerpted with permission from Carr Futures "Daily Zero to Ten" report, provides examples of how large the adjustments would have been on June 17, 2002. Contract by contract estimates of the value of the bias are shown in the column labeled "Bias."

In this exhibit, the Jun '02 contract has just expired, so the bias estimates begin with the Sep '02 contract and end with the Jun '12 contract. An examination of the convexity bias column shows the adjustment is very small for nearby contracts but increases exponentially as the time to a contract's expiration increases. Thus, the adjustment for the Sep '02 (EDU2) contract would be zero, while the adjustment for the Mar '07 (EDH7) contract would be 18.6 basis points and the adjustment for the Jun '12 (EDM2) contract would be 63.9 basis points.

The report also provides information about how sensitive the bias estimates are to changes in the level of interest rates (delta), the relative volatility of interest rates (vega), and the passing of time (theta). These sensitivity estimates are shown both for individual contracts and for swaps at key maturities. The report also includes the assumptions about interest rate volatility that have been used to calculate the bias estimates.

When pricing swaps, the results can be substantial. Exhibit 6.11 compares the results of calculating swap rates using both raw unadjusted futures rates and convexity-adjusted futures rates. And both are compared with market swap rates. For example, the 5-year swap rate (see swap maturity of Jun '07) calculated from raw futures rates would have been 4.675%, while the rate calculated from the convexity-adjusted rates would have been 4.608%. The difference was 6.7 basis points. The market swap rate was 4.58%, which is much closer to the convexity adjusted rate than to the unadjusted rate.

The difference is, of course, even more pronounced for a 10-year swap (see swap maturity of Jun '12). The rate calculated from raw futures rates was 5.584%, while the rate calculated from convexity-adjusted futures rates was 5.376%. The difference was 20.8 basis points. The market rate was 5.38%, which was almost exactly the same as our convexity-adjusted rate.

The value of the convexity bias is charted in Exhibit 6.12, which shows the value of the bias both by contract and for swaps of maturities ranging from 1 to 10 years.

COMPARING THREE YIELD CURVES: FORWARD, ZERO COUPON, AND PAR COUPON

We now have all we need to conclude this chapter by comparing the three workhorse yield curves that one commonly finds in the fixed-income world—forward, zero coupon, and par coupon. Exhibits 6.13 and 6.14 show what these curves looked like on June 17 if derived from the Eurodollar futures market. The convexity-adjusted futures rates provide the futures market's best guess about the values of the forward rates for each of the 40 3-month periods spanned by the 10 years in the table.

Next to the convexity-adjusted futures rates are the zero-coupon and par coupon yields that we have calculated from the convexity-adjusted futures rates. As one expects, with an upward-sloping yield curve, the zero-coupon yields are lower than the

EXHIBIT 6.13

Three Yield Curves: Futures, Zero Coupon and Par Coupon
June 17, 2002

		Rates and Yields (convexity adjusted)		
Contract Month	Maturity	Futures (money market)	Zero Coupon (bey)	Par Coupon (bey)
Jun '02	Sep '02	1.8788		
Sep '02	Dec '02	2.105	2.019	2.019
Dec '02	Mar '03	2.493	2.189	2.186
Mar '03	Jun '03	3.049	2.415	2.413
Jun '03	Sep '03	3.624	2.668	2.661
Sep '03	Dec '03	4.103	2.917	2.908
Dec '03	Mar '04	4.471	3.149	3.134
Mar '04	Jun '04	4.687	3.351	3.332
Jun '04	Sep '04	4.877	3.529	3.504
Sep '04	Dec '04	5.027	3.687	3.658
Dec '04	Mar '05	5.186	3.831	3.796
Mar '05	Jun '05	5.249	3.957	3.918
Jun '05	Sep '05	5.347	4.103	4.056
Sep '05	Dec '05	5.440	4.205	4.154
Dec '05	Mar '06	5.562	4.273	4.219
Mar '06	Jun '06	5.594	4.389	4.328
Jun '06	Sep '06	5.670	4.470	4.404
Sep '06	Dec '06	5.736	4.546	4.476
Dec '06	Mar '07	5.851	4.620	4.544
Mar '07	Jun '07	5.874	4.688	4.608
Jun '07	Sep '07	5.932	4.753	4.667
Sep '07	Dec '07	5.988	4.814	4.724
Dec '07	Mar '08	6.094	4.874	4.778
Mar '08	Jun '08	6.099	4.930	4.830
Jun '08	Sep '08	6.142	4.983	4.877
Sep '08	Dec '08	6.180	5.033	4.923
Dec '08	Mar '09	6.268	5.083	4.967
Mar '09	Jun '09	6.255	5.129	5.009

EXHIBIT 6.13

Continued

		Rates and Yields (convexity adjusted)		
Contract Month	**Maturity**	**Futures (money market)**	**Zero Coupon (bey)**	**Par Coupon (bey)**
Jun '09	Sep '09	6.287	5.173	5.047
Sep '09	Dec '09	6.313	5.215	5.085
Dec '09	Mar '10	6.379	5.256	5.121
Mar '10	Jun '10	6.350	5.294	5.155
Jun '10	Sep '10	6.370	5.330	5.186
Sep '10	Dec '10	6.380	5.365	5.216
Dec '10	Mar '11	6.437	5.399	5.245
Mar '11	Jun '11	6.399	5.430	5.273
Jun '11	Sep '11	6.413	5.474	5.308
Sep '11	Dec '11	6.422	5.502	5.333
Dec '11	Mar '12	6.477	5.526	5.354
Mar '12	Jun '12	6.434	5.552	5.376

Source: Carr Futures.

forward rates for each maturity, while the par coupon yields are lower than both. This is simply because the zero-coupon rates reflect a blend or average of the forward rates that go into the calculation of the term rate. In turn, a coupon rate is a weighted average of the zero-coupon yields that go into valuing each of the cash flows on a coupon-bearing bond.

The Difference between Money Market Rates and Bond Yields

The convexity-adjusted futures rates in Exhibit 6.13 are shown as quarterly money market rates, while the zero-coupon and par coupon yields are shown as semiannual bond equivalent yields (bey). We could have converted the money market rates to bond equivalent yields, or the bond equivalent yields to money market rates. We did not, however, mainly to make an important point.

EXHIBIT 6.14

Three Yield Curves: Futures, Zero Coupon, and Par Coupon
June 17, 2002

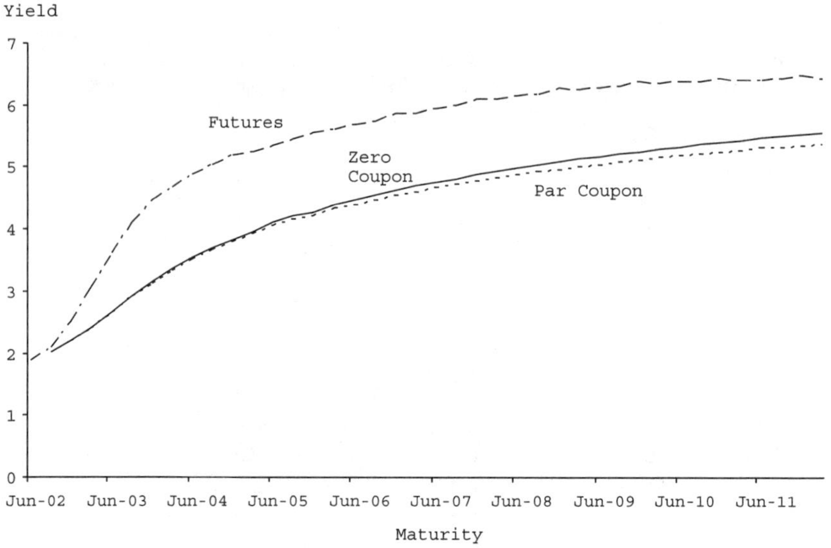

Because yields are quoted in many different ways, a basis point in one market can be worth more or less than a basis point in another market. If we simplify the relationship between quarterly money market rates and semiannual bond yields as

$$\left[1 + R\left(\frac{91.25}{360}\right)\right]^4 = \left[1 + \frac{y}{2}\right]^2$$

where R is the money market rate and y is the bond equivalent yield, we find that

$$y = \frac{91.25}{90.00}\left[1 + R\left(\frac{91.25}{720}\right)\right]R$$

which says that the semiannual bond equivalent yield, y, will tend to be higher than the quarterly money market rate, R. By the same token, changes in bond equivalent yields will be larger than changes in money market rates. Or, what is the same thing, the value of a basis point is smaller if the reference rate is a bond yield than when the reference rate is a quarterly money market rate.

What this suggests, of course, is that you should avoid the mistake of calculating the value of a basis point using bond equivalent yields and converting the results into Eurodollar hedge ratios by dividing them by $25. The resulting hedge ratios will be too small. To avoid this mistake, it is better to follow the hedging procedures outlined in these chapters and reckon all values of a basis point in terms of quarterly money market basis points.

PART THREE

Eurodollar Futures Applications

One of the great advantages of working in a research group at a futures brokerage company is that some really important questions come to you. The chapters in this part are reprints of research notes that report on the results of solving various pricing and hedging questions for our clients. Each has been chosen because it represents an important milestone in our understanding of the way Eurodollar futures should be used in practice.

CONVEXITY BIAS (Chapters 7 through 10)

Anyone who studies finance learns about convexity sooner or later. Even so, it was not until Bill Hoskins and I published "The Convexity Bias in Eurodollar Futures" (chapter 7) that the industry really seemed to sit up and take notice. Until that time, it was standard practice in the swap industry to treat futures rates as if they were forward rates. This practice produced swap rates that were much too high because, as we learned, futures rates should be higher than forward rates. For that matter, at the time we published that note in 1994, the effect of incorporating the value of the convexity bias amounted to almost 6 basis points for a 5-year swap. This was big money and the discovery resulted in a substantial and somewhat painful realignment of futures and swap rates.

Once it became generally well known that the relationship between swap rates and Eurodollar rates was a function of interest rate volatility, a natural extension was to think of the futures/swap spread in option terms. This led us to reporting "convexity bias greeks"—deltas, vegas, and thetas—which we first reported in "Convexity Bias Report Card" (chapter 8).

The steepening of the Eurodollar futures yield curve combined with a sharp inversion of the implied volatility curve for Eurodollar options in 2001 threw a monkey wrench into the way we had been calculating the theoretical value of the convexity bias for more than 5 years. The lessons learned from this episode are reported in "New Convexity Bias Series" (chapter 9), which shows how we dealt with this minor crisis. The solutions reported there were largely the contribution of Lianyan Liu.

Our daily report on the value of the convexity bias has become known as the "Daily Zero to Ten" (chapter 10), which is the successor to what we had called the "Short End."

TERM TED SPREADS (Chapters 11 and 12)

"Measuring and Trading Term TED Spreads" (chapter 11) was the result of wrestling with the problem of how to map a string of Eurodollar rates into something that could be compared with the yield on a term Treasury note. Measuring TED spreads was no problem when the basic trade was one T-bill contract against one Eurodollar futures contract. But when the industry began to trade 2-year Treasury notes against strips of 8 Eurodollar futures contracts, early efforts to quantify the spread produced wildly different answers. Our work on this note gave us a chance to sort out the real trading questions. At the same time, it allowed us to grapple with a host of real-world hassles that one encounters when dealing with different settlement conventions, day-count conventions, bad dates, and carry. The appendix to this note is especially useful for anyone who has to start coding systems to integrate coupon bonds with Eurodollar futures.

"TED Spreads: An Update" (chapter 12) provides a brief description of our daily "TED Spread" report. One of the great contributions of this report is that it shows forward TED spread values, which represent break-even values given an assumed term repo finance rate.

HEDGING AND TRADING WITH EURODOLLAR STACKS, PACKS, AND BUNDLES (Chapter 13)

We devote a lot of time and attention to deriving what I call "engineered" Eurodollar futures hedges for swaps and coupon bonds. These are the hedges that reflect the true forward rate exposure that you have in a fixed/floating swap or in a coupon bearing note. These are hedges that will work no matter what happens to the level or slope of the Eurodollar rate curve. In practice, though, there are plenty of instances in which the trader or hedger is willing to substitute speed and transactional efficiency for hedge accuracy. Moreover, given the way the structure of Eurodollar futures rates behaves, the idea of using equally weighted strips of Eurodollar futures to hedge or trade makes perfect sense. This chapter is especially useful for getting a working sense of how forward rates behave and an appreciation for just how well the yield behavior of a long-term note can be captured by a comparatively small segment of the futures rate curve.

HEDGING EXTENSION RISK IN CALLABLE AGENCY NOTES (Chapter 14)

The work that went into this note started out as an effort to find an easy and workable futures hedge for the directional exposure in callable bonds. What emerged from this research was that the value of a callable bond depends on the forward value of the note that would be called. This in turn led to our discovery that good directional hedges for callable bonds were sensitive not only to the level of yields but to the slope of the yield curve. And then, when all the dust settled, we concluded that the most efficient futures hedge for callable agency bonds would employ Eurodollar futures. I use this note as the focus of my concluding lecture in my MBA class at the University of Chicago's Graduate School of Business. It is a perfect vehicle for seeing just why derivatives are so useful to us and why the thinking that is required to understand derivatives helps us to appreciate the real power of Eurodollar futures.

OPPORTUNITIES IN THE S&P 500 CALENDAR ROLL (Chapter 15)

Many of our clients roll positions from one contract month to the next each month or quarter, depending on the expiration cycles. Knowing how best to do these rolls—knowing how to time them in particular—can have a huge effect on the transaction costs incurred in using futures. This note was the result of trying to find the best way of rolling a large S&P 500 futures position. What we found is that the financing rate implied by the S&P 500 calendar spread could be compared directly with the corresponding Eurodollar futures rate, with a comparison of the two providing a reliable guide to the spread's richness or cheapness.

TRADING THE TURN (Chapters 16 and 17)

By the time this book comes to press, this particular feature of Eurodollar futures may finally have faded into the past. Over 15 years ago, the Federal Reserve completely mismanaged year-end reserves, which led to a huge spike in the Fed funds rate for borrowing that spanned the end of the year. Since that time, from the mid-1980s to the early 2000s, all Eurodollar futures with December expirations traded at noticeably higher rates and lower prices than the normal slope of the curve would suggest. For years, "the turn" was a staple for research and trade recommendations during the months leading up to the end of the year.

CHAPTER 7

The Convexity Bias in Eurodollar Futures

Galen Burghardt and William Hoskins

Research note originally released September 16, 1994

SYNOPSIS

There is a systematic advantage to being short Eurodollar futures relative to deposits, swaps, or FRAs. Because of this advantage, which we characterize as a convexity bias, Eurodollar futures prices should be lower than their so-called fair values. Put differently, the 3-month interest rates implied by Eurodollar futures prices should be higher than the 3-month forward rates to which they are tied.

The bias can be huge. As Exhibit 7.1 shows, the bias is worth little or nothing for futures that have less than 2 years to expiration. For a futures contract with 5 years to expiration, however, the bias is worth about 17 basis points. And for a contract with 10 years to expiration, the bias can easily be worth 60 basis points.

The presence of this bias has profound implications for pricing derivatives off the Eurodollar futures curve. For example, a 5-year swap yield should be about 6 basis points lower than the yield implied by the first 5 years of Eurodollar futures. A 10-year swap yield should be about 18 basis points lower. And the differential for a 5-year swap 5 years forward should be around 36 basis points. (These estimates are explained in Exhibits 7.10, 7.14, and 7.15.)

EXHIBIT 7.1

Convexity Bias
June 13, 1994

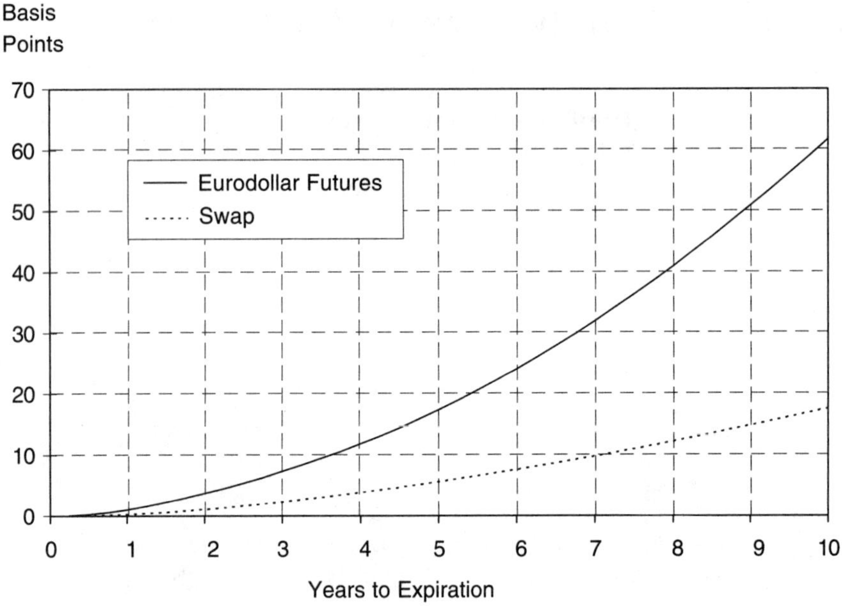

These are big numbers. A 6-basis-point spread is worth more than $200,000 on a $100 million 5-year swap. An 18-basis-point spread is worth about $1.2 million on a $100 million 10-year swap.

Although the swap market has begun to recognize this problem, swap yields still seem too high relative to those implied by Eurodollar futures rates. (See Exhibit 7.16.) If so, there is still a substantial advantage in favor of receiving fixed/paying floating on a swap and hedging with short Eurodollar futures. Also, because the value of the convexity bias depends so much on the market's perceptions of Eurodollar rate volatilities, one should be able to trade the value of the swap/Eurodollar rate spread against options on forward Eurodollar rates. The convexity bias also affects the behavior of the yield spreads between Treasury notes and Eurodollar strips.

Students of Eurodollar futures pricing should like this note. The standard approach to estimating the value of the convexity bias (also known as the financing bias) has been bound up in complex yield curve simulations and option pricing calculus. And, although such methods can yield reasonable enough answers, we show how the problem can be solved much more simply. For that matter, anyone armed with a spreadsheet program and an understanding of rate volatilities and their correlations can estimate the value of the convexity bias without recourse to expensive research facilities.

INTRODUCTION

The difference between a futures contract and a forward contract is more pronounced for Eurodollar futures, swaps, and FRAs than for any other commodity. In particular, there is a systematic bias in favor of short Eurodollar futures relative to deposits, swaps, or FRAs. As we show, the value of this bias is particularly large for futures contracts with expirations ranging from 5 to 10 years. The purpose of this note is to show:

- Why the difference is so important for Eurodollar futures
- How to estimate the value of the difference
- What traders can do about the difference

What we find is that the implications for swap traders and those who manage swap books are particularly important. Given the rate volatilities that we have observed over the past 4 years or so, it seems that market swap yields should be several basis points lower than the implied swap yields that one calculates from the rates implied by Eurodollar futures prices. Judging by current spreads between these rates, it appears that the swap market has not fully absorbed the implications of this pricing problem. As a result, there still appear to be profitable opportunities for receiving fixed/paying floating on swaps and hedging with short Eurodollar futures. By the same token, this pricing problem raises serious questions about how a swap book should be marked to market.

INTEREST RATE SWAPS AND EURODOLLAR FUTURES

Interest rate swaps and Eurodollar futures both are driven by the same kinds of forward interest rates. But the two derivatives are fundamentally different in one key respect. With an interest rate swap, cash changes hands only once for each leg of a swap, and then only in arrears. With a Eurodollar futures contract, gains and losses are settled every day. As it happens, the difference in the way gains and losses are settled affects the values of swaps and Eurodollar futures relative to one another. In particular, there is a systematic bias in favor of receiving fixed and paying floating on a swap and against a long Eurodollar futures contract. Or one can think of the short Eurodollar position as having an advantage over paying fixed and receiving floating on a swap. Either way, because swap prices are so closely tied to Eurodollar futures prices, it is important to know how much this bias is worth.

The easiest way to understand the difference between the two derivatives is through a concrete example that compares the profits and losses on a forward swap with the profits and losses on a Eurodollar futures contract.

A Forward Swap

A plain vanilla interest rate swap is simply an arrangement under which one side agrees to pay a fixed rate and receive a variable or floating rate over the life of the swap. The other side agrees to pay floating and receive fixed. The amounts of money that one side pays the other are determined by applying the two interest rates to the swap's notional principal amount.

The typical swap allows the floating rate to be reset several times over the swap's life. For example, a 5-year swap keyed to 3-month LIBOR would require the value of the floating rate to be set or reset 20 times—once when the swap is transacted and every 3 months thereafter. One can think of the swap, then, as having 20 separate segments, with the value of each segment depending on the swap's fixed rate and on the market's expectation today of what the floating rate will be on that segment's rate setting date.

The starting point for our example is the structure of Eurodollar futures prices and rates shown in Exhibit 7.2. These were the final settlement or closing prices on Monday, June 13, 1994. Each of the implied futures rates roughly corresponds to a 3-month period. The actual number of days covered by each of the futures contracts is shown in the right-hand column.

EXHIBIT 7.2

Structure of Eurodollar Futures Rates
June 13, 1994

	Eurodollar Futures			
Quarter	**Expiration**	**Price**	**Implied Futures Rate (percent)**	**Days in Period**
1	6/13/94	95.44	4.56	98
2	9/19/94	94.84	5.16	91
3	12/19/94	94.14	5.86	84
4	3/13/95	93.91	6.09	98
5	6/19/95	93.61	6.39	91
6	9/18/95	93.36	6.64	91
7	12/18/95	93.12	6.88	91
8	3/18/96	93.08	6.92	91
9	6/17/96	92.98	7.02	91
10	9/16/96	92.89	7.11	91
11	12/16/96	92.74	7.26	91
12	3/17/97	92.72	7.28	91
13	6/16/97	92.63	7.37	91
14	9/15/97	92.55	7.45	91
15	12/15/97	92.42	7.58	91
16	3/16/98	92.42	7.58	91
17	6/15/98	92.34	7.66	91
18	9/14/98	92.28	7.72	91
19	12/14/98	92.16	7.84	91
20	3/15/99	92.17	7.83	91

Note: Given these rates, the price of a $1 zero-coupon bond that matures on 6/14/99 would be 0.70667, and its semi-annual bond equivalent yield would be 7.0658%.

Now consider a swap that settles to the difference between a fixed rate and the value of 3-month LIBOR on March 15, 1999. On June 13, 1994, this would be a forward swap whose rate setting date is 4-3/4 years away and whose cash settlement date is a full 5 years away. To make the example more concrete, suppose that the forward swap's notional principal amount is \$100 million. Suppose too that the fixed rate for this swap is 7.83 percent, which is the forward value of 3-month LIBOR implied by the March 1999 Eurodollar futures contract. This may not be strictly the correct thing to do, but throughout this note we use futures rates in lieu of forward rates because we have much better information about the futures rates. And, although the purpose of this note is to explain why the two rates should be different, we can use the behavior of futures rates as an excellent proxy for the behavior of forward rates.

The Value of a Basis Point

Under the terms of this forward swap, if the value of 3-month LIBOR turns out to be 7.83 percent on March 15, 1999, no cash changes hands at all on June 14. For each basis point that 3-month LIBOR is above 7.83 percent, the person who pays fixed and receives floating on the swap receives \$2,527.78 [= 0.0001 × (91/360) × \$100,000,000] on June 14, 1999. For each basis point that 3-month LIBOR is below 7.83 percent, the person who pays fixed/receives floating on the swap pays \$2,527.78.

Thus, the nominal value of a basis point for this swap is \$2,527.78, with the cash changing hands 5 years in the future.

Eurodollar Futures

The futures market has based much of its success on a single operating principle. That is, all gains and losses must be settled up at the end of the day—in cash. This is as true of Eurodollar futures as it is of any futures contract.

Consider the March 1999 Eurodollar futures contract. When it expires on March 15, 1999, its final settlement price will be set equal to 100 less the spot value of 3-month LIBOR on that day. Before expiration, the Eurodollar futures price will be a function of the rate that the market expects. If there were no difference between a futures contract and a forward contract, and if the market expected a forward rate of 7.83 percent, for example, the futures price would be 92.17 [= 100.00 − 7.83]. If the market expected 7.84, the futures price would be 92.16. That is, a 1-basis-point increase in the value of the forward rate produces a 1-tick decrease in the futures price.

Under the Chicago Mercantile Exchange's rules, each tick or 0.01 in the price of a Eurodollar futures contract is worth \$25. This is true whether the futures contract expires 10 weeks from now, 10 months from now, or 10 years from now. The nominal value of a basis point change in the underlying interest rate is always \$25.

Reconciling the Difference in Cash Flow Dates

We now have two cash payments that are tied to the same change in interest rates. For the particular forward swap in our example, a 1-basis-point change in the expected value of 3-month LIBOR for the period from March 15 to June 14, 1999, changes the expected value of the swap settlement on June 14 by \$2,527.78. At the same time, a 1-basis-point change in the same rate produces a \$25 gain or loss that the holder of a Eurodollar futures contract must settle today. The difference in timing is illustrated in Exhibit 7.3.

The simplest way to reconcile the timing difference is to cast the two amounts of money in terms of present values. Eurodollar

EXHIBIT 7.3

Cash Consequences of a Change in a Forward Rate

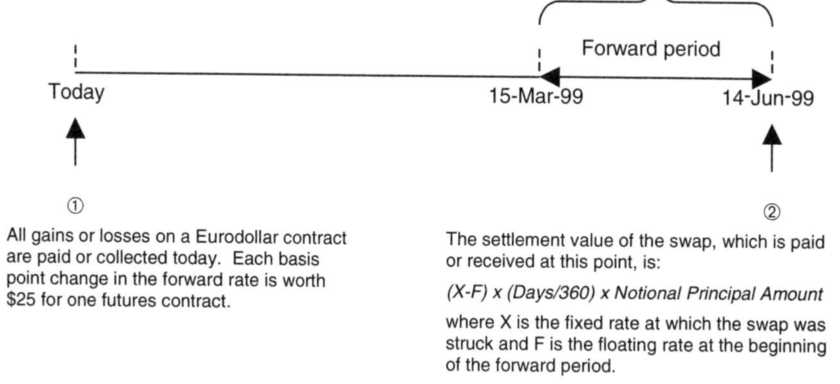
A change today in the forward interest rate covering this forward period has two cash consequences. The p/l from a change in the price of the corresponding Eurodollar contract would be realized Today. The effect on the value of an interest rate swap would be realized at the end of the period.
Forward period
Today
15-Mar-99
14-Jun-99
①
②
All gains or losses on a Eurodollar contract are paid or collected today. Each basis point change in the forward rate is worth $25 for one futures contract.
The settlement value of the swap, which is paid or received at this point, is:
(X-F) x (Days/360) x Notional Principal Amount
where X is the fixed rate at which the swap was struck and F is the floating rate at the beginning of the forward period.

futures are easy to handle. Because gains and losses are settled every day in the futures market, the present value of the $25 basis point value on a Eurodollar futures contract is always $25.

The present value of the $2,527.78 basis point value for the swap can be determined using the set of futures rates provided by a full strip of Eurodollar futures. For example, if we suppose that $1 could be invested on June 13, 1994, at the sequence of rates shown in Exhibit 7.2—for example, 4.56% for the first 98 days, 5.16% for the next 91 days and so on—the total value of the investment would grow to $1.41509 by June 14, 1999. Put differently, the present value in June 1994 of $1 to be received in June 1999 would be $0.70667 [= $1/$1.41509]. This is shown in the explanatory note at the bottom of Exhibit 7.2 as the price of a zero-coupon bond with 5 years to maturity. At this price, the present value of $2,527.78 5 years hence would be $1,786.30 [= $2,527.78 × 0.70667].

Hedging the Forward Swap with Eurodollar Futures

Given these two present values, 71.45 [= $1,786.30/$25.00] Eurodollar futures contracts would have the same exposure to a change in the March 1999 3-month forward rate as would $100 million of the forward swap. For someone who receives fixed and pays floating on the swap, the appropriate hedge against a change in the forward rate would be a short position of 71.45 Eurodollar futures. Considering what has gone into this calculation, the number of Eurodollar futures needed to hedge any leg of a swap whose floating rate is 3-month LIBOR would be

$$\textit{Hedge ratio} = \frac{NPA\left[0.0001\dfrac{Days}{360}\right]\textit{Zero-coupon bond price}}{\$25}$$

where *NPA* is the swap's notional principal amount, or $100 million in our example. The 0.0001 represents a 1-basis-point change in the forward rate. *Days* is the number of days in the period, which is 91 in our example. The *Zero-coupon bond price* is the price today of a bond that pays $1 on the same day that the swap settlement is paid. In our example, the swap settlement is 5 years away, and the price of such a bond is 0.70667. The $25 is simply the present value of a basis point for a Eurodollar futures contract.

The Other Source of Interest Rate Risk in the Forward Swap

Because any gain or loss on the swap is realized only at the end of the term, a swap can have unrealized asset value. In particular, the present value of the receive fixed/pay floating forward swap in our example can be written as

$$\textit{Swap value} = NPA\left[(X - F)\frac{Days}{360}\right]\textit{Zero-coupon bond price}$$

where X is the fixed rate at which the swap was struck originally and F is the current market value of the forward rate. From this we can see that the unrealized asset value of a swap depends both on the difference between the swap's fixed rate and the forward rate and on the present value of a dollar to be received on the swap's cash settlement date.

The practical importance of this expression is that there are really two sources of interest rate risk in a forward swap. The first, which we have dealt with already, is uncertainty about the forward rate, F. The other is uncertainty about the zero-coupon bond price, which reflects uncertainty about the entire term structure of forward rates extending from today to the swap's cash settlement date. If the forward rate is below the fixed rate, for example, the person who is receiving fixed and paying floating has an asset whose value is reduced by a general increase in interest rates. To get complete protection against interest rate risk, the swap hedger must offset not only the exposure to changes in the forward rate, but exposure to changes in the term or zero-coupon bond rate as well. The simplest way to hedge against exposure to changes in zero-coupon term rates is to buy or sell an appropriate quantity of zero-coupon bonds whose maturity matches that of the swap.

Interaction between the Two Sources of Risk

Now we have come to the heart of the difference between a swap and a Eurodollar futures contract. With Eurodollar futures, the only source of risk is the forward or futures rate. When the futures rate changes, the holder of the futures contract collects all of the gains or pays all of the losses right away. The holder of the swap, on the other hand, faces two kinds of risk—a change in the forward rate and a change in the term rate.

To see why this matters, consider what happens to a receive fixed/pay floating swap and a short Eurodollar position if all 20 of the 3-month spot and forward rates from June 1994 through March 1999 either rise or fall by 10 basis points. The results of such an exercise are shown in Exhibit 7.4. Note, first, that the $17,863 gain on the short Eurodollar position when the March 1999 futures rate rises 10 basis points is the same as the $17,863 loss when the futures rate falls 10 basis points.

Similarly, the nominal loss on the receive fixed swap—$25,278—when the March 1999 forward rate rises is equal to the nominal gain when the forward rate falls. Notice, however, that the present values of the gain and the loss on the swap are not the same. This is because the price of the zero-coupon bond falls when the forward rates rise and rises when the forward rates fall. Taking the rates in Exhibit 7.2 as our starting point, the price of the zero-coupon bond falls to $0.70315 per dollar when all of the forward rates increase 10 basis points. The price of the zero increases to $0.71020 when all of the forward rates fall 10 basis points. (Because of differences in compounding conventions, the semiannual bond equivalent yield on the zero-coupon bond changes by 10.3 basis points when the various forward rates change 10 basis points.)

With these changes in the price of the zero-coupon bond, the present value of the loss on the swap if all rates rise 10 basis points is $17,774 [= $25,278 × 0.70315], while the present value of the gain on the swap if rates fall 10 basis points is $17,952. As a result, we find that the short Eurodollar position makes $89 more than is lost on the swap if all forward rates rise and loses $89 less than is gained on the swap if interest rates fall.

A familiar way of depicting this comparison is provided in Exhibit 7.5. A receive fixed/pay floating swap, which requires the holder to pay a floating or variable rate such as 3-month LIBOR while receiving a known fixed rate, is much the same as owning a bond that is financed with short-term money. The price/yield relationship for such a position exhibits what is known in the fixed income trade as positive convexity. That is, the price increases

EXHIBIT 7.4

Swap and Eurodollar Futures P/Ls

Interest Rate Changes		*Swap P/L (Receive Fixed/Pay Floating)*				
Forward Rate	**Term Rate On Zero-Coupon Bond**	**Nominal Value (6/14/99)**	**Price of Zero-Coupon Bond**	**Present Value (6/13/94)**	**Short Eurodollar P/L**	**Net**
(basis points)		Notional principal amount = $100 million			71.45 contracts	
10	10.3	($25,278)	0.70315	($17,774)	$17,863	$89
0	0	0	0.70667	$0	$0	$0
−10	−10.3	$25,278	0.71020	$17,952	($17,863)	$89

EXHIBIT 7.5

The Convexity Difference between Swaps and Eurodollar Futures

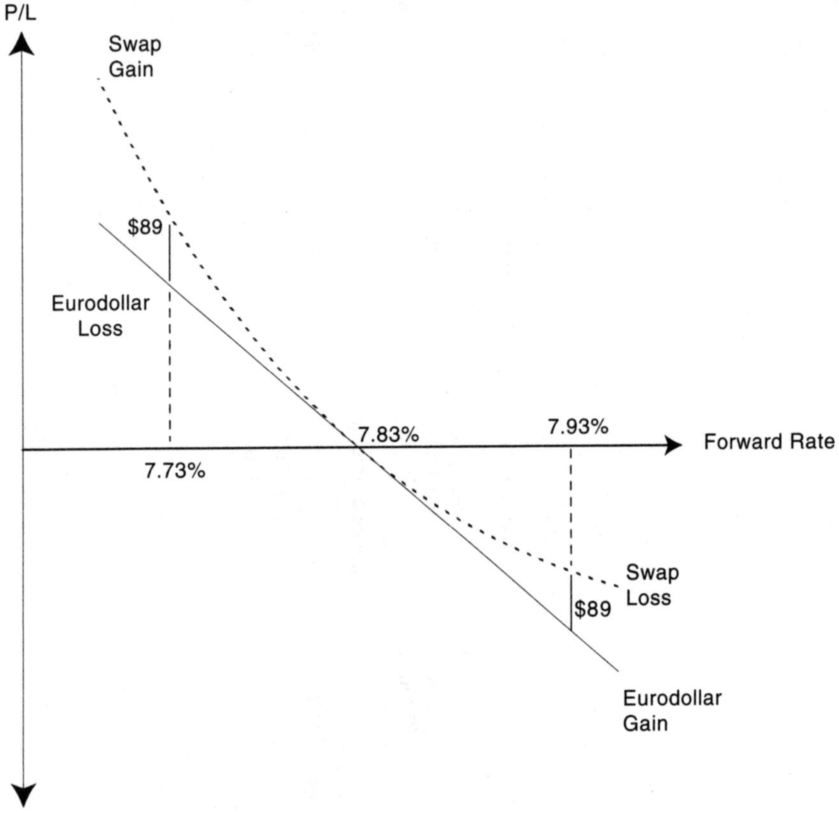

more when yields fall than the price falls when yields rise. In our example, the increase in the swap's price was $17,952 while the decrease in its price was only $17,774. A Eurodollar futures position, on the other hand, exhibits no convexity at all. Each basis point change in the forward rate is worth $25 today no matter what the level of the interest rate. The short Eurodollar position makes $17,863 for a 10-basis-point increase in rates and loses $17,863 for a 10-basis-point decline in rates.

Because of the difference in the convexities of the two instruments, a receive fixed/pay floating swap hedged with a short position in Eurodollar futures benefits from changes in the level of interest rates. As shown in Exhibit 7.5, the difference in convexities for the forward swap in our example is worth $89 if rates rise 10 basis points and $89 if rates fall 10 basis points.

Trading the Hedge

Exhibit 7.5 provides an especially useful way to illustrate the nature of the trade. For example, if interest rates fall 10 basis points, the hedger of the receive fixed swap is $89 ahead of the game. At this point, the hedger could (in principle, if not for the costs imposed by bid/asked spreads and brokerage) close out the position and pocket the $89. On the other hand, the hedger could view this as a vehicle for trading Eurodollar futures that would eventually accumulate a substantial amount of money. Notice that as rates fall, the number of futures needed to hedge the position increases, which requires selling the additional contracts at a higher price. On the other hand, as rates rise, the number of futures needed to hedge the position falls, which requires the hedger to cover some of the short futures by buying the excess contracts at a lower price.

HOW MUCH IS THE CONVEXITY BIAS WORTH?

The difference in the performance of a swap and the performance of a Eurodollar futures contract depends on three things:

- The size of the change in the forward rate
- The size of the change in the term rate (or zero-coupon bond price)
- The correlation between the two

These points are illustrated in Exhibit 7.6, which shows the net hedge P/L on our $100 million forward swap for a variety of different possible rate changes.

If both rates rise 5 basis points, the net P/L is $22. If both rates rise 10 basis points, the net gain is $86, or nearly four times as much. (The net gain in this instance is less than the $89 produced by the example illustrated in Exhibit 7.4 because the term rate in this instance has only changed by 10 basis points rather than the 10.3 basis points produced by a parallel shift in all

EXHIBIT 7.6

Net P/Ls for a Receive Fixed/Pay Floating Swap Hedged with Short Eurodollar Futures

Zero-Coupon Yield Change (bp)	*Forward Rate Change* (bp)				
	−10	−5	0	5	10
10	($86)	($43)	$0	$43	$86
5	($43)	($22)	$0	$22	$43
0	$0	$0	$0	$0	$0
−5	$43	$22	$0	($22)	($43)
−10	$86	$43	$0	($43)	($86)

Note: Based on Eurodollar futures rates in Exhibit 7.2.

3-month spot and forward rates.) Also, if the forward rate rises 10 basis points while the zero-coupon rate rises only 5 basis points, the net P/L is $43. From this we can conclude that the value of the convexity difference is greater when interest rates are volatile than when they are stable.

Exhibit 7.6 also allows us to see the importance of correlation. The net P/Ls are positive if the two interest rates both rise or both fall. If one rate falls while the other rises, the hedged position actually loses money. If one rate changes while the other does not, there is neither a gain nor a loss.

Moreover, if the zero-coupon yield is just as likely to rise as it is to fall no matter what happens to the forward rate, the expected or average net P/L is also zero. For example, if the forward rate increases 10 basis points, the net P/L is a gain of $86 if the zero-coupon rate also increases 10 basis points. The net P/L is a loss of $86, though, if the zero-coupon rate falls 10 basis points. If the probability of the zero-coupon rate rising is a half no matter what happens to the forward rate, then the expected or probability weighted average gain would be zero.

How Correlated Are the Rates?

As it happens, forward interest rates and their respective term or zero-coupon rates tend to be very highly correlated. Eurodollar futures rates and strips can be used to estimate the correlation. Exhibit 7.7 shows, for example, the relationship between changes in 3-month rates 4-3/4 years forward and changes in 5-year zero-coupon term rates. As you can see, the correlation is not perfect, but with only a few exceptions, increases in the forward rate are accompanied by increases in the term rate, and decreases in the forward rate are accompanied by decreases in the zero-coupon term rate.

Estimating the Value of the Convexity Bias

To get a rough idea of how much the convexity bias might be worth, we used actual Eurodollar futures data to calculate hedge 1-week P/Ls for 3-month forward swaps with 2 years and 5 years to final cash settlement. The calculations were much like those

EXHIBIT 7.7

Changes in 5-Year Term Rates versus Changes in the 4-3/4 Year Futures Rate
In Basis Points
(Weekly Interval, 7/10/92 through 7/1/94)

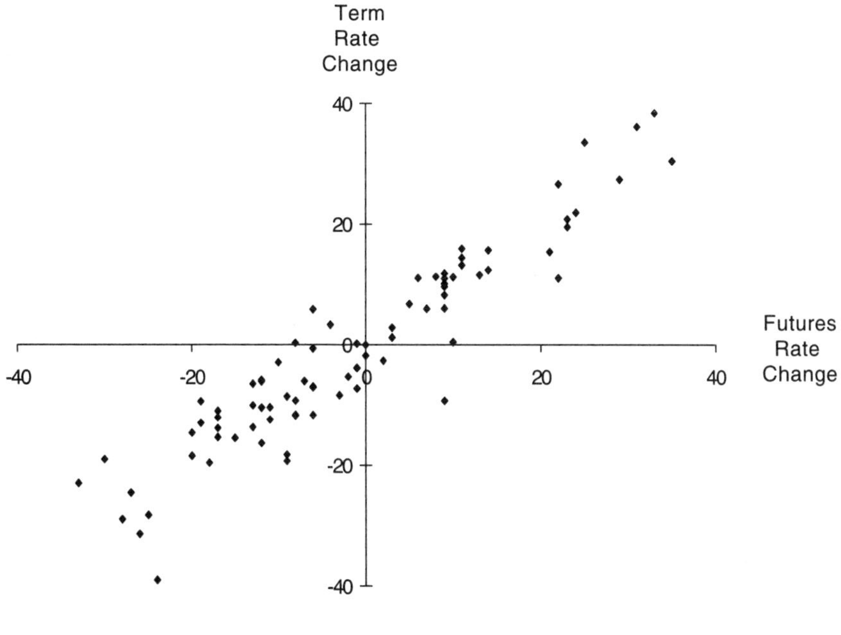

summarized in Exhibit 7.4. In particular, we used 1-week changes in the price of the eighth contract in an 8-contract strip to represent the change in a 3-month forward rate 1-3/4 years forward. We used all eight rates implied by the 8-contract strip to calculate 2-year zero-coupon bond prices and then calculated the 1-week price changes associated with 1-week changes in the 2-year term rate. For the longer-dated forward swap, we used the change in the price of the 20th contract in a 20-contract strip to represent the change in a 3-month forward rate 4-3/4 years forward and all 20 rates in the strip to calculate the price of a 5-year zero-coupon bond.

The results of these exercises for the 3-month swap 1-3/4 years forward are shown in Exhibit 7.8. The results for the 3-month swap 4-3/4 years forward are shown in Exhibit 7.9. In both cases, the hedge P/L has been divided by the number of futures contracts in the hedge so that the results are expressed in dollars per Eurodollar futures contract. In other words, Exhibit 7.8 shows the distribution of hedge P/Ls per futures for contracts that would have had 1-3/4 years to expiration, while Exhibit 7.9 shows the distribution of hedge P/Ls per futures for contracts that would have had 4-3/4 years to expiration.

Three things stand out. First, both relationships look a lot like long straddles or strangles in Eurodollar options. In fact, while the resemblance is close, the net P/L relationships in Exhibits 7.8 and 7.9 are much more like parabolas than are straddle and strangle P/Ls. Even so, the option-like quality of a swap hedged with Eurodollar futures is pronounced.

Second, the convexity is more pronounced for the 3-month swap 4-3/4 years forward than for the 3-month swap 1-3/4 years forward. This is natural enough. Longer-dated swaps exhibit greater convexity than do shorter-dated swaps, and that is what we are seeing in these two exhibits.

Third, the distribution of outcomes looks about right. As one would expect, most of the realized outcomes involved fairly small changes in the forward rate and correspondingly small net P/Ls on the hedged position. Only some of the changes were very large.

Calculating the Value of the Bias

Given the outcomes plotted in Exhibits 7.8 and 7.9, it is now a simple matter to calculate the average net P/L. Exhibit 7.8 shows

EXHIBIT 7.8

Hedge P/L for a 3-Month Swap 1-3/4 Years Forward
(Weekly Gains Per Futures Contract, 1/5/90 through 7/1/94)

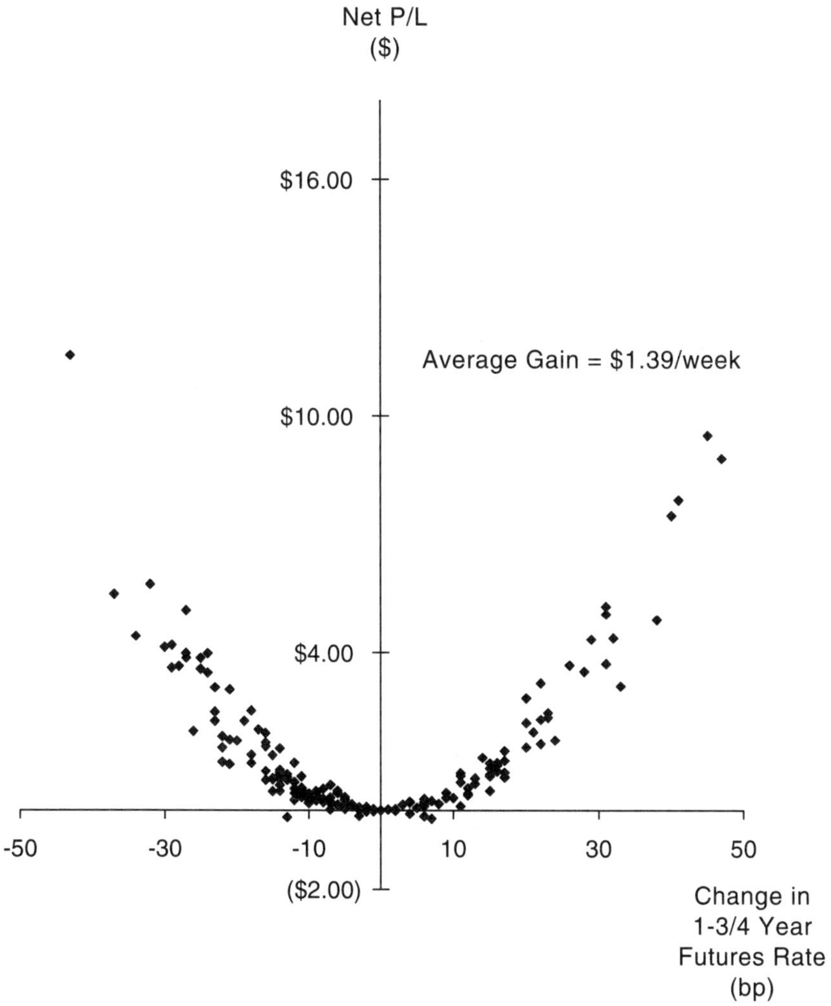

that the average outcome amounted to $1.39 per Eurodollar contract per week for futures with 1-3/4 years to expiration. Exhibit 7.9 shows that the average hedge P/L was $3.35 per Eurodollar contract per week for futures with 4-3/4 years to expiration.

EXHIBIT 7.9

Hedge P/L for a 3-Month Swap 4-3/4 Years Forward (Weekly Gains per Futures Contract, 7/10/92 through 7/1/94)

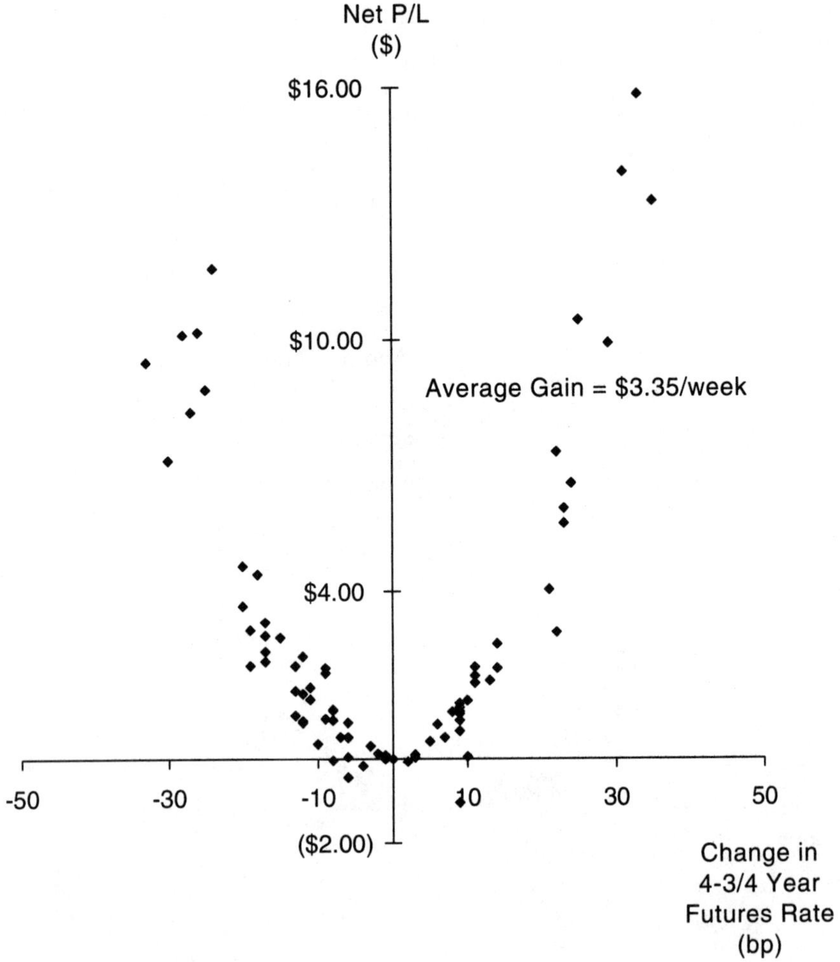

RECONCILING THE DIFFERENCE BETWEEN A SWAP AND A EURODOLLAR FUTURES CONTRACT

If you have been thinking ahead, you may see in all of this the makings of a free lunch. Exhibits 7.8 and 7.9 show all upside and no downside. As it happens, if Eurodollar futures prices were simply 100 less the appropriate forward rates, one could make money easily enough simply by receiving fixed/paying floating on swaps and hedging them with short Eurodollar futures. Unhappily for the swaps community, Milton Friedman was right in reminding us that there is no such thing as a free lunch—at least not for long.

If there is an advantage to being short Eurodollar futures, then one should be willing to pay for the advantage. The interesting questions then are how much this lunch should cost and how one should pay.

How One Would Pay for the Advantage

How one pays for the advantage is comparatively easy to describe. To make the P/L distribution shown in Exhibit 7.8 a fair bet, the whole distribution would have to be shifted down $1.39 for the week. To make the distribution in Exhibit 7.9 a fair bet, the whole distribution would have to be shifted down $3.35.

The easiest way to do this is to allow the futures rate to drift down relative to the forward rate. This would cause the futures price to drift up relative to the value of the swap. At the right rate of drift, the hedger who pays floating on the swap and is short futures would expect to give up $1.39 per week or $3.35 per week due to drift but would make it back on average because of the convexity differences. In other words, the futures rate implied by any Eurodollar futures price must start out higher than its corresponding forward rate and drift down to meet it at futures contract expiration. And, for what we are doing, it makes no particular difference how one rate converges to the other. The futures rate can fall to meet the forward rate, the forward rate can rise to meet the futures rates, or the two rates can converge to one another. They are all the same to us.

If the presence of a convexity bias means that the futures rate should be higher than the forward rate, then we have to be careful about how we calculate the so-called fair value of a futures contract. The market convention is to define the fair value of the futures as 100 less the value of the forward rate. Considering the value of the bias in favor of short Eurodollar futures, the fair value of the futures contract should be lower than is provided by the conventional definition. How much lower depends on the value of the convexity bias.

Translating the Advantage into Basis Points

In Exhibit 7.8 we found that the average net hedge gain for the 3-month swap 1-3/4 years forward was $1.39 per week per futures contract. At $25 per basis point for a Eurodollar contract, this means that the rate of drift for a Eurodollar futures contract with 1-3/4 years to expiration would have to be about 0.056 [= 1.39/25] basis points per week to compensate for the convexity bias. Over the span of a quarter, the drift would have to be about 0.73 basis points.

In Exhibit 7.9, we found that the average net hedge gain for the 3-month swap 4-3/4 years forward was $3.35 per week per futures contract. Using the same arithmetic, the rate of drift for the Eurodollar contract with 4-3/4 years remaining to expiration would have to be 0.13 basis points per week, or about 1.74 basis points per quarter.

To determine how much the difference should be between a 3-month rate 4-3/4 years forward and the 3-month interest rate implied by a Eurodollar futures contract with 4-3/4 years to expiration, the problem boils down to one of tracking a contract step by step and adding up the drift as the contract approaches expiration.

A WORKABLE RULE OF THUMB

There are a number of ways to determine the value of the convexity bias. One is the empirical approach illustrated in Exhibits 7.8 and 7.9. This is a perfectly good approach if one simply wants to look back and reconcile the historical differences between swaps and Eurodollar futures. The problem with this approach, however, is that it hides the assumptions that go into reckoning the value of the bias and makes it hard to adjust your estimates of the bias as your views about rate volatilities and correlations change.

Another approach is to undertake extensive and complex yield curve simulations that would allow you to estimate the cumulative gains associated with trading a hedged swap book or with financing the mark-to-market gains or losses on a futures contract. Such interest rate simulations can produce reasonable results, but the equipment seems much too heavy for the job and may well obscure what is really going on.

The good news in this note is that the problem can be tackled with relatively light tools. The thrust of what we have done so far is that the value of the convexity bias really depends on only three things—the volatility of the forward rate, the volatility of the corresponding term rate, and the correlation between the two. As it happens, the value of the drift in the spread between the futures and forward rates that is needed to compensate for the advantage of being short Eurodollar futures can be expressed as:

Drift = *Standard deviation of forward rate changes*
× *Standard deviation of zero-coupon bond returns*
× *Correlation of forward rate changes with zero-coupon bond returns*

where *Drift* is the number of ticks that the rate spread has to fall during any given period to compensate for the convexity bias. Those who want to know where this expression comes from will find an explanation along with tips on how to apply the rule in Appendix A.

Applying the Rule of Thumb

Exhibit 7.10 provides examples of how to apply this rule to Eurodollar futures contracts with times to expiration ranging from 3 months to 10 years. Consider, for example, the lead futures contract, which has 3 months remaining to expiration. The annualized standard deviation of changes in the lead futures price (or rate) is shown as 0.92% or 92 basis points. (Notice that this is an absolute and not a relative rate volatility like those quoted for Eurodollar options.) The annualized standard deviation of returns on a zero-coupon bond with an average of 4-1/2 months to maturity (the zero begins the quarter with 6 months to maturity and ends the quarter with 3 months remaining) is shown as 0.35% or 35 basis points. This standard deviation is itself the product of the standard deviation of changes in the yield on the zero-coupon bond and the zero's time to maturity, which is also its duration. The historical correlation between these two changes is shown as

EXHIBIT 7.10

Calculating the Value of the Convexity Bias

	Annualized Std Deviation					*Convexity Bias* (bp)	
Years to Futures Expiry (1)	ED Rate Changes (2)	Zero Yield Changes* (3)	Avg Years to Zero Maturity (avg duration) (4) = (1) + 1/8	Annualized Std Dev of Zero Returns (5) = (3) × (4)	Correlation of ED Rate Changes and Zero Returns** (6)	Per Quarter (7) = (2) × (5) × (6) / 4	Cumulative Bias (8)
1/4	0.92%	0.92%	3/8	0.35%	0.9945	0.08	0.08
1/2	1.03%	1.18%	5/8	0.74%	0.9824	0.19	0.27
3/4	1.12%	1.33%	7/8	1.16%	0.9726	0.32	0.59
1	1.18%	1.42%	1 1/8	1.60%	0.9646	0.45	1.04
1 1/4	1.22%	1.42%	1 3/8	1.95%	0.9581	0.57	1.61
1 1/2	1.23%	1.37%	1 5/8	2.23%	0.9527	0.65	2.26
1 3/4	1.23%	1.30%	1 7/8	2.44%	0.9484	0.71	2.97
2	1.22%	1.24%	2 1/8	2.64%	0.9448	0.76	3.73
2 1/4	1.21%	1.20%	2 3/8	2.85%	0.9419	0.81	4.54
2 1/2	1.20%	1.17%	2 5/8	3.07%	0.9396	0.86	5.40
2 3/4	1.18%	1.15%	2 7/8	3.31%	0.9377	0.92	6.32
3	1.17%	1.14%	3 1/8	3.56%	0.9363	0.98	7.30
3 1/4	1.16%	1.13%	3 3/8	3.81%	0.9352	1.04	8.34
3 1/2	1.15%	1.12%	3 5/8	4.06%	0.9344	1.09	9.43
3 3/4	1.14%	1.12%	3 7/8	4.34%	0.9339	1.16	10.59
4	1.14%	1.12%	4 1/8	4.62%	0.9336	1.23	11.82
4 1/4	1.13%	1.11%	4 3/8	4.86%	0.9335	1.28	13.10
4 1/2	1.13%	1.11%	4 5/8	5.13%	0.9336	1.35	14.45
4 3/4	1.12%	1.11%	4 7/8	5.41%	0.9339	1.42	15.87

5	1.12%	1.11%	5 1/8	5.69%	0.9342	1.49	17.36
5 1/4	1.11%	1.12%	5 3/8	6.02%	0.9348	1.57	18.93
5 1/2	1.11%	1.12%	5 5/8	6.30%	0.9354	1.64	20.57
5 3/4	1.11%	1.12%	5 7/8	6.58%	0.9361	1.71	22.28
6	1.11%	1.12%	6 1/8	6.86%	0.9369	1.79	24.07
6 1/4	1.11%	1.12%	6 3/8	7.14%	0.9378	1.86	25.93
6 1/2	1.11%	1.11%	6 5/8	7.35%	0.9388	1.92	27.85
6 3/4	1.11%	1.12%	6 7/8	7.70%	0.9398	2.01	29.86
7	1.11%	1.12%	7 1/8	7.98%	0.9409	2.08	31.94
7 1/4	1.11%	1.11%	7 3/8	8.19%	0.9420	2.14	34.08
7 1/2	1.10%	1.11%	7 5/8	8.46%	0.9432	2.21	36.29
7 3/4	1.10%	1.11%	7 7/8	8.74%	0.9444	2.27	38.56
8	1.10%	1.11%	8 1/8	9.02%	0.9457	2.34	40.90
8 1/4	1.10%	1.10%	8 3/8	9.21%	0.9470	2.39	43.29
8 1/2	1.09%	1.09%	8 5/8	9.40%	0.9484	2.44	45.73
8 3/4	1.09%	1.09%	8 7/8	9.67%	0.9497	2.51	48.24
9	1.09%	1.09%	9 1/8	9.95%	0.9512	2.57	50.81
9 1/4	1.09%	1.09%	9 3/8	10.22%	0.9526	2.64	53.45
9 1/2	1.08%	1.09%	9 5/8	10.49%	0.9540	2.71	56.16
9 3/4	1.08%	1.08%	9 7/8	10.67%	0.9555	2.75	58.91
10	1.08%	1.08%	10 1/8	10.94%	0.9570	2.82	61.73

* Zero-coupon yield continuously compounded.

** Equals correlation of Eurodollar rates and zero-coupon yield changes.

0.9945, which is about as highly correlated as anything can be. Taken together, we find that the required drift over a quarter of a year would be calculated as

$$Drift = \frac{0.92\% \times 0.35\% \times 0.9945}{4} = 0.08\ Basis\ points$$

In other words, for a Eurodollar futures contract with 3 months left to expiration, the rate of drift expressed in basis points per quarter would be 0.08 basis points. That is, the spread between the futures and forward rates would have to converge at this rate to compensate for the value of the convexity differential.

The Importance of Time to Contract Expiration

If we do the same exercise for a futures contract that has 6 months left to expiration, we find that the required quarterly rate of drift in the price or the rate is 0.19 basis points [= 1.03% × 0.74% × 0.9824/4], which is over twice as fast. The higher rate of drift is the combined effect of slightly higher rate volatilities, a very slightly lower correlation, and a very much higher duration of the zero-coupon bond.

As we saw in Exhibits 7.8 and 7.9, the value of the convexity bias depends directly on the convexity of the forward swap that is associated with the futures contract. This depends in turn on the price sensitivity of the zero-coupon bond that corresponds to the swap's maturity. Because the price of a zero-coupon bond with 5 years to maturity is more sensitive to a change in its yield than is the price of a zero with 2 years to maturity, the value of the bias is greater for a Eurodollar futures contract with 4-3/4 years to expiration than for a contract with 1-3/4 years to expiration.

The rule of thumb captures this effect nicely because the standard deviation of a zero-coupon bond's return is simply the product of the standard deviation of the zero's yield and its duration. If its yield is reckoned on a continuously compounded basis, then a zero-coupon bond's duration is simply its maturity. The result is a higher rate of drift for contracts with longer times remaining to expiration. For example, the rate of drift for a contract with 5 years to expiration is shown in Exhibit 7.10 to be about 1.5 basis points per quarter. For a contract with 10 years to expiration, the rate of drift is nearly 3 basis points per quarter.

The Cumulative Effect of All This Drift

We know that when the futures contract expires, its final settlement price will be set equal to 100 less the spot value of 3-month LIBOR. As a result, the implied futures rate and the spot rate have to be the same at contract expiration. We also know that the implied futures rate before expiration should be drifting down relative to the corresponding forward rate so that the two meet on contract expiration day.

The question, then, is how much different the futures and forward rates should be at any time before expiration. The answer to this question is found simply by adding up the quarterly drift estimates, which is what we have done in the last column of Exhibit 7.10. For example, if a futures contract with 3 months to expiration is drifting at a rate of 0.08 basis points per quarter, then the futures and forward rates will have to be 0.08 basis points apart if they are to meet exactly at expiration. On the other hand, if a futures contract with 6 months to expiration is drifting at a rate of 0.19 basis points per quarter for the first 3 months of its life and then at a rate of 0.08 basis points for the last 3 months of its life, the total drift in the contract's price will be 0.27 [= 0.08 + 0.19] basis points for the entire 6 months. The bias for the next contract out would be 0.59 [= 0.08 + 0.19 + 0.32] basis points, and so on down the list.

For short-dated futures contracts, all of this work adds up to comparatively little. For a contract with 1 year to expiration, for example, the total cumulative value of the bias adds up to only 1.04 basis points. Considering everything else that the market has to worry about, this is really nothing.

On the other hand, the adding up of these little bits of drift per quarter has a profound effect on the spread between futures and forward rates for contracts with several years to expiration. For example, the cumulative value of the bias for a contract with 5 years to expiration is about 17 basis points. For a contract with 10 years to expiration, the cumulative value of the bias is more than 60 basis points.

How Sensitive Are the Estimates to the Assumptions?

The rule of thumb makes it clear that the value of the bias is directly related to three things—the volatility of the forward rate, the volatility of the zero-coupon bond or term rate, and the correlation between the two. In particular, because the rate of drift is calculated simply by multiplying these numbers together, the required rate of drift is directly proportional to the value of each of these three things. If forward rate volatility doubles, the value of the bias doubles too. If term rate volatility doubles, the value of the bias doubles as well. If both double, the value of the bias quadruples. If both rate volatilities were increased by 10 percent, the value of the bias would be increased by 21 percent. In other words, the value that anyone places on the convexity bias depends clearly on his or her views about interest rate volatility.

To get an idea of how changeable these three key variables could be, we used Eurodollar futures data to estimate them for different time periods. The results of these exercises are shown in Exhibits 7.11, 7.12, and 7.13. The peculiar look of these

EXHIBIT 7.11

Standard Deviation of Eurodollar Futures Rate Changes (Annualized)

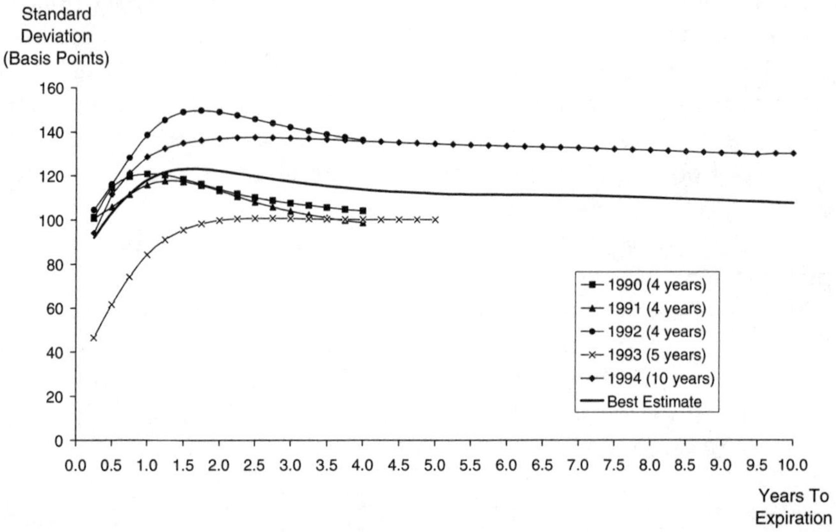

EXHIBIT 7.12

Standard Deviation of Term Yield Changes (Annualized)

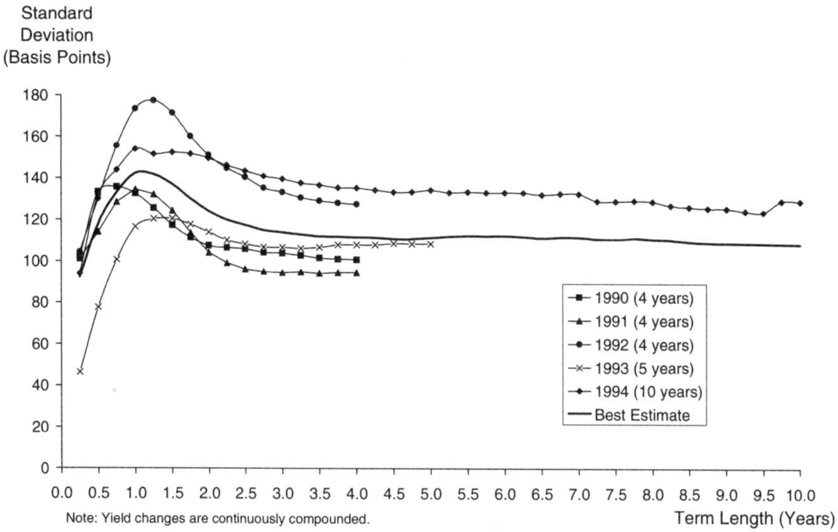

EXHIBIT 7.13

Correlation of Eurodollar Rates and Term Rates

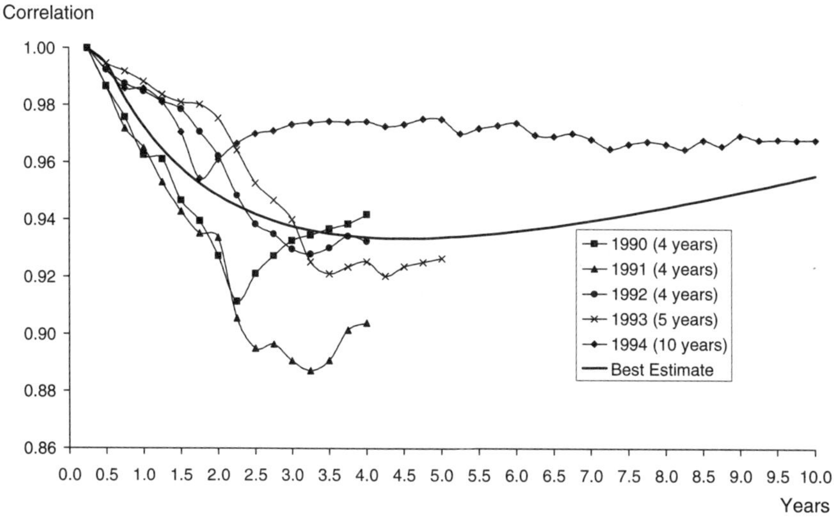

exhibits—that is, the reason the lines have different lengths—is because the Chicago Mercantile Exchange has added futures contracts with longer times to expiration in more or less discrete chunks. For example, from 1990 to 1992, futures contracts extended out to 4 years, and so our estimates of rate volatilities and correlations for these years are limited to horizons of 4 years. By the middle of 1992, however, the CME had listed the "golds," which had 5 years to expiration. Then, by the end of 1993, the exchange had listed contracts with expirations extending out a full 10 years.

Even with the mixed collection of data that were available to us, the results are instructive. Consider first the volatility of forward rates, which is represented by the standard deviation of Eurodollar futures rates in Exhibit 7.11. The annualized standard deviation of a 3-month rate 4 years forward in 1993 was around 100 basis points, or 1 percentage point. So far in 1994, the annualized standard deviation of a 4-year forward rate has been closer to 140 basis points. In Exhibit 7.10, we used 114 basis points or 1.14 percent to reckon the value of the convexity bias for a futures contract with 4 years to expiration. (See Exhibit 7.10, column 2.) The estimate of 114 basis points was taken from the solid, unmarked line in Exhibit 7.11 that extends all the way out to 10 years. This line represents our best guess about the structure of forward rate volatilities for the years 1990 through August 1994.

Because the value of the convexity bias is directly proportional to the standard deviation of forward rates and the standard deviation of term rates, the ranges of these standard deviations shown in Exhibits 7.11 and 7.12 impart substantial range to the possible value of the bias. For example, based on our best estimate of rate volatilities over the past 5 years, we reckoned that the value of the bias was 17 basis points for a contract with 5 years to expiration. Because the rule of thumb is linear in rate volatility, we can easily estimate the bias for higher or lower levels of rate standard deviations. For example, if we scale both forward and term rate standard deviations up by 15% (a reasonably high estimate given the volatility experience we saw in Exhibits 7.11 and 7.12), the bias will increase to about 22 basis points [$= 17 \times (1.15) \times (1.15)$]. On the other hand, if we scale both standard deviations down by 15% (to a low estimate), the value of the bias will decrease to about 12 basis points [= 17 × (0.85) × (0.85)]. So the true value of the bias for a contract with 5 years to expiration could easily vary between 12 and 22 basis points depending on the market's assessment of rate volatility.

Of the three key variables, the correlation between changes in forward and zero-coupon bond rates seems to be the most stable. To get a feel for these relationships, we calculated the correlations between changes in Eurodollar strip rates and changes in the rate implied by the last contract in the strip. As shown in Exhibit 7.13, the lowest of these correlations appear to have been in the low 90s or upper 80s, while the highest have been in the upper 90s. We used correlations in the mid-90s to construct the estimates in Exhibit 7.10. Given the range of correlations shown in Exhibit 7.13, changes in correlation from one year to the next would increase or decrease the value of the convexity bias by 3 or 4 percent, which is less than a basis point for a contract with 4

EXHIBIT 7.14

(a) Eurodollar and Swap Convexity Bias
June 13, 1994

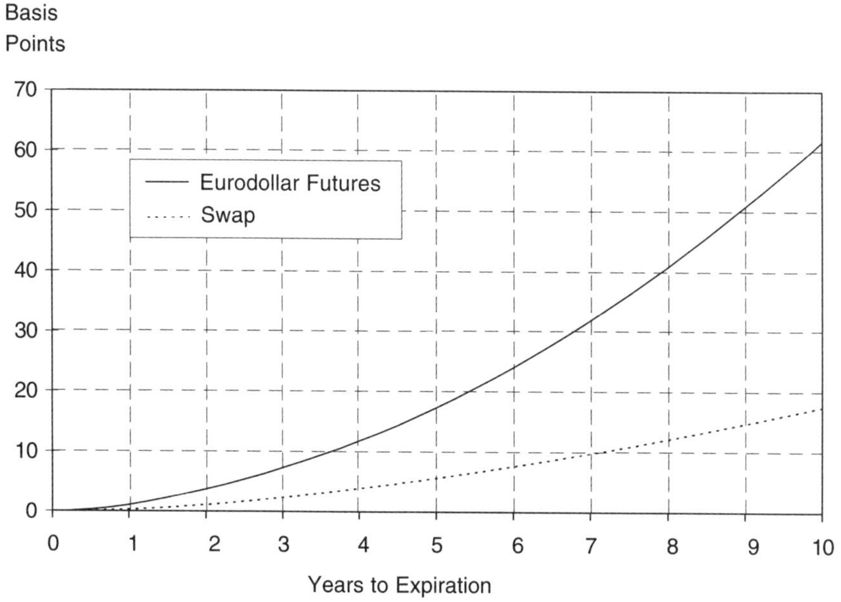

EXHIBIT 7.14

Continued
(b) Convexity Adjusted Swap Yields

	Eurodollar Rates (MM A/360)			*Calculated Term Yields* (SA 30/360)			
Years to Expiration (1)	Futures Market (2)	Convexity Bias (bp) (3)	Convexity Adjusted (4) = (2) − (3)	Eurodollar Strip* (5)	Implied Swap (6)	Convexity Adjusted Swap (7)	Swap Convexity Bias (bp) (8)
Spot	4.56	0.00	4.56				0.00
1/4	5.16	0.08	5.16				0.02
1/2	5.86	0.27	5.86	4.95	4.95	4.95	0.04
3/4	6.09	0.59	6.08				0.14
1	6.39	1.04	6.38	5.51	5.50	5.50	0.23
1 1/4	6.64	1.61	6.62				0.41
1 1/2	6.88	2.26	6.86	5.89	5.87	5.87	0.59
1 3/4	6.92	2.97	6.89				0.83
2	7.02	3.73	6.98	6.18	6.16	6.15	1.08
2 1/4	7.11	4.54	7.06				1.37
2 1/2	7.26	5.40	7.21	6.40	6.36	6.34	1.66
2 3/4	7.28	6.32	7.22				1.99
3	7.37	7.30	7.30	6.57	6.52	6.50	2.32
3 1/4	7.45	8.34	7.37				2.68
3 1/2	7.58	9.43	7.49	6.71	6.66	6.63	3.05
3 3/4	7.58	10.59	7.47				3.44
4	7.66	11.82	7.54	6.84	6.78	6.74	3.83
4 1/4	7.72	13.10	7.59				4.25
4 1/2	7.84	14.45	7.70	6.96	6.88	6.84	4.68
4 3/4	7.83	15.87	7.67				5.13

5	7.91	17.36	7.74	7.06	6.98	6.92	5.58
5 1/4	7.97	18.93	7.78				6.06
5 1/2	8.09	20.57	7.88	7.16	7.07	7.00	6.55
5 3/4	8.06	22.28	7.84				7.06
6	8.10	24.07	7.86	7.25	7.15	7.07	7.57
6 1/4	8.14	25.93	7.88				8.11
6 1/2	8.24	27.85	7.96	7.34	7.22	7.13	8.65
6 3/4	8.19	29.86	7.89				9.21
7	8.21	31.94	7.89	7.41	7.28	7.19	9.77
7 1/4	8.22	34.08	7.88				10.36
7 1/2	8.30	36.29	7.94	7.48	7.34	7.23	10.95
7 3/4	8.24	38.56	7.85				11.57
8	8.24	40.90	7.83	7.54	7.39	7.27	12.18
8 1/4	8.25	43.29	7.82				12.83
8 1/2	8.33	45.73	7.87	7.60	7.44	7.30	13.47
8 3/4	8.27	48.24	7.79				14.13
9	8.29	50.81	7.78	7.64	7.48	7.33	14.79
9 1/4	8.31	53.45	7.78				15.48
9 1/2	8.37	56.16	7.81	7.69	7.52	7.35	16.16
9 3/4	8.33	58.91	7.74				16.87
10	8.35	61.73	7.73	7.74	7.55	7.38	17.58

* Calculated from futures market Eurodollar rates on June 13, 1994.

years to expiration and only 2 or 3 basis points for a contract with 10 years to expiration.

Practical Considerations in Applying the Rule

One of the good things about the way we approach the problem of valuing the convexity bias is that anyone with a spreadsheet program and an understanding of rate volatilities and correlations can do the job. To do the job right, however, requires some attention to detail. For those who want to try their hand at it, follow the guidelines provided in Appendix A.

THE IMPORTANCE OF THE BIAS FOR PRICING TERM SWAPS

The swap industry is accustomed to pricing swaps against Eurodollar futures, chiefly because Eurodollar futures prices are thought to provide the most accurate and competitive market information about forward rates. The reasoning behind such a practice is solid because the futures market is more heavily scrutinized by interest rate traders than either the cash deposit market or the over-the-counter derivatives markets.

The problem now, however, is that swap traders are gaining a heightened appreciation for the importance of the convexity difference between swaps and Eurodollar futures. Several years ago, when futures expirations only extended out 3 or 4 years, this was not much of a problem. Today, with futures expirations extending to 10 years and with longer-dated swaps trading more actively, the problem of reconciling the differences has become more acute. The effect of the convexity bias on the pricing of swaps against Eurodollar futures is illustrated for term swaps with various maturities in Exhibit 7.14.

The interest rates shown in the second column of the table represent the spot and implied Eurodollar futures rates on June 13, 1994. If we take these rates at face value and ignore the value of the convexity differences, we can calculate two kinds of term rates. One is the Eurodollar strip rate, which is the same as the rate for a zero-coupon bond with a maturity equal to the length of the strip. Another is an implied swap yield. Examples of both are shown in columns 5 and 6.

For example, the zero-coupon rate for a 5-year Eurodollar strip is shown as 7.06 percent. The swap rate next to it is 6.98 percent. The reason for the difference, which is described in Appendix B, is that a 5-year Eurodollar strip gives equal weight to all 20 of the 3-month rates that go into its calculation. An implied 5-year swap rate, however, gives greater weight to the nearby forward rates than it does to the more distant rates. As a result, if the forward rate curve slopes upward, the implied swap rate is lower than the strip rate.

There is no need to take the futures rates at face value, however. If we are confident in our estimates of the value of the convexity bias, then we can adjust each of the futures rates before calculating the swap rates. No adjustment would be required for the spot rate. An adjustment of 0.08 basis points for the first of the Eurodollar futures rates is too small to have a noticeable effect. The adjustment to the rate implied by the futures contract with 5 years to expiration, however, is 17 basis points. As shown in columns 3 and 4 of Exhibit 7.14, the convexity-adjusted futures rate would be 7.74 [= 7.91 − 0.17] percent. Similarly, the convexity-adjusted futures rate for the longest dated futures contract, which had 10 years to expiration, would be 7.73 [= 8.35 − 0.62] percent to reflect an adjustment of 62 basis points.

These convexity-adjusted futures rates are a much better reflection of the forward rates implied by Eurodollar futures prices and are the rates that we use to calculate what we call convexity-adjusted implied swap rates. For example, the 5-year swap rate implied by the adjusted futures rates would be 6.92 percent, which is 6 basis points less than the 6.98 percent that one would get using the raw unadjusted rates. The 10-year swap rate would be 7.38 percent, which is 17 basis points less than the 7.55 percent obtained from the unadjusted futures rates.

In other words, if our estimates of the convexity biases are reliable, then a 5-year swap rate should be about 6 basis points lower than the rate implied by raw Eurodollar futures rates. A 10-year swap rate should be about 17 basis points lower. Put differently, if one wants to know whether swap yields are rich or cheap relative to Eurodollar futures, the convexity-adjusted yield spreads are the standards against which the market spreads should be compared.

Biases in Forward Swap Rates

The market for forward swaps seems to have been growing recently. For example, one can find more or less active markets for 5-year swaps 5 years forward, or for 2-year swaps 8 years forward. For such swaps, the convexity bias can loom fairly large.

Exhibit 7.15 shows what the bias would be for a wide range of spot and forward swaps given the volatility and correlation assumptions that we have used. Along the top row, for example, are the calculations for spot swaps with terms ranging from 1 to 10 years. The numbers in this row are the same as those in the right-hand column of Exhibit 7.14. Along the second row are the biases for swaps that begin 1 year in the future. For example, the value of the convexity adjustment for a 5-year swap that begins 1 year in the future is about 9 basis points. In contrast, the value of the convexity bias for a 5-year swap that begins 5 years in the future is about 36 basis points.

EXHIBIT 7.15

Convexity Bias in Forward Swaps (bp)

Years Forward	*Swap Term* (years) 1	2	3	4	5	6	7	8	9	10
Spot	0.23	1.08	2.32	3.83	5.58	7.57	9.77	12.18	14.79	17.58
1	1.99	3.49	5.23	7.21	9.44	11.88	14.55	17.42	20.48	
2	5.11	7.05	9.25	11.71	14.39	17.32	20.46	23.78		
3	9.16	11.58	14.30	17.24	20.43	23.85	27.47			
4	14.22	17.22	20.42	23.90	27.61	31.52				
5	20.48	23.94	27.71	31.73	35.95					
6	27.70	31.81	36.14	40.69						
7	36.28	40.91	45.77							
8	45.93	51.13								
9	56.76									

Note: 6-month LIBOR, SA 30/360.

THE MARKET'S EXPERIENCE WITH THE CONVEXITY BIAS

Exhibit 7.16 provides an interesting look at how the market's appreciation for convexity bias has grown over the past couple of years. We used data on 5-year swap rates to calculate the spread between market swap rates and the swap rates that can be calculated using Eurodollar futures rates. The solid line represents the spread between market swap rates and the swap rates implied by convexity-adjusted futures rates. The dashed line represents the spread between market swap rates and the swap rates implied by the raw unadjusted futures rates. Notice that in 1992, the spread between the market and raw implied swap rates was around zero. In other words, in 1992, swaps appear to have been priced right

EXHIBIT 7.16

Spreads between Market and Implied Swap Yields

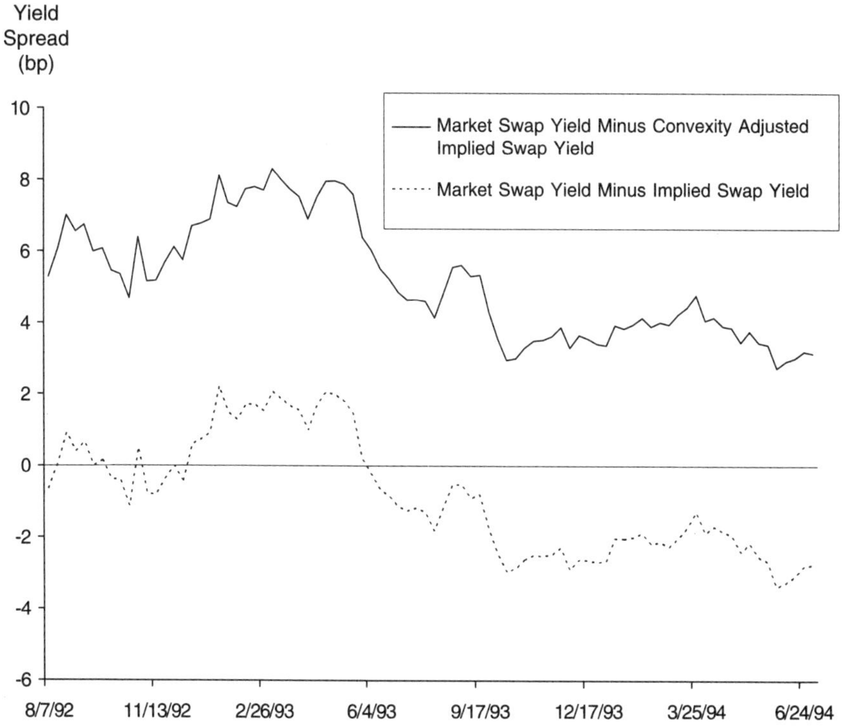

Note: Five-year swap rates courtesy of NationsBanc-CRT.

on top of the Eurodollar futures rate curve. At the same time, the spread between market swap rates and the convexity-adjusted implied swap rates was around 6 basis points.

Since then, these spreads have fallen. Market swap rates now tend to trade below those that are implied by raw, unadjusted Eurodollar futures rates. At the same time, the spread between market and convexity-adjusted rates has been drifting down toward zero. In both cases, the drop in the spread suggests that the swap market is adapting to the value of the bias in short Eurodollar futures relative to receive fixed/pay floating swaps. But the adaptation appears to be incomplete. Given our estimates of the value of the convexity bias, there still seems to be some advantage in hedging a receive fixed swap book with short Eurodollar futures.

NOW WHAT?

The natural question to ask now is what can be done with this information. Several possibilities come to mind.

Running a Receive Fixed, Pay Floating Swap Book

Given the size of the swap market, the value of knowing how to price swaps correctly against Eurodollar futures prices is enormous. If a 5-year swap is mispriced by as little as 2 or 3 basis points against Eurodollar futures, the mispricing is worth about $80,000 on a $100 million swap. If a 10-year swap is mispriced by as little as 5 basis points, and our conversations with swap traders suggest that this is possible, the mispricing is worth about $350,000 on a $100 million swap. These are large amounts of money and suggest that there is a lot at stake. For one thing, it suggests that a swap desk can still make money by receiving fixed on swaps and hedging them with short Eurodollar futures.

Marking a Swap Book to Market

Not that bank comptrollers and risk managers need any more to worry about, but the value of the convexity bias between swaps and Eurodollar futures raises a big question about how a derivatives book should be marked to market. The standard for many banks is to mark its swaps to market using Eurodollar futures rates. This standard makes good sense because Eurodollar futures prices are the result of a much more open and competitive market process than are swap yields in the over-the-counter market. The problem we find now, however, is that Eurodollar futures prices produce forward rates that are higher than the forward rates that should be used to value swaps.

This leaves comptrollers and risk managers with a difficult choice. One approach is to stick with raw, unadjusted futures rates. The advantage to this approach is that the rates are easy to calculate and to document and no one can tinker with them. The disadvantage to this approach, though, is that the true value of the swap book is misstated.

The other approach is to make what seems like a reasonable allowance for the value of the convexity bias. This has the advantage of providing better estimates of the value of the swap book and of providing correct incentives for a swap desk. The disadvantage is that convexity-adjusted Eurodollar futures rates depend so much on assumptions about rate volatilities.

Volatility Arbitrage

Because the spread between swap and Eurodollar rates should depend on expected interest rate volatilities every bit as much as the prices of caps and swaptions, one should be able to detect differences in implied rate volatilities and to construct trades that profit from differences between the two markets. For example, the spread between a 5-year swap yield and the swap yield implied by a 5-year strip of Eurodollar futures can be used to impute an expectation about interest rate volatilities from the perspective of swap and Eurodollar traders. The price of a 5-year interest rate cap, on the other hand, reflects that market's expectations about interest rate volatilities over the same period. A sharp trading desk should be able to arbitrage differences between the two markets' implied rate volatilities.

Evaluating Term TED Spreads

A trade that has gained considerable popularity over the past few years has been to spread Treasury notes against strips of Eurodollar futures. In practice, the market has viewed this trade as a way of trading the yield spread between private bank paper and Treasury paper. Now we find that the rates implied by Eurodollar futures prices reflect a convexity bias, which means that these trades have a volatility component as well. For notes with 5 to 10 years to expiration, the value of the convexity bias can loom fairly large. The imputed credit spread between the yield on a 5-year Eurodollar strip and a 5-year Treasury note really should be about 6 basis points narrower than it appears to be. In light of the comparatively tight spreads at which Eurodollars have been trading against Treasury notes anyway, such an adjustment would make the imputed credit spread appear to be paper-thin rather than merely narrow.

APPENDIX A

Deriving the Rule of Thumb

The rule of thumb for calculating the rate of drift in Eurodollar rates relative to forward rates stems directly from calculating the expected gain when a forward swap is hedged with Eurodollar futures and applying the "no free lunch" principle.

SWAP VALUE

The net present value of a forward swap that receives fixed and pays floating for a 3-month period is:

$$NPV = NPA \times (X - F) \times \frac{Days}{360} \times Z$$

where

NPA is the swap's notional principal amount
X is the fixed rate at which the swap is struck
F is the forward rate
Days is the actual number of days in the swap period to which the floating and fixed rates apply
Z is the fractional price of a zero-coupon bond that matures on the swap payment date (which is *Days* following the swap rate setting date)

The interest rates in this expression are expressed in percent (that is, 7 percent would be 0.07). If we multiply and divide this expression by \$1,000,000 as well as by 90, we get

$$NPV = \frac{NPA}{\$1MM} \times [(X - F)\, 10{,}000] \times \left[\left(\frac{Days}{90} \right) \left(\frac{90}{360} \right) \$100 \right] \times Z$$

which is fairly messy but allows us to arrive at

$$NPV = \frac{NPA}{\$1MM} \times (X^* - F^*) \times \frac{Days}{90} \times \$25 \times Z$$

in which X^* and F^* are expressed in basis points. We also find the \$25, which corresponds nicely to the value of a tick or basis point on a Eurodollar futures contract. The value of *Days*/90 compensates for the actual length of the swap period.

When a typical swap is transacted, we begin with $X^* = F^*$ so that the net present value of the swap is zero. When interest rates change, both F^* and Z change, and both contribute to the swap's profit or loss.

SWAP P/L AND HEDGE RATIO

For a change of ΔF^* in the forward rate and ΔZ in the price of the zero, the profit on the forward swap is

$$\Delta NPV = -\left(\frac{NPA}{\$1MM} \right) \times \frac{Days}{90} \times \$25 \times \Delta F^* \times (Z + \Delta Z)$$

Because the change in the value of one Eurodollar futures contract is equal to $-\$25 \times \Delta F^*$, the number of futures contracts needed to hedge against unexpected changes in rates would be

$$Hedge\ ratio = -\left(\frac{NPA}{\$1MM} \right) \times \frac{Days}{90} \times Z$$

This hedge ratio makes sense. The minus sign indicates that the hedger must short the contracts, *NPA*/\$1*MM* captures the nominal number of contracts required, *Days*/90 reflects the importance of the day count in the swap, and Z provides the present value correction for the difference in timing of the cash flows on the futures and the swap.

EURODOLLAR P/L

Given this hedge ratio, the profit on the short Eurodollar futures position would be

$$\left(\frac{NPA}{\$1MM}\right) \times \frac{Days}{90} \times Z \times (\Delta F^* + Drift) \times \$25$$

where *Drift* represents the systematic change in the Eurodollar futures rate relative to the forward rate needed to compensate for the convexity difference between the swap and the futures contract.

EXPECTED HEDGE P/L

To eliminate any possibility of a free lunch in this hedge, the expected profit of the hedged swap must be zero. Put differently, the expected profit on the swap must exactly offset the expected profit on the Eurodollar position. Because the $[(NPA/\$1\text{MM}) \times (Days/90) \times \$25]$ is common to both the profit on the swap and the profit on the Eurodollar position, this part of both expressions cancels out. The result of setting the two combined profits equal to zero and rearranging shows us that

$$E[\Delta F^* \times (Z + \Delta Z)] = E[Z \times (\Delta F^* + Drift)]$$

where $E[\;]$ represents the market's expectation today of whatever is contained inside the brackets. Because Z is a known number, we can solve for the drift by dividing through by Z within the expectations to get

$$E[Drift] = E\left[\Delta F^* \times \frac{\Delta Z}{Z}\right]$$

If we combine this expression with the fact that the average move in forward rates and term rates will be zero and use the formula for correlation, we arrive at the rule of thumb:

$$E[Drift] = stdev(\Delta F^*) \times stdev\left(\frac{\Delta Z}{Z}\right) \times correlation\left(\Delta F^*, \frac{\Delta Z}{Z}\right)$$

This rule of thumb assumes nothing, by the way, about the distribution of rate changes.

PRACTICAL CONSIDERATIONS

- The drift is expressed in basis points per period if the standard deviation of ΔF^* is in basis points per period.
- To use volatilities from the options market, relative or percentage rate volatilities must be converted to absolute rate volatilities by multiplying by the level of the interest rate.
- $\Delta Z/Z$ is the *unexpected* return on a zero-coupon bond over the period. It should be expressed as a fraction (for example, as 0.015). The easiest way to compute the standard deviation of $\Delta Z/Z$ is to break it into two parts: the standard deviation of the zero's continuously compounded yield and duration. (See Appendix B for the method used to compute continuously compounded zero-coupon yields from Eurodollar futures rates.)
- The length of the period over which you calculate changes in rates is not terribly important as long as the duration for the zero-coupon bond is chosen to be its average years to maturity over the period. A period of one day would be theoretically correct, because mark-to-market actually occurs daily in the futures market. But this would be computational overkill. Using a quarterly period produces almost the same result as daily calculations but involves a lot less work.

APPENDIX B

Calculating Eurodollar Strip Rates and Implied Swap Rates

EURODOLLAR STRIP RATES

A Eurodollar strip is a position that contains one each of the contracts in a sequence of contract months. For example, a 1-year strip might contain one each of the June '94, September '94, December '94, and March '95 contracts. A 2-year strip would contain these plus one each of the June '95, September '95, December '95, and

March '96 contracts. The rates implied by a strip of Eurodollar futures prices together with an initial spot rate can be used to calculate the terminal value of $1 invested today. For example,

$$TW_T = \left(1 + R_0 \frac{D_0}{360}\right)\left(1 + F_1 \frac{D_1}{360}\right) \times \cdots \times \left(1 + F_n \frac{D_n}{360}\right)$$

where

TW_T is the terminal value (i.e., terminal wealth) of $1 invested today for T years
R_0 is spot LIBOR to the first futures expiration
F_1 is the lead futures rate [= 100 − lead futures price]
F_n is the futures rate for the last contract in the strip
D_i is the actual number of days in each period, $i = 0, \ldots, n$

From this value of terminal wealth, we can calculate Eurodollar strip rates in several forms including money market, semiannual bond equivalent, and continuously compounded. All three are zero-coupon bond rates implied by a strip of Eurodollar futures prices.

MONEY MARKET STRIP YIELD

The money market strip yield is the value of R_{MM} that satisfies

$$\left(1 + R_{MM} \frac{365}{360}\right)^N \left(1 + R_{MM} \frac{D_f}{360}\right) = TW_T$$

where N is the whole number of years in the strip and D_f is the number of days in a partial year at the end of the strip.

SEMIANNUAL BOND EQUIVALENT YIELD

The semiannual bond equivalent strip yield is the value of R_{SA} that satisfies

$$\left(1 + \frac{R_{SA}}{2}\right)^{2T} = TW_T$$

which provides R_{SA} as

$$R_{SA} = [(TW_T)^{\frac{1}{2T}} - 1]\,2$$

CONTINUOUSLY COMPOUNDED YIELD

For computing returns on zero-coupon bonds, continuously compounded yields are the most convenient because the duration of a zero-coupon bond is equal to its maturity when yield changes are continuously compounded. The continuously compounded yield is the value of R_{CC} for which

$$e^{T \times R_{CC}} = TW_T$$

where e is the base for natural logarithms. This can be solved as

$$R_{CC} = \frac{ln(TW_T)}{T}$$

where $ln(\,)$ is the natural log.

ZERO-COUPON BOND PRICE

The price of a \$1 par value zero-coupon bond that matures at T is:

$$Z = \frac{1}{TW_T}$$

IMPLIED SWAP RATES

A conventional fixed/floating interest rate swap typically is priced as if it contains a long position in a floating rate note and a short position in a fixed rate note. At the time of the transaction, the fixed and floating rates are set so that the net present value of the swap is zero. If the initial floating rate is set equal to the market rate for the term of the floater—for example, equal to 3-month LIBOR if the swap has 3-month reset dates—then one can assume the hypothetical floater would trade at par. As a result, one can assume that the fixed rate on the swap must be set so that the hypothetical fixed rate note would also trade at par. The swap yield is simply the coupon rate that would accomplish this. For example, the swap yield for a 1-year swap with semiannual reset dates would be the value of C that satisfied the following

$$\left[\frac{C}{2} \times Z_6\right] + \left[\left(\frac{C}{2} + 100\right) Z_{12}\right] = 100$$

where Z_6 is the price of a zero-coupon bond that matures in 6 months, and Z_{12} is the price of a zero-coupon bond that matures in 12 months. If one happens to be pricing a swap on a futures expiration date, the zero-coupon prices would be calculated as

$$Z_6 = \frac{1}{\left[\left(1 + F_1 \frac{D_1}{360}\right)\left(1 + F_2 \frac{D_2}{360}\right)\right]}$$

$$Z_{12} = \frac{1}{\left[\left(1 + F_1 \frac{D_1}{360}\right)\left(1 + F_2 \frac{D_2}{360}\right)\left(1 + F_3 \frac{D_3}{360}\right)\left(1 + F_4 \frac{D_4}{360}\right)\right]}$$

and so forth. Note that F_1 and F_2 appear both in Z_6 and Z_{12} while F_3 and F_4 appear only in Z_{12}. From this, one can see that the swap yield implied by a sequence of Eurodollar futures rates is a weighted average of these rates that gives greater weight to the nearby rates than to the more distant rates.

CHAPTER 8

Convexity Bias Report Card

Galen Burghardt, William Hoskins, and Niels Johnson
Research note originally released April 15, 1997

The purpose of this note is to review the performance of the convexity bias estimates and to introduce the "convexity bias greeks."

WHAT IS THE CONVEXITY BIAS?[1]

If you are long Eurodollar futures, you make exactly the same amount of money if yields fall 10 basis points as you lose if yields rise 10 basis points. In contrast, if you receive fixed on a forward position (e.g., on an FRA), you make more when yields fall than you lose when yields rise. Thus, if the Eurodollar futures rate were the same as the FRA rate, you would rather receive fixed on the FRA. To compensate for the disadvantage of being long Eurodollar futures, the Eurodollar futures price must be lower and the implied futures interest rate higher than the FRA rate would suggest. By the same token, the swap rate that one would calculate using a strip of Eurodollar futures rates should be higher than the swap rate in the market.

1. For a full explanation of the convexity bias, see "The Convexity Bias in Eurodollar Futures," chapter 7.

Just how much this "convexity bias" is worth depends largely on the volatility of interest rates.

HOW HAVE WE DONE?

Exhibit 8.1 compares just over a year's worth of our theoretical values with the market's values of the convexity biases for 5-year and 10-year swaps. We find the results both interesting and encouraging.

In the first place, while the swap market's valuation of the convexity bias has not always agreed with ours, it has generally converged to our estimates over the past year and a half. Thus, our estimates seem to provide a reliable standard of fair value for pricing swaps against Eurodollar futures.

Second, it is apparent that the swap market is now comfortable with the idea that the value of the convexity bias can change with both the level and volatility of interest rates. Thus, we see

EXHIBIT 8.1

Eurodollar/Swap Convexity Adjustments
Theoretical vs. Market

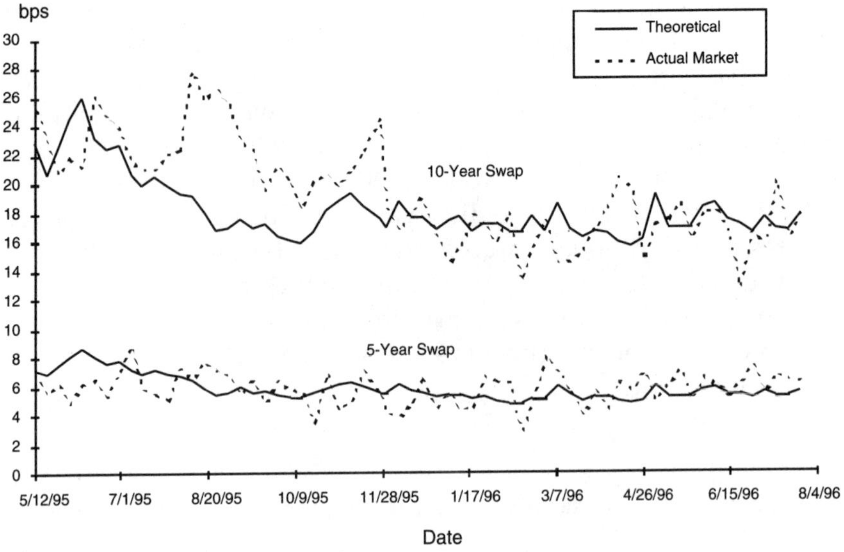

that both the market's valuation of the convexity bias and our theoretical estimate of the bias have drifted down over time, as interest rate volatilities have fallen.

CONVEXITY BIAS GREEKS

As we showed in our original research note, the value of the bias depends chiefly on two absolute interest rate volatilities and their correlation. While the correlation is comparatively stable, the rate volatilities are not. Moreover, the bias depends on absolute or basis point rate volatilities rather than relative rate volatilities. The relationship between the two is:

$$\textit{Absolute rate volatility} = \textit{Rate level} \times \textit{Relative rate volatility}$$

Thus, the value of the convexity bias can increase because interest rates go up or because implied relative rate volatilities go up. These effects can be thought of as convexity bias deltas and vegas respectively.[2]

Convexity Bias Delta

The deltas shown in Exhibits 8.2 and 8.3 represent the effect on the convexity bias of a 1-basis-point increase in the level of interest rates, holding implied relative rate volatility fixed. The estimates in Exhibit 8.2 show the effect on the bias for single futures contracts. For example, a 1-basis-point parallel increase in all forward rates would, under the market conditions for April 14, 1997, increase the value of the bias 0.029 basis points for the June '01 (EDM1) futures contract.

The estimates in Exhibit 8.3 show the total effect on the bias for swaps of various key maturities. For example, a 1-basis-point increase in the level of rates would increase the value of the bias for a 5-year swap by 0.012 basis points (or 1.2 basis points for a 100-basis-point increase in rates).

2. Delta and vega are terms commonly associated with options. Delta represents the change in the option value given a change in the underlying price (or rate). Vega represents the change in the option value given a change in volatility. See chapter 19 for more on options.

EXHIBIT 8.2

Eurodollar Convexity Bias Greeks
April 14, 1997

	Fut	Exp	Bias (bps)	1 bp Delta (bps)	1% Vega (bps)	1 day Theta (bps)
I	EDM7	6/16/97	0.0	0.000	0.007	0.000
M	EDU7	9/15/97	0.1	0.000	0.021	0.001
M	EDZ7	12/15/97	0.3	0.001	0.044	0.001
	EDH8	3/16/98	0.5	0.001	0.080	0.002
E	EDM8	6/15/98	0.9	0.003	0.128	0.003
U	EDU8	9/14/98	1.4	0.004	0.190	0.004
R	EDZ8	12/14/98	1.9	0.005	0.257	0.005
O	EDH9	3/15/99	2.5	0.007	0.333	0.006
D	EDM9	6/14/99	3.1	0.009	0.420	0.006
O	EDU9	9/13/99	3.9	0.011	0.517	0.007
L	EDZ9	12/13/99	4.7	0.013	0.626	0.008
L	EDH0	3/13/00	5.6	0.015	0.744	0.009
A	EDM0	6/19/00	6.6	0.018	0.874	0.010
R	EDU0	9/18/00	7.6	0.021	1.012	0.010
	EDZ0	12/18/00	8.6	0.024	1.154	0.011
F	EDH1	3/19/01	9.6	0.026	1.302	0.012
U	EDM1	6/18/01	10.7	0.029	1.458	0.012
T	EDU1	9/17/01	11.8	0.032	1.625	0.013
U	EDZ1	12/17/01	13.1	0.036	1.811	0.014
R	EDH2	3/18/02	14.5	0.040	2.006	0.014
E	EDM2	6/17/02	16.0	0.044	2.210	0.015
S	EDU2	9/16/02	17.5	0.048	2.426	0.016
	EDZ2	12/16/02	19.1	0.052	2.653	0.017
	EDH3	3/17/03	20.7	0.056	2.887	0.017
	EDM3	6/16/03	22.3	0.060	3.121	0.018
	EDU3	9/15/03	23.9	0.065	3.364	0.019
	EDZ3	12/15/03	25.6	0.069	3.618	0.019
	EDH4	3/15/04	27.2	0.073	3.878	0.020
	EDM4	6/14/04	29.0	0.078	4.145	0.020
	EDU4	9/13/04	30.7	0.082	4.422	0.021
	EDZ4	12/13/04	32.5	0.087	4.709	0.022
	EDH5	3/14/05	34.3	0.092	5.001	0.022
	EDM5	6/13/05	36.2	0.096	5.300	0.023
	EDU5	9/19/05	38.1	0.101	5.613	0.023
	EDZ5	12/19/05	40.4	0.107	5.958	0.024
	EDH6	3/13/06	42.7	0.113	6.310	0.025
	EDM6	6/19/06	45.1	0.119	6.674	0.025
	EDU6	9/18/06	47.5	0.126	7.052	0.026
	EDZ6	12/18/06	50.1	0.132	7.444	0.027
	EDH7	3/19/07	52.7	0.139	7.842	0.027

EXHIBIT 8.3

Convexity Bias Greeks for Swaps
April 14, 1997

	Term	Est Bias (bps)	1 bp Delta (bps)	1% Vega (bps)	1 day Theta (bps)
S	2 yr	0.8	0.002	0.104	0.002
W	3 yr	1.7	0.005	0.234	0.004
A	4 yr	3.0	0.008	0.408	0.005
P	5 yr	4.6	0.012	0.620	0.007
S	7 yr	8.4	0.022	1.161	0.009
	10 yr	15.2	0.037	2.189	0.012

Convexity Bias Vega

The estimates in the vega columns of Exhibits 8.2 and 8.3 show the effect of a 1-percentage-point increase in all of the relevant cap and swaption volatilities that go into producing our estimates. For example, a 1-percentage-point increase in relative rate volatilities would increase the theoretical value of the bias by 0.620 basis points for a 5-year swap and by 2.189 basis points for a 10-year swap.

Convexity Bias Theta

A position that receives fixed on a swap or FRA and is short Eurodollar futures should lose money gradually over time as futures rates fall to converge with forward rates. Just how much a position should lose each day is shown under the theta columns of Exhibits 8.2 and 8.3. If you receive fixed on a 10-year swap and are short an appropriately weighted strip of Eurodollar futures, you should expect to lose 0.012 basis points a day.

CHAPTER 9

New Convexity Bias Series

Galen Burghardt and Lianyan Liu
Research note originally released February 1, 2002

The purpose of this note is to introduce a new convexity bias series that corrects an apparent shortcoming in the original Carr Futures convexity bias estimates. The original series worked well when both the yield curve and volatility curve were comparatively flat. This past year, however, the Fed's aggressive campaign to cut interest rates produced an unusually steep Eurodollar futures rate curve and a steeply inverted implied volatility curve. (See the upper and lower charts in Exhibit 9.1.) As a result, our estimates of the convexity at key maturities began to fall well below market values. (See Exhibit 9.2.)

The new series, which employs implied cap and floor volatilities together with estimated correlations between Eurodollar futures rates and corresponding zero-coupon rates, has been designed to be more robust in the face of unusual changes either in the slope or curvature of the Eurodollar rate curve or in the shape of the implied volatility curve.

The effect of our improved approach on estimates of the bias for 5-year and 10-year swaps can be seen in Exhibit 9.2, which plots both the new series and the original series against the market value of the bias for the past 6 years. For most of these 6 years, the two series produced roughly the same estimates. Over the past

EXHIBIT 9.1

Eurodollar Futures Rates
January 4, 2001, and January 4, 2002

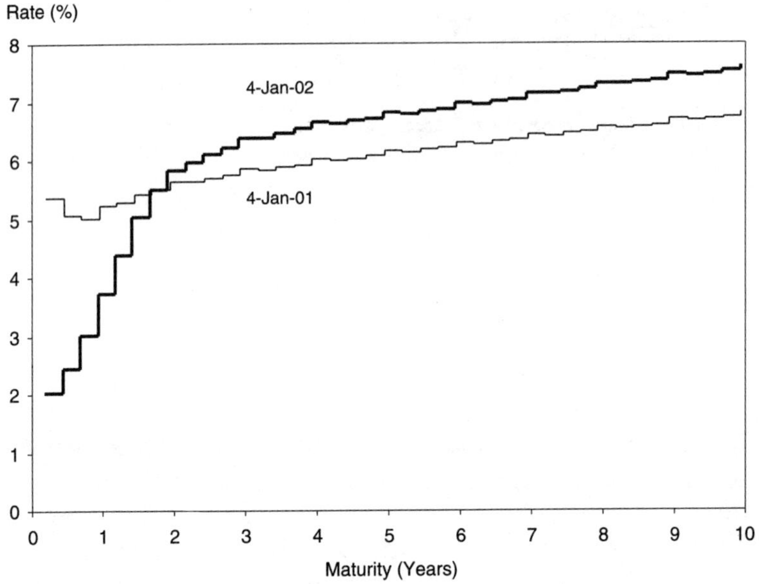

Eurodollar Futures Implied Volatilities
January 4, 2001, and January 4, 2002

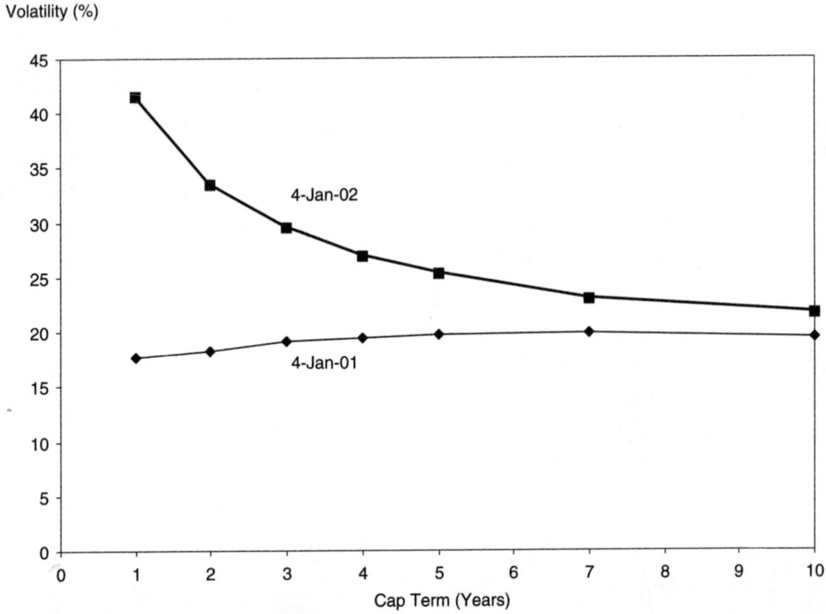

EXHIBIT 9.2

Convexity Bias Values for 5-Year Swaps
January 26, 1996, through December 31, 2001

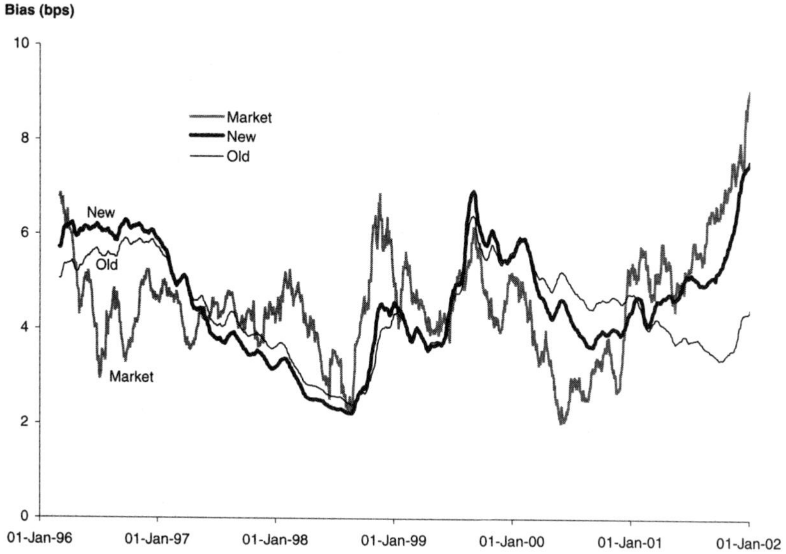

Convexity Bias Values for 10-Year Swaps
January 26, 1996, through December 31, 2001

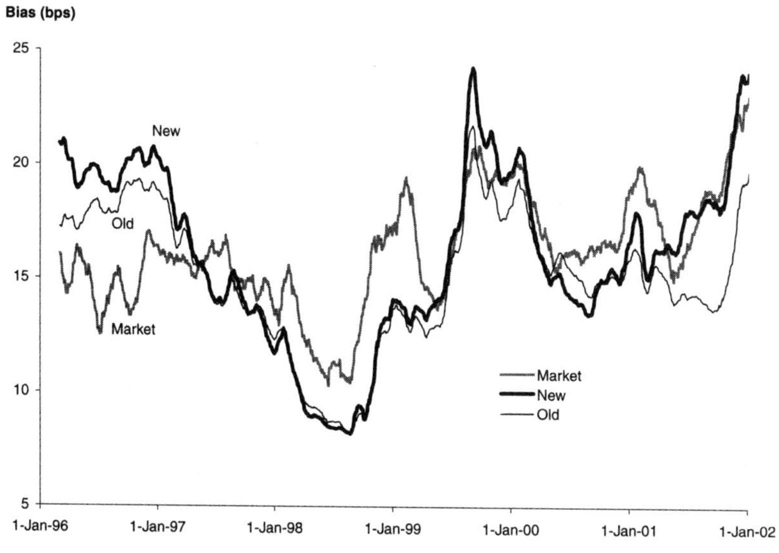

year, however, the new series does a much better job of tracking the market. While the original series actually showed declining bias values over the past year, the new series not only catches the change in direction of the market bias but tracks the market values as well.

CHAPTER 10

Convexity Bias: An Update

Chapters 7, 8, and 9 reproduce 3 research notes:

- The Convexity Bias in Eurodollar Futures (1994)
- Convexity Bias Report Card (1997)
- New Convexity Bias Series (2002)

These three notes describe the work we have done to gain an understanding of the relationship between Eurodollar futures rates and the forward rates that one would use to price interest rate swaps. The "Daily Zero to Ten," a four-page daily report produced by Carr Futures, is the working tool that has emerged from these notes. We reproduce a copy of this report, taken from the close of business September 10, 2002, in Exhibit 10.1.

For swap traders, the two most important pages are the first and fourth. The first page compares swap rates derived from three sources: the market; raw, unadjusted Eurodollar futures rates; and convexity-adjusted futures rates. For swap traders, the upper part of the lower panel is most relevant day to day. There you will find mid-market swap rates as reported by Reuters, a Eurodollar implied swap rate (as calculated from unadjusted futures rates) and an estimated convexity-adjusted Eurodollar implied swap rate (from convexity-adjusted rates). For example, the mid-market 5-year swap rate in the attached report was 3.640%. The Euro-

EXHIBIT 10.1

Daily Zero to Ten

CARR FUTURES — **Daily Zero to Ten (New Bias)** — Tuesday, Sep 10, 2002

Chicago

Data as of 3:00 PM NY CLOSE

Euro Strips: Strip and Convexity Adjusted Strip Rates

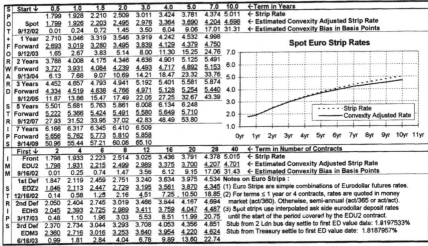

	Start ↓	0.5	1.0	1.5	2.0	3.0	4.0	5.0	7.0	10.0	←Term in Years
P		1.799	1.928	2.210	2.509	3.011	3.424	3.781	4.374	5.011	← Strip Rate
O	Spot	1.799	1.926	2.203	2.495	2.976	3.364	3.690	4.204	4.698	← Estimated Convexity Adjusted Strip Rate
T	9/12/02	0.01	0.24	0.72	1.45	3.50	6.04	9.06	17.01	31.31	← Estimated Convexity Bias in Basis Points
+	1 Year	2.710	3.046	3.319	3.546	3.919	4.242	4.532	4.998		
F	Forward	2.693	3.019	3.280	3.495	3.839	4.129	4.379	4.750		
O	9/12/03	1.65	2.67	3.83	5.14	8.00	11.30	15.25	24.76		
R	2 Years	3.788	4.008	4.175	4.346	4.636	4.901	5.125	5.491		
W	Forward	3.727	3.931	4.084	4.239	4.493	4.717	4.892	5.153		
A	9/13/04	6.13	7.68	9.07	10.69	14.21	18.47	23.32	33.76		
R	3 Years	4.452	4.657	4.793	4.941	5.192	5.401	5.581	5.874		
D	Forward	4.334	4.519	4.638	4.766	4.971	5.128	5.254	5.440		
	9/12/05	11.87	13.86	15.47	17.49	22.05	27.25	32.67	43.39		
S	5 Years	5.501	5.681	5.763	5.861	6.008	6.134	6.248			
T	Forward	5.222	5.366	5.424	5.491	5.580	5.649	5.710			
R	9/12/07	27.93	31.52	33.95	37.02	42.83	48.49	53.80			
I	7 Years	6.166	6.317	6.345	6.410	6.509					
P	Forward	5.656	5.762	5.773	5.810	5.858					
S	9/14/09	50.96	55.44	57.21	60.08	65.10					

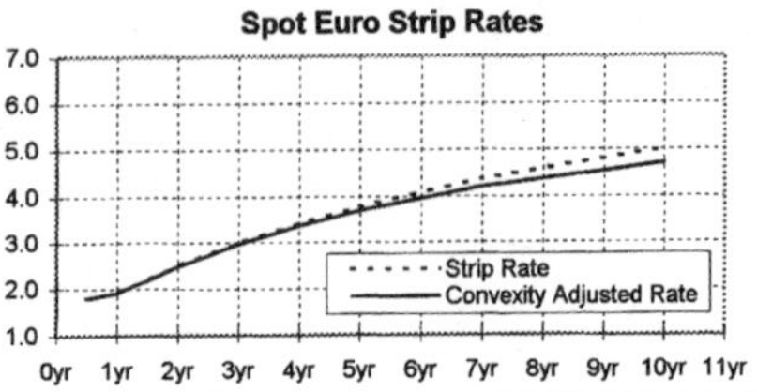

	First ↓	2	4	6	8	12	16	20	28	40	← Term in Number of Contracts
I	Front	1.798	1.933	2.223	2.514	3.025	3.436	3.791	4.378	5.015	← Strip Rate
M	EDU2	1.798	1.931	2.215	2.499	2.989	3.375	3.700	4.207	4.701	← Estimated Convexity Adjusted Strip Rate
M	9/16/02	0.01	0.25	0.74	1.47	3.56	6.12	9.15	17.06	31.43	← Estimated Convexity Bias in Basis Points
	1st Def	1.847	2.119	2.459	2.751	3.240	3.634	3.975	4.534		
S	EDZ2	1.846	2.113	2.447	2.729	3.195	3.561	3.870	4.345		
T	12/16/02	0.14	0.58	1.25	2.16	4.51	7.25	10.50	18.85		
R	2nd Def	2.050	2.404	2.745	3.019	3.466	3.844	4.167	4.694		
I	EDH3	2.045	2.393	2.725	2.989	3.411	3.759	4.047	4.487		
P	3/17/03	0.48	1.10	1.96	3.03	5.53	8.51	11.99	20.75		
S	3rd Def	2.370	2.734	3.044	3.293	3.708	4.053	4.356	4.851		
	EDM3	2.360	2.716	3.016	3.253	3.640	3.954	4.220	4.624		
	6/16/03	0.99	1.81	2.84	4.04	6.78	9.89	13.60	22.74		

Notes on Euro Strips :

(1) Euro Strips are simple combinations of Eurodollar futures rates.
(2) For terms ≤ 1 year or 4 contracts, rates are quoted in money market (act/360). Otherwise, semi-annual (act/365 or act/act).
(3) Spot strips use interpolated ask side eurodollar deposit rates until the start of the period covered by the EDU2 contract.

Stub from 2 Ldn bus day settle to first ED value date: 1.8197533%
Stub from Treasury settle to first ED value date: 1.8187957%

Interest Rate Swaps: Implied, Convexity Adjusted and Market Swap Rates

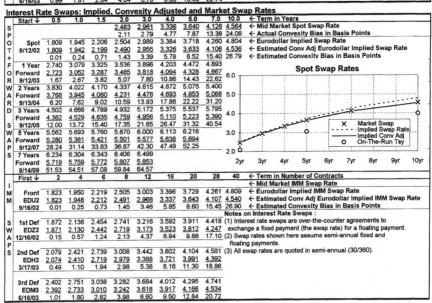

	Start ↓	0.5	1.0	1.5	2.0	3.0	4.0	5.0	7.0	10.0	← Term in Years
S					2.483	2.961	3.336	3.640	4.126	4.564	← Mid Market Spot Swap Rate
P					2.11	2.79	4.77	7.87	13.38	24.08	← Actual Convexity Bias in Basis Points
O	Spot	1.809	1.945	2.206	2.504	2.989	3.384	3.718	4.260	4.804	← Eurodollar Implied Swap Rate
T	9/12/02	1.809	1.942	2.199	2.490	2.955	3.326	3.633	4.106	4.536	← Estimated Conv Adj Eurodollar Implied Swap Rate
+		0.01	0.24	0.71	1.43	3.39	5.78	8.52	15.40	26.79	← Estimated Convexity Bias in Basis Points
F	1 Year	2.740	3.079	3.325	3.536	3.896	4.203	4.472	4.893		
O	Forward	2.723	3.052	3.287	3.485	3.818	4.094	4.328	4.667		
R	9/12/03	1.67	2.67	3.82	5.07	7.80	10.86	14.43	22.62		
W	2 Years	3.830	4.022	4.170	4.337	4.615	4.872	5.075	5.400		
A	Forward	3.768	3.945	4.080	4.231	4.476	4.693	4.853	5.088		
R	9/13/04	6.20	7.62	9.02	10.59	13.93	17.88	22.22	31.20		
D	3 Years	4.502	4.666	4.789	4.932	5.172	5.375	5.537	5.795		
	Forward	4.382	4.529	4.635	4.759	4.956	5.110	5.223	5.390		
S	9/12/05	12.00	13.72	15.40	17.35	21.65	26.47	31.32	40.54		
W	5 Years	5.562	5.693	5.760	5.870	6.000	6.113	6.216			
A	Forward	5.280	5.381	5.421	5.501	5.577	5.638	5.694			
P	9/12/07	28.24	31.14	33.83	36.87	42.30	47.49	52.25			
S	7 Years	6.234	6.304	6.343	6.406	6.499					
	Forward	5.719	5.759	5.772	5.807	5.853					
	9/14/09	51.53	54.51	57.08	59.84	64.57					

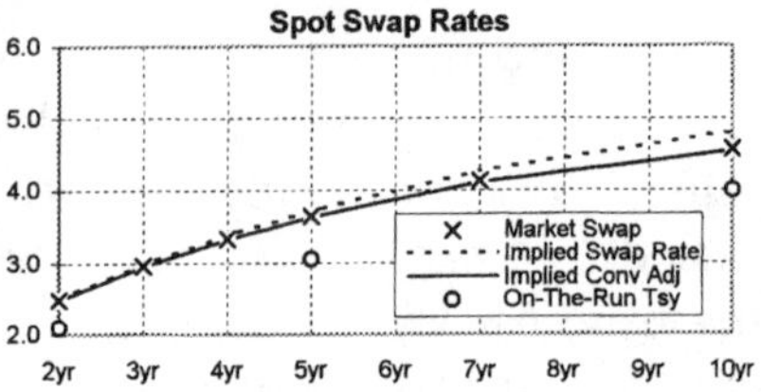

	First ↓	2	4	6	8	12	16	20	28	40	← Term in Number of Contracts
I											← Mid Market IMM Swap Rate
M	Front	1.823	1.950	2.219	2.505	3.003	3.396	3.729	4.261	4.809	← Eurodollar Implied IMM Swap Rate
M	EDU2	1.823	1.948	2.212	2.491	2.968	3.337	3.643	4.107	4.540	← Estimated Conv Adj Eurodollar Implied IMM Swap Rate
	9/16/02	0.01	0.25	0.73	1.45	3.46	5.85	8.60	15.45	26.90	← Estimated Convexity Bias in Basis Points
S	1st Def	1.872	2.136	2.454	2.741	3.216	3.592	3.911	4.418		
W	EDZ2	1.871	2.130	2.442	2.719	3.173	3.523	3.812	4.247		
A	12/16/02	0.15	0.57	1.24	2.13	4.37	6.94	9.88	17.10		
P											
S	2nd Def	2.079	2.421	2.739	3.008	3.442	3.802	4.104	4.581		
	EDH3	2.074	2.410	2.719	2.979	3.388	3.721	3.991	4.392		
	3/17/03	0.49	1.10	1.94	2.98	5.38	8.16	11.30	18.86		
	3rd Def	2.402	2.751	3.038	3.282	3.684	4.012	4.295	4.741		
	EDM3	2.392	2.733	3.010	3.242	3.618	3.917	4.166	4.534		
	6/16/03	1.01	1.80	2.82	3.98	6.60	9.50	12.84	20.72		

Notes on Interest Rate Swaps :

(1) Interest rate swaps are over-the-counter agreements to exchange a fixed payment (the swap rate) for a floating payment.
(2) Swap rates shown here assume semi-annual fixed and floating payments.
(3) All swap rates are quoted in semi-annual (30/360).

Page 1 of 4

EXHIBIT 10.1

Continued

CARR FUTURES — *Chicago*

Daily Zero to Ten (New Bias)

Tuesday, Sep 10, 2002
Data as of 3:00 PM NY CLOSE

Market Data, Treasury Hedges and Term TEDs

		3:00 PM NY CLOSE				Convexity	
I			IMM Market			Bias	Adj
M	Fut	Exp	Price	+/-	Rate	(bps)	Rate
M	EDU2	9/16/02	98.19	+1	1.81	0.0	1.81
	EDZ2	12/16/02	98.22	+1	1.78	0.0	1.78
E	EDH3	3/17/03	98.09	+1	1.91	0.3	1.91
U	EDM3	6/16/03	97.82	-1	2.18	0.7	2.17
R	EDU3	9/15/03	97.46	-2	2.54	1.3	2.53
O	EDZ3	12/15/03	97.11	-2	2.89	2.1	2.87
D	EDH4	3/15/04	96.79	-2	3.21	3.0	3.18
O	EDM4	6/14/04	96.54	+0	3.46	4.2	3.42
L	EDU4	9/13/04	96.33	+1	3.67	5.4	3.62
L	EDZ4	12/13/04	96.12	+3	3.88	6.8	3.81
A	EDH5	3/14/05	95.95	+4	4.05	8.1	3.97
R	EDM5	6/13/05	95.79	+6	4.21	9.6	4.11
	EDU5	9/19/05	95.64	+6	4.36	11.1	4.25
F	EDZ5	12/19/05	95.47	+6	4.53	12.7	4.40
U	EDH6	3/13/06	95.33	+6	4.67	14.3	4.53
T	EDM6	6/19/06	95.19	+6	4.81	16.0	4.65
U	EDU6	9/18/06	95.08	+6	4.92	17.8	4.74
R	EDZ6	12/18/06	94.93	+6	5.07	19.7	4.87
E	EDH7	3/19/07	94.82	+6	5.18	21.8	4.96
S	EDM7	6/18/07	94.70	+6	5.30	24.1	5.06
	EDU7	9/17/07	94.60	+6	5.40	26.5	5.14
	EDZ7	12/17/07	94.46	+6	5.54	29.0	5.25
	EDH8	3/17/08	94.38	+6	5.62	31.7	5.30
	EDM8	6/16/08	94.29	+6	5.71	34.5	5.36
	EDU8	9/15/08	94.22	+6	5.78	37.4	5.41
	EDZ8	12/15/08	94.12	+6	5.88	40.3	5.48
	EDH9	3/16/09	94.07	+6	5.93	43.2	5.50
	EDM9	6/15/09	93.99	+6	6.01	46.0	5.55
	EDU9	9/14/09	93.92	+6	6.08	48.9	5.59
	EDZ9	12/14/09	93.84	+6	6.16	51.7	5.64
	EDH0	3/15/10	93.81	+6	6.19	54.5	5.65
	EDM0	6/14/10	93.75	+6	6.25	57.2	5.68
	EDU0	9/13/10	93.69	+6	6.31	60.0	5.71
	EDZ0	12/13/10	93.63	+6	6.37	62.6	5.74
	EDH1	3/14/11	93.61	+6	6.39	65.1	5.74
	EDM1	6/13/11	93.56	+6	6.44	67.5	5.77
	EDU1	9/19/11	93.51	+6	6.49	69.7	5.79
	EDZ1	12/19/11	93.44	+6	6.56	71.9	5.84
	EDH2	3/19/12	93.43	+6	6.57	74.0	5.83
	EDst	6/18/12	93.43	+6	6.57	76.0	5.81

		ED Contracts Per $100 Million Face Amount				
O	Fut	10-Year	5-Year	3-Year	2-Year	1-Yr Bill
N	Stub	8.0	7.9		7.8	7.7
	EDU2	104.3	102.0		100.8	99.8
T	EDZ2	103.6	101.5		100.6	93.3
H	EDH3	102.1	100.3		99.8	0.0
E	EDM3	101.2	99.7		99.5	0.0
	EDU3	99.7	98.5		98.6	
R	EDZ3	98.9	97.9		98.3	
U	EDH4	97.4	96.8		97.4	
N	EDM4	96.7	96.2		81.3	
	EDU4	95.2	95.1			
T	EDZ4	94.5	94.5			
R	EDH5	93.0	93.4			
E	EDM5	99.2	99.9			
A	EDU5	90.9	91.9			
S	EDZ5	83.3	84.4			
U	EDH6	95.5	97.2			
R	EDM6	88.0	89.7			
Y	EDU6	86.7	88.8			
	EDZ6	86.0	88.2			
H	EDH7	84.8	87.3			
E	EDM7	84.0	53.7			
D	EDU7	82.8				
G	EDZ7	82.1				
E	EDH8	80.9				
S	EDM8	80.2				
	EDU8	79.1				
	EDZ8	78.5				
	EDH9	77.3				
	EDM9	76.7				
	EDU9	75.6				
	EDZ9	75.0				
	EDH0	73.9				
	EDM0	73.3				
	EDU0	72.2				
	EDZ0	71.7				
	EDH1	70.6				
	EDM1	75.3				
	EDU1	69.1				
	EDZ1	68.5				
	EDH2	67.6				
	EDst	41.6				

		Rate (act/360)	
E	Mat	Bid	Ask
U	ON	1.750	1.813
R	TN	1.750	1.813
O	SN	1.750	1.813
D	1W	1.770	1.820
O	2W	1.770	1.820
L	3W	1.770	1.820
L	1M	1.770	1.820
A	2M	1.760	1.810
R	3M	1.750	1.800
	4M	1.750	1.800
D	5M	1.750	1.800
E	6M	1.750	1.800
P	7M	1.770	1.830
O	8M	1.790	1.850
S	9M	1.800	1.860
I	10M	1.830	1.890
T	11M	1.860	1.920
S	1Y	1.900	1.960
	18M	2.188	2.313
	2Y	2.500	2.625
	3Y	3.000	3.125
	4Y	3.375	3.500
	5Y	3.688	3.813

	Term	ED Shift	Implied ED*	
	TED	Business	Nominal	Business
T	1yr Bill	14.5	14.8	14.8
E	2yr Tsy	37.5	38.3	38.3
D	3yr Tsy			
S	5yr Tsy	63.6	65.0	65.0
	10yr Tsy	80.1	81.4	81.5

*Business method:cash flows on business days
Nominal method: cash flows on stated days

	Term	Maturity	Coupon	Mid Price	BEY
T	3mo Bill	10/3/02	n/a	1.68	1.705
R	6mo Bill	12/12/02	n/a	1.65	1.680
E	1yr Bill	3/13/03	n/a	1.64	1.677
A	2yr Tsy	8/31/04	2 1/8	100-01+	2.101
S	3yr Tsy				
U	5yr Tsy	8/15/07	3 1/4	100-29	3.050
R	10yr Tsy	8/15/12	4 3/8	103-03+	3.992
Y	30yr Tsy	2/15/31	5 3/8	108-13	4.828

Spot and Forward Rate Comparisons: Euro Strips, Swaps, Deposits and Treasuries**

	Term	Spot Euro$ Strip (a)	Mid Market Swap Rate (b)	Euro$ Implied Swap Rate (c)	Convex Adjusted Swap Rate (d)	Ask Market Euro$ Deposits (e)	Mid Market Treasury Yield (f)			Euro$ Strip v Market Swap (a-b)	Convex Adjusted v Market Swap (d-b)	Convex Adjusted v Implied Swap (d-c)	Mid Market Swap Spread (b-f)	Convex Adjusted Spread (d-f)	Euro$ Strip Credit Spread (a-f)
	1 Year	1.928		1.928	1.925	1.960	1.661					-0.2		+26.4	+26.7
S	2 Year	2.509	2.479	2.504	2.490	2.625	2.101		S	+3.0	+1.1	-1.4	+37.9	+38.9	+40.9
P	3 Year	3.011	2.955	2.989	2.955	3.125	2.417	interp	P	+5.7	+0.0	-3.4	+53.8	+53.8	+59.4
O	4 Year	3.424	3.327	3.384	3.326	3.500	2.734	interp	R	+9.7	-0.1	-5.8	+59.4	+59.2	+69.0
T	5 Year	3.781	3.629	3.718	3.633	3.813	3.050		E	+15.2	+0.4	-8.5	+57.9	+58.3	+73.1
	7 Year	4.374	4.119	4.260	4.106		3.427	interp	A	+25.5	-1.4	-15.4	+69.3	+67.9	+94.7
	10 Year	5.011	4.563	4.804	4.536		3.992		D	+44.7	-2.7	-26.8	+57.1	+54.4	+101.9
	Z7-Z8	1.933		1.933	1.930	1.977			S			-0.2			
I	Z7-M9	2.223		2.219	2.212	2.358						-0.7			
M	Z7-Z9	2.514		2.505	2.491	2.664			B			-1.4			
M	Z7-Z0	3.025		3.003	2.968	3.187			P			-3.5			
	H8-H9	2.119		2.118	2.112	2.287			S			-0.6			
	M8-M9	2.404		2.402	2.391	2.602						-1.1			
	U8-U9	2.734		2.732	2.714	2.996						-1.8			

**Term ≤ 1 year (or 4 contracts): money market yield (act/360); Otherwise: semiannual bond equivalent yield (act/act, act/365 or 30/360)

EXHIBIT 10.1

Continued

CARR FUTURES
Chicago

Daily Zero to Ten (New Bias)

Tuesday, Sep 10, 2002
Data as of 3:00 PM NY CLOSE

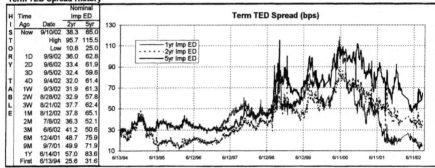

Term TED Spread History

	Time Ago	Date	Nominal Imp ED 2yr	Nominal Imp ED 5yr
H				
I				
S	Now	9/10/02	38.3	65.0
T		High	95.7	115.5
O		Low	10.8	25.0
R	1D	9/9/02	36.0	62.8
Y	2D	9/6/02	33.4	61.9
	3D	9/5/02	32.4	59.6
T	4D	9/4/02	32.0	61.4
A	1W	9/3/02	31.9	61.3
B	2W	8/28/02	32.9	57.8
L	3W	8/21/02	37.7	62.4
E	1M	8/12/02	37.8	65.1
	2M	7/8/02	36.3	52.1
	3M	6/6/02	41.2	50.6
	6M	12/4/01	48.7	75.9
	9M	9/7/01	49.9	71.9
	1Y	6/14/01	57.0	83.6
	First	6/13/94	25.6	31.6

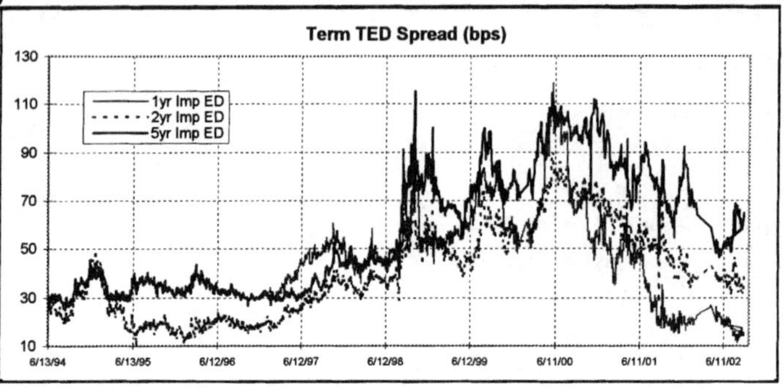

Rich/Cheap Analysis

	Fut	IMM Market Price	Std Fair Value	Convex Adj. Fair Value	Market Rich/Cheap vs. Standard Fair Value	Market Rich/Cheap vs. Cnvx Adj Fair Value
S						
I						
N						
G	EDU2	98.19	98.20	98.20	1 cheap	1 cheap
L	EDZ2	98.22	98.19	98.19	3 rich	3 rich
E	EDH3	98.09	98.03	98.03	6 rich	6 rich
	EDM3	97.82	97.72	97.72	10 rich	10 rich
C	EDU3	97.46	96.98	96.97	47 rich	49 rich
O	EDZ3	97.11	96.95	96.93	15 rich	17 rich
N	EDH4	96.79	96.49	96.46	31 rich	34 rich
T	EDM4	96.54	96.47	96.43	7 rich	11 rich
R	EDU4	96.33	95.87	95.82	46 rich	51 rich
A	EDZ4	96.12	95.87	95.81	25 rich	31 rich
C	EDH5	95.95	95.87	95.79	8 rich	16 rich
T	EDM5	95.79	95.82	95.73	3 cheap	6 rich
	EDU5	95.64	95.36	95.24	29 rich	40 rich
	EDZ5	95.47	95.36	95.23	11 rich	24 rich
	EDH6	95.33	95.35	95.21	2 cheap	12 rich
	EDM6	95.19	95.31	95.15	12 cheap	4 rich
	EDU6	95.08	94.88	94.70	20 rich	38 rich
	EDZ6	94.93	94.88	94.68	4 rich	24 rich
	EDH7	94.82	94.88	94.66	7 cheap	15 rich

	Strip of 4 Contracts	Market Strip Rate	Convex Adj. Strip Rate	Fair Value	Rich / Cheap Market vs. Fair Value	Rich / Cheap Cnvx Adj Market vs. Fair Value
4						
C						
O	EDU2-M3	1.93	1.93	1.98	4 rich	5 rich
N	EDZ2-U3	2.12	2.11	2.29	17 rich	17 rich
T	EDH3-Z3	2.40	2.39	2.60	20 rich	21 rich
R	EDM3-H4	2.73	2.72	3.00	26 rich	28 rich
A	EDU3-M4	3.06	3.03	3.32	26 rich	28 rich
C	EDZ3-U4	3.35	3.31	3.60	25 rich	29 rich
T	EDH4-Z4	3.60	3.55	3.88	28 rich	33 rich
	EDM4-H5	3.82	3.75	4.04	22 rich	28 rich
S	EDU4-M5	4.02	3.94	4.21	19 rich	26 rich
T	EDZ4-U5	4.19	4.10	4.34	15 rich	24 rich
R	EDH5-Z5	4.35	4.24	4.46	11 rich	22 rich
I	EDM5-H6	4.51	4.39	4.60	9 rich	21 rich
P	EDU5-M6	4.67	4.53	4.74	7 rich	21 rich
	EDZ5-U6	4.82	4.66	4.86	4 rich	20 rich
	EDH6-Z6	4.95	4.78	4.98	3 rich	20 rich
	EDM6-H7	5.09	4.90	5.11	1 rich	21 rich

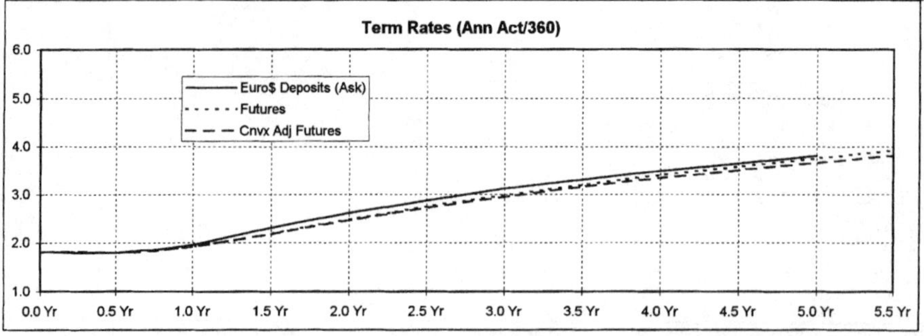

EXHIBIT 10.1

Continued

CARR FUTURES
Chicago

Daily Zero to Ten (New Bias)

Tuesday, Sep 10, 2002
Data as of 3:00 PM NY CLOSE

Convexity Bias Greeks

IMM EURODOLLAR FUTURES

Fut	Exp	Bias (bps)	1 bp Delta (bps)	1% Vega (bps)	1 day Theta (bps)
EDU2	9/16/02	0.0	0.000	0.000	0.000
EDZ2	12/16/02	0.0	0.001	0.000	-0.001
EDH3	3/17/03	0.3	0.003	0.007	-0.002
EDM3	6/16/03	0.7	0.007	0.023	-0.003
EDU3	9/15/03	1.3	0.010	0.049	-0.004
EDZ3	12/15/03	2.1	0.015	0.084	-0.006
EDH4	3/15/04	3.0	0.020	0.130	-0.008
EDM4	6/14/04	4.2	0.026	0.185	-0.009
EDU4	9/13/04	5.4	0.033	0.249	-0.011
EDZ4	12/13/04	6.8	0.039	0.323	-0.013
EDH5	3/14/05	8.1	0.045	0.406	-0.014
EDM5	6/13/05	9.6	0.051	0.498	-0.016
EDU5	9/19/05	11.1	0.058	0.599	-0.017
EDZ5	12/19/05	12.7	0.064	0.710	-0.018
EDH6	3/13/06	14.3	0.070	0.829	-0.019
EDM6	6/19/06	16.0	0.076	0.958	-0.020
EDU6	9/18/06	17.8	0.083	1.098	-0.021
EDZ6	12/18/06	19.7	0.090	1.251	-0.022
EDH7	3/19/07	21.8	0.097	1.417	-0.024
EDM7	6/18/07	24.1	0.105	1.596	-0.025
EDU7	9/17/07	26.5	0.113	1.789	-0.026
EDZ7	12/17/07	29.0	0.121	1.994	-0.027
EDH8	3/17/08	31.7	0.131	2.213	-0.029
EDM8	6/16/08	34.5	0.140	2.444	-0.030
EDU8	9/15/08	37.4	0.150	2.683	-0.031
EDZ8	12/15/08	40.3	0.159	2.925	-0.033
EDH9	3/16/09	43.2	0.169	3.169	-0.034
EDM9	6/15/09	46.0	0.179	3.415	-0.035
EDU9	9/14/09	48.9	0.188	3.663	-0.036
EDZ9	12/14/09	51.7	0.198	3.913	-0.037
EDH0	3/15/10	54.5	0.207	4.166	-0.037
EDM0	6/14/10	57.2	0.217	4.422	-0.038
EDU0	9/13/10	60.0	0.226	4.683	-0.039
EDZ0	12/13/10	62.6	0.234	4.953	-0.039
EDH1	3/14/11	65.1	0.242	5.233	-0.040
EDM1	6/13/11	67.5	0.249	5.523	-0.040
EDU1	9/19/11	69.7	0.256	5.821	-0.040
EDZ1	12/19/11	71.9	0.262	6.130	-0.040
EDH2	3/19/12	74.0	0.267	6.448	-0.040
EDM2	6/18/12	76.0	0.272	6.775	-0.040

SWAPS

Term	Est Bias (bps)	1 bp Delta (bps)	1% Vega (bps)	1 day Theta (bps)
2 yr	1.4	0.010	0.059	-0.004
3 yr	3.4	0.020	0.160	-0.007
4 yr	5.8	0.031	0.304	-0.010
5 yr	8.5	0.042	0.493	-0.012
7 yr	15.4	0.066	1.017	-0.017
10 yr	26.8	0.102	2.016	-0.022

SWAP RATE

Term	Rate
1 yr	1.92
2 yr	2.46
3 yr	2.94
4 yr	3.32
5 yr	3.62
6 yr	3.89
7 yr	4.11
8 yr	4.28
9 yr	4.42
10 yr	4.54

VOLATILITY

Term	Cap
1 yr	47.50
2 yr	49.50
3 yr	44.40
4 yr	39.60
5 yr	35.80
6 yr	
7 yr	31.30
8 yr	
9 yr	
10 yr	27.60

dollar implied swap rate was 3.718%, and the convexity-adjusted Eurodollar implied swap rate was 3.633%. The actual convexity bias was then 7.87 basis points [≈ 3.718% − 3.640%], while the estimated or theoretical convexity bias was 8.52 basis points [≈ 3.718% − 3.633%].

The fourth page is especially useful to risk managers, who often need convexity bias estimates from a disinterested source. Carr Futures can be this source, since it is a specialist futures firm and has, as a result, no swap book to value. This page is also useful to those who want to know what assumptions have gone into our calculations and how sensitive the estimates are to changes in rate levels and rate volatilities.

CHAPTER 11

Measuring and Trading Term TED Spreads

Galen Burghardt, William Hoskins, and Susan Kirshner
Research note originally released July 26, 1995

SYNOPSIS

The spread between Treasury and Eurodollar rates, which we know as the TED spread, has been a staple trade in the futures markets ever since the Eurodollar contract was listed in 1981. As a measure of the credit spread between high-grade bank debt and Treasury debt, the TED spread often has responded sharply to financial crises that have threatened to harm the credit quality of the banking system.

Although the world has become less skittish over the years and tends to react less violently to financial crises than it once did, the basic TED spread is still an active part of the trading scene. And over the past several years, the trade has extended into more sophisticated territory. The original TED was simply the spread between the price of a Treasury bill futures contract and the price of a Eurodollar futures contract. Now we find a growing interest in trading Treasury notes (or note futures) against strips of Eurodollar futures. We call these term TED spreads.

The basic TED spread is the easiest thing in the world to trade. Because a basis point is worth a flat $25 for both Treasury bill and Eurodollar futures contracts, buying the TED spread involves nothing more than buying Treasury bill futures and selling an equal number of Eurodollar futures in the same contract month.

Term TED spreads, however, are trickier both to measure and to trade, and the purpose of this note is to lay out as neatly as we can the various ways of approaching the trade. In the process, we show that simple zero-coupon (unweighted) measures of the spread are sensitive to changes in the slope of the yield curve while coupon (weighted) measures of the spread are not, and we show how to construct the two kinds of trades correctly. We show that the trade is not as directional as a lot of traders think. We show that measures of term TED spreads can be very sensitive to seemingly innocuous assumptions or mistakes that one might make when dealing with Eurodollar and Treasury markets. We also discuss in some detail the choices that traders can make when dealing with exposure to the "stub" rate and the consequences of the choices they make.

I should mention that this note is not as imposing as its size might make it seem. The main body of the note is comparatively short and contains most of what a trader needs to know about how term TED spreads are measured and traded. The technical appendix, on the other hand, is a hefty piece of work that contains everything anyone might want to know about the intricacies of relating markets for coupon-bearing notes and bonds to the Eurodollar futures market. As such, it will serve as a technical document for anyone who wants to know how to reconcile settlement dates and date mismatches in different markets, and how to calculate hedge ratios.

TED SPREADS

The spread between Eurodollar and Treasury rates has been one of the great staples of trading ever since the Eurodollar futures contract was listed in 1981. As a measure of the difference in credit quality between prime London banks and the U.S. Treasury, the TED spread has widened with each new financial crisis and narrowed as fears have died down. As shown in Exhibit 11.1, the TED spread has become much less volatile than it once was, but it is still an actively watched measure of the credit quality of the banking system.

EXHIBIT 11.1

History of the TED Spread, 1970–1995
3-Month LIBOR Less 3-Month Treasury Bill Rate

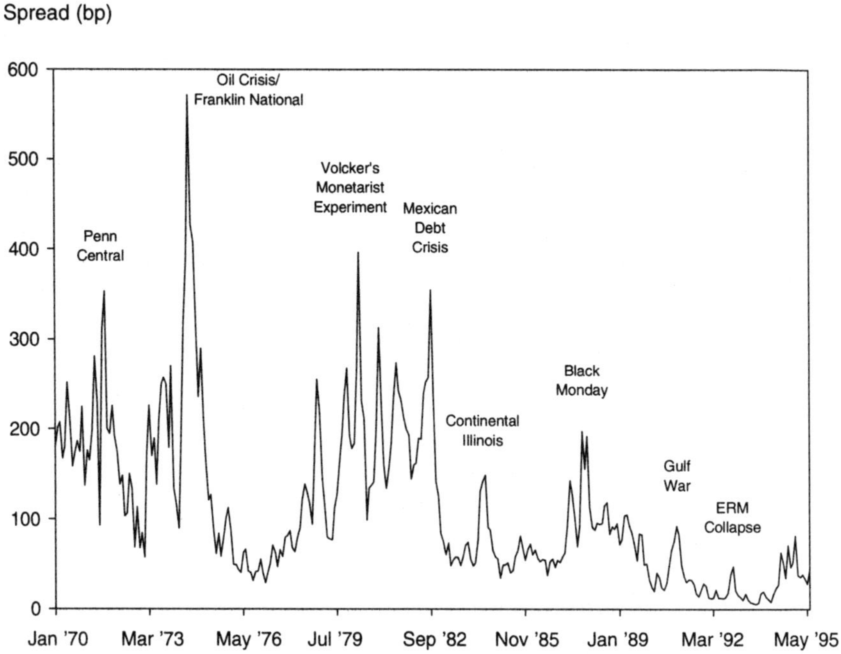

Simple TED Spreads

From the outset, the most actively traded TED spread has been the difference between the *Treasury bill* and *Eurodollar (ED) futures prices*. Because of the way these two contract prices are quoted,

$$\textit{Treasury bill futures price} = 100 - \textit{3-month Treasury bill rate}$$

$$\textit{ED futures price} = 100 - \textit{3-month ED rate}$$

The spread between the T-bill and Eurodollar futures prices is the difference between the market's expectations of 3-month LIBOR and the 3-month Treasury bill rate as of the expiration of the futures contract. That is,

$$\textit{Bill futures price} - \textit{ED futures price} = \textit{3-month ED rate} - \textit{3-month bill rate}$$

This is a very simple trade to execute because the value of a basis point is $25 for both of these contracts. Therefore, if you think the TED spread will increase, you can simply buy Treasury bill futures and sell an equal number of Eurodollar futures, and the value of a basis point change in the spread will be $25 times the number of spreads. For example, if you buy 100 T-bill futures and sell 100 Eurodollar futures, each basis point increase in the TED spread will produce a gain of $2,500.

Term TED Spreads

Over the past several years, the market has taken an interest in the spread between longer-term Treasury and Eurodollar rates. These spreads are known generally as term TED spreads, and Exhibit 11.2 shows how the 2-year TED spread has behaved over the past several years. Given their volatility, these are highly tradable spreads. But unlike the simple TED spread between Treasury bill

EXHIBIT 11.2

2-Year Term TED

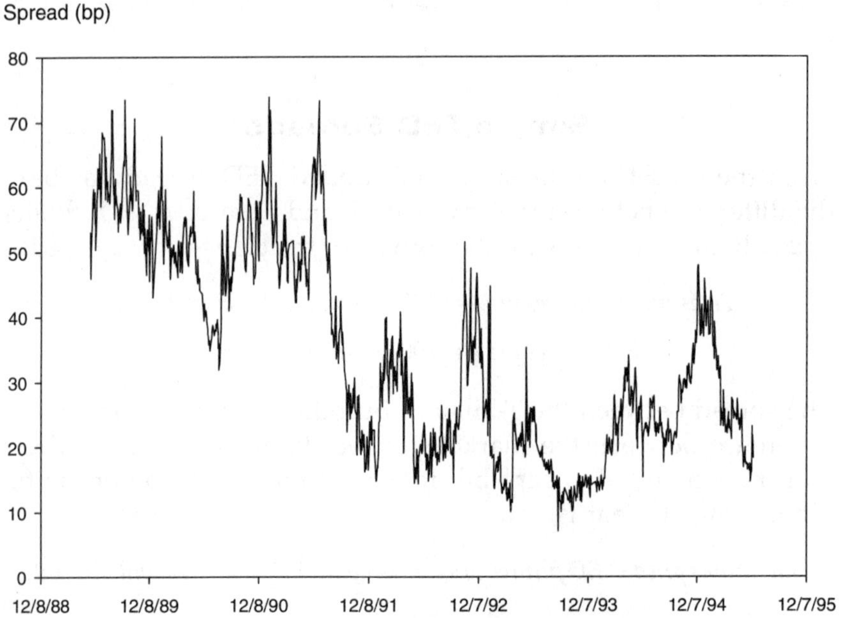

and Eurodollar futures prices, term TED spreads are both harder to measure and harder to execute properly.

TWO KINDS OF TERM TED SPREADS

While everyone computes Treasury yields using well-accepted standards, there are several ways to compute the yield on the Eurodollar side of the spread. The two most widely used measures of the Eurodollar yield are those that use a zero-coupon rate and those that make an effort to translate Eurodollar futures rates into a yield on a coupon bearing instrument. We will refer to the first of these as unweighted Eurodollar strip yields and the second of these as weighted Eurodollar strip yields.

Unweighted Eurodollar Strip Yields versus Treasury Yields

This form of the term TED spread is easy to calculate and easy to trade. In its most basic form, a Eurodollar strip yield is simply the bond equivalent yield on a zero-coupon bond where the price of a $1 zero-coupon bond is

$$\textit{Eurodollar zero price} = \frac{1}{\left(1+S\left(\frac{D_{spot}}{360}\right)\right)\left(1+F_1\left(\frac{D_1}{360}\right)\right)\left(1+F_2\left(\frac{D_2}{360}\right)\right)\times\cdots\times\left(1+F_n\left(\frac{D_n}{360}\right)\right)}$$

In the denominator is the amount to which $1 would grow at maturity if invested at today's spot rate, S, and Eurodollar futures rates, F_i. The weights given these rates are the days in their respective periods, D_i. Because most Eurodollar futures contracts cover a 91-day period, this calculation gives nearly equal weight to each rate.[1]

This method has one important shortcoming: it produces term TED spreads that are sensitive to changes in the slope of the

1. Exceptions to this equal weighting are the spot "stub" rate, which covers the period from the settlement date to the value date for the first futures expiration, and the final futures rate in the strip, which typically covers only a partial period. Just how we handle the stub rate, date mismatches, and partial periods is explained in considerable detail in the technical appendix to this note.

yield curve. If one calculates the present value of a coupon bearing note using Eurodollar futures rates, it is easy to see that the note's present value or price is more sensitive to changes in the nearby rates than to changes in more distant rates.

$$Full\ price = \frac{\dfrac{Coupon}{2}}{\left(1+S\left(\dfrac{D_{spot}}{360}\right)\right)\left(1+F_1\left(\dfrac{D_1}{360}\right)\right)\left(1+F_2\left(\dfrac{D_2}{360}\right)\right)} + \cdots$$

$$+ \frac{100+\dfrac{Coupon}{2}}{\left(1+S\left(\dfrac{D_{spot}}{360}\right)\right)\left(1+F_1\left(\dfrac{D_1}{360}\right)\right)\times\cdots\times\left(1+F_8\left(\dfrac{D_8}{360}\right)\right)}$$

In this expression, the nearby futures rates (for example, F_1 and F_2) appear in all of the present value calculations, while the more distant rates (for example, F_8) appear only in the calculation of later cash flows. Because of this, one can imagine a simple rotation of the forward rate curve that would have no effect on the price of a zero-coupon note (for example, raising the first two futures rates 10 basis points and lowering the last two futures rates 10 basis points) but that would lower the price of a coupon note. Such a rotation would have no effect on an unweighted Eurodollar strip yield but would increase the yield on a coupon bearing note.

Weighted Eurodollar Strip Yields versus Treasury Yields

To produce measures of the term TED spread that depend only on the credit spread and not on the slope of the yield curve, one must find a way to give greater weight to nearby futures rates and less weight to the more distant futures rates. We calculate two such measures. One is the spread between implied Eurodollar yields and Treasury yields. The other is the fixed basis point spread against Eurodollar rates needed to reconcile Eurodollar rates with Treasury note prices.

Implied Eurodollar Yield versus Treasury Yield

This approach to measuring the spread begins by finding what the note would yield if it were issued by a bank of LIBOR quality.

We call this the implied Eurodollar yield. From this we subtract the note's actual yield to produce the spread.

The implied Eurodollar yield on the note is found by calculating the present value of the Treasury note's cash flows using discount factors derived from spot LIBOR and Eurodollar futures rates and then finding the note's yield at that present value. Because Eurodollar rates are higher than corresponding Treasury yields, the present value of the note at these rates is lower than its full market price, and the implied Eurodollar yield is higher than the note's actual market yield. When measured this way, the term TED spread is expressed as a semiannual bond equivalent yield.

Fixed Basis Point Spread to Eurodollar Futures Rates

Another way to give greater weight to nearby futures rates when computing the term TED spread is to answer the question "What fixed number of basis points must be subtracted from each Eurodollar futures rate to produce a present value of the Treasury note that is equal to its actual full market price?" When measured this way, the spread is expressed in quarterly money market basis points, which uses an Actual/360 day-count convention.

Complete operating instructions for calculating the different measures of the term TED spread are provided in the technical appendix, which covers day-count conventions, date mismatches, and various other real-world headaches that make life in the markets so interesting.

HOW DO THESE RATES COMPARE?

The three approaches to reckoning the term TED spread are illustrated in Exhibit 11.3, which provides on-the-run 2-year and 5-year spreads for June 5, 1995. Exhibit 11.4 provides a history of all three measures of the 5-year term TED spread since September 1993.

The differences between the three measures of the spread have two main causes. First, as shown in Exhibit 11.4, the Eurodollar strip measure of the spread can be quite a bit larger than either of the other two measures. When the yield curve is positively sloped, the Eurodollar strip yield is higher than the implied Eurodollar yield because relatively greater weight is given to the

EXHIBIT 11.3

Term TED Spreads
June 5, 1995

Term	Eurodollar Strip	*Weighted* Implied Eurodollar	*Weighted* Fixed Spread to Eurodollars
2 years	16.8	15.2	16.3
5 years	35.5	31.9	31.1

EXHIBIT 11.4

5-Year Term TED Spreads
September 1993 through May 1995

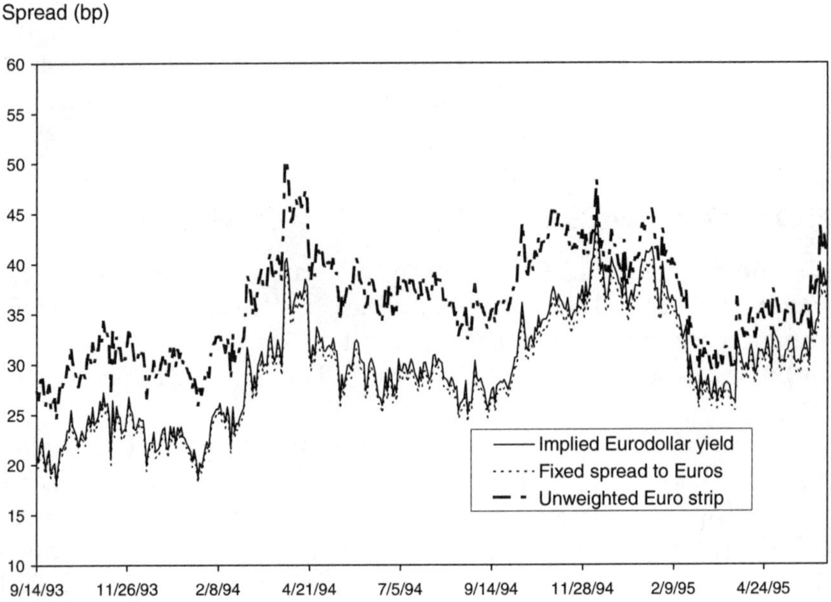

higher rates found on the more distant parts of the forward rate curve. This is the same effect as zero-coupon bonds yielding more than coupon bonds when the yield curve is positively sloped.

This difference is illustrated more forcefully in Exhibit 11.5, which charts the difference between the Eurodollar strip and implied Eurodollar measures of the 5-year term TED spread (on the vertical axis) against the slope of the yield curve as measured by the difference between the fifth year and lead Eurodollar futures rates (on the horizontal axis). Notice that when the yield curve is steep, the difference between the unweighted and weighted measures of the spread is quite large. When the yield curve is nearly flat, on the other hand, the difference between the two measures is almost zero. And, if the yield curve were to invert, the Eurodollar strip rate version of the spread would actually be smaller than that given by the implied Eurodollar yield spread.

The chief lesson here is that if one wants to trade the straight credit spread between Eurodollar futures and Treasury notes,

EXHIBIT 11.5

Effect of Yield Curve Slope on the Difference between Unweighted and Weighted TED Spreads (5-Year)

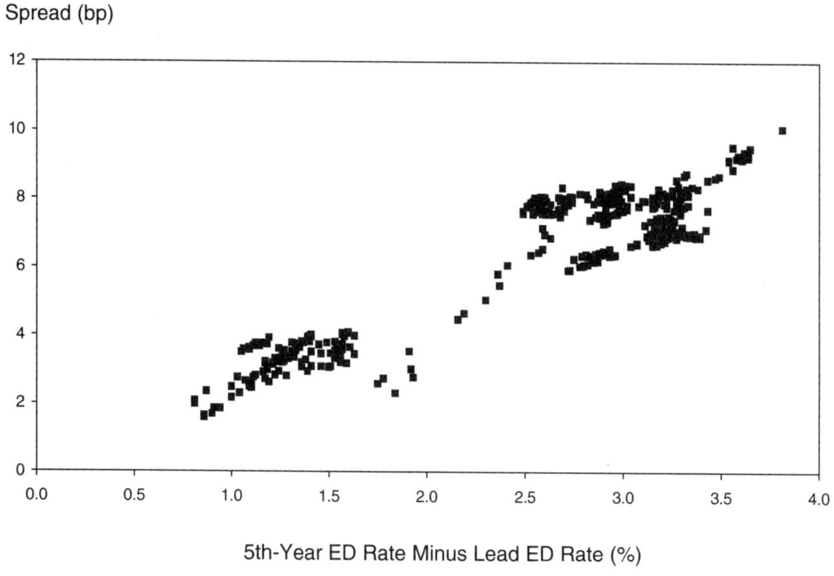

without interference from the slope of the yield curve, one should focus on term TED spreads that give appropriately greater weight to the nearby contracts.

A second difference between the spreads stems from Treasury issues that have so-called bad dates. Some Treasury notes have coupons or principal payments that are scheduled to fall on weekends or holidays. In these cases, the actual cash payments are made on the first following business day. This is a well known problem in the Treasury market, and the effect of delaying these cash payments is to lower the price of the note. Because the note's yield is calculated without regard to these delays, however, its yield will appear to be higher than it really is. The swap market compensates for this effect, which can be worth as much as 1.5 basis points or more, by reducing the quoted swap spread over Treasuries if the relevant on-the-run note has bad dates. The way we calculate the implied Eurodollar/Treasury spread produces the same effect, so this measure of the term TED spread is the best for making comparisons between term TED spreads and swap spreads.

In contrast, we calculate the fixed basis point spread to Eurodollars version of the spread assuming that all of the Treasury note's cash flows fall on actual business days. As a result, the fixed basis point spread to Eurodollars version is perhaps the cleanest version of the pure credit spread. It is not influenced by the slope of the yield curve, and it is not confused by bad dates. On the other hand, it does not lend itself as well to comparisons with swap spreads, which are influenced by the timing of cash flows on the Treasury note.

HOW DIRECTIONAL IS THE SPREAD?

There is a strong sense among traders that the term TED spread is highly directional. This view is seemingly borne out in Exhibit 11.6, which charts the value of the 2-year term TED spread against the yield on a 2-year Treasury note. On average, this spread has been comparatively wide when note yields have been high and comparatively narrow when note yields have been low. A closer examination of the relationship suggests, however, that term TED spreads are much less directional than Exhibit 11.6 seems to imply.

EXHIBIT 11.6

2-Year TED Spread versus 2-Year Note Yield
1989 through 1995

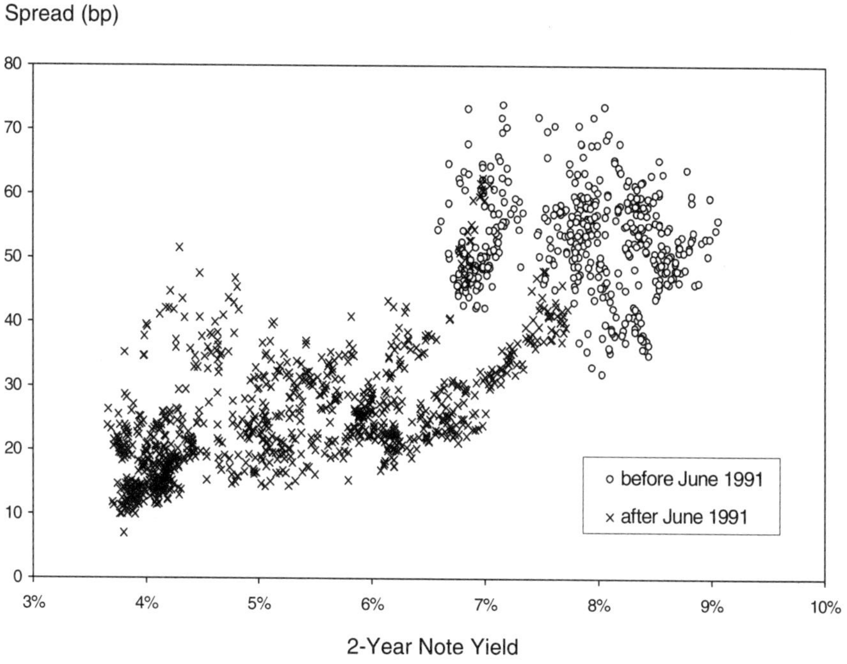

Notice first how the observations are clumped. If you focus on the period before June 1991, when 2-year note yields were trading between 6.50 percent and 9.00 percent, the values of the term TED spread (which are shown as circles) seem to be more or less randomly scattered. Or if you focus on the period after June 1991, when 2-year note yields were trading in a much lower range, the values of the term TED spread seem again to be more or less randomly scattered.

The lack of any significant directional relationship between the size of the spread and the level of note yields is driven home even more forcefully in Exhibit 11.7, which shows 1-month changes in the value of the 2-year term TED spread against 1-month changes in the level of 2-year Treasury note yields. If you look hard enough, you can see a slight positive relationship, but

EXHIBIT 11.7

Change in 2-Year Term TED Spread versus Change in 2-Year Treasury Yield
Monthly Intervals, May 1989 through May 1995

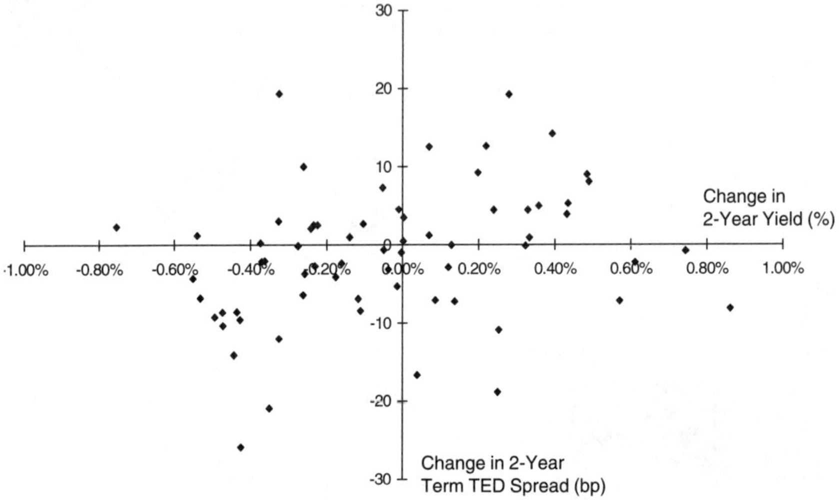

any trades based on this kind of relationship would be subject to a lot of noise.

TRADING THE SPREADS

How you trade the spread depends entirely on how you measure the spread. Suppose that on June 5, 1995, you think that the 2-year term TED spread is too narrow and will widen. To take advantage of this market view, you might buy $100 million face value of the current on-the-run 2-year Treasury note, which is the 6-1/8s of 5/31/97, and sell an appropriately weighted strip of Eurodollar futures.

Just what constitutes an appropriately weighted strip of futures depends, however, on which version of the TED spread you want to trade. Whatever your approach to the trade, you want a position whose P/L can be explained by changes in your measure of the spread. For example, if you want to trade the Eurodollar strip measure of the spread, you want a position that will make money when this measure of the spread widens and will lose money when it narrows. Because the Eurodollar strip measure of the spread is sensitive to changes in the slope of the yield curve, you want your trade's P/L to have the same sensitivity. On the other hand, if you just want to trade the credit spread, you want a trade construction that is insulated from changes in the slope of the yield curve.

Hedge Ratios

The appropriate Eurodollar combinations for the unweighted and weighted measures of the spread are shown in Exhibit 11.8, both for the trade date of June 5 and one week later (assuming rates unchanged). Consider first the difference between the unweighted and weighted hedge ratios for June 5. In both cases, the total num-

EXHIBIT 11.8

Eurodollar Futures Hedge Ratios for a 2-Year Term TED
$100 Million of the 6-1/8s of 5/31/97

	*Hedges on June 5**		*Hedges 1 Week Later*	
Contract Month	**Unweighted Spread**	**Weighted Spread****	**Unweighted Spread**	**Weighted Spread****
Stub	16.1	16.8	8.6	9.0
Jun '95	96.5	100.8	96.5	101.0
Sep '95	96.5	100.3	96.6	100.4
Dec '95	96.6	98.0	96.6	98.1
Mar '96	96.6	97.4	96.7	97.5
Jun '96	96.6	95.1	96.6	95.2
Sep '96	96.6	94.6	96.6	94.7
Dec '96	96.5	92.2	96.6	92.3
Mar '97	79.5	76.0	79.6	76.1
Total	771.5	771.2	764.4	764.3

* June 6 settlement.

** Fixed basis point spread to Eurodollar rates method.

ber of contracts is either 771 or 772 (depending on how you round) because the hedges were designed to keep the trade direction neutral.

The allocation of contracts across contract months, however, is very different. If you are trading the Eurodollar strip version of the spread, the interest rate on the Eurodollar leg of the spread is the yield on a zero-coupon note. Because there is only one cash flow on a zero-coupon note, the present value of that cash flow depends equally on the futures rates that make up its term discount factor. As a result, the appropriate hedge for this version of the spread gives equal weight to each of the contracts. The main exceptions to this rule stem from differences in the days covered by each of the contracts. For example, Eurodollar futures periods may include as many as 98 days or as few as 84 days, and our calculated hedge ratios will reflect these differences. Also, the last contract in the strip is almost always an exception because it is being asked to cover only the number of days from its corresponding value date to the maturity of the note.

If you are trading either of the weighted versions of the spread, then the hedge is designed to give a weight to each contract that is proportional to the effect of its rate on the value of the note. Because nearby futures rates have a greater effect on the price of a coupon bearing note than do more distant futures rate, we give relatively greater weight to the nearby contracts.

The two sets of hedge ratios are designed to perform differently because of the differences in the way the unweighted and weighted TED spreads are calculated. We know that the Eurodollar strip version of the spread is sensitive to changes in the slope of the forward rate curve. An equally weighted strip of Eurodollar futures captures this effect by giving too little weight to the front contracts and too much weight to the back. As a result, a flattening of the forward rate curve will decrease the price of the coupon bearing Treasury note relative to the price of the corresponding zero-coupon note, which is represented by the Eurodollar strip. The resulting loss should track the decrease in the Eurodollar strip measure of the TED spread.

In contrast, if you want to focus only on the value of the credit spread, you want to sell more of the nearby Eurodollar contracts and fewer of the more distant contracts. For the trade on June 5, the correct numbers of contracts are shown in the weighted term TED spread column of Exhibit 11.8. Anyone who trades swaps against Eurodollar futures recognizes this kind of weighting scheme. When constructed this way, the trade captures only changes in the credit spread and is largely insulated from changes in the slope of the yield curve.

What to Do with the Stub

How you handle exposure to the stub rate depends on how you handle the financing of your note position. In turn, the way you finance your note position can have an effect on the break-even conditions for a term TED spread trade.

Overnight Financing

Consider, first, the problem of financing. If you finance your Treasury position in the overnight RP market, you are exposed to changes in the value of the stub rate. You can hedge this exposure by adding an appropriate number of Eurodollar futures to your position in the lead contract. For our June 5 trade, we would add 16 or 17 contracts to our June '95 position. Taking this approach introduces some slippage in the P/L of the trade because the June '95 contract is a cross-hedge for exposure to the stub rate. Also, this approach requires you to adjust your hedge by small amounts each day if you want to avoid any directional exposure in the trade. As shown in Exhibit 11.8, the number of contracts needed to hedge against exposure to the stub rate is only 9 contracts 1 week later. To compensate for this decline, you would have to remove one contract a day from your hedge.

Or you can choose not to hedge your stub exposure at all. If you take this route, then you are combining a small financing trade with the TED spread trade. By not hedging the stub exposure, you are earning a term rate on the Treasury note and paying overnight financing. You are riding the yield curve, and the risks and returns to such a trade are well known.

Term Financing

You can instead choose to finance your Treasury note position in the term RP market to the first Eurodollar futures expiration. If you do, your term financing hedges your exposure to the stub rate, and you can ignore the 16 or 17 contracts that Exhibit 11.8 indicates as the hedge for the stub rate.

Carry and Convergence

However you choose to finance your position, carry affects the break-even conditions for a term TED trade. Consider a long position in the 2-year term TED spread on June 5, 1995. The term RP rate at which one could have financed a Treasury note position to the expiration of the June '95 Eurodollar futures contract was about 5.95 percent, which was only 5 basis points lower than the Eurodollar stub rate of 6.0009 percent. The 2-year implied Eurodollar term TED spread was trading on June 5 at 15.2 basis points. As a result, the value of the TED spread for the stub period was smaller than the value of the term TED spread for the entire life of the note.

The effect of carry and the passing of time on the value of a term TED spread trade can be determined by reckoning a forward value of the term TED spread. The first step is to find a forward price for the note. If you want to remove the influence of the stub period from the trade, the appropriate forward date will be the value date for the first Eurodollar futures expiration. This forward price, given the RP rate at which you can finance the note, is a break-even price. Given the forward price, you can easily determine the forward yield on the note. The second step is to calculate the implied Eurodollar price of the note as of the forward date. From this you would calculate the forward yield implied by Eurodollar rates. The difference between the two is a forward TED spread and represents the value to which the spot term TED spread must converge if the trade is to break even.

On June 5, for example, the spot value of the 2-year term TED spread was 15.2 basis points. The term RP rate to the first Eurodollar futures expiration was 5.95 percent. Using this RP rate to find the 2-year note's forward price and converting this forward price to a yield, we find that its forward yield is 5.530 percent. For the same forward date, we find that its implied Eurodollar yield is 5.684 percent. Thus, the note's forward term TED spread is 15.4 basis points, and this is its break-even value. That is, if you buy the note on June 5, finance it term, and sell an appropriate combination of Eurodollar futures to hedge the note, the position will just break even if the TED spread widens 0.2 basis points, from its initial value of 15.2 basis points to its forward value of 15.4 basis points.

In this instance, the spread has to widen for the trade to break even because the spread between the Eurodollar stub rate and the term RP rate is smaller than the full 2-year term TED spread. If the difference between the stub and term RP rates were larger than the full term TED spread, the break-even term TED spread would be lower than the spot spread.

Convexity

Because a Treasury note exhibits positive convexity, while Eurodollar futures exhibit no convexity, you will find yourself having to adjust your hedges as rates rise and fall. If you are long the term TED spread, this will work in your favor because a decrease in rates will require you to sell additional Eurodollar futures while an increase in rates will require you to buy back some of your short Eurodollar futures. Because you are selling Eurodollar futures when rates fall and buying Eurodollar futures when rates rise, you will find yourself systematically selling high and buying low. Just how much this is worth to you depends on how much convexity the note exhibits and how much rate volatility the market delivers. (Exhibit 11.12 shows how much we estimated the convexity bias to be worth over the entire lives of notes with maturities ranging from 2 to 10 years.)

FORWARD TERM TED SPREADS

One can also measure and trade forward term TED spreads. Exhibit 11.9 provides various examples of such spreads for standard Treasury maturities. For example, the 2 × 5 term TED spread (that is, the 3-year term TED spread 2 years forward) on June 5 was 44.4 basis points. The value of the 5 × 10 term TED spread (that is, the 5-year term TED 5 years forward) was 117.2 basis points.

Forward term TED positions may afford interesting trading opportunities. The upper panel of Exhibit 11.10 shows, for example, that over recent weeks, the 2-year term TED spread has been trading somewhat cheap while the 5-year term TED has been trading at the upper end of its range. As a result, the 2 × 5 term TED spread, which is shown in the lower panel of Exhibit 11.10, has become comparatively rich.

EXHIBIT 11.9

Forward Term TED Spreads
Implied Eurodollar/Treasury Spreads for June 5, 1995 (in bps)

	To: (final maturity in years)		
From: (years forward)	**3**	**5**	**10**
2	26.2	44.4	82.1
3		54.0	93.2
5			117.2

Just how one would sell such a position is illustrated in Exhibit 11.11. There is no active forward market for Treasury notes, but one can construct synthetic forwards in the cash market. On June 5, for example, one could have sold $99.155797 million par amount of the on-the-run 5-year note (the 6-1/4s of 5/00) and bought $100 million par amount of the on-the-run 2-year note (the 6-1/8s of 5/97). Given the full prices of these notes, one would be long and short equal market values of the two notes. The appropriate Eurodollar futures hedge for this position would be a long strip in which the first expiration would be the March '97 contract. This hedge is simply the net of the Eurodollar hedges for the two note positions, a short 2-year strip for the 2-year note and a long 5-year strip for the 5-year note.

TERM TED SPREADS AND SWAP SPREADS

Term TED spreads are closely related to swap spreads. *Swap spreads* measure the spread of swap rates over Treasury note yields, while term TED spreads capture the difference between Eurodollar futures rates and Treasury note yields. If swaps were priced right on top of the Eurodollar curve—that is, if swap rates were equal to those implied by Eurodollar futures rates—the two spreads would be the same. As it is, swap rates are slightly lower than those implied by Eurodollar futures rates because of the value of the convexity difference between Eurodollar futures and interest

EXHIBIT 11.10

2-Year versus 5-Year Term TED Spreads

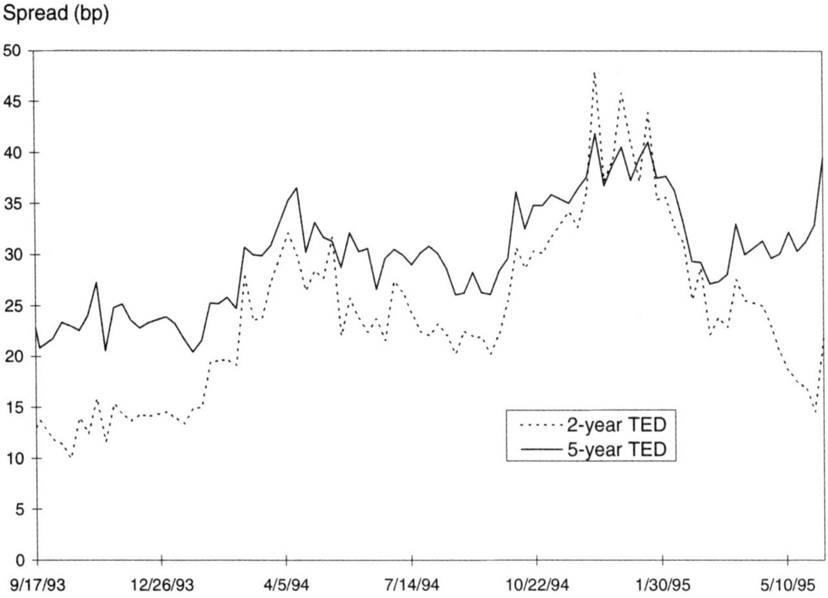

2 × 5 Forward Term TED

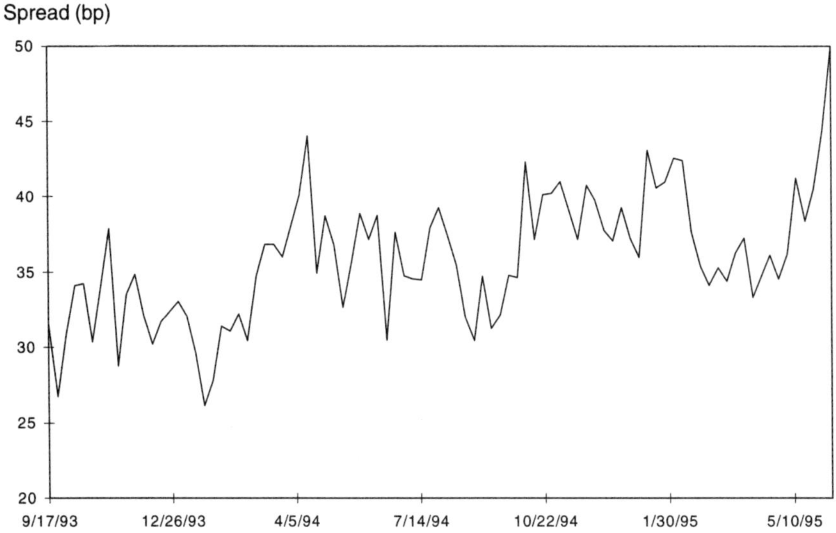

EXHIBIT 11.11

Eurodollar Hedge for a 2 × 5 Term TED Spread
June 5, 1995

Contract Month	2-Year Note Hedge	5-Year Note Hedge	Net Eurodollar Futures Hedge
Stub	−17	17	0
Jun '95	−101	101	0
Sep '95	−100	100	0
Dec '95	−98	98	0
Mar '96	−97	97	0
Jun '96	−95	95	0
Sep '96	−95	95	0
Dec '96	−92	92	0
Mar '97	−76	92	16
Jun '97		89	89
Sep '97		89	89
Dec '97		87	87
Mar '98		86	86
Jun '98		84	84
Sep '98		83	83
Dec '98		81	81
Mar '99		81	81
Jun '99		79	79
Sep '99		78	78
Dec '99		76	76
Mar '00		65	65
Total	−771	1765	994

Position:
Short $99,155,797 par ($101,178,535 market) amount of the 6-1/4s of 5/00.
Long $100,000,000 par ($101,178,535 market) amount of the 6-1/8s of 5/97.

rate swaps.[2] Because of this convexity bias, the term TED spread is slightly larger than the swap spread. In particular, if we use the

2. See chapter 7, "The Convexity Bias in Eurodollar Futures," for a full explanation of this convexity bias and the way we estimate its value.

implied Eurodollar/Treasury form of the term TED spread, we can write the term TED spread as

$$\textit{Term TED spread} = \textit{Swap spread} + \textit{Value of the convexity bias}$$

Exhibit 11.12 shows how much the convexity bias can influence the difference between term TED spreads and conventional swap spreads. Notice that the influence of the convexity bias increases rapidly with maturity. On June 5, the value of the convexity bias for a 2-year horizon was only 1.6 basis points. For a 5-year horizon, though, the convexity bias was worth 8.3 basis points and for a 10-year horizon was worth 25.6 basis points.

The term TED spread, then, is a composite trade whose value depends both on the market's assessment of the swap spread and on the market's assessment of the value of the convexity bias. As shown in Exhibit 11.13, the parts can add up to more or less than the whole. On June 5, for example, the 5-year swap spread was trading at 27.5 basis points, while our estimate of the value of the convexity was 8.3 basis points. Taken together, these two numbers suggest that the term TED spread should have been trading at 35.8 basis points. As it was, the term TED spread was trading at 31.9 basis points, or 3.9 basis points less than its theoretical value.

A situation like this affords opportunities for traders. Taken together, for example, the term TED spread market and the

EXHIBIT 11.12

Components of the Term TED Spread
June 5, 1995

		Components	
Maturity (Years)	Term TED Spread*	Swap Spread**	Convexity Bias
2	15.2	13.6	1.6
3	19.5	16.1	3.4
5	31.9	23.6	8.3
10	63.4	37.8	25.6

* Implied Eurodollar/Treasury spread.

** Theoretical fair value of the swap spread.

EXHIBIT 11.13

Parsing the 5-Year Term TED Spread
Basis Points

			Theoretical Spread		
Date	Market Term TED Spread (1)	Swap Spread (2)	Theoretical Convexity Bias (3)	Theoretical Term TED Spread (4) = (2) + (3)	Rich/Cheap (mkt − th) (5) = (1) − (4)
6/5/95	31.9	27.5	8.3	35.8	−3.9
6/12/95	36.5	30.5	8.4	38.9	−2.4
6/19/95	39.8	31.5	7.8	39.3	0.5

swap market think that the value of the convexity bias is only 4.4 [= 31.9 − 27.5] basis points. At the same time, the term TED market, given our estimate of the value of the convexity bias, thinks that swaps should be trading at only 23.6 [= 31.9 − 8.3] basis points. And, of course, the term TED spread appears cheap from the perspective of the swap market for those who are confident that convexity is really worth 8.3 basis points. As it was, these apparent mispricings resolved themselves over the next two weeks, in part because the term TED spread increased relative to swap rates, and in part because the estimated value of the convexity bias fell somewhat.

APPENDIX

Complete Operating Instructions for Calculating Term TED Spreads and Hedge Ratios

Calculating term TED spreads requires far greater attention to detail than one might think. Seemingly innocuous simplifying assumptions can affect the calculated value of the spread by 2 or 3 basis points, and when the spread is trading between 15 and 20 basis points, such errors can loom large. At the same time, because calculated values of the spread are so sensitive to both the assumptions and the data, traders should take care not to confuse precision with accuracy. Just because one can calculate a spread to a tenth of a basis point does not mean that one can trade it at that level of precision.

The purpose of this appendix is to spell out just how we calculate the various measures of the term TED spread and to show where the various pitfalls are. In the process, we show how to

- Calculate zero-coupon note prices (discount factors) from spot LIBOR and Eurodollar futures interest rates
- Handle the integration of cash and futures rates, the reconciliation of value dates across markets, the problem of date mismatches, and the issue of nominal versus actual cash flow dates
- Calculate hedge ratios for term TED spread trades

The following operating instructions couch everything in terms of the 2-year term TED spread for June 5, 1995, when the current on-the-run 2-year note was the 6-1/8s of 5/31/97. All prices and rates were taken at 3:00 p.m. New York time.

ZERO-COUPON NOTE PRICES

As shown in the main section of this note, there are several ways to calculate term TED spreads. All of these methods require one or more zero-coupon note prices that can be used either to find the yield on a zero-coupon note or to find the present values of the various cash flows on a Treasury note. To calculate zero-coupon note prices, we use money market conventions to find the value to which $1 today would grow if invested at a sequence of spot LIBOR and Eurodollar futures interest rates. These values represent terminal wealths. The inverse of terminal wealth is the zero-coupon note price or discount factor for $1 to be received on a particular date in the future.

Terminal Wealth

Using the LIBOR deposit market to supply the spot rate and the Eurodollar futures market to supply forward rates, terminal wealth at time t is calculated as

$$TW_t = \left(1 + S\left(\frac{D_{spot}}{360}\right)\right)\left(1 + F_1\left(\frac{D_1}{360}\right)\right) \times \cdots \times \left(1 + F_n\left(\frac{D_n}{360}\right)\right)$$

where

- S is the spot ("stub") deposit rate from the Treasury value date to the first Eurodollar futures expiration value date
- F_i is the implied forward deposit rate, calculated as 100 minus the Eurodollar futures price, divided by 100
- D_i is the number of days associated with the ith spot or forward term

Exhibit 11.A1 shows the terminal wealths and associated discount factors that we calculated using spot LIBOR and Eurodollar futures rates for June 5, 1995. For example, the terminal wealth on December 20, 1995, for $1 invested on June 6, 1995 (our value date) is calculated as

$$TW_{20Dec95} = \left(1 + 0.0600093\left(\frac{15}{360}\right)\right)\left(1 + 0.0586\left(\frac{91}{360}\right)\right)\left(1 + 0.0551\left(\frac{91}{360}\right)\right)$$

$$= 1.03152$$

EXHIBIT 11.A1

Terminal Wealths and Discount Factors
June 5, 1995

Futures Expiration	Value Date	Rate	Days	Terminal Wealth	Discount Factor*
Stub	6/6/95	6.00093	15	1.00000	1.00000
6/19/95	6/21/95	5.86	91	1.00250	0.99751
9/18/95	9/20/95	5.51	91	1.01735	0.98295
12/18/95	12/20/95	5.44	91	1.03152	0.96944
3/18/96	3/20/96	5.35	91	1.04570	0.95629
6/17/96	6/19/96	5.41	91	1.05985	0.94353
9/16/96	9/18/96	5.50	91	1.07434	0.93080
12/16/96	12/18/96	5.69	91	1.08928	0.91804
3/17/97	3/19/97	5.75	91	1.10494	0.90502
6/16/97	6/18/97	5.86	91	1.12100	0.89206

* Discount factor = 1/(Terminal wealth).

Zero-Coupon Note Prices and Discount Factors

The price of a zero-coupon note that matures on any given date is simply the inverse of terminal wealth for that date. And, because the fractional price of a zero-coupon note is the present value of $1 to be received on the same date, the zero's price can be used as a discount factor as well. In this example, the fractional price on June 5, 1995, of a zero-coupon note that settles on June 6 and matures on December 20, 1995, was 0.96944 [= 1/1.03152].

Exhibit 11.A1, which is the starting point for all of the work that follows, provides terminal wealths and discount factors for value dates ranging from June 6, 1995, through June 18, 1997. This horizon is just long enough to work with a Treasury note that matures May 31, 1997. The first value date was chosen to conform to a June 5 trade in the Treasury market. The remaining value dates fall two days after each of the respective Eurodollar futures expirations.

FOUR GENERAL PROBLEMS IN CALCULATING TERM TED SPREADS

Because the term TED spread involves a comparison of two instruments with different day-count, yield, and settlement conventions, four kinds of practical problems must be addressed:

- Reconciling differences in value dates between Treasury and LIBOR markets
- Finding the spot "stub" rate from the value date to the first Eurodollar futures value date
- Handling date mismatches between cash flows and Eurodollar futures value dates
- Coping with differences between nominal and actual Treasury cash flow dates

Value Dates and Stub Rates

The first two general problems can be illustrated with the time line shown in Exhibit 11.A2. The first problem is that value dates in the Treasury and LIBOR markets are different. For example, standard settlement in the Treasury market is next business day

EXHIBIT 11.A2

Time Line 1: Calculating a Spot Stub Rate

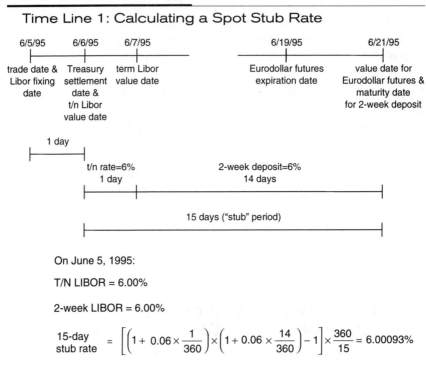

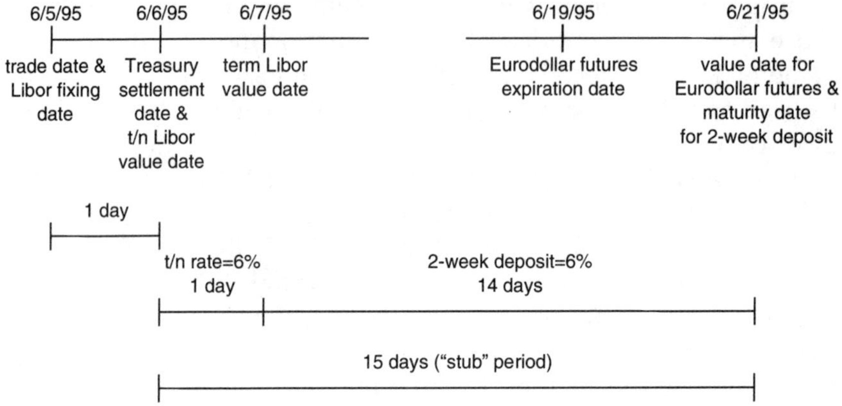

On June 5, 1995:

T/N LIBOR = 6.00%

2-week LIBOR = 6.00%

$$\text{15-day stub rate} = \left[\left(1 + 0.06 \times \frac{1}{360}\right) \times \left(1 + 0.06 \times \frac{14}{360}\right) - 1\right] \times \frac{360}{15} = 6.00093\%$$

in the United States. The standard value date for the LIBOR market is the second following business day in London. In our example, if a trade is done on June 5 (a Monday), settlement for the Treasury note is June 6. Thus, any present values we calculate should be done as of Tuesday, June 6. The value date for a term LIBOR deposit, however, is Wednesday, June 7. To reconcile the difference between the 6th and the 7th, we must use the tomorrow/next (T/N) rate to fill in the gap between the two dates.

The second problem is to get from June 6 to the value date for the first Eurodollar futures contract. In our example, the first Eurodollar futures contract expires on Monday, June 19, 1995. The value date for the 3-month rate against which this contract is cash settled at expiration is Wednesday, June 21, 1995. Thus, we need a spot rate (a.k.a. stub rate) from Tuesday, June 6 to Wednesday, June 21. Given deposit rates of 6.00 percent for tomorrow/next and 6.00 percent for a two-week deposit, we would calculate a 15-day spot stub rate of 6.00093 percent as shown in Exhibit 11.A2.

Handling Date Mismatches

The cash one receives on a Treasury note rarely if ever falls exactly on the value date for a Eurodollar futures contract. As a result, we must have a way of reckoning discount factors for cash flows that fall between Eurodollar futures value dates.

Consider, for example, the 6-1/8s of 5/31/97 note, whose next coupon payment on November 30, 1995, is shown along the time line in Exhibit 11.A3. Our challenge is to find a discount factor for this coupon payment that allows us to calculate its present value as of the June 6 value date. Using our stub rate of 6.00093 percent and the June and September Eurodollar futures rates of 5.86 percent and 5.51 percent, we can calculate terminal wealths for September 20, 1995, and December 20, 1995, which are the value dates for the September and December 1995 contracts. As shown in Exhibit 11.A1, the discount factor for any cash received on September 20 would be 0.98295 [= 1/1.01735]. The discount factor for any cash received on December 20 would be 0.96944.

EXHIBIT 11.A3

Time Line 2: Calculating a Discount Factor for a Particular Cash Flow

Eurodollar futures	Price	Implied forward
stub		6.00093
Jun-95	94.14	5.86
Sep-95	94.49	5.51

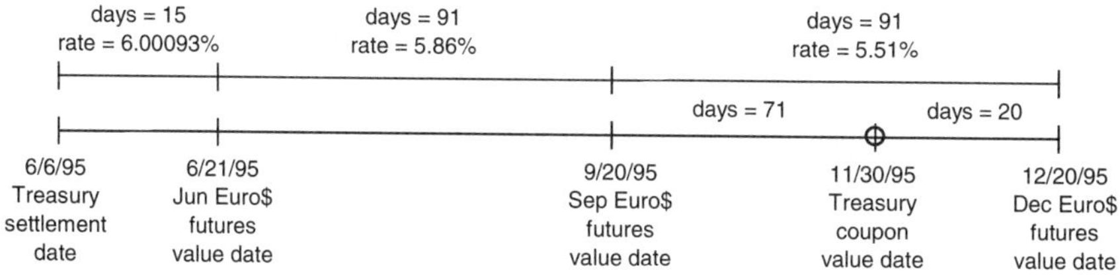

What Is the Appropriate Discount Factor for a Treasury Coupon Received on November 30?

Interpolating between September 20 and December 20 can be done in any number of ways. In the upper part of Exhibit 11.A4, you can see the results of linearly interpolating between the terminal wealth values for September 20 and December 20. The result is a terminal wealth that seems higher than it ought to be and, as a result, a discount factor (the inverse of terminal wealth) that seems lower than it ought to be.

Much of this problem can be handled by interpolating between the natural logarithms of the terminal wealth values for September 20 and December 20. The Ln(terminal wealth) schedule flattens out the curvature in the exponential terminal wealth curve (all of the curvature if all forward rates are the same). By interpolating Ln(terminal wealth) values, then, one gets a somewhat better approximation of what terminal wealth at November 30 would be if it were a stop along the way from September 20 to December 20. In this case, the resulting terminal wealth value would be 1.02839, which is slightly lower than the 1.02841 one obtains by simply interpolating between terminal wealths. Also, the corresponding discount factor is somewhat higher.

Nominal and Actual Treasury Payment Dates

The fourth problem is the actual timing of cash flows in the Treasury market. Coupon dates and a note's maturity fall on 6-month anniversaries, regardless of whether these are business days, weekends, or holidays. So, for example, the nominal and actual cash flow dates for the 6-1/8s of 5/31/97 would be

Nominal Cash Flow Dates	Actual Cash Flow Dates
November 30, 1995 (Thursday)	November 30, 1995 (Thursday)
May 31, 1996 (Friday)	May 31, 1996 (Friday)
November 30, 1996 (Saturday)	December 2, 1996 (Monday)
May 31, 1997 (Saturday)	June 2, 1997 (Monday)

The problem is that November 30, 1996, and May 31, 1997, are both Saturdays. As a result, any coupon or principal amount

EXHIBIT 11.A4

Interpolating Terminal Wealths

Linear Interpolation of Terminal Wealth

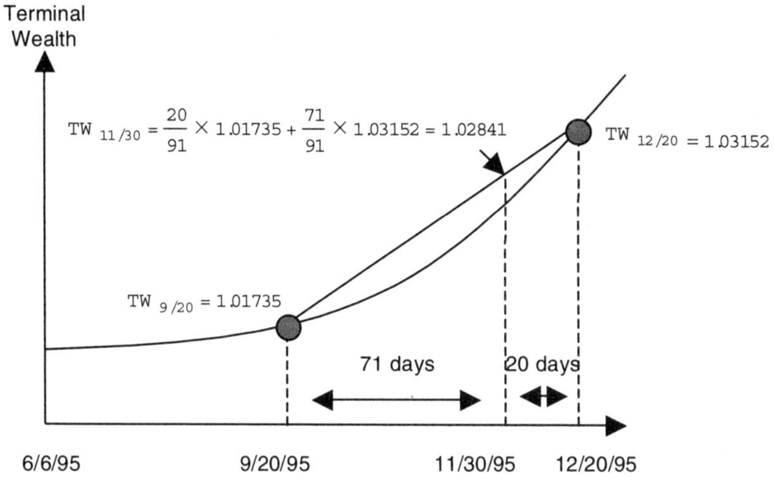

Linear Interpolation of Natural Log of Terminal Wealth

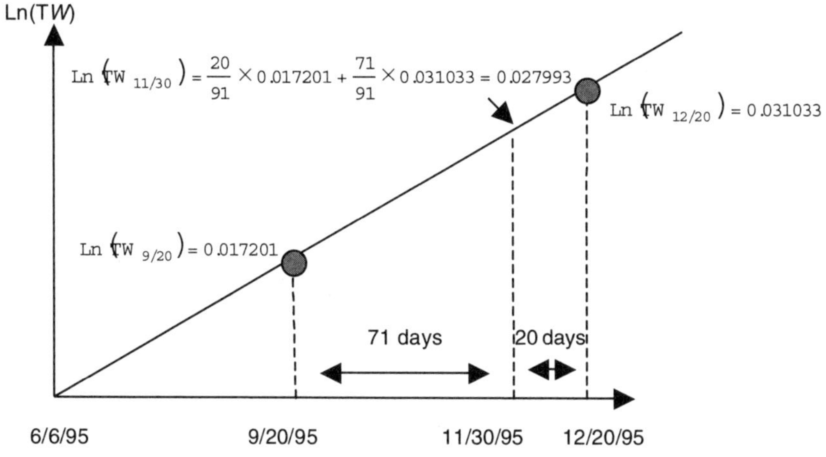

After finding the interpolated natural log of terminal wealth, find the associated terminal wealth on November 30:

$$TW_{11/30} = e^{0.027993} = 1.02839$$

A more direct approach to this interpolation is:

$$TW_{11/30} = 1.01735^{20/91} \times 1.03152^{71/91} = 1.02839$$

scheduled for these dates would be received the following Monday. Standard yield calculations, however, ignore the effects of cash flows occurring on holidays or weekends. And, while the difference of a couple of days may not sound like much, the effect on the credit spread can be large. In our example, illustrated in Exhibit 11.A5, the effect of shifting the cash flows from Saturday to Monday changes the note's yield by about 1.5 basis points. This looms large against 2-year credit spreads that have recently been under 20 basis points.

In the examples that follow, we take particular care to point out how we handle these so-called bad dates (i.e., coupon or principal dates that fall on non-business days) and the consequences of what we do. Note especially that we construct one measure of the term TED spread that is affected by bad dates and two measures that are not. The measure that is affected by bad dates (the implied Eurodollar/Treasury spread) is designed to suit the purposes of the swap market, which deals with this problem by changing the spread at which swap rates are quoted over the on-the-run Treasury rate.

TWO BASIC APPROACHES TO CALCULATING TERM TED SPREADS

In the main section of this note, we described two fundamentally different approaches to calculating TED spreads. One approach compared unweighted Eurodollar strip yields with Treasury note yields. The other involved weighted Eurodollar strips in which the weights given the various Eurodollar futures contracts reflect the sensitivity of the price of the Treasury note to changes in the respective futures rates. Here we list the steps involved for calculating each of these TED spreads.

Eurodollar Strip Rate versus Treasury Yield (Unweighted)

This measure of the spread is the result of calculating a strip yield from the spot stub rate and successive Eurodollar futures rates and finding the difference between this and the yield on the note. Specifically, we compute a zero-coupon note yield from the Eurodollar market. This allows us to translate the Eurodollar money

EXHIBIT 11.A5

Time Line 3: Tracking the Cash Flows on a Treasury Note

Note market data:	
Trade date	6/5/95
Settle date	6/6/95
Coupon	6.125%
Maturity	5/31/97
Clean price	101-2+
Accrued interest	0.100410
Full price	101.178535

Yields:	
Nominal cash flow dates	5.543%
Actual cash flow dates	5.528%

Cash flows:	coupon/2	coupon/2	coupon/2	100 + coupon/2
Nominal cash flow dates:	11/30/95	5/31/96	11/30/96	5/31/97
Actual cash flow dates:	11/30/95	5/31/96	12/2/96	6/2/97

market rates into a semiannual bond equivalent yield, which is directly comparable to the Treasury note yield. The steps to find this spread are:

1. Calculate the terminal wealth as of the note's final cash flow date, which, because of weekends and holidays, may differ from the note's maturity date.
2. Set the price of a zero-coupon note equal to the inverse of this terminal wealth
3. Calculate the semiannual bond equivalent yield of this zero-coupon note
4. Subtract the Treasury note yield from the zero-coupon yield

This approach is illustrated in Exhibit 11.A6 for the 2-year TED spread. In this example, the final coupon and principal for the 6-1/8s of 5/31/97 actually fall on June 2, 1997. Given terminal wealths for March 19, 1997, and June 18, 1997, shown in Exhibit 11.A1, the interpolated value of terminal wealth for June 2 would be 1.11816. The corresponding fractional price of the zero-coupon note that matures on June 2 would be 0.89433 [= 1/1.11816]. We then calculate the semiannual bond equivalent yield for this zero-coupon note assuming that it nominally matures on May 31, 1997.

The reason for pricing the zero-coupon note to the note's actual maturity and then calculating its yield as if it matures on the note's nominal maturity is that this is what the market does with the note itself. The market prices the note knowing that the actual cash will be received on a weekday (June 2 in this example) rather than on a weekend. Even so, the note's yield typically is calculated using its nominal maturity date. The effect of this practice is to produce a yield for the note that is somewhat higher than it really ought to be. By calculating the zero-coupon yield the same way, we impart nearly the same bias to both yields. The spread, as a result, should be nearly unbiased.

As shown in Exhibit 11.A6, the zero-coupon note's yield is 5.711 percent. The note's yield was 5.543 percent. Thus, this version of the 2-year term TED spread on June 5, 1995, was 0.168% [= 5.711% − 5.543%], or 16.8 basis points.

EXHIBIT 11.A6

TED Spread: Eurodollar Strip Rate versus Treasury Yield

Step 1. Calculate terminal wealth on the final cash flow date.

The note matures on May 31, 1997, which is a Saturday. The final cash flow takes place on June 2, 1997.

Futures Expiration	Value Date	Days between Value Dates	Terminal Wealth
3/17/97	3/19/97		1.10494
	6/02/97	75	?
6/16/97	6/18/97	16	1.12100

Interpolate the two surrounding terminal wealths:

$$TW_{02Jun97} = (TW_{19Mar97})^{16/91}\,(TW_{18Jun97})^{75/91}$$

$$TW_{02Jun97} = (1.10494)^{16/91}\,(1.12100)^{75/91} = 1.11816$$

Step 2. Calculate a zero-coupon note price using 1/*TW*.

$$\textit{Zero-coupon price} = \frac{1}{1.11816} = 0.89433$$

Step 3. Calculate a semiannual bond equivalent yield.

$$\textit{Zero-coupon yield} = \left[\left(\frac{1}{ZCP}\right)^{\left(\frac{1}{CP - 1 + \frac{Days_{SC}}{Days_{CP}}}\right)} - 1\right] \times 2$$

where

- ZCP Zero-coupon price
- CP Number of hypothetical "coupon periods" from settlement to maturity; round fractional amount up to next whole number
- $Days_{SC}$ Number of days from settlement to next hypothetical "coupon"
- $Days_{CP}$ Number of days in "coupon period" in which settlement date falls

For our example,

$ZCP = 0.89433$
$CP = 4$
$Days_{SC} = 11/30/95 - 6/6/95 = 177$
$Days_{CP} = 11/30/95 - 5/31/95 = 183$

Zero-coupon bond equivalent yield = 5.711%

Step 4. Calculate the TED spread.

$$\textit{TED spread} = \textit{Zero-coupon yield} - \textit{Note yield}$$

$$\textit{TED spread} = 5.711\% - 5.543\% = 16.8 \text{ bp}$$

Implied Eurodollar Yield versus Treasury Yield (Weighted)

One approach to measuring the weighted spread between Eurodollars and Treasuries begins by asking what the Treasury note's price and yield would be if it had been issued instead by a bank with LIBOR quality credit. This is done by finding the present value of the Treasury note using discount factors calculated from spot LIBOR and Eurodollar futures rates. The resulting present value is the implied full price of what can be thought of as a Eurodollar-credit-quality bond. This full price, reduced by accrued interest on the note, is then converted to a yield that can be compared with the yield on the Treasury note. The steps in this approach, which are shown in Exhibit 11.A7 for our 2-year TED spread, are:

1. Calculate the nominal dates (rather than the actual dates) and dollar amounts of the Treasury note's cash flows.
2. Calculate discount factors for each of these cash flows using (interpolated) terminal wealths.
3. Find the present value (i.e., the full price) of the note's cash flows using these discount factors.
4. From this present value, subtract accrued interest on the note to produce the note's hypothetical clean price.
5. Plug this clean price into a standard yield calculator to find the yield on the note. This yield value is the note's "implied Eurodollar yield."
6. Subtract the Treasury note's actual yield from its implied Eurodollar yield.

In our example, the present value of the 6-1/8s of 5/97 when reckoned using discount factors calculated from Eurodollar rates is 100.895, which is less than the note's market full price of 101.1785. Subtracting 0.100 to adjust for accrued interest on the note, we find the note's implied Eurodollar clean price is 100.795, which gives us a yield of 5.695 percent.

The value of the term TED spread would be 0.152% [= 5.695% − 5.543%], or 15.2 basis points.

This approach can have a curious effect on the computed value of the spread if the Treasury note has any bad dates, which

EXHIBIT 11.A7

TED Spread: Implied Eurodollar Yield versus Treasury Yield

Step 1. List note cash flows.

Step 2. Find corresponding terminal wealths.

Step 3. Find implied Eurodollar full price of note.

Nominal T-Note Cash Flow date (1)	Interpolated Terminal Wealth (2)	Nominal Cash Flow (3)	Discounted Cash Flow (4) = (3)/(2)
11/30/95	1.028389	3.0625	2.978
05/31/96	1.056878	3.0625	2.898
11/30/96	1.086306	3.0625	2.819
05/31/97	1.117808	103.0625	92.201
			Implied full price = 100.895

Step 4. Subtract accrued interest from implied Eurodollar full price.

Clean price = *Full price* − *Accrued interest*

Clean price = 100.895 − 0.100 = 100.795

Step 5. Calculate the implied Eurodollar yield. Use 5/31/97 as the maturity date.

Implied Eurodollar yield = 5.695%

Step 6. Calculate the TED spread.

TED spread = *Implied Eurodollar yield* − *Treasury market yield*

TED spread = 5.695% − 5.543% = 15.2 bp

are coupon or principal payment dates that are scheduled to fall on weekends or holidays. The note itself is priced by a market that knows full well that the cash will actually be paid out on the first business day following a bad date. The effect of delaying these cash flows is to lower the note's market price. And, because the note's yield is calculated using its nominal maturity date, the effect of lowering its price is to increase its apparent yield. Both the present value and the yield of the hypothetical note, however, are calculated using the note's nominal (as opposed to actual) payment dates. The result is a more or less unbiased reckoning of what the note would yield if issued by a LIBOR quality bank.

When taken together, the spread between the unbiased implied Eurodollar yield and the upward biased yield on the Treasury note is smaller than it would be without the bad dates. This smaller spread is consistent with the way the swap market works around bad dates on Treasury issues.

Fixed Spread to Eurodollars (Weighted)

A second approach to calculating a weighted term TED spread is to find the amount by which spot LIBOR and Eurodollar futures rates must be adjusted to produce appropriate Treasury spot and forward rates. As the above example shows, if you use Eurodollar rates to calculate the present value of a Treasury note, the resulting value is lower than the full market price of the note because the discount rates are too high to suit a Treasury credit. This can be corrected by reducing each of the spot and futures rates by an appropriate number of basis points:

$$\begin{aligned}\textit{Market full price} &= \frac{\frac{Coupon}{2}}{\left(1+(S-s)\frac{D_0}{360}\right)\left(1+(F_1-s)\frac{D_1}{360}\right)\left(1+(F_2-s)\frac{D_2}{360}\right)}+\cdots \\ &+ \frac{100+\frac{Coupon}{2}}{\left(1+(S-s)\frac{D_0}{360}\right)\left(1+(F_1-s)\frac{D_1}{360}\right)\times\cdots\times\left(1+(F_n-s)\frac{D_n}{360}\right)}\end{aligned}$$

In this method, we solve for the value, s, that sets the present value of the cash flows equal to the note's actual full market price. The steps in finding this spread are:

1. Calculate the date and size of the Treasury note's cash flows, looking out for odd first coupon dates and taking care to place cash flows on business days.
2. Calculate discount factors for each of these cash flows.
3. Calculate the present value of the note using these discount factors and compare with the note's current full market price.

4. If the present value is not equal to the note's full market price, find (through an optimized trial and error procedure) the single fixed number of basis points that must be subtracted from each of the Eurodollar rates to produce a present value of the note that equals its full market price.

The resulting adjustment to spot LIBOR and Eurodollar futures rates is a measure of the weighted term TED spread.

In this example, as shown in Exhibit 11.A8, we find that we have to subtract 16.3 basis points from each of the spot and Eurodollar futures rates that go into calculating the discount factors

EXHIBIT 11.A8

TED Spread: Fixed Spread to Eurodollar Rates

Two-year note market data

Settlement	6/6/95
Coupon	6-1/8
Maturity	5/31/97
Clean price	101-2+ or 101.078125
Full price	101.179

Adjusting the spot rate and each Eurodollar futures rate in Exhibit 11.A1 by 16.3 basis points gives the following terminal wealths and discounted cash flows:

Actual T-Note Cash Flow Date (1)	Interpolated Adjusted TW (2)	Nominal Cash Flow (3)	Discounted Cash Flow (4) = (3)/(2)
	1.0000000		
11/30/95	1.0275769	3.0625	2.980
05/31/96	1.0551814	3.0625	2.902
12/02/96	1.0839959	3.0625	2.825
06/02/97	1.1145423	103.0625	92.471
			Actual full price = 101.179

With the 16.3 basis point credit spread, the calculated full price of the note is equal to its market full price.

for the note's cash flows. This measure of the value of the term TED spread, unlike the spreads calculated using the other methods, is quoted in annual money market basis points rather than bond equivalent basis points. Bad dates and the slope of the yield curve have no affect on this measure of the spread. It is, as a result, perhaps the cleanest measure of the pure credit spread.

FORWARD TERM TED SPREADS

One can also calculate and trade forward term TED spreads. And, if there were an active forward market for term Treasury notes—say, a market for 3-year notes 2 years forward—one could calculate term TED spreads in any of the three ways described above.

In practice, if one wants to trade a forward Treasury position against anything, one has to create the forward position using spot notes. For example, a long position in a 3-year note 2 years forward can be constructed more or less well by buying a 5-year note and financing the purchase by selling an equal market value amount of a 2-year note. Because the coupons of the available notes are apt to differ, the construction of the forward note is unlikely to be perfect, but the approximation should be fairly good.

If we approach the problem of measuring and trading forward term TED spreads from this practical trading standpoint, the simplest way to measure the spread entails these steps for a 3-year note 2 years forward:

1. Establish long and short positions of equal full market value in a 5-year Treasury note and a 2-year Treasury note. This position is self financing and its net present value is zero.
2. Determine the positive and negative cash flows associated with this position. Place cash flows on business days.
3. Find the single internal rate of return that sets the net present value of this position (long the 5-year note, short the 2-year note) equal to zero. This is the approximate yield on the 3-year note 2 years forward.
4. Calculate the present value of the same position using discount factors derived from spot LIBOR and Eurodollar futures rates. Because these rates are higher than Treasury rates, the resulting note prices will be

lower. And, because you are long the 5-year note and short the 2-year note, the net present value of the position will now be negative.

5. Find the single internal rate of return that sets the net present value of your position equal to the negative value calculated in the previous step.
6. The difference between this rate and the rate calculated in step 3 is a semiannual bond equivalent measure of the forward term TED spread.

Consider how this works using the on-the-run 2-year and 5-year Treasury notes on June 5, 1995, as shown in Exhibit 11.A9.

EXHIBIT 11.A9

Forward Term TED Spread

Settlement June 6, 1995

	Two-Year Note	Five-Year Note
Coupon	6-1/8	6-1/4
Maturity	5/31/97	5/31/00
Clean price	101-2+	101-30
	101.078125	101.9375
Full price	101.1785	102.0400

Step 1. Establish long and short positions of equal market value.

$$\frac{\textit{2-year full price}}{\textit{5-year full price}} = \frac{101.1785}{102.0400} = 0.99156$$

Use \$0.99156 par amount of the 5-year note for every \$1 par amount of the 2-year note.

Step 2. Determine cash flow dates and amounts, placing flows on business days.

Step 3. Find the IRR of the cash flows, setting the net present value = 0.

Step 4. Discount the cash flows by terminal wealths, finding the new net present value.

Step 5. Find the IRR of Step 4's cash flows, setting the net present value = Step 4's present value.
(See table below.)

Step 6. Find the forward term TED by taking the difference of the two IRR values.

6.442% − 5.998% = 0.444% or 44.4 *basis points*

EXHIBIT 11.A9

Continued

		Cash Flows			*Present Value of Combined Cash Flows*		
Actual Cash Flow Date	**Terminal Wealth**	**Long 5-Year Note ($99.156 par)**	**Short 2-Year Note ($100 par)**	**Combined**	**Discounted Using IRR = 5.998%**	**Discounted Using ED Terminal Wealths**	**Discounted Using IRR = 6.442%**
11/30/95	1.028389	3.09862	−3.0625	0.03612	0.03510	0.03512	0.03502
5/31/96	1.056878	3.09862	−3.0625	0.03612	0.03407	0.03417	0.03393
12/02/96	1.086635	3.09862	−3.0625	0.03612	0.03307	0.03324	0.03286
6/02/97	1.118163	3.09862	−103.0625	−99.96388	−88.86285	−89.40012	−88.10351
12/01/97	1.151692	3.09862		3.09862	2.67453	2.69049	2.64598
6/01/98	1.187472	3.09862		3.09862	2.59686	2.60942	2.56363
11/30/98	1.225270	3.09862		3.09862	2.52145	2.52893	2.48384
5/31/99	1.265252	3.09862		3.09862	2.44823	2.44901	2.40654
11/30/99	1.307675	3.09862		3.09862	2.37675	2.36956	2.33124
5/31/00	1.352515	102.25442		102.25442	76.14280	75.60319	74.52350
					0.00000	−1.04697	−1.04697 NPV

On that day, the 6-1/8s of 5/31/97 were trading at a net price of 101-2+/32nds (101.078125) and a full price including accrued interest of 101.1785. The 6-1/4s of 5/31/00 were trading at a net price of 101-30/32nds (101.9375) and a full price of 102.0400. At these prices, one could establish a short position of $100 million par amount in the 2-year note (the 6-1/8s) against a long position of $99,155,797 [= $100 million × (101.1785/102.0400)] par amount in the 5-year note (the 6-1/4s). Altogether, one would be long and short $101,178,535 market value of the respective notes so that the net value of the position would be zero.

Given the cash flows associated with this position—positive for the 5-year note, negative for the 2-year note—the internal rate of return that sets the net present value of the position equal to zero is 5.998 percent.

We next calculate the net present value of the position using discount factors derived from the spot LIBOR and Eurodollar futures rates. Given the market rates on June 5, the net present value of the position would be −$1,046,967. If we then solve for the single internal rate of return that sets the net present value of the position equal to this negative number, we get 6.442 percent.

Our estimate of the 2 × 5 forward term TED spread is then 0.444 percent [= 6.442 percent − 5.998 percent] percent or 44.4 basis points. These calculations are done so that the spread is unaffected by bad dates in the Treasury issue.

CALCULATING HEDGE RATIOS

The objective in calculating hedge ratios is to construct trades whose profit or loss can be explained by the change in the term TED spread. To trade the spread between the unweighted Eurodollar strip yield and the Treasury yield, for example, one needs a Eurodollar futures position that gives roughly equal weight to each of the contracts in the strip. In contrast, to trade either of the weighted measures of the term TED spread, one needs a Eurodollar position that gives greater weight to nearby contracts than to more distant contracts.

The basic approach to finding how many of any given Eurodollar futures contract you need to include in your term TED spread trade is always the same. Hold your measure of the term TED spread constant and increase the relevant Eurodollar futures rate 1 basis point. Determine how much this reduces the total market value of your Treasury note position and divide this reduction by $25. The ratio is the number of that particular futures contract you need. Repeat for each of the relevant futures rates (as well as for the stub rate) until you have answers for all of the contracts.

Hedge Ratios for Unweighted Strip Spreads

In our example, the Eurodollar strip version of the 2-year term TED spread is 16.8 basis points. To find the number of Eurodollar futures contracts needed to hedge against a change in the stub rate, we

1. Increase the stub rate 1 basis point and recalculate the terminal wealth for the actual maturity of the note (Monday, June 2, 1997, in this example).
2. Invert this terminal wealth to find the new price of a zero-coupon note that matures on the same date as the Treasury note.
3. From this price, calculate the new—and higher—yield on the zero-coupon note.
4. From this yield, subtract 16.8 basis points to find what the new—and higher—yield on the note would have to be to keep the TED spread constant.
5. At this higher yield, find the new—and lower—price of the Treasury note.
6. Calculate the change in the full market value of the note position.
7. Divide this change by $25 to find the number of Eurodollar contracts needed.

Repeat this process for each of the Eurodollar futures rates. The resulting hedge ratios will be those shown in the second column of Exhibit 11.A10.

For example, to determine the number of Eurodollar contracts needed to hedge against changes in the stub rate, we begin by increasing the stub rate one basis point from 6.00093 percent to 6.01093 percent. The terminal wealth on June 2, 1997, increases from 1.118163 to 1.118167. The zero-coupon price is 0.89432 and the associated zero-coupon yield, given the actual note maturity

EXHIBIT 11.A10

Hedge Ratios for TED Spread Trades
$100 Million of the 6-1/8s of 5/31/97
Trade June 5, 1995, Settle June 6, 1995

	Eurodollar Futures Hedge Ratios		
Future Contract	**Eurodollar Strip**	**Implied Eurodollar***	**Fixed Basis Point Spread to ED Rates**
Stub	16.09	16.83	16.82
Jun '95	96.46	100.88	100.84
Sep '95	96.54	100.31	100.27
Dec '95	96.56	98.00	97.97
Mar '96	96.58	97.42	97.39
Jun '96	96.57	95.11	95.08
Sep '96	96.55	94.53	94.56
Dec '96	96.50	92.22	92.20
Mar '97	79.52	73.97	75.97
Total	771.37	769.27	771.10

*The implied Eurodollar method does not shift cash flows to business days.

of May 31, 1997, is 5.710720. Subtracting the TED spread of 16.76513 basis points gives us a new yield on the Treasury note of 5.5430687. This yield translates into a Treasury note price of 101.077723. The difference between this value and the original clean price of 101-2+ is $402 per $100 million par amount. Dividing $402 by $25 gives 16.1, the number of Eurodollar contracts needed to hedge the stub rate.

Hedge Ratios for Weighted Eurodollar Strip Hedges

If you are trading the implied Eurodollar/Treasury version of the TED spread, the steps for hedging are similar to those above. The main differences are in Steps 1–3. For example, for our 2-year note, the implied Eurodollar TED spread is 15.2 basis points. To find the number of Eurodollar futures needed to hedge against a change in the stub rate:

1. Increase the stub rate 1 basis point and recalculate terminal wealths for the nominal cash flow dates of the note (in this case, 11/30/95, 5/31/96, 11/30/96, and 5/31/97).
2. Place the note's cash flows on the nominal payment dates and calculate the present value of the cash flows. This value is the full price of the note discounted at Eurodollar rates.
3. Subtract accrued interest from this full price, then calculate the new implied Eurodollar yield.
4. From this implied Eurodollar yield, subtract 15.2 basis points (the TED spread) to find the new yield on the Treasury note. This ensures that the TED spread remains constant.
5. Using the Treasury note's new yield, calculate its new clean price.
6. Find the change in the clean price of the note from the market clean price.
7. Divide this change by $25 to find the number of Eurodollar contracts needed to hedge.

If you are trading the fixed spread against Eurodollar rates, there are fewer steps because there is no need to calculate a new Treasury note yield. Instead, when you increase any one of the Eurodollar rates one basis point, you get the new full market price of the note directly. Thus, to calculate a hedge ratio for the stub:

1. First find the spread, s, that correctly prices the Treasury note's cash flows (see Exhibit 11.A11, top equation).
2. Add one basis point to the stub rate and calculate the new present value of the note (see Exhibit 11.A11, lower equation).
3. Calculate the change in the present value of the note (i.e., the DV01, which will be a negative number in this case).
4. Divide this change by $25 to find the number of Eurodollar futures needed in the hedge.

Notice that because the spot and nearby futures rates affect the present values of all of the note's cash flows, while the more

EXHIBIT 11.A11

Hedge Ratios: Fixed Spread against Eurodollar Rates

$$\textit{Treasury note full market value} = \frac{\textit{Par amount}}{100}\left[\frac{\frac{\textit{Coupon}}{2}}{\left(1+(S-s)\frac{D_0}{360}\right)\left(1+(F_1-s)\frac{D_1}{360}\right)\left(1+(F_2-s)\frac{D_2}{360}\right)}+\cdots\right.$$
$$\left.+\frac{100+\frac{\textit{Coupon}}{2}}{\left(1+(S-s)\frac{D_0}{360}\right)\left(1+(F_1-s)\frac{D_1}{360}\right)\times\cdots\times\left(1+(F_n-s)\frac{D_n}{360}\right)}\right]$$

$$\textit{New present value} = \frac{\textit{Par amount}}{100}\left[\frac{\frac{\textit{Coupon}}{2}}{\left(1+(S-s+1bp)\frac{D_0}{360}\right)\left(1+(F_1-s)\frac{D_1}{360}\right)\left(1+(F_2-s)\frac{D_2}{360}\right)}+\cdots\right.$$
$$\left.+\frac{100+\frac{\textit{Coupon}}{2}}{\left(1+(S-s+1bp)\frac{D_0}{360}\right)\left(1+(F_1-s)\frac{D_1}{360}\right)\times\cdots\times\left(1+(F_n-s)\frac{D_n}{360}\right)}\right]$$

distant futures rates affect only the present values of later cash flows, this approach will produce hedges that contain more nearby futures than distant futures. The uneven weighting reflects the greater sensitivity of a coupon bearing note to changes in nearby forward rates than to changes in distant forward rates.

The two sets of hedge ratios for weighted versions of the TED spread are shown in the third and fourth columns of Exhibit 11.A10. Because the procedures for finding the two are different, the hedge ratios are different as well. But the differences are so slight that there is no need to calculate both sets of weighted hedges. In practice, we distinguish only between weighted and unweighted hedge ratios when constructing term TED spread trades.

All three hedges contain nearly the same total number of contracts because all three sets of hedges were constructed with an eye to making the position direction neutral. The only thing that should affect the net value of any of the positions is a change in the relevant measure of the term TED spread.

An important consequence of constructing the hedges this way, however, is that the unweighted version of the spread trade contains fewer of the nearby contracts and more of the distant contracts. By comparing the two, it is easy to see how a change in the slope of the yield or forward rate curve will affect the unweighted version of the trade. A steepening of the forward rate curve tends to reduce the value of the Eurodollar strip version of the TED spread relative to either of the weighted versions of the spread. This is because a steepening of the curve tends to reduce the value of a coupon-bearing note relative to the price of a zero-coupon note. This effect is captured by the smaller weight given the nearby contracts.

Hedges for Forward Term TED Spreads

The hedge for a forward term TED position is, for all practical purposes, the same as the net hedge for a long position in one note and a short position in the other. For example, the Eurodollar futures hedge for a long position in a 5-year note would be a short, weighted 5-year strip of Eurodollar futures. The hedge for a short position in a 2-year note would be a long, weighted 2-year strip of Eurodollar futures. Except for small differences in coupons and prices, the long 2-year strip will largely offset the first 2 years of the short 5-year strip. The resulting net hedge will be a short, weighted 3-year Eurodollar futures strip, 2 years forward. See Exhibit 11.11 in the main body of the note for an example of a hedge for selling the forward term TED spread.

CHAPTER 12

TED Spreads: An Update

Chapter 11 reproduces the research note:

- Measuring and Trading Term TED Spreads (1995)

Since this note was written, we have tracked the values of 1-year, 2-year, and 5-year TED spreads. We report time series of these spreads in Carr Futures "Daily Zero to Ten" report, shown earlier on page four of Exhibit 10.1.

We also developed a special report, "TED Spreads," that provides two key insights into the structure of TED spreads:

- Term structure of TED spreads
- Comparison of forward and spot values of the TED spread

We have reproduced a copy of the "TED Spreads" report in Exhibits 12.1 and 12.2 as of the close on September 10, 2002. Exhibit 12.1 shows the values of TED spreads for original issue 2-year Treasury notes, which are listed in order of increasing time to maturity. You can see in this report, for example, that the TED spread for the 2-1/8s of 8/31/04 was 37.51 basis points (measured in quarterly money market basis points). In contrast, the 3-5/8s of 8/31/03, which were one year closer to maturity, traded at a spread of 21.13 basis points. This gives insight into the term structure of the TED spread.

EXHIBIT 12.1

2-Year Note TED Spreads
Plus Forward TEDs to September 18, 2002
September 10, 2002

CARR FUTURES
Chicago

Ted Spreads

Tuesday, Sep 10, 2002
Data as of 3:00 PM NY CLOSE

Note TED Table (settle: 9/11/02)

			Mid Market		Repo	Spot TED Spread			Forward		Fwd Start TED			Fwd Start TED: RP+1bp		
Original					to	ED	Implied ED		9/18/2002		ED	Implied ED		ED	Implied ED	
Issue	Cpn	Maturity	Price	Yield	09/18	Shift	Nom	Work	Prc (dec)	Yield	Shift	Nom	Work	Shift	Nom	Work
2 yr	5 3/4	10/31/02	100-17+	1.681%	1.74	16.82	17.17	17.17								
2 yr	5 5/8	11/30/02	100-27	1.723%	1.74	16.02	12.01	16.70								
2 yr	5 1/8	12/31/02	101-01	1.672%	1.74	17.39	17.80	17.80								
2 yr	4 3/4	1/31/03	101-05	1.724%	1.74	11.66	11.95	11.95	101.10	1.721%	11.83	12.12	12.12	+0.05	+0.05	+0.05
2 yr	4 5/8	2/28/03	101-12+	1.639%	1.74	17.03	17.19	17.19	101.34	1.634%	17.40	17.56	17.56	+0.04	+0.04	+0.04
2 yr	4 1/4	3/31/03	101-14	1.622%	1.74	20.19	20.51	20.51	101.39	1.616%	20.62	20.95	20.95	+0.04	+0.04	+0.04
2 yr	4	4/30/03	101-15+	1.641%	1.74	19.27	19.53	19.53	101.44	1.637%	19.62	19.87	19.87	+0.03	+0.03	+0.03
2 yr	4 1/4	5/31/03	101-26+	1.677%	1.74	18.82	17.77	19.29	101.78	1.674%	19.11	18.02	19.59	+0.03	+0.03	+0.03
2 yr	3 7/8	6/30/03	101-23	1.705%	1.74	16.52	16.80	16.80	101.68	1.703%	16.73	17.00	17.00	+0.02	+0.03	+0.03
2 yr	3 7/8	7/31/03	101-28+	1.714%	1.74	18.95	19.29	19.29	101.85	1.712%	19.19	19.52	19.52	+0.02	+0.02	+0.02
2 yr	3 5/8	8/31/03	101-26	1.731%	1.74	21.13	20.41	21.65	101.78	1.731%	21.39	20.65	21.92	+0.02	+0.02	+0.02
2 yr	2 3/4	9/30/03	101-02	1.726%	1.74	23.93	24.38	24.38	101.04	1.725%	24.23	24.68	24.68	+0.02	+0.02	+0.02
2 yr	2 3/4	10/31/03	101-04	1.744%	1.74	26.74	27.26	27.26	101.11	1.744%	27.06	27.58	27.58	+0.02	+0.02	+0.02
2 yr	3	11/30/03	101-14+	1.788%	1.74	26.64	26.60	27.22	101.43	1.788%	26.93	26.90	27.52	+0.02	+0.02	+0.02
2 yr	3 1/4	12/31/03	101-27	1.809%	1.74	28.62	29.21	29.21	101.82	1.809%	28.93	29.52	29.52	+0.02	+0.02	+0.02
2 yr	3	1/31/04	101-18	1.852%	1.74	30.51	30.13	31.28	101.54	1.853%	30.83	30.44	31.61	+0.01	+0.01	+0.01
2 yr	3	2/29/04	101-19+	1.884%	1.74	30.40	30.46	31.01	101.59	1.886%	30.70	30.76	31.32	+0.01	+0.01	+0.01
2 yr	3 5/8	3/31/04	102-18+	1.930%	1.74	30.33	30.94	30.94	102.54	1.932%	30.61	31.23	31.23	+0.01	+0.01	+0.01
2 yr	3 3/8	4/30/04	102-08+	1.960%	1.74	32.15	32.77	32.77	102.24	1.962%	32.45	33.06	33.06	+0.01	+0.01	+0.01
2 yr	3 1/4	5/31/04	102-03	2.003%	1.74	33.22	33.42	33.96	102.07	2.006%	33.51	33.70	34.25	+0.01	+0.01	+0.01
2 yr	2 7/8	6/30/04	101-15+	2.031%	1.74	34.59	35.28	35.28	101.46	2.033%	34.88	35.57	35.57	+0.01	+0.01	+0.01
2 yr	2 1/4	7/31/04	100-11	2.063%	1.74	37.48	37.34	38.36	100.33	2.066%	37.78	37.64	38.67	+0.01	+0.01	+0.01
2 yr	2 1/8	8/31/04	100-01+	2.101%	1.74	37.51	38.29	38.30	100.04	2.104%	37.80	38.59	38.60	+0.01	+0.01	+0.01
2 yr																
2 yr																

The information contained herein is based on sources that we believe to be reliable, but we do not represent that it is accurate or complete. Nothing contained herein should be considered as an offer to sell or a solicitation of an offer to buy any financial instruments discussed herein. All references to prices and yields are subject to

Early on in our work with traders, we learned about the importance of reckoning the forward values of TED spreads so that we could understand why trades made or lost money. The structure of the report shown in Exhibit 12.2 stems from the insight that forward values are break-even values. In this example, we calculated the forward prices of all the notes shown in the table as of December 18, 2002, using a term repo rate of 1.68 percent. Using these forward prices for the notes plus the Eurodollar futures rates beginning with the Dec '02 contract, we calculated forward starting TEDs for all of the issues.

These forward-starting TEDs can be used in various ways. For example, they represent the spread values at which a trade initiated on September 10, 2002, would break even if the Treasury leg of the trade were financed at the term repo rate shown in the report.

They can also be used to assess possible convergence trades. For example, the December 18 forward-starting TED for the 2-1/8s of 8/31/04 was 41.48 basis points assuming a term repo rate of 1.68 percent. The spot TED spread for the 3-1/4s of 5/31/04 was 33.22 basis points. If one reasons that the 2-1/8s in December will have the same remaining time to maturity that the 3-1/4s had on September 10 and if one assumes that the term structure of spot TED spreads will remain unchanged, then one could sell the forward TED spread of the 2-1/8s and look for 8.26 [= 41.48 − 33.22] basis points of convergence. And the trader knows that the spot TED spread of a Treasury note that has 1-3/4s years to maturity can widen 8.26 basis points and still break even.

The forward spread calculations are sensitive to the term repo assumption. The lower is the term repo rate, the lower is the forward price of the note and the higher is its forward yield. If a note is on special in the term repo market at a rate lower than the general collateral rates shown in the report, the forward TED for that note would be smaller than the value shown. To adjust for this, the report shows how sensitive each forward TED spread is to changes in the assumed term repo rate. For example, reducing the term repo rate for the 2-1/8s by 10 basis points would decrease the forward starting TED by 1.6 [$= -10 \times 0.16$] basis points.

EXHIBIT 12.2

TED Spreads

Plus Forward TEDs to December 18, 2002
September 10, 2002

CARR FUTURES
Chicago

Ted Spreads

Tuesday, Sep 10, 2002
Data as of 3:00 PM NY CLOSE

Note TED Table (settle: 9/11/02)

Original			Mid Market		Repo	Spot TED Spread			Forward		Fwd Start TED			Fwd Start TED: RP+1bp		
					to	ED	Implied ED		12/18/2002		ED	Implied ED		ED	Implied ED	
Issue	Cpn	Maturity	Price	Yield	12/18	Shift	Nom	Work	Prc (dec)	Yield	Shift	Nom	Work	Shift	Nom	Work
2 yr	2 3/4	9/30/03	101-02	1.726%	1.68	23.93	24.38	24.38	100.79	1.732%	27.78	28.31	28.31	+0.35	+0.35	+0.35
2 yr	2 3/4	10/31/03	101-04	1.744%	1.68	26.74	27.26	27.26	100.85	1.755%	31.09	31.72	31.72	+0.31	+0.32	+0.32
5 yr	4 1/4	11/15/03	102-28	1.768%	1.68	27.29	26.77	27.97	102.21	1.784%	31.64	30.90	32.45	+0.30	+0.31	+0.31
20 yr	11 7/8	11/15/03	111-23+	1.750%	1.68	28.57	28.11	29.27	109.08	1.761%	33.50	32.82	34.35	+0.31	+0.32	+0.32
2 yr	3	11/30/03	101-14+	1.788%	1.68	26.64	26.60	27.22	101.12	1.809%	30.57	30.49	31.24	+0.29	+0.29	+0.29
2 yr	3 1/4	12/31/03	101-27	1.809%	1.68	28.62	29.21	29.21	101.45	1.831%	32.80	33.43	33.43	+0.27	+0.27	+0.27
2 yr	3	1/31/04	101-18	1.852%	1.68	30.51	30.13	31.28	101.23	1.882%	34.81	34.25	35.68	+0.24	+0.25	+0.25
5 yr	4 3/4	2/15/04	104-03	1.829%	1.68	34.80	34.51	35.69	103.31	1.853%	40.00	39.55	41.01	+0.24	+0.24	+0.24
10 yr	5 7/8	2/15/04	105-21	1.839%	1.68	33.72	33.39	34.58	104.58	1.865%	38.70	38.20	39.67	+0.24	+0.24	+0.24
2 yr	3	2/29/04	101-19+	1.884%	1.68	30.40	30.46	31.01	101.26	1.927%	34.39	34.48	35.17	+0.23	+0.23	+0.23
2 yr	3 5/8	3/31/04	102-18+	1.930%	1.68	30.33	30.94	30.94	102.07	1.978%	34.07	34.78	34.78	+0.21	+0.22	+0.22
2 yr	3 3/8	4/30/04	102-08+	1.960%	1.68	32.15	32.77	32.77	101.83	2.010%	36.05	36.74	36.74	+0.20	+0.21	+0.21
5 yr	5 1/4	5/15/04	105-13	1.955%	1.68	35.51	35.25	36.31	104.49	2.002%	40.01	39.66	40.93	+0.20	+0.20	+0.20
10 yr	7 1/4	5/15/04	108-22	1.955%	1.68	35.08	34.82	35.87	107.25	2.003%	39.56	39.20	40.47	+0.20	+0.21	+0.21
20 yr	12 3/8	5/15/04	117-02+	1.966%	1.68	33.12	32.82	33.87	114.31	2.018%	37.35	36.94	38.21	+0.21	+0.21	+0.21
2 yr	3 1/4	5/31/04	102-03	2.003%	1.68	33.22	33.42	33.96	101.69	2.058%	37.06	37.28	37.89	+0.19	+0.19	+0.19
2 yr	2 7/8	6/30/04	101-15+	2.031%	1.68	34.59	35.28	35.28	101.19	2.085%	38.51	39.23	39.23	+0.18	+0.18	+0.18
2 yr	2 1/4	7/31/04	100-11	2.063%	1.68	37.48	37.34	38.36	100.21	2.119%	41.64	41.41	42.60	+0.17	+0.17	+0.17
5 yr	6	8/15/04	107-13+	2.050%	1.68	39.49	39.80	40.37	106.32	2.105%	44.02	44.30	44.97	+0.17	+0.17	+0.17
10 yr	7 1/4	8/15/04	109-24	2.061%	1.68	38.14	38.41	39.00	108.33	2.118%	42.49	42.72	43.40	+0.17	+0.18	+0.18
20 yr	13 3/4	8/15/04	121-31	2.059%	1.68	36.85	37.03	37.68	118.87	2.118%	41.16	41.29	42.05	+0.18	+0.18	+0.18
2 yr	2 1/8	8/31/04	100-01+	2.101%	1.68	37.51	38.29	38.30	99.93	2.166%	41.48	42.42	42.43	+0.16	+0.16	+0.16
5 yr	5 7/8	11/15/04	107-28	2.151%	1.68	42.41	43.29	43.33	106.80	2.215%	46.83	47.81	47.86	+0.15	+0.15	+0.15
10 yr	7 7/8	11/15/04	112-01	2.183%	1.68	38.58	39.36	39.41	110.44	2.254%	42.50	43.36	43.42	+0.15	+0.16	+0.16
20 yr	11 5/8	11/15/04	119-31	2.178%	1.68	37.82	38.56	38.63	117.41	2.251%	41.74	42.56	42.65	+0.16	+0.16	+0.16
10 yr	7 1/2	2/15/05	112-11	2.244%	1.68	45.23	46.16	46.26	110.86	2.313%	49.59	50.58	50.69	+0.13	+0.14	+0.14
[illegible]	[illegible]	[illegible]	[illegible]	[illegible]	[illegible]	[illegible]	[illegible]	[illegible]	[illegible]	[illegible]	[illegible]	[illegible]	[illegible]	[illegible]	[illegible]	[illegible]

EXHIBIT 12.2

Continued

20 yr	12	5/15/05	124-31	2.322%	1.68	46.47	47.00	47.44	122.34	2.399%	50.77	51.35	51.84	+0.13	+0.13	+0.13
10 yr	6 1/2	8/15/05	111-16+	2.401%	1.68	52.14	53.16	53.23	110.30	2.475%	56.46	57.54	57.62	+0.11	+0.11	+0.11
20 yr	10 3/4	8/15/05	123-13	2.417%	1.68	48.32	49.22	49.33	121.11	2.495%	52.39	53.34	53.47	+0.11	+0.12	+0.12
5 yr	5 3/4	11/15/05	109-27	2.506%	1.68	52.70	53.80	53.84	108.81	2.585%	56.71	57.91	57.95	+0.10	+0.10	+0.10
10 yr	5 7/8	11/15/05	110-07	2.507%	1.68	52.48	53.58	53.61	109.16	2.586%	56.48	57.67	57.71	+0.10	+0.10	+0.10
10 yr	5 5/8	2/15/06	109-28+	2.589%	1.68	54.69	55.86	55.91	108.90	2.669%	58.57	59.81	59.87	+0.09	+0.09	+0.09
20 yr	9 3/8	2/15/06	122-00	2.619%	1.68	49.08	50.07	50.16	120.07	2.705%	52.60	53.65	53.75	+0.10	+0.10	+0.10
5 yr	4 5/8	5/15/06	106-23+	2.688%	1.68	54.67	55.77	55.80	105.99	2.771%	58.26	59.44	59.47	+0.09	+0.09	+0.09
10 yr	6 7/8	5/15/06	114-17	2.696%	1.68	52.02	53.04	53.08	113.22	2.782%	55.49	56.59	56.64	+0.09	+0.09	+0.09
10 yr	7	7/15/06	115-12+	2.750%	1.68	53.18	53.70	54.35	114.06	2.837%	56.61	57.14	57.85	+0.08	+0.09	+0.09
10 yr	6 1/2	10/15/06	114-03	2.828%	1.68	54.56	55.41	55.75	112.87	2.917%	57.86	58.79	59.15	+0.08	+0.08	+0.08
5 yr	3 1/2	11/15/06	102-15+	2.864%	1.68	56.91	58.14	58.16	102.02	2.949%	60.17	61.49	61.51	+0.07	+0.08	+0.08
10 yr	6 1/4	2/15/07	113-22	2.930%	1.68	56.05	57.23	57.28	112.55	3.017%	59.21	60.45	60.50	+0.07	+0.07	+0.07
5 yr	4 3/8	5/15/07	105-29	3.011%	1.68	57.81	58.99	59.01	105.22	3.098%	60.84	62.11	62.13	+0.07	+0.07	+0.07
10 yr	6 5/8	5/15/07	115-23	2.996%	1.68	56.47	57.58	57.61	114.48	3.086%	59.53	60.73	60.76	+0.07	+0.07	+0.07
5 yr	3 1/4	8/15/07	100-29	3.050%	1.68	63.64	64.99	65.02	100.50	3.132%	66.81	68.23	68.26	+0.06	+0.06	+0.06
10 yr	6 1/8	8/15/07	113-24+	3.091%	1.68	55.78	56.90	56.94	112.66	3.180%	58.62	59.80	59.84	+0.07	+0.07	+0.07

CHAPTER 13

Hedging and Trading with Eurodollar Stacks, Packs, and Bundles

Galen Burghardt, George Panos, and Fred Sturm
Research note originally released December 15, 1999

SYNOPSIS

Eurodollar futures are the financial building blocks of the dollar interest rate market. With 40 quarterly contract expirations, the Eurodollar futures contract complex is a financial engineer's dream. One can create or offset exposure to forward interest rates in 3-month segments out to a horizon of 10 years.

In practice, though, the flexibility afforded by individual contract expirations comes at a cost that is not always warranted. In many cases, traders and hedgers find it better to put all their eggs in one basket and use a single contract month (a stack). Or they may prefer to buy or sell packages of Eurodollar futures that the CME calls packs or bundles. A pack represents a sequence of 4 consecutive expiration dates that can be bought or sold simultaneously. A bundle is similar to a pack but spans 2 or more years' worth of contract expirations.

Perhaps 15 percent or so of all trading in the first year's expirations (that is, the white contracts) is done in the form of packs. Roughly half or more of all trading in expirations from 6 to 10 years (that is, the purple through copper years) is done in the form of packs or bundles. This suggests quite plausibly that the flexibility afforded by quarterly contract expirations is more important in the front months than in the more distant back months.

Three Objectives

We do three things in this note. The first is to provide a basic guide to the language and quote conventions of packs and bundles—the color coding of contracts and the way packs and bundles are bid and offered. The second is to take a look at the way pack and bundle hedges for Treasury notes perform. The third is to tackle the question of how a TED spread trade behaves when the trader introduces yield curve exposure by using a stack, pack, or bundle hedge in place of a hedge that is engineered to eliminate forward rate exposure.

How Good Are Stack, Pack, and Bundle Hedges?

Under normal circumstances, Eurodollar packs can do a very good job of capturing changes in the value of Treasury notes. The best pack hedges can provide correlations with daily changes in the prices of key Treasury notes that exceed 95 percent (see Exhibit 13.1). And, as we show later, you can get similar results with

EXHIBIT 13.1

Treasury Note Correlations with ED Packs
Daily Price Changes, June 1994 to June 1999

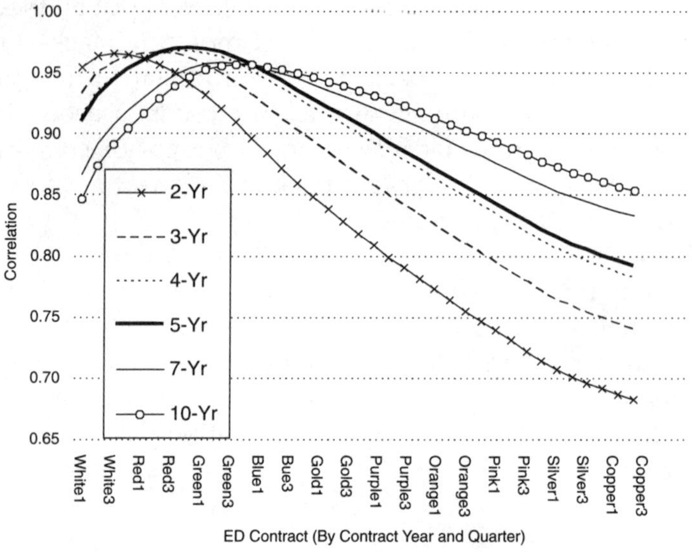

stacks and bundles. We also show how to scale a stack, pack, or bundle hedge to get a minimum variance hedge.

Curve-Augmented TED Spreads?

The decorrelation that accompanies a change in the slope or shape of the forward rate curve is a nuisance for hedgers but can be an opportunity for traders. For example, by hedging a Treasury note with a stack, pack, or bundle of Eurodollar futures, the trader can augment a standard TED spread with a yield curve trade. And because so many traders do just this, we take some time at the end of this note to tackle the problem of how one should measure the performance of a "curve TED" and to provide some evidence on how various curve spreads have behaved.

HEDGING AND TRADING WITH EURODOLLAR STACKS, PACKS, AND BUNDLES

Exhibit 13.2 shows five different Eurodollar hedges for the 5-1/2s of July 31, 2001, which was the on-the-run 2-year Treasury note

EXHIBIT 13.2

Eurodollar Hedges for a 2-Year Note
5-1/2s of 7/31/01 as of August 4, 1999

		Hedge Approach				
	Contract Month	**Engineered (weighted)**	**Stack**	**Single Pack**	**Tandem Packs**	**Bundle**
	stub	45				
White	Sep '99	100			99	90
	Dec '99	98			99	90
	Mar '00	104			99	90
	Jun '00	95			99	90
Red	Sep '00	94	717	179	80	90
	Dec '00	93		179	80	90
	Mar '01	92		179	80	90
	Jun '01	41		179	80	90
	Total (net of stub)	717	717	716	716	720

on August 4, 1999. All five hedges have roughly the same number of Eurodollar contracts (net of whatever is needed to hedge the stub), but differ from one another in two key respects—ease of execution and yield curve exposure.

The engineered hedge is the most difficult to execute but is the combination of Eurodollar futures that is designed to capture as completely as possible the forward rate exposure in the 2-year note. A trader who buys $100 million of the note and sells this combination of Eurodollar futures will be long the term TED spread as conventionally defined. This position will profit from increases in the credit spread between the LIBOR and Treasury markets and will be almost completely unaffected by changes in the slope or curvature of the forward rate curve.

The stack, pack, and bundle hedges, in contrast, provide ease and economy of execution. Instead of the eight separate transactions required to put on the weighted hedge, the stack hedge requires only one transaction (the sale of 717 "red Seps") as does the bundle hedge (the sale of 90 "2-year bundles"). The hedge can be done with the sale of 179 of a single pack such as "red Sep." Or one could hedge with tandem packs with only two transactions (i.e., the sale of 99 "white packs" and the sale of 80 "red packs"). The drawback of these simpler hedges is a reduction in the quality of the hedge. Put differently, these simpler hedges inject curve exposure into the position, which will be an advantage to some hedgers and traders and a drawback to others.

BASICS: DATES, NAMES, PACKS, BUNDLES, AND QUOTES

On any given day, the Chicago Mercantile Exchange lists 40 Eurodollar futures contract expirations in the March/June/September/December quarterly cycle. As Exhibit 13.3 shows, these 40 quarterly contracts, each of which is tied to its own value of 3-month LIBOR, span 10 years of the forward rate curve.

Contract Colors

Keeping track of 40 contracts in terms of expiration year and month is potentially very cumbersome. To simplify matters, at least for people who trade these contracts for a living, the CME

EXHIBIT 13.3

Eurodollar Futures Contract Rates
Closing Levels, August 4, 1999

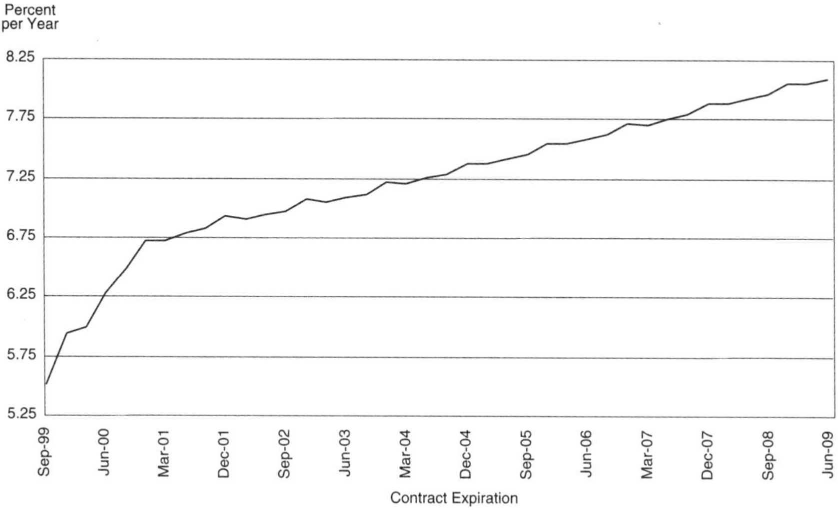

defines expiration years in terms of a color-coded grid, with 4 contract expirations per color. On any trading day the first 4 quarterly contracts (the lead contract and the next 3 contracts that expire thereafter) are collectively dubbed the white year, or the whites. The next 4 quarterly expirations beyond the whites are called the reds. The 4 quarterly expirations beyond the reds are called the greens, and so on. As we move out to more distant expirations, the coding system vaguely resembles a 1965-vintage color TV. Exhibit 13.4 illustrates the complete color-coded grid, using contract expirations available on August 4, 1999. Note that the grid is dictated purely by the order in which futures contracts expire, not the calendar years in which they expire. Indeed, in only one quarter out of every four—the interval between mid-December and mid-March—will color-coded expiration years coincide with calendar years.

For generic purposes, we can reference a Eurodollar contract by color code of expiration year and contract position within expiration year, e.g., first red, or third green. That is the convention we will follow in the remainder of this note. Market transactors,

EXHIBIT 13.4

Contracts by Color
August 4, 1999

Expiration Year	First	Second	Third	Fourth
White	Sep '99	Dec '99	Mar '00	Jun '00
Red	Sep '00	Dec '00	Mar '01	Jun '01
Green	Sep '01	Dec '01	Mar '02	Jun '02
Blue	Sep '02	Dec '02	Mar '03	Jun '03
Gold	Sep '03	Dec '03	Mar '04	Jun '04
Purple	Sep '04	Dec '04	Mar '05	Jun '05
Orange	Sep '05	Dec '05	Mar '06	Jun '06
Pink	Sep '06	Dec '06	Mar '07	Jun '07
Silver	Sep '07	Dec '07	Mar '08	Jun '08
Copper	Sep '08	Dec '08	Mar '09	Jun '09

however, typically name the contracts by color code of expiration year and month of expiration.

EXAMPLE

On August 4, 1999, we refer to the second blue contract as "blue Dec." If we are also transacting in the first red contract, we refer to it as "red Sep." The 4 contracts in the white year are generally referenced by only their month of expiration. Thus, if we are dealing in "March" on August 4, 1999, we are understood to be trading the third white contract.

Packs and Bundles

Frequently market practitioners wish to buy or sell entire sequences of Eurodollar futures contracts at once rather than transacting one contract expiration at a time. To accommodate such participants, the CME has introduced a variety of bulk transaction mechanisms, in the form of packs and bundles, that permit the simultaneous purchase or sale of equally weighted consecutive sequences of Eurodollar contracts.

Thus, a *pack* is a sequence of 4 futures contracts with consecutive expiration dates that can be bought or sold simultaneously. Market practitioners reference a pack by the member contract that expires soonest. On any given trading day, there are 37 packs available, ranging from first white out to first copper, and spanning all possible starting points in between.

EXAMPLE

On August 4, 1999, the red March pack comprises one each of the contracts expiring in March, June, September, and December of 2001 (i.e., red March, red June, green Sep, and green Dec). The gold Dec pack consists of one each of the contracts expiring in December 2003 and March, June, and September of 2004.

Any pack that is named simply by color code, without an expiration month, refers to the sequence of 4 contracts within the corresponding expiration year.

EXAMPLE

A broker who quotes a market in "the purple pack" is implicitly referring to the sequence of 4 contracts within the purple expiration year. On August 4, 1999, that comprises the contracts expiring between September 2004 and June 2005, making it identical in this case to the purple Sep pack.

A *bundle* is mechanically similar to a pack, the chief difference being that the bundle spans 2 or more years' worth of Eurodollar contract expirations, whereas the pack spans only 1 year's worth. With a 5-year bundle, for example, a market participant can buy or sell one each of 20 consecutive Eurodollar futures contracts simultaneously (i.e., 5 years times 4 contract expirations per year). Market practitioners reference a bundle by (1) the member contract that expires first and (2) the length of the bundle in years. Exhibit 13.5 summarizes the types of bundles currently available.

EXHIBIT 13.5

The Menu of Eurodollar Bundles

Bundle Type	Number of Consecutive ED Contracts	Number of Bundles Available on Any Trading Day	Bundle Can Start with Any ED Contract Ranging From
2-year	8	33	First white to first silver
3-year	12	29	First white to first pink
4-year	16	25	First white to first orange
5-year	20	21	First white to first purple
7-year	28	13	First white to first blue
10-year	40	1	First white

EXAMPLE

On August 4, 1999, the red June 2-year bundle comprises 1 each of the 8 contracts that expire in June, September, and December of 2001, March through December of 2002, and March 2003. The green Sep 7-year bundle contains one each of the 28 contracts found in the 7 expiration years from green out to silver (i.e., all contracts from first green through fourth silver). The 10-year bundle—there can be only one—represents the sale or purchase of one each of the 40 quarterly Eurodollar contracts.

Any bundle that is named simply by year-length, without reference to any particular expiration month, is understood to refer to the lead (first white) bundle.

EXAMPLE

On August 4, 1999, a trader dealing in the "2-year bundle" is understood to have an interest in the bundle that comprises 1 each of the first 8 futures expirations, i.e., September 1999 through June 2001.

There are 122 possible bundles listed for trading on any given day.[1] In practice, the more liquid of these are, with the exception of the 10-year, bundles within 5 years. At this writing, however, liquidity tends to be concentrated in just seven bundle configurations. Six of these are the lead (first white) versions of the basic bundle types listed in Exhibit 13.5. The seventh is the first purple 5-year bundle. Market practitioners call this bundle "L5" because it encompasses the last 5 years' worth of contract expirations (first purple through fourth copper).

Note that market practitioners also are in the habit of referring to the pack that contains the first 4 contracts as the "1-year bundle," not as the "white pack." Early in the history of the pack/bundle trading facility, this distinction was meaningful. Today, however, it is purely an artifact of terminology. Thus, for convenience and consistency, we will call it the white pack throughout this note.

QUOTE PRACTICES 1: TICKS

The concept of tick is fundamental to understanding how markets are quoted in Eurodollar futures. One tick represents a move of 0.01 on a price base of 100.00. In interest rate (i.e., LIBOR) terms this corresponds to one basis point. A one tick move on a Eurodollar contract is always worth $25, regardless of the contract's expiration date.

EXAMPLE

If a Eurodollar futures contract price moves from 93.20 to 93.25, it has rallied 5 ticks. The corresponding contract rate (in LIBOR terms) has declined 5 basis points, from 6.80 percent per year to 6.75 percent. If we own 100 of this contract, then we will collect a variation margin adjustment of $12,500 [= $25/tick × 5 ticks/contract × 100 contracts]. Conversely, if we have a short position in the same 100 contracts, then we must pay $12,500 in variation margin adjustment.

1. Update 2002: The CME now offers bundles with maturities from 1 to 10 years, making the available number of bundles 190.

The value of a 1-tick move for a pack or a bundle is simply \$25 times the number of contracts in the pack or bundle.

EXAMPLE

If we have a short position in 100 4-year bundles (any 4-year bundle) that has risen in price from 93.18 to 93.195, then we are liable for a variation margin payment of \$60,000 [= \$25/tick × 1.5 ticks/contract × 16 Eurodollar contracts/bundle × 100 bundles].

QUOTE PRACTICES 2: USE PRICE LEVEL FOR INDIVIDUAL CONTRACTS

Individual Eurodollar contracts are traded in terms of price, with the tick as the basic unit of measure.

EXAMPLE

On the afternoon of August 4, 1999, market players bid the Dec '99 contract at a price of 94.06 and offer it at 94.07. Traders and brokers will quote this as a "six-seven" market. If the market tightens to 94.06 bid versus 94.065 offered, they will quote it as "six-six-and-a-half" or "six to the half."

Though the tick is the basic unit of measure, it is not the smallest unit. On most days all Eurodollar contracts trade in half ticks. The sole exception is the lead contract, which is permitted to trade in quarter ticks during the 4-week interval immediately preceding its expiration. (To be more precise, the lead contract trades in quarter ticks during the interval starting with the Monday before the third Wednesday of the previous month, i.e., the expiration day of the previous month's serial futures contract, and ending with the contract's own expiration. Though this interval typically spans 4 weeks, the vagaries of the calendar sometimes stretch it to 5.)

QUOTE PRACTICES 3: USE PRICE CHANGES FOR PACKS AND BUNDLES

The daily settlement prices that are established at 2:00 p.m. Chicago time play a pivotal role in how packs and bundles are quoted, for two reasons. First, it is at this point in the trading day that actual price levels are set for all packs and bundles. The price of each pack or bundle is simply the arithmetic average of the prices of its member contracts.

EXAMPLE

On August 4, 1999, the CME records the following closing price levels:

Red Sep	93.525
Red Dec	93.285
Red Mar	93.295
Red Jun	93.220

To determine the closing price level of the red pack, CME officials compute the arithmetic average of the closing prices on these 4 individual contracts, which is 93.33125.

Second, and more important, is that over the ensuing 24 hours the market price of any pack or bundle will be quoted in terms of tick change versus the previous day's 2:00 p.m. Chicago time settlement level. (It is useful to recall here that the Eurodollar futures market trades more or less continuously—by open outcry during regular trading hours [7:20 a.m. to 2:00 p.m. Chicago time], and on GLOBEX nearly continuously [4:30 p.m. to 4:00 p.m. next day, Chicago time].)

As with Eurodollar futures contracts, packs and bundles trade in smaller increments than one tick. However, the finest permissible price move for any pack or bundle is a quarter tick versus the half tick minimum move that applies to individual contracts.

EXAMPLE

It is early on August 5, 1999, and mid-market prices for contracts in the red pack are as follows—

Contract	Aug 5 Price	Tick Change versus Aug 4 Close
Red Sep	93.55 0	+2.5
Red Dec	93.30 5	+2.0
Red Mar	93.31 5	+2.0
Red Jun	93.24 0	+2.0

The average price change across these 4 contracts is a gain of +2.125 ticks. That is where market participants will be inclined to price the red pack. However, they will be unable to quote it as "up two and an eighth" because the pack is constrained to move in price increments of a quarter tick or more. Thus, they will have to quote it as "up two," or as "up two and a quarter," or as a bid/offer spread, e.g., "up two to the quarter."

UNPACKING PACKS, UNBUNDLING BUNDLES

A pack or bundle exists only up to the point that it has been transacted. It does not show up as a package on the books of its buyer and seller. Rather, the Eurodollar contracts in the package are booked individually, at transaction prices that are consistent with the average price at which the pack or bundle changed hands. For this reason, anyone who employs these bulk transaction mechanisms should have a clear understanding of how their prices get translated into individual contract prices.

Once a buyer and a seller have agreed upon the price of a pack or a bundle, they must assign mutually acceptable prices to each of the contracts in the package. In principle, the transactors may set these component prices arbitrarily, subject to two restrictions.

The first and more obvious one is that the average price change among the contracts (versus their previous 2:00 p.m. CT closing levels) must equal the price change at which the pack or bundle has been priced.

Second, the price of at least one Eurodollar contract must lie within that contract's trading range for the day (assuming that at least one of the Eurodollar contracts in the pack or bundle has established a trading range). This rule ensures that the prices of bulk transaction devices remain tethered to the price action of the underlying individual Eurodollar contracts.

EXAMPLE

Suppose we have sold the 2-year bundle (i.e., 1 each of the 8 contracts in the white and red expiration years) to a buyer at the price of +5 ticks. In principle, we can agree with the buyer to unbundle this average price change as +10 ticks on each of the 4 white contracts and zero price change for each of the 4 red contracts (assuming of course that such pricing fulfills the trading-range constraint mentioned above). Alternatively—again, in principle—we can agree with the buyer to exchange each of these 8 contracts at a price change of +5 ticks.

Rarely in practice do market participants spend time dickering over how to price the individual members of the packs or bundles that they have traded among each other. The objective in using these devices, after all, is to save time. Instead, they almost always rely on a computerized system furnished by the CME that automatically assigns individual prices to the contracts in any pack or bundle.

The algorithm employed by the CME's pricing system is guided by the following principle: To the extent that adjustments are necessary to bring the average price of the pack's or bundle's components into conformity with the bundle's own price, these price adjustments should begin with the most deferred contract in the bundle and should work forward to the nearest contract.

EXAMPLE

Suppose that a buyer and a seller who are transacting in the 3-year bundle have agreed upon a net price change of −2.75 ticks versus the previous day's settlement level. The CME algorithm distributes

E X A M P L E Continued

this price change among the bundle's 12 member contracts in two steps, dealing first with the integer portion of the −2.75 tick trade price (the "2"), and then with the fractional portion (the "0.75"). Specifically, the algorithm begins by assigning to each of the 12 contracts in the bundle a net price change of −2 ticks from the previous day's close. Then it adjusts these price changes downward, proceeding one contract at a time—beginning with the bundle's most deferred contract and working forward—until the average net price change for the bundle is the agreed-upon −2.75 ticks. Following this procedure results in the bundle's nearest 3 contracts being booked at prices that are −2 ticks below their respective closing levels for the previous day, while the bundle's 9 most deferred contracts are each booked at net price changes of −3 ticks. The average price change across the 12 contracts is $(9 \times -3 + 3 \times -2)/12 = -2.75$ bps, as desired.

Note that although futures contracts trade in half ticks, the CME price-distribution algorithm works only through whole-tick price adjustments.

The relentless efficiency of the Eurodollar futures market means that the price change quoted for a pack or a bundle will almost never deviate systematically from the actual average price change across the individual contracts within the pack or bundle. However, the two are apt to exhibit frequent short-lived deviations, ranging in size from as much as 1/4 contract tick to as little as 1/80 contract tick (on a 10-year bundle). These will arise as natural artifacts of the restrictions on minimum price increments—half ticks for individual Eurodollar contracts versus quarter ticks for packs and bundles.

E X A M P L E

Just before 2:00 p.m. Chicago close on August 5, 1999, we want to buy 1 each of the first 8 Eurodollar futures. Price changes among these contracts versus their August 4 closing levels range from +3 ticks on white Sep to +9-1/2 ticks on white Mar. Their average

EXAMPLE Continued

price move is +6-5/16 ticks. We can buy them individually, but we also consider buying them as a 2-year bundle. Since the bundle is constrained to trade in increments of 1/4 tick, it cannot be priced at +6-5/16 ticks. Rather it is apt to be quoted at either +6-1/4 ticks or +6-1/2 ticks. If we can buy the bundle at +6-1/4 ticks, then we enjoy an overall discount of −1/16 tick per contract by using the bundle instead of purchasing the 8 contracts individually. (By contrast, if the Eurodollar pit offers the 2-year bundle at +6-1/2 ticks, then it is not such a great deal. We would pay a premium of +3/16 tick per contract to buy our futures contracts in bundle form instead of individually.) Having bought the bundle at +6-1/4 ticks, suppose we apply the CME's price distribution algorithm in unbundling it. If we do this, we will pay +6 ticks for the first 6 contracts (white Sep through red Dec) and +7 ticks for the last 2 (red Mar and red Jun).

For more on the basics of Eurodollar futures, packs, and bundles, see "CME Interest Rate Futures: The Basics," from the Chicago Mercantile Exchange.

HEDGING WITH STACKS, PACKS, AND BUNDLES

The engineered hedge shown in Exhibit 13.2 is designed to eliminate as completely as possible any yield curve exposure in the hedged position. All the risk that remains stems from changes in the credit spread, which in this case would be the 2-year term TED spread.

Simple stack, pack, and bundle hedges will work less well than will engineered hedges. This is because rate changes across contract months are not perfectly correlated.

Also, the total number of contracts needed to produce the "best" stack, pack, or bundle hedge—that is, the hedge with the smallest variance—may well be more or less than the number required for the engineered hedge. For one thing, a hedger faced with imperfect correlations can improve things by underhedging. For another thing, rate changes tend to be larger for some contract months—for example, the red months—than for others. As a result, the hedger will want to scale the size of the hedge up or down to compensate for any regular differences in rate variability.

What Happens to the Correlations?

Exhibit 13.6 shows how changes in the values of various stack, pack, and bundle hedges correlate with changes in the values of on-the-run 2-year, 5-year, and 10-year Treasury notes. One can see easily which of these hedges provided the best protection and how much the correlations fall off if the hedger chooses something other than the best spot on the curve.

These rankings are based on correlations between day-to-day changes in (clean) prices of Treasury notes and day-to-day changes in the prices of Eurodollar futures contracts or packs or bundles. The "best" futures hedge for a given Treasury note is simply the ED package most highly correlated with it. (Specifically, the data we use to compute these correlations are daily changes—from futures close to futures close—in prices of ED futures and (clean) prices of Treasury notes over the 5-year interval from mid-June 1994 to mid-June 1999. Note that this span of history is sufficiently long to embrace a broad variety of market environments—bullish, bearish, stable, volatile. At the same time, it is reasonably homogeneous in terms of the Fed's operating procedures and policy announcement protocols.)

Three things are apparent from Exhibit 13.6. First, the best of these stack, pack, and bundle hedges are really quite good, at least under normal circumstances. In all cases, the highest correlations are between 0.95 and 1.00. If one allows for the fact that even the engineered hedge would exhibit a correlation that is less than 1.00 because of residual credit spread or TED spread risk, the hedger does not lose much at all.

Second, the best stack, pack, or bundle hedge is found at different, and in some cases surprising, places on the Eurodollar curve. For example, although it is impossible to see in Exhibit 13.6, the best 2-year bundle hedge for the on-the-run Treasury began with the second white contract, not with the lead, or first, white contract. As shown in Exhibit 13.7, the best stack hedge for the 2-year note was the first red contract, and the best pack hedge was the third white pack.

EXHIBIT 13.6

Best Pack and Bundle Hedges

2-Year Note

———Individual contracts — — —Packs ▬▬ Bundles

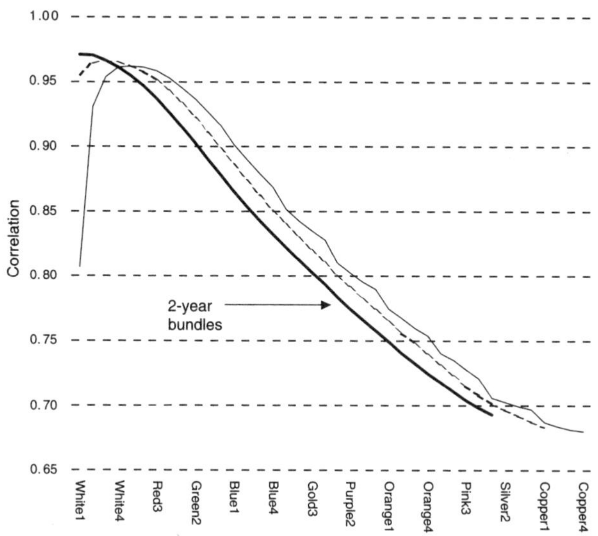

5-Year Note

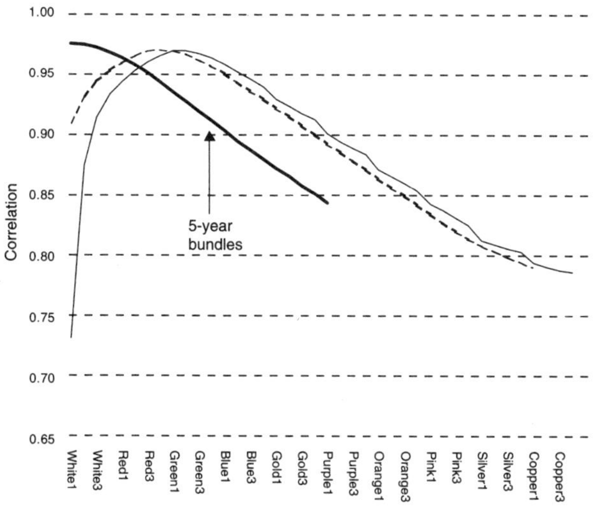

EXHIBIT 13.6

Continued
10-Year Note

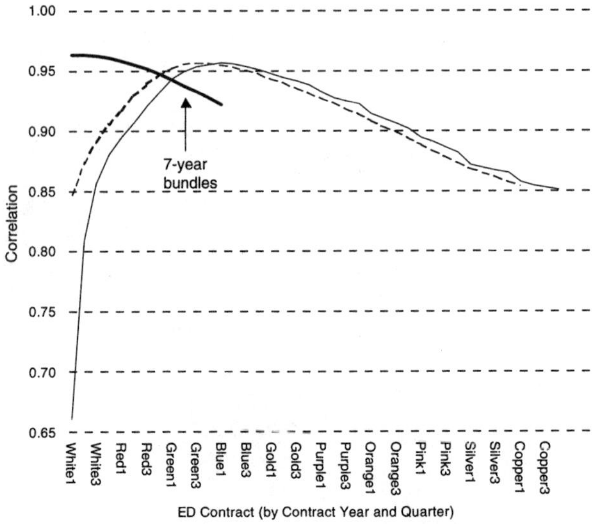

EXHIBIT 13.7

Best Single Contract, Pack, and Bundle Hedges

	Best Single		
Treasury Issue	**Contract**	**Pack**	**Bundle**
On-the-run 2-year	First red	Third white	Second white 2-year
Current 3-year	Third red	Second red	First white 3-year
Current 4-year	First green	Fourth red	First white 4-year
On-the-run 5-year	First green	Fourth red	Second white 4-year
Current 7-year	Fourth green	Second green	First white 7-year
On-the-run 10-year	First blue	Third green	First white 7-year

As one would expect, the best stack, pack, or bundle hedge for a 5-year or 10-year note is further out along the Eurodollar curve than is the best hedge for the 2-year note. As shown in Exhibit 13.7, the best stack hedges would be the first green and first blue contracts for these notes. The best pack hedges began with the fourth red and third green contracts.

Third, the term of the best bundle does not always correspond to the maturity of the note. For example, the best bundle hedge for the on-the-run 5-year note was not, as one might expect, a 5-year bundle. Rather, the second white 4-year bundle produced a slightly higher correlation than did any of the 5-year bundles.

Best Pack Proxies for Key Treasury Maturities

How well can Eurodollar packs capture the behavior of yields at key points along the Treasury curve? The high correlations of the best pack hedges shown in Exhibit 13.8 would suggest that packs can do a very good job of representing Treasurys.

EXHIBIT 13.8

Treasury Note Correlations with ED Packs
Daily Price Changes, June 1994 to June 1999

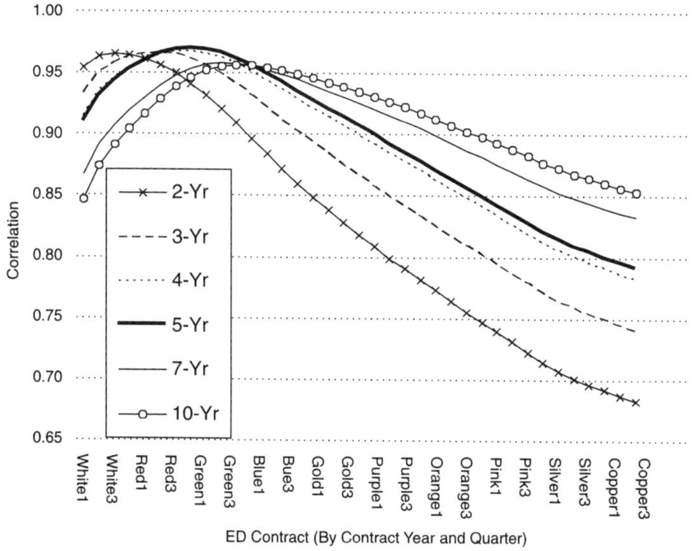

A closer look tells us, though, that they would not do a very good job of discriminating. For example, the best pack hedge for the current 4-year note and the on-the-run 5-year note is the fourth red pack. Note, too, that the best pack hedge for the on-the-run 10-year note is the third green pack, which is only 3 contracts, or 9 months, farther out on the Eurodollar curve than the fourth red pack. Thus, using correlation alone to find the best proxy for a Treasury note would be no help at all in trading the 4-year/5-year Treasury spread, and would be comparatively little help in the trading the 5-year/10-year spread.

Horizon Matters

When using changes in rates or prices to estimate correlations, it makes sense to us to match the period over which one calculates changes with the hedging horizon. For example, if a typical position is held for a day, then daily changes seem best. If a position is held for a week, then weekly changes seem best.

As shown in Exhibit 13.9, the best stack or pack hedges depends somewhat on the hedging horizon. For example, the best 1-day pack hedge for the on-the-run 5-year Treasury was the fourth red pack. The best 1-week pack hedge was the second red. The differences shown in Exhibit 13.9 are not especially large, but the best hedges using weekly changes do tend to be closer in on the Eurodollar curve.

EXHIBIT 13.9

Hedge Horizon and Best Hedges

	Best Stack		*Best Pack*	
Treasury Issue	**1 Day**	**1 Week**	**1 Day**	**1 Week**
On-the-run 2-year	First red	Fourth white	Third white	Third white
Current 3-year	Third red	Third red	Second red	First red
Current 4-year	First green	Third red	Fourth red	Second red
On-the-run 5-year	First green	Third red	Fourth red	Second red
Current 7-year	Fourth green	First green	Second green	Fourth red
On-the-run 10-year	First blue	First green	Third green	Fourth red

The Dangers of Decorrelation

Whoever said that the only thing that goes up in a crash is correlations was not thinking of stack, pack, and bundle hedges.

In recent years, short-run estimates of correlation between Treasury notes and Eurodollar futures have rarely strayed too far from their long-run benchmarks. Consider, for example, the relationship between the Treasury 5-year note and the 5-year Eurodollar bundle, as depicted in Exhibit 13.10. The jagged line represents a running correlation of daily changes estimated over 20-day periods. The solid straight line represents the full period correlation, which was 0.975. And, over most of the 5 years covered by Exhibit 13.10, the running 20-day correlation was higher than this.

Exhibit 13.10 also shows what can happen to correlations if things go badly, as they did in the autumn of 1998 when credit

EXHIBIT 13.10

Short-Term versus Long-Term Correlation between Price Changes in 5-Year Treasurys and First White 5-Year Bundle

Daily, June 14, 1994 to June 14, 1999

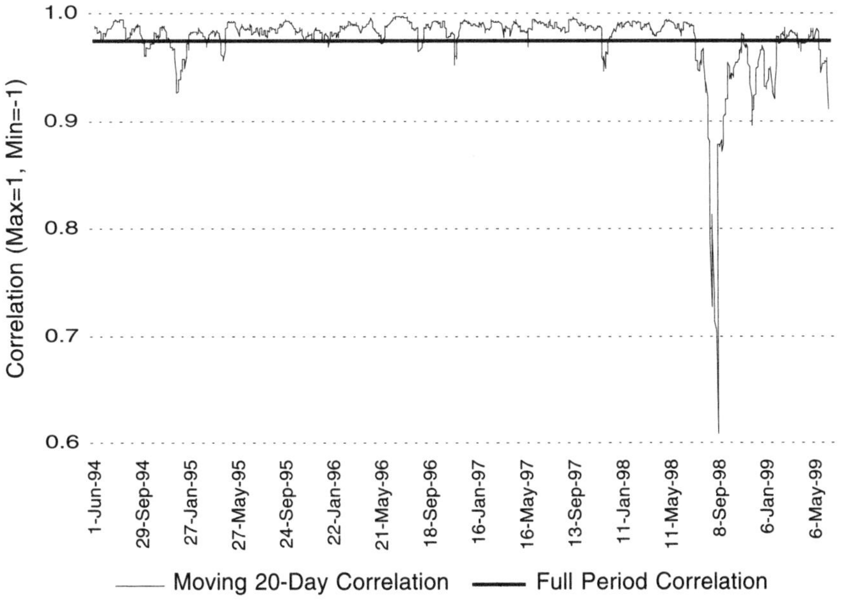

markets were roiled by Russia's financial meltdown and the failure of Long-Term Capital Management. The typically rock-steady relationship between the 5-year T-note and the 5-year ED bundle deteriorated abruptly, with the correlation between them plunging almost to 0.60 from values that were almost 1.00.

What this means in dollars and cents is shown in Exhibit 13.11, which depicts daily hedge errors for a hypothetical trader who is always long the on-the-run 5-year T-note and is short an appropriate number of 5-year Eurodollar bundles. Through the 4 years from mid-June 1994 to mid-June 1998, the hedge errors on this trade ran reliably close to zero, typically less than 2/32nds. The plunge in correlation in late summer and early fall of 1998 caused a correspondingly sharp jump in range and variability of hedge errors.

EXHIBIT 13.11

The Consequences of Decorrelation:
Errors from DV01-Hedging OTR 5-Year Treasury Note with First White 5-Year Bundle
Daily, June 14, 1994 to June 14, 1999

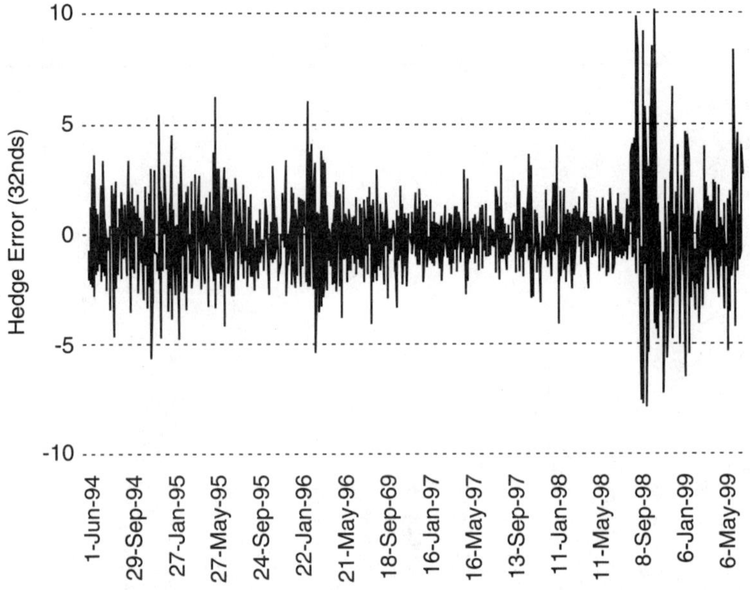

Scaling Your Hedges to Reduce Hedge Error

Once you decide to use a stack, pack, or bundle in lieu of an engineered hedge, you may want to consider scaling the hedge to compensate for two things—differences in rate variability and a loss of correlation. It is useful to think of a hedge ratio as the product of two things—the correlation between the two variables and the ratio of their respective standard deviations (i.e., beta). For example, if you want to hedge y with x, the hedge ratio that you would find by regressing y on x would be:

$$\textit{Hedge ratio} = \rho_{y,x}\left(\frac{\sigma_y}{\sigma_x}\right)$$

where $\rho_{y,x}$ is the correlation between y and x, and σ_y and σ_x are the standard deviations of y and x respectively.

The handy thing about this way of expressing the hedge ratio is that two things are readily apparent. First, if the two variables are perfectly correlated, the hedge ratio is simply the ratio of the two standard deviations. Second, if the two variables are less than perfectly correlated, the hedge ratio will be smaller than the ratio of the standard deviations.

Both forces come into play when hedging with stacks, packs, and bundles. Consider the results shown in Exhibit 13.12. The curve represents the standard deviation of daily changes in individual Eurodollar contract rates. The two solid squares represent the standard deviation of daily changes in the yields of hypothetical 2-year and 5-year Eurodollar bonds.

The shape of the curve illustrates three key features of Eurodollar rate volatility. First, the lead contract (i.e., the first white contract) is the least variable of all. The red contracts tend to be the most volatile of all. And once you get past the greens, all rates exhibit roughly the same variability.

The practical consequences for hedgers are clear. If you want to hedge a 2-year note with any red stack or red pack, you will need fewer contracts than are called for in the engineered hedge. Or if you want to hedge a 5-year note with a gold stack or pack, you will need more contracts than are called for in the engineered hedge.

EXHIBIT 13.12

Volatility of Daily Changes in ED Contract Rates and Term TED Yields

Standard Deviations, Mid-1994 to Mid-1999

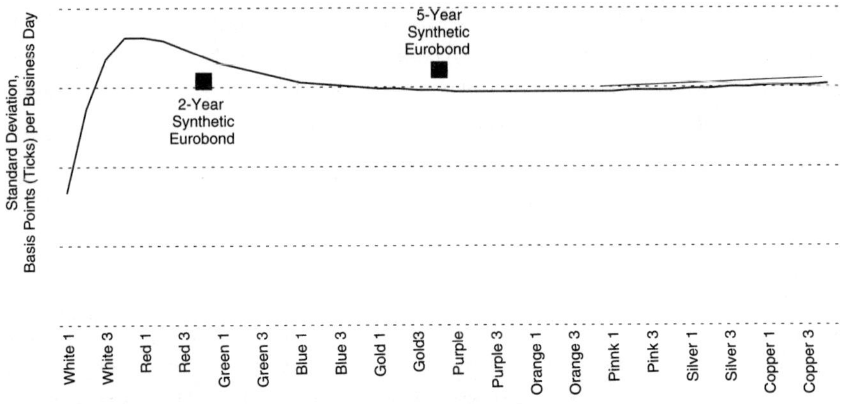

Taken together, imperfect correlations and differences in variability of rate changes across contract months encourage the scaling of hedges. For example, as shown in Exhibit 13.13, the engineered hedge for the on-the-run 2-year note would eliminate nearly all of the forward rate exposure in the note. (The percent risk reduction shown in Exhibit 13.13 applies only to rate risk, not to credit spread risk.) As shown, the engineered hedge would require 738 contracts. In contrast, the best red pack hedge would use only 548 contracts and at this size would reduce the forward rate risk in the position by 20 percent. More or less than this number of contracts would add risk to the hedge. By the same token, the hedger would require only 544 of the first red contract to get a minimum risk hedge.

TRADING CURVE TEDs

Some people look at the curve mismatches implied by stack, pack, and bundle hedges for Treasurys and see opportunities instead of problems.

Up to this point, we have assumed that the practitioner wants to construct a hedge with whatever Eurodollar futures package (contract, pack, or bundle) is most highly correlated with his

EXHIBIT 13.13

Scaled Hedges for a 2-Year Treasury Note
5-5/8s of 9/30/01 as of October 27, 1999,
Daily Standard Deviation = $227,618

	Number of Contracts		
Contract Month	**Engineered**	**First Red Pack**	**First Red Stack**
stub	54		
Dec '99	99		
Mar '00	105		
Jun '00	97		
Sep '00	94		
Dec '00	94	137	544
Mar '01	92	137	
Jun '01	91	137	
Sep '01	12	137	
Total contracts	738	548	544
Daily standard deviation	$61	$46,406	$40,026
Percent risk reduction	99.97%	79.61%	82.42%

Treasury note. For a hedger interested in minimizing basis risk, this is the right approach. It may not, however, suit the purposes of a speculative trader for whom a certain amount of decorrelation between Treasurys and Eurodollar futures is necessary for profitable trading opportunities to exist.

The challenge then for the speculator—or for the hedger who wants to improve the odds—is to identify, for any given Treasury note, which curve TEDs are out of line and whether they are sufficiently out of line to offer the prospect of a profitable trade.

The best way to understand how a *curve TED* spread trade works is to break it down into its two components—a standard weighted TED spread trade and a Eurodollar curve spread trade.

$$\textit{Curve TED} = \textit{Standard TED} + \textit{Curve spread}$$

Consider, for example, the curve TED trade illustrated in Exhibit 13.14. In this case, the trader buys a 2-year Treasury note and

EXHIBIT 13.14

Deconstructing a Curve TED Spread

	ED Contract Month	*A curve TED spread . . .* Tsy	ED	*. . . equals a standard TED spread . . .* Tsy	ED	*. . . plus a curve spread* ED
White	Sep '99	Long		Long	−100	100
	Dec '99	the		the	−98	98
	Mar '00	2-year		2-year	−104	104
	Jun '00	note		note	−95	95
Red	Sep-00		−179		−94	−85
	Dec '00		−179		−93	−86
	Mar '01		−179		−92	−87
	Jun '01		−179		−41	−138
	Total		−716		−717	1

sells 179 of the red pack. This trade can (and should) be thought of as the sum of two separate trades. First, as shown in the middle column, the trader is long the standard 2-year term TED spread, which is long the 2-year note and short a weighted strip of Eurodollar futures. Second, as shown in the right-hand column, the trader is long the white contracts and short the red contracts and is, as a result, long the slope of the 2-year Eurodollar curve. The standard 2-year term TED will profit from an increase in the pure credit spread between LIBOR and Treasury yields. The curve spread will profit if the 2-year segment of the Eurodollar futures rate curve steepens as shown in Exhibit 13.15. For this part of the trade to profit, "red" futures rates must rise relative to "white" futures rates.

Calculating the Hybrid Spread

Tracking the performance of a curve TED requires a consistent measure of the value of the hybrid spread. Perhaps the best and simplest way to do this is to begin with a measure of the standard

EXHIBIT 13.15

The Curve Trade Implied by a Red Pack Hedge for a 2-Year Treasury Note

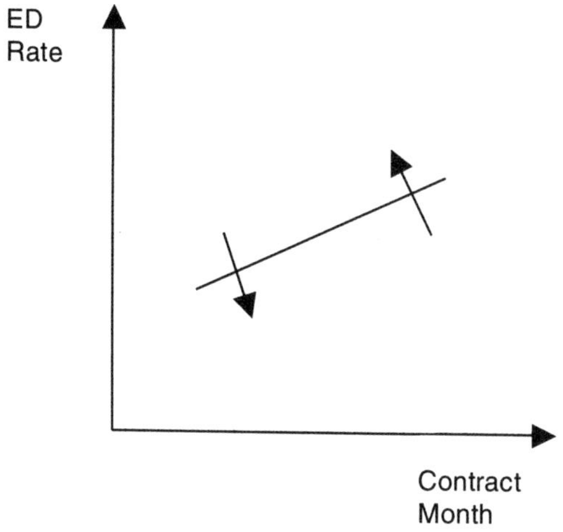

TED spread. To this can be added the difference between the average rate at which the trader is short Eurodollar futures and the average rate at which the trader is long Eurodollar futures in the curve part of the trade. For this kind of addition to work correctly, the two spreads should be quoted in like terms. Since the curve spread is an average of quarterly money market rates, any measure of the TED spread that is measured in semiannual bond equivalent yield terms (for example, the implied yield and implied price TEDs that one finds on Bloomberg) should be converted to quarterly money market basis points. Or one could use the spread-adjusted TED (what we call the fixed basis point spread to Eurodollar rates), which is quoted in quarterly money market basis points by definition. Or, finally, one could convert the Eurodollar curve spread from quarterly money market basis points into semiannual bond equivalent basis points. In this note, we express everything in money market terms.

A correct reckoning of the curve spread requires only that the value of a basis point change in the value of the curve spread be the same as the value of a basis point change in the standard TED spread. In this example, the standard weighted hedge for the Treasury note has a total of 717 Eurodollar contracts so that the value of a basis point is $17,925 [= 717 contracts × $25 per contract per basis point]. Thus, for the purposes of calculating the curve spread, we should think of the curve trade in terms of the gross trades needed to add the curve trade.

As shown in Exhibit 13.16, the curve trade we are adding to the TED trade could be accomplished by buying the strip of Eurodollar futures shown under the "long" column and selling the strip of Eurodollar futures shown under the "short" column. (The actual trade would simply be the net of these two strips.) Given these contracts and the closing values of the Eurodollar contract rates for August 4, the average rate at which the trader is short is 6.669 percent, and the average rate at which the trader is long is 6.244 percent. The difference is 0.425%, or 42.5 basis points, which can be added to the value of the 2-year term TED spread, which was 71.4 basis points. Taken together, the value of the curve TED spread would be 113.9 basis points [= 71.4 + 42.5].

Similar adaptations of the standard TED spread can be done for other kinds of TED hedges. For example, if the trader decided to hedge the 2-year note with the first red stack, the curve exposure would be an odd sort of butterfly, as shown in Exhibit 13.17.

EXHIBIT 13.16

Calculating the Curve Spread

Contract Month	Contracts Long	Contracts Short	Rate
Sep '99	100		5.495
Dec '99	98		5.935
Mar '00	104		5.980
Jun '00	95		6.270
Sep '00	94	−179	6.475
Dec '00	93	−179	6.715
Mar '01	92	−179	6.705
Jun '01	41	−179	6.780
Total contracts	717	−716	
Average rate	6.244	6.669	
Curve spread	0.425		

EXHIBIT 13.17

Curve Exposure

	Contract Month	Hedge Approach		
		Stack	Pack	Bundle
White	Sep '99	100	100	10
	Dec '99	98	98	8
	Mar '00	104	104	14
	Jun '00	95	95	5
Red	Sep '00	−623	−85	4
	Dec '00	93	−86	3
	Mar '01	92	−87	2
	Jun '01	41	−138	−49
	Net	0	1	−3

To achieve this, the trader could be thought of as buying back the original Eurodollar strip and selling 717 of the first red contract (red Sep in this case). Thus, the trader would be short at a rate of 6.475 percent (the rate for the red Sep contract in Exhibit 13.16) and long at an average rate of 6.244 percent. The curve spread would then be 0.231 percent, or 23.1 basis points.

Looking for Opportunities

If the trader wants to augment a standard TED spread with a curve spread, the next challenge is to find the best opportunities. One perspective is provided by the change in a particular kind of curve spread through time. Exhibit 13.18, for example, shows how generic versions of the stack, pack, and bundle curve spreads described in Exhibit 13.17 behaved over the past 5 years. Not too surprisingly, the curve spread produced by substituting a 2-year bundle for the engineered hedge was very stable. Rarely, for that matter, was this curve spread more than 2 or 3 basis points.

The stack and pack spreads, on the other hand, proved to be really quite volatile. In the stack curve spread, for example, you can see the curvature of the forward rate curve increase and de-

EXHIBIT 13.18

Generic Eurodollar Curve Spreads

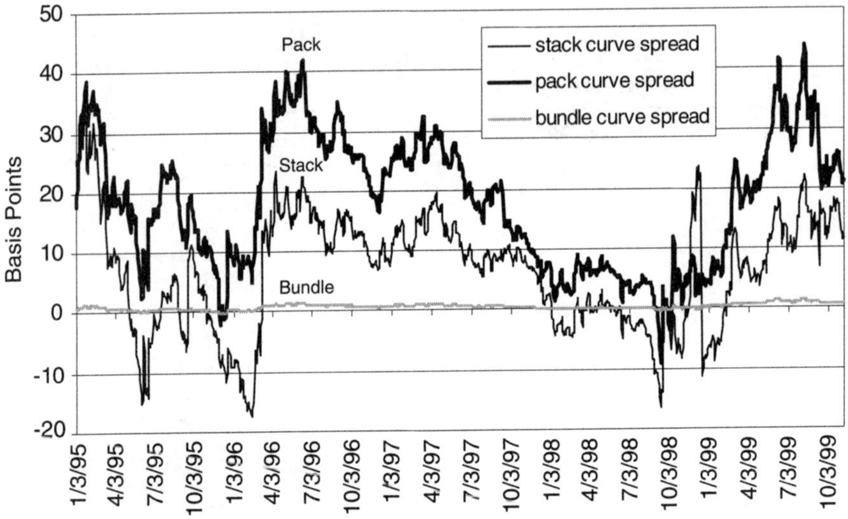

crease as the value of the spread rises and falls. And, in the pack curve spread, you can see the slope of the forward rate curve increase and decrease as the value of the spread rises and falls.

The effect of appending the pack curve spread to a conventional 2-year TED spread is illustrated in Exhibit 13.19. The lightest line tracks the value of the 2-year TED spread, and the darkest line tracks the value of the pack curve spread. The value of the augmented pack curve TED is traced out by the third line. In this history, the two components of the pack curve TED exhibit a considerable degree of independence. Over the period shown, the correlation of weekly changes in the values of the 2-year TED spread and the pack curve spread was 0.10.

To the extent the two components of the pack curve TED spread are uncorrelated, the pack curve TED spread will have desirable risk/return characteristics. A curve TED spread represents a diversified portfolio of two separate spreads—namely the pack curve spread and the conventional TED spread. Thus, during those intervals when the pack curve spread and the conventional TED spread are uncorrelated with each other, the pack curve TED

EXHIBIT 13.19

Augmenting a 2-Year TED Spread

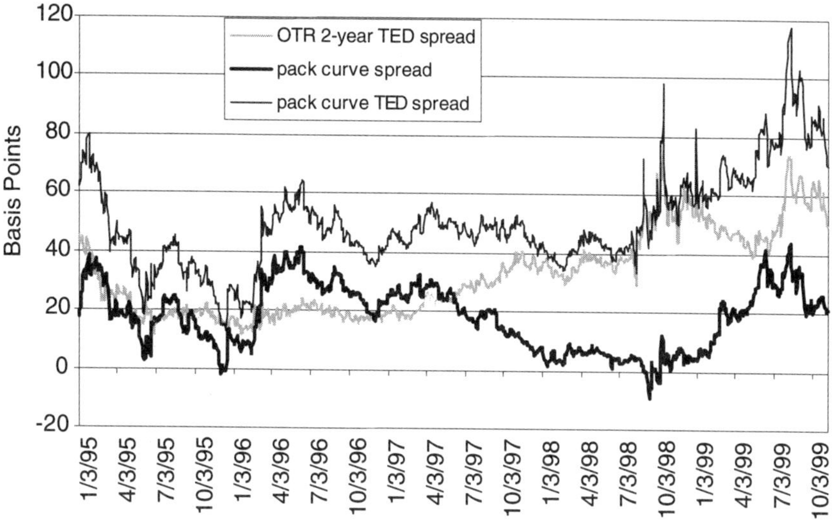

should exhibit less risk for any given expected return than will the conventional TED spread by itself.

Consider the recent experience with both parts of the spread trading at historically rich levels—that is, the 2-year TED spread above 60 basis points and the pack curve spread above 40 basis points. At these values, a trader could have sold either of the spreads by themselves. Combining them, though, by selling a Treasury note and buying red packs could have produced a trade with the same potential gain but with less risk.

In this case, the trade opportunity is presented by a steepening of the Eurodollar rate curve in the white and red years. In augmenting a TED trade, one has a much longer menu of curve trades from which to choose.

CHAPTER 14

Hedging Extension and Compression Risk in Callable Agency Notes

Galen Burghardt and William Hoskins
Research note originally released March 24, 1995

SYNOPSIS

The federal financing agencies have raised well over $150 billion by issuing callable notes, and some of these issues have been large. In January, for example, the Federal National Mortgage Agency (FNMA) issued a $1 billion global bond that was offered to the world at large.

The street's experience with hedging these issues has been hugely disappointing. Because of the embedded call options, these issues behave like short-term notes when yields are low and falling. But when yields are high and rising, the calls drop out of the money and the notes begin to behave like long-term notes. The result is a compression of capital gains when rates fall and an acceleration of capital losses when rates rise. The risk in this kind of note is known variously as compression risk (when yields are already high) and extension risk (when yields are already low). In either case, the consequences of rate changes can be ugly. Also, underwriters and market makers complain that the spreads between the yields on callable agency notes and the yields on Treasury notes are far too variable to allow effective hedging.

Much of this disappointment almost certainly stems from the practice of treating a 10-year note that can be called anytime after 5 years as if its maturity and duration are simply somewhere between those of a 10-year note and those of a 5-year note. The mistake is in treating the call provision as if it does nothing more than shorten the maturity and lower the effective duration of the note. This approach may work well enough when the yield curve rises or falls in parallel, but it does nothing to capture the yield curve exposure that is contained in a callable note.

An effective hedge can be constructed only by taking apart the risk exposure and dealing with the different sources of risk separately. This note shows how to isolate the forward yield risk exposure in the embedded call options from the spot yield risk exposure in the bullet part of the issue. In the process, we show how to capture yield curve risk as well as yield level risk. Examples of what these hedges look like are shown in Exhibit 14.9 (using Treasury futures) and in Exhibits 14.14 and 14.15 (using Eurodollar futures).

We also find that much of the apparent volatility of yield spreads over Treasurys can be explained by changes in the slope and shape of the yield curve. Exhibit 14.1, which shows the spread for a 10-year note callable in 5, illustrates this quite vividly.

INTRODUCTION

Although some callable agency notes have no call protection, a typical note will specify a period during which it cannot be called. The note illustrated in Exhibit 14.2, for example, has an original maturity of 10 years. During the first 5 of these years, the agency cannot call the note. Once the 5-year mark has been passed, the

EXHIBIT 14.1

Callable Agency Yield Spread over 10-Year Treasury
Yield Spread in Basis Points

5-Year Yield Shift (bps)	*10-Year Yield Shift* (bps)				
	−50	**−25**	**0**	**25**	**50**
−50	90	75	63	53	45
−25	100	84	70	59	49
0	110	93	78	65	55
25	121	103	87	73	61
50	133	114	96	81	68

EXHIBIT 14.2

Structure of a Callable Agency Security

10-Year Note That Cannot Be Called During the First 5 Years of Its Life

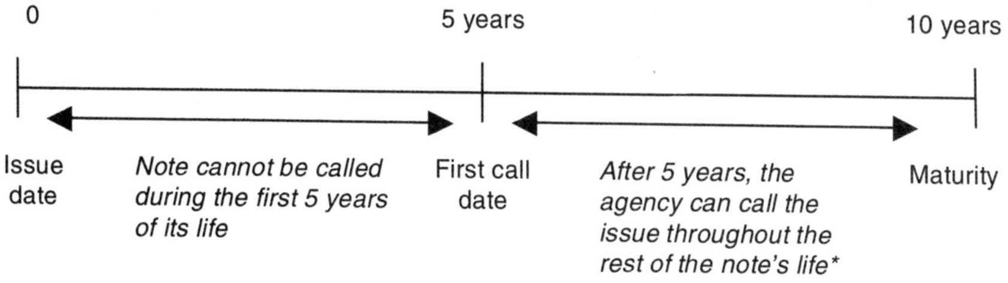

*Call provisions vary from agency to agency and, in some instances, from note to note. Some notes are callable only on coupon dates with appropriate notice, while others are callable anytime with appropriate notice.

agency has the right to redeem or call the note at par throughout the remaining life of the note. Notes issued by the Federal Home Loan Banks typically are callable on coupon dates with 10 days notice. Notes issued by the Federal National Mortgage Agency (FNMA) typically are callable any time during the call period with 30 days notice. Typical maturities and no-call periods for these agency issues are shown in Exhibit 14.3.

The key to hedging notes like these effectively is to think of a callable note as a package that combines a noncallable bullet note with one or more call options. This approach allows the

EXHIBIT 14.3

Standard Maturities and Call Features

Years to Maturity	*Number of Years of Call Protection*				
2	1				
3	1	2			
5	1	2	3		
7	1	2	3	4	
10	1	2	3		5

hedger to separate the term yield risk in the bullet from the forward yield risk in the forward notes that underlie the embedded call options. Once this is done, it is easy to construct durable hedges using either cash instruments or futures contracts. Also, we find that much of the apparent yield spread risk between callable notes and Treasurys can be explained by changes in the relationship between term and forward yields. The main steps in this process include:

- Finding the yield curve exposure in a callable note
- Structuring robust delta hedges with cash instruments
- Substituting Treasury note futures or Eurodollar futures for cash instruments

Along the way, we explain the risks in delta hedging and what can be done about them, and what to do if the note has little or no call protection.

Much of the success of this approach hinges on finding the most likely call date. For issues with a lot of call protection, the most likely call date is the first call date. For issues with little or no call protection, the most likely call date depends, among other things, on both the level and volatility of interest rates. To simplify the presentation, we begin with a comparatively simple example in which the issue has 10 years to maturity and 5 years of call protection. In this example, the issuer's right to call at 5 years is far and away the most valuable option.

What Is the Exposure in a Callable Agency Issue?

For anyone who owns these issues, however briefly, the embedded call options can pose particularly ugly exposure problems. If interest rates fall, the likelihood that the issuing agency will redeem the note at par goes up and the note begins to behave as if it matures on the first call date rather than at the maturity. If interest rates fall enough, a 10-year note callable after 5 years would exhibit the price behavior of a 5-year note because the financial world would be confident that the issuing agency will redeem or call the note at the 5-year mark. On the other hand, if interest rates rise enough, the agency would not be expected to call the note, and the note would exhibit the price behavior of a 10-year note.

Extension and Compression Risk

The result is a note whose price rises more like that of a 5-year note when yields are low and falling and falls like that of a 10-year note when yields are high and rising. This kind of behavior, which is the worst of both worlds, can be described as either extension risk, or compression risk depending on your point of view. When yields are low and the issue is behaving like a short-term note, the risk is that yields will rise and the issue will begin to behave like a longer-term note. This is the extension risk. When yields are high, on the other hand, and the issue is behaving like a long-term note, the risk is that yields will fall, the call features will kick in, and the issue will begin to behave like a short-term note. This is the compression risk.

A Packaged Deal

The best way to understand the risks in a callable note is to think of it as a package that combines a noncallable note with a short option on a forward note. The noncallable note's coupon and maturity would be the same as those of the agency note. The underlying for the short option would be a noncallable note with the same coupon as the agency's and a maturity equal to the remaining life of the agency issue at the time the option can be exercised. In Exhibit 14.2, the noncallable note has a maturity of 10 years, and the underlying for the short option is a 5-year note, 5 years forward.

A package like this is illustrated in Exhibit 14.4.

What Is the Package Worth?

The value of the package is simply the sum of the values of the parts. The investor's position is like that of someone who is long a noncallable note and short a strip of call options. As a result, to price a callable agency issue, all we have to do (in principle) is price a noncallable note with a coupon and maturity equal to that

EXHIBIT 14.4

Components of Risk in a Callable Note
10-Year Note, Callable in 5 Years

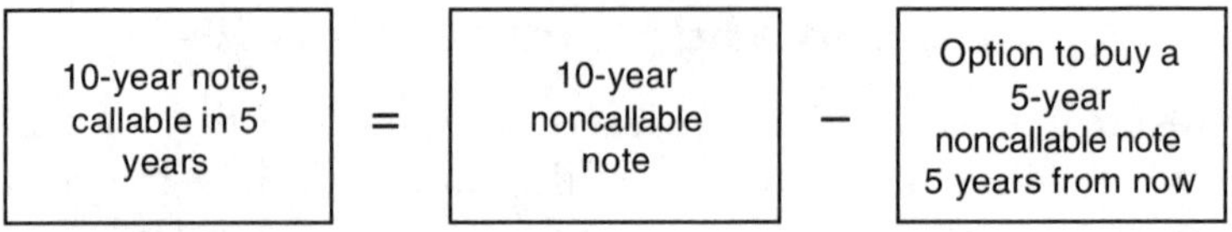

of the callable note and subtract from that the total value of the option package.

What Is the Risk Exposure?

Looking at the issue this way makes plain what has to be done to hedge it. In particular, we see that we have two kinds of instruments—one a note and one an option on a note. Also, we see that we face two different underlying sources of interest rate risk. For the agency issue in Exhibit 14.4, the price of the 10-year note is driven by the term yield on a 10-year note. The price of the embedded option is driven by the yield on a 5-year note 5 years forward. An effective hedge, then, will tackle these risks separately.

STRUCTURING A HEDGE

How you hedge such an instrument will depend on which of the risks most worry you and on whether you can lay your hands on the right hedging tools. For example, offsetting the risk in the noncallable part of the note is a comparatively straightforward task that entails little more than selling a Treasury note or noncallable agency note with a similar coupon and maturity. One also can hedge this risk with Treasury note futures or, in many instances, with strips of Eurodollar futures.

The Option Is Tougher

The most straightforward hedge for the embedded short option positions would be a long position in an identical package of options, which would be a forward-starting American-style swaption. Such a package could be purchased in the over-the-counter (OTC) market. This strategy would make sense if the objective in buying the callable notes were to profit from a mispricing of the embedded options. That is, if the embedded options were more expensive than the offsetting OTC package, the hedged position would provide a higher yield than a conventional noncallable note.

Buying an offsetting package of OTC options might not be the best strategy, however, for a dealer whose business is underwriting agency debt. Once the issue has been sold and is out the door, the underwriter no longer needs the hedge. To unwind the option part, though, the underwriter would have to sell an OTC option package identical to the one it bought as part of the hedge. And because this also has to be done in the OTC market, the underwriter would be left with both long and short OTC options and a trailing credit exposure in the long option package until it expires.

For anyone who wants a temporary hedge, the challenge is to find a hedge that adequately captures the risk in the callable note, that can be put on and taken off at low cost, and that leaves no trailing credit exposure once the need for the hedge has passed. As it is, such a hedge is too good to be true. But we can, by focusing on the sources of yield curve exposure in the note, produce delta hedges that should do a first-rate job of capturing the directional risk in a callable agency note.

Focus on Delta Hedging

In general, the directional exposure in a callable note can be expressed approximately as

$$\textit{Callable note exposure} \approx \textit{Noncallable note } DV01 - (\textit{Embedded call delta} \times \textit{Forward note } DV01)$$

where $DV01$ represents the dollar value of a basis point change in the underlying yield and the call delta is the delta today of the agency's option to redeem the note at par when the no-call period is over. One good thing about writing out the exposure this way is that it underscores the separate sources of risk in the issue. A common mistake people make when hedging callable issues is to assume that noncallable and forward note yields rise and fall in parallel. With this assumption, one can calculate a hybrid *DV*01 for the callable note that makes it look as if it behaves like a note whose maturity is somewhere between the note's first call date and its final maturity. And having done this, one can easily make the mistake of hedging the callable note as if it were simply a noncallable note with a shorter maturity.

We know, however, that parallel shifts in the yield curve are an exception rather than the rule. The only hedges that will prove effective in the face of yield changes while the curve is steepening or flattening are those that address the separate sources of risk separately.

Consider, for example, a 10-year issue that is callable in 5 years. Suppose, too, that the embedded call is around the money so that its delta is 0.50. In a case like this, the directional risk in $10 million of the callable issue would be the same as the directional risk in a long position of $10 million of a noncallable 10-year note combined with a short position of, say, $5 million of a 5-year note 5 years forward. The best way to hedge the directional exposure in this case would be to sell $10 million of a 10-year noncallable note and to buy $5 million of a 5-year noncallable note 5 years forward. In both cases, the spot and forward notes would have coupons equal to the callable note's coupon. Done this way, the hedge provides protection against the 10-year bullet exposure and against the callable note's exposure to changes in 5-year rates 5 years forward.

Synthetic Forward Notes

The main hurdle to doing this hedge is that there is not much of a market for the forward note the hedger needs to put this kind of delta hedge together. A substitute for the missing security, however, is fairly easy to create. As shown in Exhibit 14.5, the equivalent of a 5-year note 5 years forward can be constructed by combining a long position in a 10-year note with a short position in a 5-year note.

The effect of using the synthetic equivalent of the forward note is illustrated in Exhibit 14.6 for a case in which the delta of the embedded call is 0.5. Hedge 1 shows the direct hedge, which deals with the problem by offsetting each source of exposure separately. The 10-year exposure is hedged by selling $10 million of

EXHIBIT 14.5

Constructing a Synthetic Forward Note

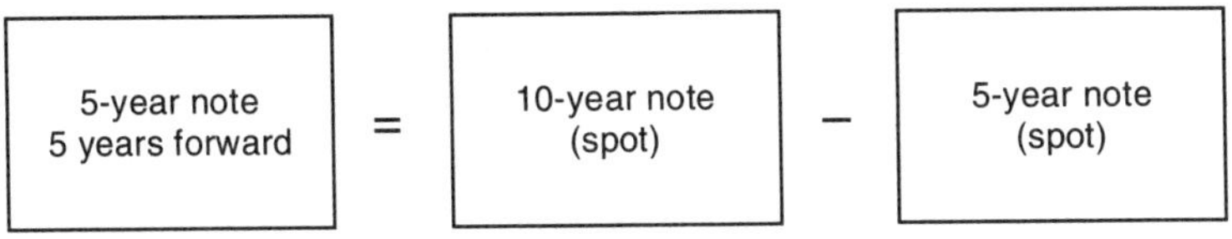

EXHIBIT 14.6

Alternative Hedges for a 10-Year Note Callable in 5 Years

Call Option's Delta = 0.5

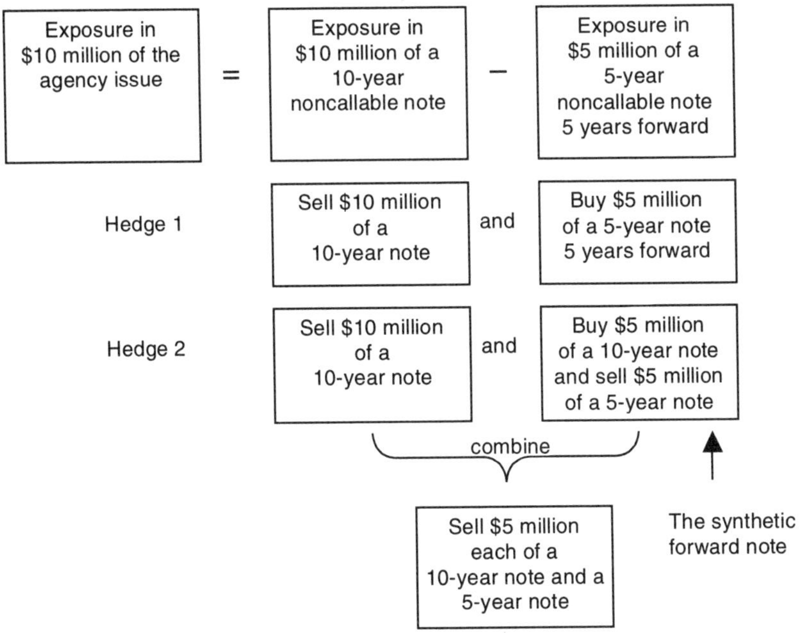

a noncallable 10-year note, and the exposure to the 5-year note 5 years forward is hedged by buying $5 million of the 5-year note 5 years forward. Such a hedge would leave the position with no directional exposure.

Hedge 2 shows what happens if we substitute a long position in a synthetic forward note for the actual forward note. In this case, the synthetic forward would include a long position of $5 million in a 10-year note and a short position of $5 million in a 5-year note instead of a long position of $5 million in a 5-year note 5 years forward. If we buy the synthetic note, notice that the $5 million of the 10-year note that we buy to construct the synthetic forward note offsets half of the $10 million of the 10-year note that we would sell to hedge the exposure to the 10-year noncallable note. Netting the two, we find that we can sell just $5 million of the 10-year note. And, if we do, the combined net hedge would comprise short positions of $5 million each in the 10-year and 5-year notes.

This is not the same, of course, as selling $10 million of something like a 7.5-year note, even though the average maturity or duration may be the same as that of the best hedge. By selling 10s and 5s, the hedger captures exposure to changes in the slope of the yield curve as well as to changes in the general level of yields.

Different Deltas

This kind of financial algebra is extremely useful for constructing economical and effective hedges. Consider how things look if the embedded call delta is 1.00. In this case, yields are so low that there is no question in anyone's mind (at least not in the mind of anyone in the options market) that the issuing agency will redeem the note at the first possible opportunity. If this is the case, then the market will trade the agency issue as if it were a 5-year note. If you wanted no directional price exposure, you would have to sell $10 million of a noncallable 5-year note.

Or suppose that the call's delta is 0.25. In this case, yields are high and the likelihood that the issuing agency will call the note is about one in four. As a result, the note is behaving as if it were a combination of $7.5 million of a 10-year noncallable note and $2.5 million of a 5-year noncallable note. In this case the hedger would have to sell $7.5 million of a 10-year note and sell $2.5 million of a 5-year note.

If the call's delta is zero, the option market's guess is that the agency will never call the note. In this case, the market will treat the issue as if it were a 10-year noncallable note, and it can be hedged simply by selling $10 million of a 10-year note.

EXHIBIT 14.7

Delta Hedges for $10 Million of a Callable Agency Note
10-Year Maturity, Callable in 5 Years

Call Delta	Hedge	
1.00	Sell $10 5-year	↑ If the embedded option's delta is greater than 0.5, the hedger's concern is extension risk
0.75	Sell $2.5 10-year, Sell $7.5 5-year	
0.50	Sell $5 10-year, Sell $5 5-year	
0.25	Sell $7.5 10-year, Sell $2.5 5-year	↓ If the embedded option's delta is less than 0.5, the hedger's concern is compression risk
0.00	Sell $10 10-year	

In general, as the marginal comments in Exhibit 14.7 indicate, the kind of risk the hedger faces hinges on the delta of the embedded call. If the embedded call's delta is greater than 0.50 because interest rates are low, then the issue is behaving mainly like a 5-year note, and the hedger is concerned with extension risk. On the other hand, if the delta is less than 0.50 because interest rates are high, then the issue is behaving more like a 10-year note, and the hedger's big concern is compression risk.

EXAMPLE OF HEDGING A 10-YEAR, 8.5 PERCENT COUPON NOTE, CALLABLE IN 5 YEARS

A lot can be learned by working through an example of how one would construct a hedge. For this example, we will work with a 10-year, 8.5 percent coupon note with 5 years of call protection. This resembles the FNMA global issue that was brought to market in January 1995. The steps in finding the hedge are:

- Find the forward price of the note underlying the embedded call
- Find the embedded option's delta for changes in the forward price

- Calculate spot market hedge ratios
- Calculate futures hedge ratios
- Adjust the hedge as interest rates change

All of the information we need to work through this example is displayed in Exhibit 14.8, which shows how to price a forward note using spot bullet issues, and Exhibit 14.9, which is an example of our hedge report.

Step 1: Find the Price of the Forward Note

To value the embedded call option, you have to know the price of the underlying, which is a 5-year note, 5 years forward. That

EXHIBIT 14.8

How to Price a Forward Note

10-year note (spot)	–	5-year note (spot)	=	5-year note 5 years forward

Today	
Pay	103.19 to buy a 10-year, 8.5% coupon noncallable agency issue
Receive	102.28 on the sale of a 5-year, 8.5% coupon noncallable agency issue
Net pay	0.91 [= 103.19 – 102.28] per $100 par amount of the transaction
Sell	1.35 [= 0.91/0.6774] par amount of a 5-year zero-coupon bond at 0.6774 to finance this outlay
Between Today and 5 Years from Now	
	The 8.5% coupon received on the 10-year note just offsets the 8.5% coupon paid on the 5-year note
5 Years from Today	
Pay	100.00 to redeem the 5-year issue that you sold today
Pay	1.35 to redeem the 5-year zero you sold today
Total pay	101.35 [= 100.00 + 1.35] is the final price of the 5-year, 8.5% coupon noncallable agency issue 5 years from today

EXHIBIT 14.9

Callable Agency Hedge: 10-Year Callable in 5
Trade January 20, 1995, Settlement January 30, 1995

A: Callable Agency Specs

					Call Dates		
Coupon	Maturity	Spread	YTM	Price	First	Most Likely	Size ($MM)
8.50%	2/1/05	78 bps	8.54%	99.73	2/1/00	2/1/00	100

B: Treasury Data / No-Call Agency Spread

Term	Coupon	Maturity	YTM	No-Call Sprd (bps)
5 yr	7.75%	1/31/00	7.74%	20 bps
10 yr	8.75%	11/15/95	7.76%	27 bps

C: No-Call Agency Forward Price

Instrument	Interp Tsy Yld	Interp Tsy Sprd	YTM	Price
5 yr bullet	7.74%	20 bps	7.94%	102.28
10 yr bullet	7.76%	27 bps	8.03%	103.19
5 yr zero coupon			7.74%	67.74
5 yr bullet, 5 yrs fwd			8.17%	101.35

D: Option Valuation

		Volatility		Delta		Vega	
Value	Days	Yield	Price	Fwd px	Spot px	Price	Yield
3.46	1828	14.74%					
assumed volatility →		12.85%	4.20%	0.39	0.58	0.61	0.20

E: Hedge Quantities

Agency Hedge $MM		DV01s for $100,000 par amount: Agency bullets		DV01s for $100,000 par amount: March Futures		Futures Hedge #	
5 yr	10 yr	5 yr	10 yr	5 yr	10 yr	5 yr	10 yr
57.5	42.5	41.21	69.32	37.20	57.52	637.3	511.9

Note: All prices are in decimal.

F: Spot Price Delta

5 yr Treasury Yield Shift			10 yr Treasury Yield Shift: 7.26% -50 bps	7.51% -25 bps	7.76% 0 bps	8.01% 25 bps	8.26% 50 bps
	7.24%	-50 bps	0.657	0.554	0.447	0.343	0.249
	7.49%	-25 bps	0.714	0.617	0.511	0.405	0.304
	7.74%	0 bps	0.766	0.676	0.575	0.468	0.364
	7.99%	25 bps	0.812	0.732	0.637	0.533	0.426
	8.24%	50 bps	0.852	0.782	0.695	0.596	0.490

G: Cash Market Hedge (short 5yr / 10 yr Agency bullets $MM par)

5 yr Treasury Yield Shift			10 yr Treasury Yield Shift: 7.26% -50 bps	7.51% -25 bps	7.76% 0 bps	8.01% 25 bps	8.26% 50 bps
	7.24%	-50 bps	65.7/34.3	55.4/44.6	44.7/55.3	34.3/65.7	4.9/75.1
	7.49%	-25 bps	71.4/28.6	61.7/38.3	51.1/48.9	40.5/59.5	30.4/69.6
	7.74%	0 bps	76.6/23.4	67.6/32.4	57.5/42.5	46.8/53.2	36.4/63.6
	7.99%	25 bps	81.2/18.8	73.2/26.8	63.7/36.3	53.3/46.7	42.6/57.4
	8.24%	50 bps	85.2/14.8	78.2/21.8	69.5/30.5	59.6/40.4	49.0/51.0

H: Note Futures Hedge Quantities (Short 5 yr / 10 yr Futures)

5 yr Treasury Yield Shift			10 yr Treasury Yield Shift: 7.26% -50 bps	7.51% -25 bps	7.76% 0 bps	8.01% 25 bps	8.26% 50 bps
	7.24%	-50 bps	728/413	614/538	495/667	380/792	276/905
	7.49%	-25 bps	791/345	683/462	566/589	448/718	337/839
	7.74%	0 bps	848/282	749/390	637/512	519/641	403/767
	7.99%	25 bps	899/227	811/323	706/437	590/563	472/692
	8.24%	50 bps	943/179	866/263	770/367	661/486	543/614

is, you have to know how much you would pay 5 years from now for a note with the appropriate coupon and that matures 5 years later, or 10 years from now. To find this price, consider what it would cost to construct such a note using noncallable 5-year and 10-year notes. As shown in Exhibit 14.8, the price of a 5-year, 8.5 percent noncallable note yielding 20 basis points over the 5-year Treasury yield of 7.74 percent on January 20, 1995, is 102.28 (decimal). The price of a 10-year, 8.5 percent coupon noncallable note yielding 27 basis points over the 10-year Treasury yield of 7.76 percent is 103.19. Note, too, that the price of a 5-year, zero-coupon issue is 67.74 per $100 par amount.

At these prices, you can construct today a synthetic 5-year, 8.5 percent coupon note 5 years forward by buying the 10-year issue and selling the 5-year issue. At the prices on January 20, this would require a net cash outlay of $0.91 [= 103.19 − 102.28] per $100 face amount of the transaction. For the purposes of this exercise, you would finance this cash outlay by selling a 5-year zero-coupon bond, which allows you to borrow for 5 years without making any cash interest payments between now and 5 years from now. As shown in Exhibit 14.8, you would have to sell $1.35 [= 0.91/0.6774] par amount of the zero to cover the difference in the two prices. Notice that because you borrow the difference between the purchase of the 10-year note and the sale price of the 5-year note, your net cash outlay today is zero.

For the next 5 years, the two coupon streams just offset one another. That is, the coupon income on your long position in the 10-year bullet just covers the coupon outlay on your short position in the 5-year bullet.

At the 5-year mark, you have to pay out two amounts of money—$100.00 to cover the bullet payment on the 5-year note that you sold at the outset and $1.35 to redeem the zero-coupon bond that you sold. Taken together, your total cash outlay in 5 years is $101.35 per $100 par amount, and you are left with the last 5 years of the original 10-year issue.

The price, then, of the noncallable 5-year, 8.5% coupon note 5 years forward is simply $101.35. This is the price of the underlying that we plug into an option pricing model to find the embedded call's delta.

Before we do this, though, it is important to lay out the relationship between this forward price and the spot prices of the notes used in the forward note's construction. In particular, we can write the price of the forward note as

$$\textit{Forward price} = 100 + \left[\frac{\textit{10-yr spot price} - \textit{5-yr spot price}}{\textit{5-yr zero price}}\right]$$

where 100 is the par value of the note. The expression in brackets is the forward value of the difference between the spot prices of the 10-year and 5-year notes. This expression will prove to be especially useful because it is the link between the price of the forward note that underlies the embedded option and the spot prices of the notes we will use to construct the actual delta hedge.

Step 2: Find the Embedded Option's Delta

To calculate the option's delta, we need a measure of the implied volatility of the 5-year forward note's price. We can get a first approximation of this by comparing the price of the callable note, which is 99.73 (or 99-23/32nds) in this example, with the price of a 10-year noncallable note, which is 103.19. These prices are shown in panels A and C of Exhibit 14.9. The difference between the two, or 3.46, is what the issuing agency is paying for the right to call the note and is shown as the value of the option in panel D. Using 3.46 as the option price, 101.35 as the price of the underlying forward note, and the Black model for pricing European calls on forwards, we get an implied price volatility of 4.84 percent. This level of price volatility corresponds to a yield volatility for the forward note of 14.74 percent.

In practice, we want to use a slightly smaller implied volatility for calculating the option's theoretical delta. This is because the issuing agency has more than a simple European call on the issue at 5 years. Rather, the agency has a string of options that allow it to call the note almost any time between 5 years and maturity. These "backup" calls contribute a small amount to the value of the package of calls. For this example, we make a reasonable allowance for their contribution and use an implied volatility of 4.20 percent, or a yield volatility of 12.85 percent, for calculating the delta of the first—and most important—of the note's embedded call options.

With these assumptions, we find that the option's delta for changes in the forward note's price is 0.39. That is, a $1 increase in the forward price of the forward note would increase the value of the embedded call by $0.39. This delta may seem small for an option that is in the money, but the delta represents the change in the present value of the right to exercise the option. If we were close enough to the call date, the delta would be greater than 0.50, but 5 years of discounting reduces the present value a great deal.

If we plan to use 5-year and 10-year bullet notes, however, we need a measure of the embedded option's spot price delta. That is, we need to know the change in the value of the option for a $1 change in the prices of the 5-year and 10-year notes. To find the spot price deltas, all we need is the linkage between the spot and forward prices, which we already know is:

$$\textit{Forward price} = 100 + \left[\frac{\textit{10-yr spot price} - \textit{5-yr spot price}}{\textit{5-yr zero price}}\right]$$

From this, we see that a $1 increase in the spot price of the 10-year note increases the forward price by $1 divided by the price of a 5-year zero. In our example, this would be 1.48 [= $1.00/ $0.6774]. Chaining this together with the option's forward price delta of 0.39, we find that the option's spot price delta is 0.58 [= 0.39 × 1.48] for changes in the price of the 10-year note. Similarly, we see that a $1 increase in the spot price of the 5-year note decreases the forward price by $1.48. As a result, the option's spot price delta for changes in the price of the 5-year note would be −0.58 [= 0.39 × −1.48]. The only difference between the deltas for changes in the 10-year and 5-year notes' prices is the sign. In general, the option's spot deltas are simply

$$\textit{10-yr spot price delta} = \left[\frac{\textit{Forward price delta}}{\textit{5-yr zero price}}\right]$$

$$\textit{5-yr spot price delta} = -\left[\frac{\textit{Forward price delta}}{\textit{5-yr zero price}}\right]$$

where the forward price deltas are the standard output from an option pricing model.

Step 3: Calculate Spot Market Hedge Ratios

Now we can use the simple hedge algebra illustrated in Exhibit 14.6. The owner of this callable note can think of it as a long position in an 8.5 percent coupon, 10-year noncallable note together with a short call option on an 8.5 percent coupon, 5-year note, 5 years forward. With spot deltas of 0.58 for the 10-year note and −0.58 for the 5-year note, the effect of being short the embedded call is like that of selling 0.58 of the 10-year note and buying 0.58 of the 5-year note. Thus, the investor's net exposure in the callable note can be summarized as

$$10\text{-}yr\ note\ exposure = 1.00 - 0.58 = 0.42$$

$$5\text{-}yr\ note\ exposure = 0.00 + 0.58 = 0.58$$

In other words, the risk exposure in $100 million of the callable note is like the risk exposure in a position that combines $42 million of the 10-year noncallable note with $58 million of the 5-year noncallable note.

And, if our interest in hedging the callable note is to remove any directional exposure to changes in 5-year and 10-year interest rates, we would sell $42 million of the 10-year noncallable note and sell $58 million of the 5-year noncallable note. This hedge, with slightly greater precision, is shown in the center of panel G of Exhibit 14.9.

As a reasonableness check, we should satisfy ourselves that these measures of risk exposure make sense. We know that the forward note price is above par so the issuer's call option is in the money. As a result, the callable note should tend to behave more like a 5-year note than a 10-year note. Thus, finding that the risk equivalent of the callable note is $58 million of a 5-year note and $42 million of a 10-year note should seem right.

Step 4: Calculate Futures Hedge Ratios

The spot hedges in Step 3 would be done with noncallable agencies or Treasury notes with appropriate coupons and maturities. The next step is to do the best possible job of hedging the position with futures. In some cases, especially those involving maturities over 5 years, the best available hedging tools would be Treasury note futures. In other cases, especially those involving issues with shorter maturities or those with little or no call protection, Eurodollar futures can provide a better match. In all cases, though, the problem of hedging with futures comes down to nothing more than replicating adequately the 5-year and 10-year bullets with futures.

This example provides a good opportunity to use Treasury note futures. We can, for example, sell 10-year Treasury note futures as a reasonable proxy for selling the 10-year noncallable note. And we can use 5-year Treasury note futures in lieu of selling the 5-year noncallable note. To find the appropriate number of contracts in each case, we simply calculate the standard hedge ratios for each issue. For example, the 8.5 percent coupon 5-year noncallable note has a dollar value of a basis point (*DV*01) of \$41.21 per \$100,000 face amount. The *DV*01 for \$57.5 million of this issue would then be \$26,695.75 [= \$57,500,000 × (\$41.21/\$100,000)]. As shown in panel E, the *DV*01 of a single 5-year Treasury note futures contract on January 20 was \$37.20. Thus, the number of 5-year note futures that we would need in place of the 5-year notes would be

$$\textit{5-yr futures hedge} = \frac{DV01 \textit{ of 5-yr note}}{DV01 \textit{ of 5-yr futures}} = \frac{\$26{,}695.75}{\$37.20}$$

$$= 637 \textit{ of the 5-yr Treasury note futures}$$

which we would short. Similarly, with a *DV*01 of \$29,461.00 [= \$42,500,000 × (\$69.32/\$100,000)] for \$42.5 million of an 8.5 percent coupon, 10-year noncallable note, and a *DV*01 of \$57.52 for a 10-year Treasury note futures contract, the 10-year note futures hedge would be

$$\textit{10-yr futures hedge} = \frac{DV01 \textit{ of 10-yr note}}{DV01 \textit{ of 10-yr futures}} = \frac{\$29{,}461.00}{\$57.52}$$

$$= 512 \textit{ of the 10-yr Treasury note futures}$$

These hedge ratios are shown as a pair of numbers in the center of panel H in Exhibit 14.9.

Step 5: Adjust the Hedge as Interest Rates Change

Any change in the price of the forward note will cause the delta of the embedded call to change. For example, if the forward note price rises, the call delta increases, and we will have to adjust our hedge to include more 5-year notes and fewer 10-year notes. If the forward price falls, the call delta decreases, and we will have to reduce our 5-year note position and increase our 10-year note position to reflect the change.

The hedge pairs in Exhibit 14.9 provide some indication of how the hedge ratios would change in response to changes in the spot yields of the 10-year and 5-year notes that we use to construct the synthetic forward.

Consider what happens, for example, if the 10-year yield rises while the 5-year yield remains unchanged. If this were to happen, the yield on a 5-year note 5 years forward would rise and the price of the forward note would fall. This would cause the embedded option's delta to fall, causing the callable issue to behave more like a 10-year note and less like a 5-year note. In Exhibit 14.9, we find that if the 10-year noncallable note's yield were to increase 25 basis points while the 5-year noncallable note's yield is held fixed, the appropriate hedge would be 519 of the 5-year note futures and 641 of the 10-year note futures. In other words, because of a decrease in the likelihood of call, the note would behave more like a 10-year note and less like a 5-year note. The decrease in the number of 5-year futures and the increase in the number of 10-year futures reflects this shift in behavior.

In contrast, an increase in the 5-year note's yield with no change in the 10-year note's yield would cause the forward note's yield to fall. The resulting increase in the forward note's price would cause the embedded call's delta to rise and would, as a result, tip the hedge more towards 5-year note futures and away from 10-year note futures. For example, if the 5-year note's yield were to increase 25 basis points with no change in the 10-year note's yield, the new hedge pair would include 706 5-year note futures and 437 10-year note futures.

THE COSTS AND RISKS OF DELTA HEDGING

The main costs of delta hedging a short option are incurred when rebalancing the hedge. For example, an increase in the 5-year note's yield would cause the hedger to sell more 5-year notes and to scale back the short position in 10-year notes. Similarly, a decrease in the 5-year note's yield would cause the hedger to scale back the short position in 5-year notes and to sell additional 10-year notes.

Only some of this rebalancing is costly. For example, an increase in the 5-year note's yield forces the hedger to sell more 5-year notes, and these must be sold at a lower price. On the other hand, if it is only the 5-year note's yield that has changed, the price of the 10-year notes that the hedger has to buy is the same as it was. The only cost of transacting in the 10-year notes would be transactions costs.

And, to the extent changes in 5-year and 10-year note yields are correlated, at least some of the hedge rebalancing will actually be done at favorable prices. Consider what happens, for instance, if 5-year and 10-year note yields both increase 25 basis points. As shown in Exhibit 14.9, this increase would force the hedger to buy 47 [= 637 − 590] 5-year note futures and to sell 51 [= 563 − 512] 10-year note futures. Because both futures prices will have fallen with the rise in 5-year and 10-year note yields, the cost of having to sell the 10-year futures at a lower price is offset somewhat by being able to buy the 5-year contracts at a lower price.

In any case, the costs of delta hedging the note are offset by the time decay earned on the short options embedded in the callable note.

Risks in the Hedge

Delta hedging an option is risky business for at least two reasons. First, delta hedges do not capture the gamma in the option. As a result, a large, unexpected change in the underlying price can produce large hedge errors. Because the investor in the callable note is short the embedded call, the gamma in the position is negative. Any large rate changes, then, hurt the investor.

Second, delta hedges afford no protection against changes in implied volatility. Because the investor is short the embedded call, any increase in implied volatility increases the value of the call and reduces the value of the callable note. In Exhibit 14.9 panel D, the callable note is shown to have a price vega of 0.61 and a yield vega of 0.20. That is, an increase in implied price volatility from 4.20 percent to 5.20 percent would increase the value of the issuer's call option by 0.61. Or, an increase in implied yield volatility from 12.85 percent to 13.85 percent would increase the value of the call by 0.20.[1]

At least some of these risks can be offset by including some long options in the hedge. Long options would bring with them positive gamma, which would help offset the risks of large and unexpected price changes. Long options would also afford some protection against increases in implied volatilities. The chief difficulties in using options lie in their availability. The long-dated options on forward bonds or swaps that would provide the right mix of gamma, vega, and theta are available only in the over-the-counter market. The short-dated options that trade on the Chicago exchanges can be used to offset gamma exposure but their relatively small vegas would do little to offset the implied volatility exposure in the callable notes.

THE YIELD SPREAD BETWEEN AGENCIES AND TREASURYS

Some hedgers worry about not being able to hedge changes in the yield spread between callable notes and Treasurys. The approach to hedging that we take here, however, makes it possible to hedge much of the apparent risk in this spread. The reason is that much of the yield spread reflects nothing more than the value of the embedded call options. And if we can hedge the embedded calls, then we can hedge that part of the yield spread risk that is produced by changes in the values of the embedded calls.

The yield spread between a callable agency note and a Treasury note with the same maturity reflects two main differences between the two notes. One is the apparent credit of the issuer. However badly our country manages its fiscal affairs, the U.S. Treasury is less likely to default than are any of the Federal financing agencies. This difference is reflected in the higher yields paid on noncallable agency bullet issues.

---

1. The link between price volatility and yield volatility for a noncallable note can be represented roughly as:

$$\textit{Price volatility} = [\textit{Modified duration} \times \textit{Yield}] \times \textit{Yield volatility}$$

The other difference is in the call features. The holder of the callable note pays a lower price for the callable note as compensation for giving the agency the right to call the note. The result of the lower price is a seemingly higher yield to maturity. As a result, anything that increases the value of the embedded calls should increase the callable note's yield spread over Treasurys.

In particular, consider an increase in the yield on the 5-year note with no change in the yield on the 10-year note. Such a change would cause the yield on the 5-year note 5 years forward to fall and the forward price of the note to rise. The embedded calls would increase in value, the price of the callable note would fall, and its measured yield to maturity would rise. Thus, even with no change in the bullet spreads over Treasurys, the yield spread between the callable note and a 10-year Treasury note would increase. In Exhibit 14.10, we see that a 25-basis point increase in the yield of the 5-year note with no change in the yield of the 10-year note would increase the spread over 10-year Treasurys from 78 to 87 basis points.

Similarly, any decrease in the yield on the 10-year note with no change in the yield on the 5-year note would decrease the yield on the forward note and, as a result, increase its price. The resulting increase in the value of the embedded calls would increase the agency's spread over 10-year Treasurys. In Exhibit 14.10, we find that a 25-basis point decrease in the yield of the 10-year note

EXHIBIT 14.10

Callable Agency Yield Spread over 10-Year Treasury
8.5 Percent Coupon, 10-Year Callable in 5
Yield Spread in Basis Points

5-Year Yield Shift (bps)	*10-Year Yield Shift* (bps)				
	−50	**−25**	**0**	**25**	**50**
−50	90	75	63	53	45
−25	100	84	70	59	49
0	110	93	78	65	55
25	121	103	87	73	61
50	133	114	96	81	68

would increase the callable note's yield spread from 78 to 93 basis points.

WHAT IF THERE IS LITTLE OR NO CALL PROTECTION?

The problem of hedging a 10-year note that has 5 years of call protection is comparatively easy because the most valuable of the agency's rights to call the note is the very first option. As a result, even though the agency's right to call the note any time after 5 years is worth something to the agency, the hedger can ignore these backup options and treat the note as if it could only be called at the 5-year mark without any really serious consequences to the effectiveness of the hedge.

In many cases, however, the note that one wants to hedge has little or no call protection. What should one do then?

The main question is this. If the agency can call the 10-year note anytime, what is the appropriate underlying for the embedded call option? The answer is that it depends. The agency, for example, has the right to call the note 1 year from now. For this particular option, which has 1 year to expiration, the underlying is a 9-year note 1 year forward. The agency also has the right to call the note 3 years from now. For this option, which has 3 years to expiration, the underlying is a 7-year note 3 years forward. Which of these is the more valuable option? The option to call the note in 1 year benefits from having an underlying note whose price is relatively volatile for any given level of yield volatility. But the option itself only has 1 year to expiration. The option to call the note in 3 years suffers from having an underlying—a 7-year note 3 years forward—whose price is less volatile than that of the 9-year note underlying the 1-year option. But the option has more time to expiration.

Which of these is the more valuable option depends to a large extent on the level of rates. As shown in Exhibit 14.11, if yields are low enough, the agency can be counted on to call the note at the earliest opportunity. The most valuable option would be the option with the nearest expiration, which in this example would be the option to call in 1 year. If yields are high enough, on the other hand, the most valuable option would be a longer-dated option on a shorter maturity note. In Exhibit 14.11, the most val-

EXHIBIT 14.11

Value of American Option versus European Options

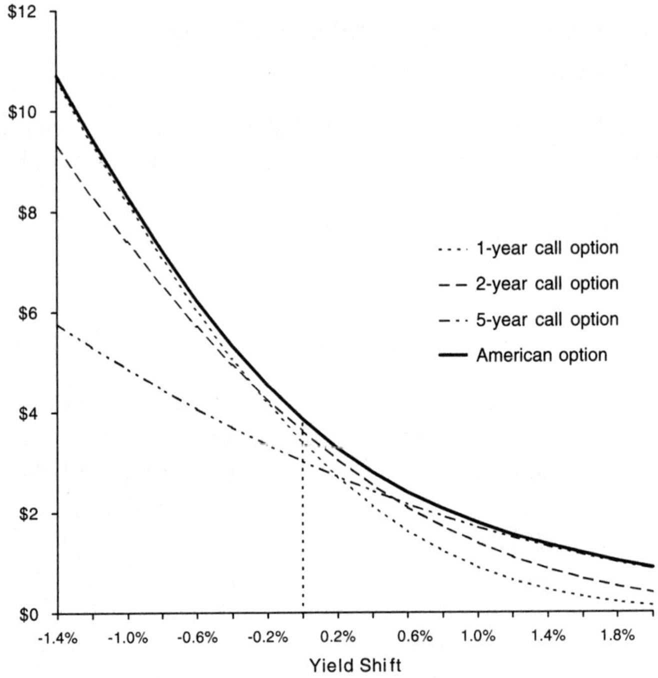

uable option is the right to call the note in 2 years. At higher yields still, the most valuable option might be the right to call the note in 5 years.

For any given level of yields and yield volatilities, then, there is one option that is more valuable than all the others. In Exhibit 14.12, which shows the values of the option to call the note at various points throughout the note's life, we find that the most valuable option is the agency's right to call the note in 2 years. For this particular setting, then, the agency is most likely to call the note in 2 years. And because the delta of the agency's European-style option to call the note in 2 years is very close to the delta of the American-style option that comprises all of the agency's call options (see Exhibit 14.11), we can hedge the note as if this were the only option embedded in the note. If we do, our task is to price an 8-year note 2 years forward, value the embed-

EXHIBIT 14.12

European Call Option Values
No Call Protection

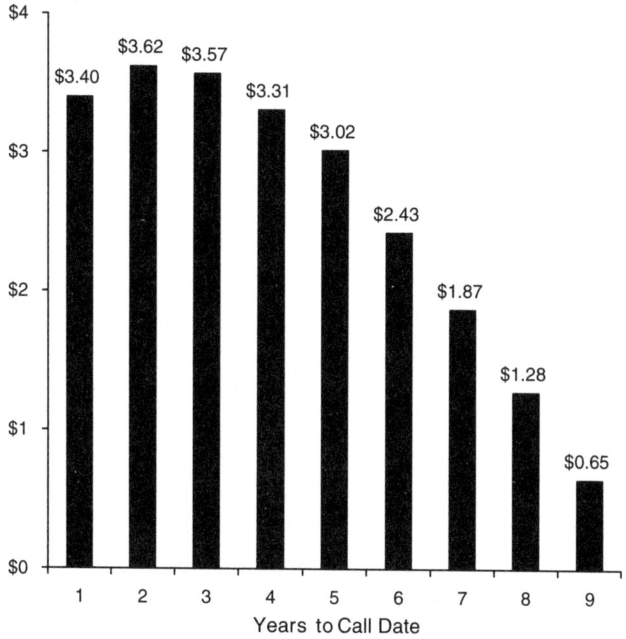

ded option, find its delta, and construct an appropriate delta hedge along the lines laid out in this note.

As rates rise or fall, one can expect shifts in the most likely call date and corresponding shifts in the appropriate underlying for the embedded call. As rates fall, for example, we would find the underlying shifting away from an 8-year note 2 years forward to a 9-year note 1 year forward. As rates rise, on the other hand, we find the underlying shifting toward a 7-year note 3 years forward. It is easy enough to adjust the hedges to suit changing circumstances.

Exhibit 14.13 illustrates the value of call protection. If the agency provides 5 years of call protection on a 10-year note, for example, it gives up the most valuable of the call options. The exhibit also shows that the most valuable of the remaining options is the right to call the note at the 5-year mark, which is the first possible opportunity. The values of the backup options trail off

EXHIBIT 14.13

European Call Option Values
5 Years of Call Protection

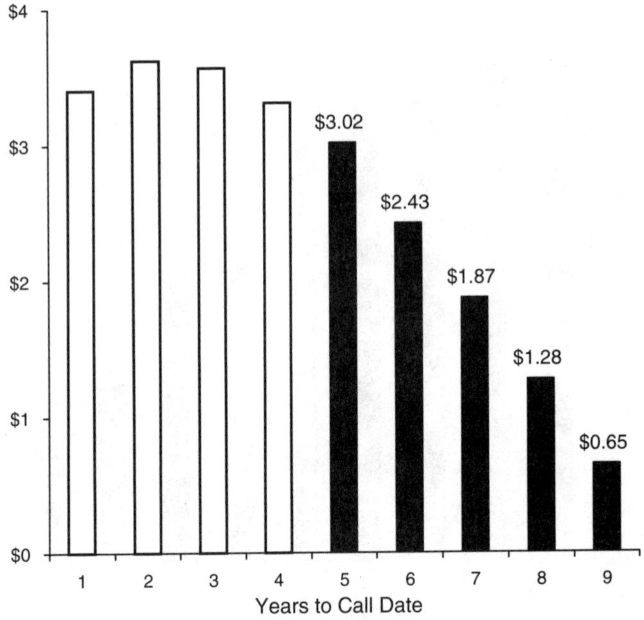

fairly quickly. And, because they would come into play only at very high yields or high implied volatilities, these backup options can be ignored without doing serious harm to our hedge constructions. Thus, if the note has enough call protection, the business of hedging the note is simplified considerably.

SOMETIMES STRIPS OF EURODOLLAR FUTURES PROVIDE BETTER HEDGES

Eurodollar futures offer clear-cut advantages in many cases. They are especially well suited to hedging notes that have less than 5 years to maturity or for which the most likely call date is under 5 years. Eurodollar futures hedges can be easier to maintain in the face of changing yield levels and changing yield curve slopes. Also, hedging with Eurodollar futures may offer an added advantage by capturing some of the credit spread between yields on bullet agency issues and on Treasury notes.

An example of what a Eurodollar hedge for an agency issue would look like is provided in Exhibit 14.14. The hedge is for $10 million of a 3-year 6.8 percent coupon note callable in 2 years. In this case, the embedded call is out of the money so that its delta is less than 0.50. As a result, the note behaves more like a 3-year than a 2-year note. And, for the purposes of this illustration, one would hedge it by shorting $6.8 million of a 3-year note and $3.2 million of a 2-year note.

Netting Positions

Exhibit 14.14 provides two different ways of interpreting the hedge that one would construct using Eurodollar futures. In the

EXHIBIT 14.14

Hedging with Eurodollar Futures
3-Year Callable Note with 2 Years of Call Protection

	Number of Eurodollar Futures					
	Spot Hedge			*Bullet/Option Hedge*		
Contract Month	**3-Year Note ($6.8 MM)**	**2-Year Note ($3.2 MM)**	**Net**	**3-Year Bullet**	**Option**	**Net**
Mar '95	−7.9	−3.7	−11.6	−11.6	0.0	−11.6
Jun '95	−6.6	−3.2	−9.8	−9.8	0.0	−9.8
Sep '95	−6.4	−3.1	−9.5	−9.5	0.0	−9.5
Dec '95	−6.4	−3.0	−9.4	−9.4	0.0	−9.4
Mar '96	−6.2	−3.0	−9.2	−9.2	0.0	−9.2
Jun '96	−6.2	−2.9	−9.1	−9.1	0.0	−9.1
Sep '96	−6.0	−2.9	−8.9	−8.9	0.0	−8.9
Dec '96	−6.0	−2.8	−8.8	−8.8	0.0	−8.8
Mar '97	−5.9	−0.4	−6.3	−8.6	2.3	−6.3
Jun '97	−5.8		−5.8	−8.5	2.7	−5.8
Sep '97	−5.6		−5.6	−8.3	2.7	−5.6
Dec '97	−5.6		−5.6	−8.2	2.6	−5.6
Mar '98	−0.9		−0.9	−1.3	0.4	−0.9
Total			−100.5			−100.5

left hand part of the exhibit, we show the number of Eurodollar contracts, by expiration month, that one would short instead of shorting the bullet issues. The weighted strip of Eurodollar futures with expirations extending out to March '98 would capture fully the rate exposure of a short position of $6.8 million of the 3-year note. The weighted Eurodollar strip with expirations reaching out to March '97 would stand in for a short position of $3.2 million of the 2-year note. Adding them together provides the combined strip shown under the "Net" column.

One could arrive at exactly the same answer by hedging the components of the note separately. That is, the callable note can be thought of as a 3-year bullet combined with a 2-year option on a 1-year note, 2 years forward. In the right-hand part of Exhibit 14.14, we show the hedges for these two components. To hedge the bullet part of the exposure, we would short the weighted strip of Eurodollar futures shown in the 3-year bullet column. The underlying for the embedded option is a 1-year note 2 years forward. Given the option's delta, we can offset this delta by buying a strip of Eurodollar futures beginning with the March '97 contract and extending out to include the March '98 contract. Notice that when we add these two hedges together, the combined net hedge is exactly the same as the hedge shown in the left hand part of the exhibit.

Adjusting the Hedges

Exhibit 14.15 shows how Eurodollar futures can simplify the problem of adjusting to changing market conditions. In this example, to make things especially interesting, we consider an issue that has no call protection at all. The left-hand panel shows what the hedge for a 3-year 6.8 percent coupon note with no call protection would look like at the current level of interest rates. In this instance, the most likely call date is 1.5 years away and the Eurodollar futures used to hedge the embedded call begin with the September '96 contract.

Two things happen to the hedge as rates rise or fall. For one thing, the price sensitivity or *DV*01 of the bullet component of the agency note changes—falling as rates rise and rising as rates fall. As a result, if rates rise 50 basis points, we need fewer contracts to hedge the bullet, and if rates fall 50 basis points, we need more.

EXHIBIT 14.15

Hedging with Eurodollar Futures
3-Year Callable Note with No Call Protection

	Number of Eurodollar Futures								
	Current Rates[1]			*Rates Up 50 bps*[2]			*Rates Down 50 bps*[3]		
Month	**Bullet**	**Option**	**Net**	**Bullet**	**Option**	**Net**	**Bullet**	**Option**	**Net**
Mar '95	−11.6	0.0	−11.6	−11.4	0.0	−11.4	−11.8	0.0	−11.8
Jun '95	−9.8	0.0	−9.8	−9.6	0.0	−9.6	−9.9	0.0	−9.9
Sep '95	−9.5	0.0	−9.5	−9.4	0.0	−9.4	−9.6	3.3	−6.3
Dec '95	−9.4	0.0	−9.4	−9.3	0.0	−9.3	−9.6	3.8	−5.8
Mar '96	−9.2	0.0	−9.2	−9.0	0.0	−9.0	−9.3	3.7	−5.6
Jun '96	−9.1	0.0	−9.1	−9.0	0.0	−9.0	−9.3	3.7	−5.6
Sep '96	−8.9	2.0	−6.9	−8.7	0.0	−8.7	−9.0	3.6	−5.4
Dec '96	−8.8	2.4	−6.4	−8.7	0.0	−8.7	−9.0	3.6	−5.4
Mar '97	−8.6	2.3	−6.3	−8.4	1.5	−6.9	−8.7	3.5	−5.2
Jun '97	−8.5	2.3	−6.2	−8.4	1.8	−6.6	−8.7	3.5	−5.2
Sep '97	−8.3	2.2	−6.1	−8.2	1.7	−6.5	−8.4	3.4	−5.0
Dec '97	−8.2	2.2	−6.0	−8.1	1.7	−6.4	−8.4	3.4	−5.0
Mar '98	−1.3	0.3	−1.0	−1.2	0.3	−0.9	−1.3	0.5	−0.8
Total			−97.5			−102.4			−77.0

[1] Most likely call in 1.5 years.
[2] Most likely call in 2.0 years.
[3] Most likely call in 9 months.

For another thing, the most likely call date and the option delta change. For example, if rates rise 50 basis points, the most likely call date is extended to 2 years and the delta declines. If rates fall 50 basis points, the most likely call date is brought forward to 9 months and the delta increases. As a result, a change in rates changes both the number and expirations of the contracts needed to hedge the embedded call options.

Taken together, an increase in rates would increase the hedger's net short position by about 5 contracts. As a practical matter, 4 of these 5 would be sold to increase the hedger's short position in September '96 and December '96. A decrease in rates would reduce the hedger's short position by about 20 contracts. Most of this adjustment would be made by buying 3 or 4 contracts in each of the contract months from September '95 through December '96, with the remainder made up in later months.

In either case, adjusting the Eurodollar hedge is simpler than adjusting a cash market hedge, which requires three separate transactions. For example, if the most likely call date falls from 1.5 years to 9 months, the hedger would have to reduce the size of the short position in the 3-year bullet, cover entirely the short position in the 1.5-year bullet, and short a 9-month instrument. This would almost certainly be more expensive than simply adjusting the Eurodollar hedge.

CHAPTER 15

Opportunities in the S&P 500 Calendar Roll

Galen Burghardt and George Panos
Research note originally released June 7, 1999

SYNOPSIS

Anyone who uses S&P 500 futures to maintain a standing long or short position in the equity market must face the problem of when to roll out of the expiring contract month and into a deferred contract month. If futures were always fairly priced, the roll would hardly be an issue. As it is, however, the evidence suggests that one can improve a portfolio's performance by choosing the best time to do the roll.

Exhibit 15.1 shows three measures of the value of the spread—the spread itself, the actual spread less the theoretical spread, and the implied financing rate less the lead Eurodollar rate—against business days remaining to expiration of the lead contract. The top panel of Exhibit 15.1 shows that the spread between the deferred contract price and the lead contract price has, over the past 3 years, tended to widen as the lead contract approaches expiration. The two lower panels show, in different ways, that the spread has become overvalued in the last days of the expiring contract's life.

Save 15 Basis Points per Year on the Roll

This increasing richness of the spread as expiration approaches suggests that anyone who maintains a standing long position in

EXHIBIT 15.1

Average S&P 500 Futures Calendar Spreads (First Deferred – Lead) versus Business Days to Lead Contract Expiry

1Q 1996 through 4Q 1998

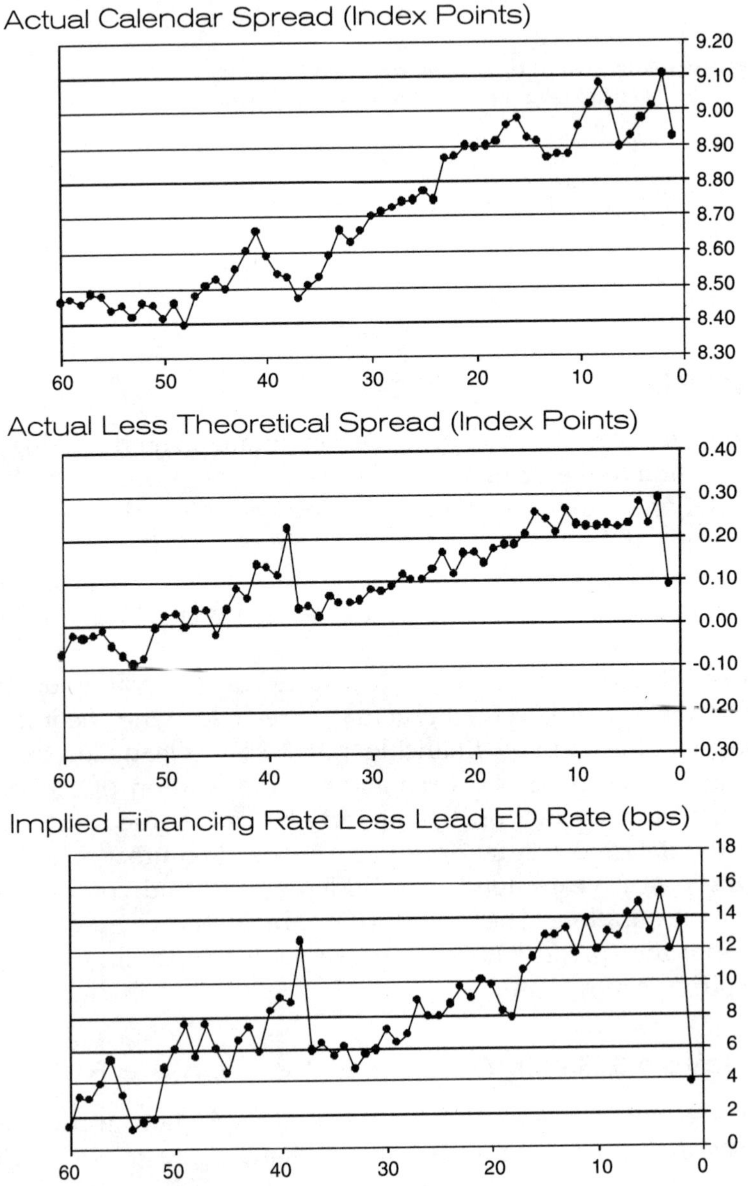

S&P 500 futures should undertake the roll as early as possible. In contrast, anyone who maintains a standing short position should wait as long as possible.

The results in Exhibit 15.1 suggest that one could save as much as 15 basis points annualized by timing the roll correctly. On a $1 billion position, this would amount to $1.5 million a year, which makes the problem worth tackling.

Eliminate Interest Rate Risk in the Roll

We also find that much of the risk in the calendar roll comes from changes in short-term money market rates. At the current level of futures prices, a 10-basis-point change in the lead Eurodollar futures rate produces a 0.33-point change in the value of the calendar spread. On a $1 billion position, such a change in rates could produce a gain or loss of about $250 thousand, which may also be worth dealing with by buying or selling an appropriate number of Eurodollar futures.

Earn Superior Money Market Returns

For cash managers, the systematic richness in the calendar spread as the lead contract approaches expiration affords an opportunity to earn above-LIBOR money market returns with comparatively little risk. In particular, if a money manager were to combine a long stock position with a short deferred S&P 500 futures position just before the expiration of the nearby or lead contract, such a position would promise to yield as much as 15 basis points over LIBOR.

THE VALUE OF THE CALENDAR SPREAD

The relationship between the spot value of the S&P 500 index and any futures price is:

$$Futures = Spot\left[1 + R\left(\frac{Days}{360}\right)\right] - Div$$

where

R is an appropriate money market interest rate
$Days$ is days between the settlement date for a spot transaction in equities and futures expiration
Div, if handled correctly, is the forward value of expected dividends (that is, dividends plus interest earned on dividends) during the period

A similar expression describes the relationship between two futures prices:

$$F_D = F_L\left[1 + R_f\left(\frac{Days_f}{360}\right)\right] - Div_f$$

where

F_D is the deferred contract price
F_L is the lead contract price
R_f is the forward money market rate
$Days_f$ is days between contract expirations
Div_f is the expected forward value of dividends to be received during the period between contract expirations

Fair Value of the Spread

Armed with this relationship, the value of the spread between two futures prices can be written as:

$$F_D - F_L = F_L R_f\left(\frac{Days_f}{360}\right) - Div_f$$

which shows that the value of the spread depends on the level of the lead futures price, the forward financing rate, days in the period, and the value of forward dividends. If you know the forward financing rate and have a solid expectation about the value of forward dividends, you can use this expression to calculate the fair value of the futures spread. The difference between the market value of the spread and the fair value of the spread would then be a measure of richness or cheapness in the spread.

Implied Financing Rate

Another way to look at things is to calculate the financing rate implied by two futures prices. The implied financing rate is:

$$IR_f = \left[\frac{(F_D + Div_f)}{F_L} - 1\right]\left(\frac{360}{Days_f}\right)$$

The difference between this implied financing rate and the rate that one believes to be the relevant financing rate is another way of judging the richness or cheapness of the spread. If the implied financing rate is higher than the relevant market rate, for example, the deferred contract will be rich relative to the lead contract.

Exhibit 15.2 provides a history of the difference between the implied financing rate and the value of the rate implied by the corresponding Eurodollar futures contract. That is, if the implied rate is calculated for the June and September futures contracts, the rate implied by the June Eurodollar futures contract is used for purposes of comparison. The Eurodollar contract expires on the Monday before the third Wednesday of the contract month, while the S&P 500 futures contract expires on the third Thursday (for cash settlement on the third Friday) of the contract month. Thus, the overlap in days is not perfect, but is quite good enough for these purposes.

The history of this relationship is worth noting. In the late 1980s, the implied financing rate traded substantially below the corresponding Eurodollar futures rate. Then, throughout the early 1990s, the implied rate traded around but generally below the futures rate. During the past few years, though, the implied fi-

EXHIBIT 15.2

Implied Financing Rate Less Lead ED Rate
1988–1998

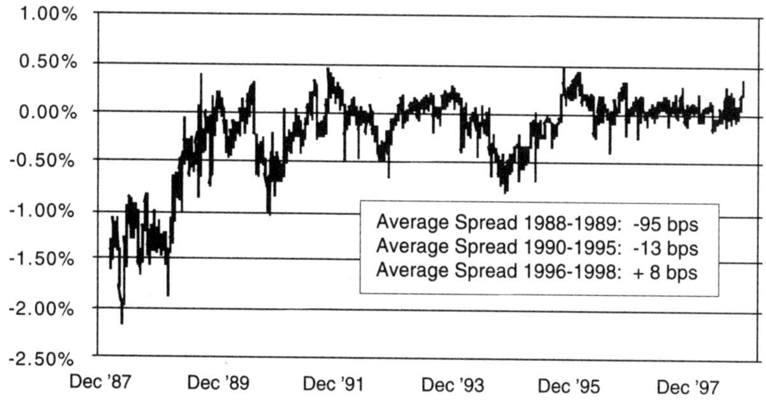

nancing rate has traded in a fairly narrow range just above the Eurodollar futures rate.

HOW THE CALENDAR SPREAD HAS BEHAVED

Over the past 3 years (1996 through 1998), the average value of the calendar spread has tended to widen during the 3 months leading up to the expiration of the lead futures contract. As shown in the upper panel of Exhibit 15.1, the value of the spread increased from 8.40 to 9.00 on average during these months. By itself, the value of the spread tells you nothing about richness or cheapness. This experience could have been the result of increasing futures prices or increasing interest rates.

The lower two panels of Exhibit 15.1 show, however, that the tendency of the spread to increase reflects a tendency for the contract to become rich as the lead contract approaches expiration. In the middle panel, for example, we see that when the lead contract has about 3 months (or 60 business days) to expiration, the calendar spread is just about fairly priced. The difference between the market value of the spread and the theoretical value of the spread (calculated using a financing rate equal to the rate implied by the lead Eurodollar futures contract) is about zero. Then, as time passes, the difference between market and theoretical increases until it trades between 0.20 and 0.30 index points during the month before the lead contract expires.

The bottom panel, which shows the difference between the implied financing rate in the spread and the market financing rate (again, the rate implied by the lead Eurodollar futures contract), provides a different way of seeing exactly the same thing. With 3 months to expiration of the lead contract, the implied and market rates are nearly identical. Then, as the spread ages, the implied financing rate rises relative to the market rate until the difference is in the neighborhood of 12 to 16 basis points.

In practice, this increasing richness suggests that anyone who maintains a standing long position in S&P 500 futures should strive to roll into the deferred contract month as early as possible. Anyone who maintains a standing short position, on the other hand, should wait as long as possible to do the roll.

The increasing richness of the spread also produces opportunities for those who manage short-term money market portfolios. Because we are using Eurodollar futures to establish the fair value of the spread, the evidence in the bottom panels of Exhibit 15.1 suggests that a money manager could earn LIBOR plus 12 to 16 basis points by selling the rich deferred contract against a long position in an S&P 500 equity portfolio.

WHAT IS YOUR EXPOSURE TO INTEREST RATES?

Because the fair value of the spread is simply the forward cost of financing less the forward value of expected dividends, most of the day-to-day variability in the spread will be explained either by changes in the level of the lead futures price or in the relevant financing rate. To get an idea of your exposure to a change in the interest rate, consider this example.

At the close of business on Tuesday, June 1, 1999, the June '99 S&P 500 futures contract closed at a price of 1291.50. At this value, given 91 days between the expirations of the June and September contracts, the effect of a 10 basis point change in the financing rate would be worth 0.33 futures price points [$= 1291.50 \times 0.0010 \times (91/360)$], which would be worth about \$82.50 [$= 0.33 \times \$250$]. The same change in rates would be worth \$250 for the June '99 Eurodollar futures contract.

The history of daily changes in Eurodollar rates shown in Exhibit 15.3 helps put this source of risk in perspective. The standard deviation of daily rate changes over the past 3 years has been about 2.8 basis points, which would translate into a change in the spread of 0.09 price points. The history of daily rate changes is dotted with some fairly large moves, however. On several days the change was as much as 10 basis points, and on at least one occasion the rate fell 26 basis points on a single day.

Handling Rate Exposure in the Roll

Perhaps the single most important determinant of the lead Eurodollar futures rate is the market's expectations about where the Fed will set its target for overnight Fed funds. As shown in Exhibit

EXHIBIT 15.3

Daily Changes in the Lead ED Futures Rate

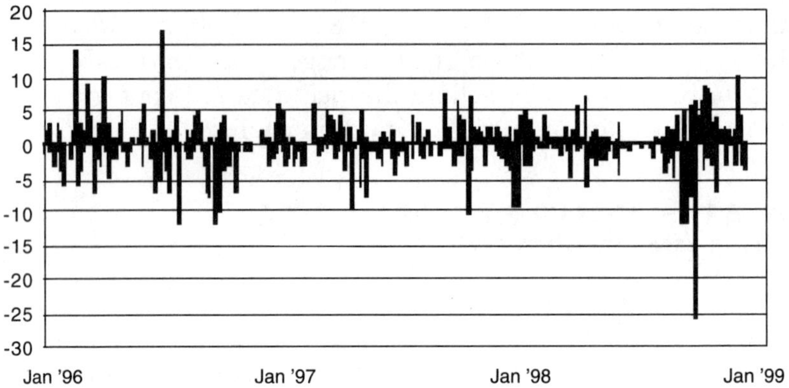

15.4, the Fed changes its target rate in discreet jumps. The market's expectations about changes in the target rate change every day and are reflected in the spread at which LIBOR trades over the target funds rate.

The typical spread, as shown in Exhibit 15.5, is about 24 basis points. The spread is wider if the market expects a rate increase and is narrower if the market expects a rate decrease.

EXHIBIT 15.4

Target Fed Funds Rate

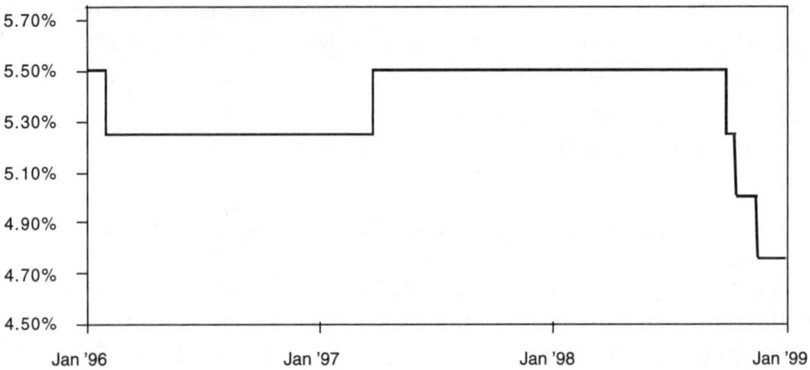

EXHIBIT 15.5

Lead ED Futures Rate Less Target Fed Funds Rate (bps)

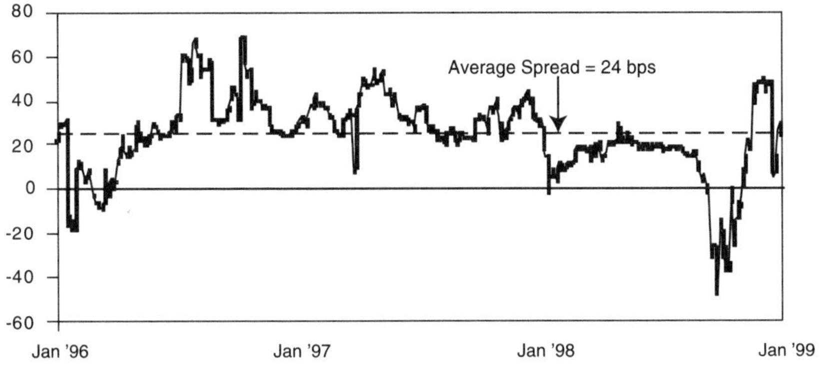

At the close on Tuesday, June 1, the June '99 Eurodollar rate was 5.1375 percent, which was 38.75 basis points over the Fed's target overnight Fed funds rate of 4.75 percent and about 14 basis points over the normal spread. At this spread, one can infer that the market's guess about the probability of a 25-basis-point rate increase at the June 30 FOMC meeting is slightly greater than half—that is, about 14 bps/25 bps.

Consider now the problem faced by a portfolio manager who must roll a long S&P 500 futures position from the June to the September contract. If anything caused the market to think that a 25-basis-point rate increase would be a sure thing, the June Eurodollar rate likely would increase by about 10 basis points and the calendar spread would increase by 0.33 price points. If this happened before doing the roll, the portfolio manager would miss out on this increase.

On the other hand, if the Fed made it plain that there would be no rate increase at its June 30 meeting, the June Eurodollar rate could easily fall by 10 basis points (or more), in which case the value of the calendar spread would fall by 0.33 price points. If this happened after doing the roll, the portfolio manager would lose this much from having rolled too early.

The timing of the roll, therefore, is in large part a bet on interest rates. A portfolio manager who has a superior understanding of interest rates can outperform the S&P 500 by handling this bet well. At the same time, most equity portfolio managers are not paid to take interest rate risk and would prefer to take this kind of risk out of the equation.

Hedging against Interest Rate Risk

The easiest way to hedge against interest rate risk in the calendar spread is to combine the roll with a Eurodollar hedge. In this example, the portfolio manager who would like to wait as long as possible to roll a long position could hedge against the possibility of a rate increase by selling the appropriate number of lead Eurodollar futures. By the same token, the portfolio manager who wants to do the roll as early as possible could buy Eurodollar futures to protect against the possibility of a fall in the interest rate. In general, the correct number of Eurodollar futures contracts is:

$$\textit{Eurodollars per S\&P 500} = F_L \times 0.0001 \times \left(\frac{Days}{360}\right)\left(\frac{\$250}{\$25}\right)$$

At the current level of futures prices, this is about 0.33 Eurodollar contracts per S&P 500 contract.

CASH MANAGEMENT AND PORTFOLIO REPLICATION

As a general rule, when one combines a money market investment with a long futures position to create a portfolio that will replicate a real asset, the term of the money market investment should correspond as closely as possible to the expiration of the associated futures contract.

Timing the roll poses a challenge for cash management, then, because you may want to roll out of one contract month and into the next before the lead contract expires. If you have matched the maturity of your money market investment to the lead contract's expiration, you have two choices for handling the cash-management problem. The first would be to sell the asset you have and replace it with one whose maturity matches the expiration of your new, longer-dated futures contract.

If the secondary market for your money market asset is illiquid, however, you have another choice, and that is to buy the lead Eurodollar futures contract. This long Eurodollar futures position will fill in the 3 months of rate exposure that you need until your current asset matures and you can roll over your investment into a new 3-month asset.

Whatever you choose to do, you cannot avoid having a few days of rate mismatch. For example, the true value date for an expiring S&P 500 futures contract is 3 business days after the final settlement value of the contract is determined. Thus, if you choose a money maturity equal to the final settlement date for the futures contract, you will have 3 business days of rate mismatch. Also, if you choose to gain flexibility in your roll strategy by using the Eurodollar contract to provide you with the rate coverage you need, you might choose to have the money market asset mature on the value date for the expiring Eurodollar contract. Since this is the third Wednesday of the contract month, it would fall 2 days before the final settlement value of the expiring S&P 500 futures contract. Thus, you might have as much as 6 days of mismatch in your money market rate exposure.

CHAPTER 16

Trading the Turn: 1993

Galen Burghardt, Mike Bagatti, and Kevin Ferry
Research note originally released October 25, 1993

SYNOPSIS

The last time there was any serious pressure on year-end financing rates was 1986. Even so, the memory lives on, and "the turn" still has an effect on people's thinking about the way they finance positions over year end. Exhibit 16.1, for example, shows a huge change last November in the spread between the December '92 and January '93 LIBOR contracts. Given the rules of thumb developed in this note, the 60-tick drop in the spread suggests that the market briefly expected a 500-basis-point increase in the turn premium.

"The turn" is a 2-, 3-, or 4-day period from the last business day of one year through the first business day of the next. Just how many days the turn contains depends on where the New Year's holiday falls and how it is treated. This year (i.e., 1993), the turn will be unusual because it will be 3 days for some banks and 4 days for others. In the United States, for example, the turn is just like any other weekend for most U.S. banks. The Fed wire is open on both Friday, December 31, and on Monday, January 3, so that any financing done over year end will be done for 3 days. In the United Kingdom on the other hand, Monday the 3rd is a holiday so that London banks will have to choose between financing their positions for 4 days and arranging for their U.S. branches

EXHIBIT 16.1

LIBOR Futures Calendar Spread
December 1992/January 1993

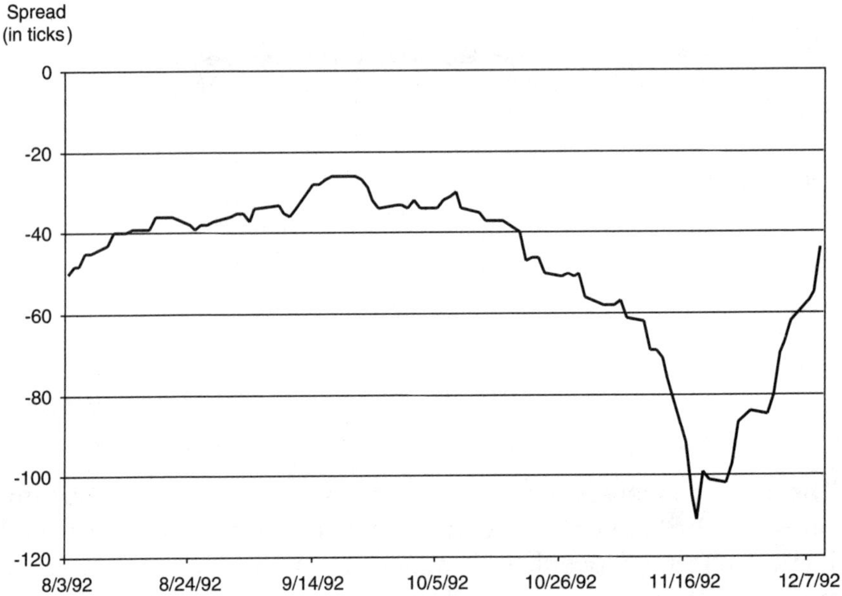

(for those that have them) to do their financing for 3 days over the turn and then for 1 day at the overnight rate.

The effect of all this on the December LIBOR and Eurodollar contracts will depend on how banks reconcile these differences. The final settlement prices of these two contracts will depend on the December 13 values of 1-month and 3-month LIBOR, which will be quoted by London banks for whom the turn is a 4-day event. As things now stand, many banks are quoting both 3-day and 4-day turn rates, and as the distinction between the two becomes clear to all market participants, competitive forces should cause the 4-day turn rate to be nothing more than a simple weighted average of the 3-day turn rate and a regular 1-day overnight rate. In this note, therefore, we treat the turn as if it is a 3-day event. This seems compatible with the way banks that are aware of the different holiday schedules are treating year-end financing.

In any case, people's understanding of the turn has been sufficiently clouded by misunderstandings about year-end holiday schedules that everyone with an interest in the event should take special care when quoting turn rates and arranging year-end financing.

WHAT IS "THE TURN"?

"The turn" is the period of time between the last business day of the current calendar year and the first business day of the new year. Because New Year's Day is a holiday, the number of days in the turn is at least 2 calendar days and can be 3 or 4.

Two-Day Turns

The turn lasts 2 days if December 31 falls on a Monday, Tuesday, or Wednesday. In each of these cases, the next calendar day is a holiday so that money borrowed on Monday would be paid back on Wednesday, 2 days later. Money borrowed Tuesday is paid back Thursday, and money borrowed Wednesday is paid back Friday.

Three-Day Turns

This year, the turn lasts 3 days because December 31 falls on a Friday and the Fed wire is open on both Friday and on the following Monday, January 3. Similarly, if December 31 fell on a Saturday so that January 1 is on Sunday, the turn likely would last 3 days as well, although the Fed wire might be closed on Monday. If it were, the turn would last 4 days.

Four-Day Turns

The turn lasts 4 days if December 31 falls on either a Thursday or a Sunday. In either of these cases, any money borrowed on the last business day of the year must be kept for 4 days. For example, if December 31 is on Thursday, money borrowed then is paid back on Monday, the 4th, or 4 days later. Similarly, if December 31 is on Sunday, money borrowed on Friday the 29th is paid back on Tuesday the 2nd.

Exhibit 16.2 shows a time line of the turn for the end of 1993. The last business day is Friday, the 31st. A bank looking to borrow overnight funds on Friday would normally repay those funds the

EXHIBIT 16.2

Time Line for the 1993 Turn

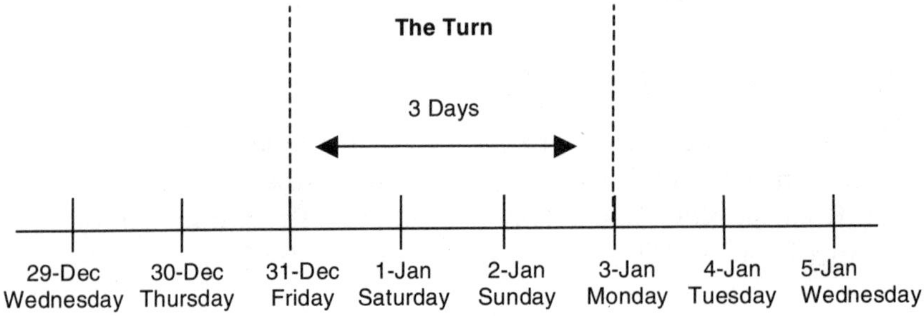

following Monday, which is the next business day. In this respect, this year's turn is just like a normal weekend. New Year's Day falls on Saturday, and the Fed wire is open for business as usual on Monday, the 3rd.

Turn financing rates can be obtained both in the forward deposit market and in the FRA (forward rate agreement) market. At this writing, the markets are still thin and rate indications seem to depend heavily on the nationality of the counterparty. For U.S. banks, the turn premium is very small, while for European and Japanese banks, turn financing rates are offered around 9 to 10 percent, which implies turn premiums in the neighborhood of 5 to 6 percent.

RATE BEHAVIOR AROUND THE TURN

The turn has gained notoriety among bankers because of the pressures that have, in years past, been brought to bear on year-end financing rates. The source of this pressure is said to be the demand by banks for cash that can be used to dress up their balance sheets at the end of the calendar year. Although the Federal Reserve does what it can to accommodate this year-end increase in demand for liquid balances, and does an excellent job most of the time, it appears to have misjudged the size of the shift at least twice since 1984.

As shown in Exhibit 16.3, the turn rate and the average rate around the turn appear to have been fairly close to one another in most of the past 8 years. In 1984, for example, normal financing

EXHIBIT 16.3

Fed Funds Behavior around Year-End

Year	Average Rate around the Turn (1)	Turn Rate (2)	Turn Premium (3) = (2) − (1)	Turn Rate (4) = (2)/(1)
1984	8.37	8.74	0.37	1.04
1985	8.14	13.46	5.32	1.65
1986	7.57	14.35	6.78	1.90
1987	6.96	6.89	−0.07	0.99
1988	9.14	9.04	−0.10	0.99
1989	8.52	7.97	−0.55	0.94
1990	7.73	5.53	−2.20	0.72
1991	4.25	4.09	−0.16	0.96
1992	3.16	2.66	−0.50	0.84
Mean	7.09	8.08	0.99	1.11
Standard deviation	2.04	3.92	2.98	0.39

rates during the 5 days before and after the turn were around 8.37 percent. For the turn between 1984 and 1985, the turn rate increased to 8.74 percent, for a turn premium of 0.37 percent. The "turn ratio," which is simply the ratio of the turn rate to the nonturn rate and which we will use later when we examine the effect of the turn on rate volatility, was only 1.04.

At the end of 1985, however, the turn premium was more than 5 percentage points, and at the end of 1986 the turn premium was nearly 7 percentage points. The effect of such large turn premiums on year-end financing costs must have had a riveting effect on bankers at the time. The effect of a 7-percentage-point turn premium on the cost of funding $1 billion over year end, even for a turn period as short as 2 days, is $389 thousand. This is serious money in anybody's book.

Since 1986, realized rate behavior around the turn has been unremarkable. Even so, the possibility of a large premium still looms large, and wide swings in the market's expectations about turn financing rates can have dramatic effects on forward deposit rates. In late November 1990, for example, fear of extreme pressure on year-end financing rates greatly depressed both December LIBOR and Eurodollar futures prices for about a week.

EFFECTS ON EURODOLLAR AND LIBOR FUTURES PRICES

Because the 1-month LIBOR and 3-month Eurodollar futures contracts that expire in December settle to deposit rates that span the end of the year, changes in the turn rate affect the final settlement value of these two contracts. This year, for example, the December LIBOR and Eurodollar contracts expire on December 13. The final settlement price of the 1-month LIBOR contract on that day will be $100 - R_{1m}$, where R_{1m} is the 1-month deposit rate on December 13 for the 34-day deposit period that runs from Wednesday, December 15, through Tuesday, January 18. (See Exhibit 16.4.) The final settlement price of the 3-month Eurodollar contract will be $100 - R_{3m}$, where R_{3m} is the 3-month deposit rate on December 13 for the 90-day period that runs from December 15 through Tuesday, March 15.

The relationship between the turn rate and the deposit rates to which the LIBOR and Eurodollar futures contracts will settle can be determined by comparing two borrowing transactions. In the first, money is borrowed for the full term at a term lending

EXHIBIT 16.4

How the Turn Fits In

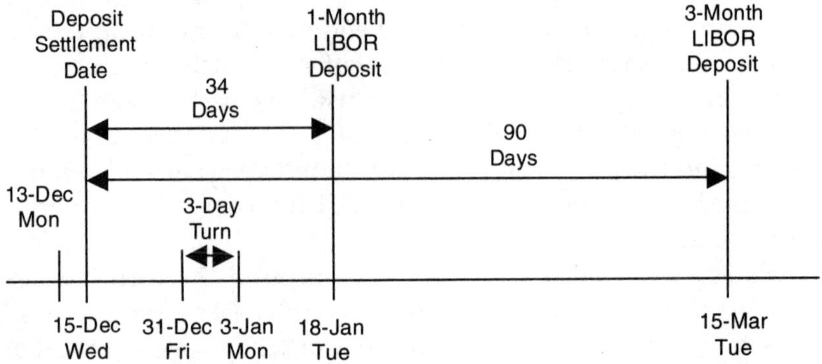

rate. In the second, money is borrowed in three legs—one that runs from December 15 through December 30, one that runs from December 31 through January 3, and one that runs from January 4 through the end of the term. Under the first strategy for borrowing 1-month money, one dollar borrowed on December 15 would call for

$$\$1\left[1 + R_{1m}\frac{34}{360}\right]$$

to be repaid on January 18. Under the second strategy, one dollar borrowed on December 15 would require a repayment of

$$\$1\left[1 + R_b\frac{D_b}{360}\right]\left[1 + R_t\frac{D_t}{360}\right]\left[1 + R_a\frac{D_a}{360}\right]$$

where R_b, R_t, and R_a are the rates that apply to the days before, during, and after the turn and where D_b, D_t, and D_a are the actual number of days in the periods before, during, and after the turn. For a bank financing a position over this period to be indifferent between the two strategies, the two amounts of money must be the same. If we collapse the rates before and after the turn into a single, non-turn deposit rate, the two strategies cost the same if

$$R_{1m} = \left[\left(1 + R_{nt}\frac{D_{nt}}{360}\right)\left(1 + R_t\frac{D_t}{360}\right) - 1\right]\left[\frac{360}{34}\right]$$

The 3-month term deposit rate can be expressed the same way. The only difference is that the non-turn rate for the 90-day period would be different from the non-turn rate for the 34-day period.

To get a sense of how large an effect the turn can have on December LIBOR and Eurodollar futures prices, suppose first that the turn and non-turn rates are the same, say 3.50 percent. In this case, both 1-month and 3-month deposit rates would be (except for a trivial amount of compounding) 3.50 percent. December LIBOR and Eurodollar futures prices would both be 96.50 [= 100.00 − 3.50].

Suppose now that the turn rate increases 200 basis points to 5.50 percent, while the non-turn rate stays at 3.50 percent. At these rates, and given the day counts shown in Exhibit 16.4, the 1-month forward deposit rate for December 13 would be

$$F_{1m} = \left[\left(1 + 0.035\frac{31}{360}\right)\left(1 + 0.055\frac{3}{360}\right) - 1\right]\left[\frac{360}{34}\right]$$

$$F_{1m} = 0.0368$$

which is 18 basis points higher than the 1-month forward rate with the turn rate at 3.50 percent. The 3-month or 90-day forward deposit rate would be

$$F_{3m} = \left[\left(1 + 0.035\frac{87}{360}\right)\left(1 + 0.055\frac{3}{360}\right) - 1\right]\left[\frac{360}{90}\right]$$

$$F_{3m} = 0.0357$$

which is 7 basis points higher than the 3-month forward rate with the turn at 3.50. At these rates, the fair value of the December LIBOR contract would be 96.32 [= 100.00 − 3.68], and the fair value of the December Eurodollar contract would be 96.43 [= 100.00 − 3.57]. Thus, the effect of a 200 basis point spread between the turn and non-turn rates is to decrease the fair value of the December LIBOR contract by 18 basis points and the fair value of the December Eurodollar contract by 7 basis points.

Although the effect of any given turn/non-turn rate spread on the fair value of the December LIBOR and Eurodollar futures contracts depends to some extent on the actual number of days in the forward periods and on the level of rates, we have what we need for excellent working rules of thumb.

Rule of Thumb for a 4-Day Turn

With a 4-day turn, the effect of each 100-basis-point increase in the spread between the turn and non-turn forward deposit rates is a 12-tick decrease in the fair value of the December LIBOR contract and just over a 4-tick decrease in the fair value of the December Eurodollar contract.

Rule of Thumb for a 3-Day Turn

With a 3-day turn, the effect of each 100-basis-point increase in the spread between the turn and non-turn forward deposit rates is a 9-tick decrease in the fair value of the December LIBOR contract and just over a 3-tick decrease in the fair value of the December Eurodollar contract.

Rule of Thumb for a 2-Day Turn

With a 2-day turn, each 100-basis-point increase in the spread between the turn and non-turn forward deposit rates reduces the fair value of the December LIBOR contract by about 6 ticks and the fair value of the December Eurodollar contract by just over 2 ticks.

These rules of thumb are borne out by Exhibit 16.5, which shows the effect of various rate spreads on the fair value of both the December LIBOR and Eurodollar futures contracts given a 3-day turn. For example, if the non-turn forward deposit rate were 3 percent and the turn rate were 9 percent, the effect of the 600-basis-point spread would be a 53-tick reduction in the fair value of the December '93 LIBOR futures contract. The same spread would produce a 20-tick reduction in the fair value of the December '93 Eurodollar futures contract. Because the effect of the turn rate is roughly proportional to the length of the turn, the effects of these rate spreads on the fair values of the LIBOR and Euro-

EXHIBIT 16.5

Effect of Turn Rate on the Fair Values of Dec '93 LIBOR and Eurodollar Futures Prices (3-Day Turn)

Forward Turn Rate	*Effect on 1-Month LIBOR Futures with Non-Turn Rates at*			*Effect on 3-Month Eurodollar Futures with Non-Turn Rates at*		
	3%	**5%**	**7%**	**3%**	**5%**	**7%**
3%	0	18	35	0	7	13
5%	−18	0	17	−7	0	6
7%	−35	−18	0	−14	−7	0
9%	−53	−36	−18	−20	−14	−7
11%	−71	−53	−36	−27	−20	−14
13%	−89	−71	−54	−34	−27	−21

dollar futures contracts given 2-day and 4-day turns can be determined easily enough from the figures shown in Exhibit 16.5.

Implied Turn Rates

With these rules of thumb, it is easy to get a reading on the spread between turn and non-turn rates by looking at the pattern of rates implied by the 1-month LIBOR contracts, which have serial expirations extending out 6 months at any one time. On September 13, for example, there were 1-month LIBOR futures with expirations ranging from October 1993 through March 1994, not counting the expiring September 1993 contract. Exhibit 16.6 shows the strip of 1-month forward deposit rates implied by their September 13 settlement prices. The effect of the turn on the pattern of rates stands out clearly in this exhibit. The 1-month deposit rate for the November contract, which spans the period from mid-November to mid-December, was 3.16 percent. The 1-month deposit rate for the January contract, which spans the period from mid-January to mid-February, was 3.27 percent. In between, the 1-month deposit rate for the December contract was 3.69 percent, which was about

EXHIBIT 16.6

Implied 1-Month Forward Deposit Rates
September 13, 1993

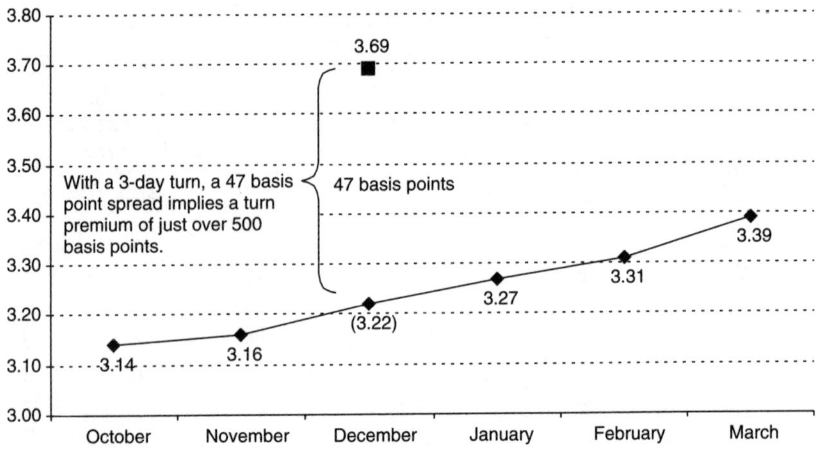

47 basis points higher than the 3.22 percent that the surrounding rates would suggest for a 1-month December deposit rate.

From this 47-basis-point differential, we can determine the spread between turn and non-turn financing rates that is implied by the LIBOR futures contract. Using the rule of thumb that each 100 basis points in the spread reduces the fair value of the December LIBOR contract by about 9 basis points, the 47-basis-point differential that we see in the December contract implied a spread of just over 500 basis points between the turn and non-turn rates.

This implied rate spread can be compared easily with the spreads quoted in the forward deposit market as a way of comparing the pricing of the turn in the two markets. If you find, for example, that the implied turn rate differential is larger than the actual, then you know that the December LIBOR contract is cheap relative to cash.

IMPLICATIONS FOR FUTURES SPREADS

Because the turn rate affects both the December LIBOR and Eurodollar futures contracts, it affects the values of several key futures spreads including the:

December LED Spread

In this spread, you are long the LIBOR contract and short the Eurodollar contract. Given the rule of thumb for a 3-day turn, each 100-basis-point increase in the turn premium translates roughly into a 6-tick decrease in the value of this spread. Thus, the December LED spread is about 30 ticks lower than it would be if the turn premium were zero.

December/January LIBOR Spread

In this spread, you are long the December and short the January LIBOR contracts. Because the turn premium affects only the December contract, each 100-basis-point increase in the turn premium is worth about 9 ticks in this spread. As shown in Exhibit 16.6, this spread is 47 or so ticks lower than it would be if there were no turn premium.

December/March Eurodollar Spread

Here you are long the December and short the March Eurodollar contracts, and with a 3-day turn, each 100-basis-point increase in the turn premium decreases the value of this spread by about 3 ticks.

December TED Spread

In this spread, you are long the 3-month December Treasury bill contract and short the December Eurodollar contract. Because you are short the Eurodollar contract, each 100-basis-point increase in the turn premium increases the value of this spread by about 3 ticks.

One can work out similar implications for the Nov/Dec/Jan LIBOR butterfly and for the December/March TED tandem as well.

Of the various spreads, the December/January LIBOR spread is one of the better vehicles for trading the turn because the effect of the turn premium on the December contract price is both large and fairly direct, and the calendar risk in the trade is about as small as it can be without actually trading the cash deposits themselves. If the turn premium falls to zero by the time the December LIBOR contract expires on the 13th, a long position in the spread would gain 47 ticks, or $1,175 per spread. Exhibit 16.7 shows how this spread behaved last year, and Exhibit 16.8 shows how the spread has performed so far this year.

The dangers in this spread are three. One is that the turn rate is not realized until 2 or 3 weeks after the December contract expires. A second is that there is considerable fluctuation in the market's perception of the turn premium throughout the months leading up to the end of the year. A third is that you are exposed to a flattening of the near-term yield curve.

The other spreads may be less attractive for trading the turn premium, but the effect of the turn on these spreads certainly cannot be ignored when evaluating trades that involve them. The December TED spread, for example, as well as the December/March TED tandem, are greatly influenced by the turn premium. With an implied turn premium of around 500 basis points, December Eurodollar futures trade 15 ticks or so lower than they

EXHIBIT 16.7

LIBOR Futures Calendar Spread
December 1992/January 1993

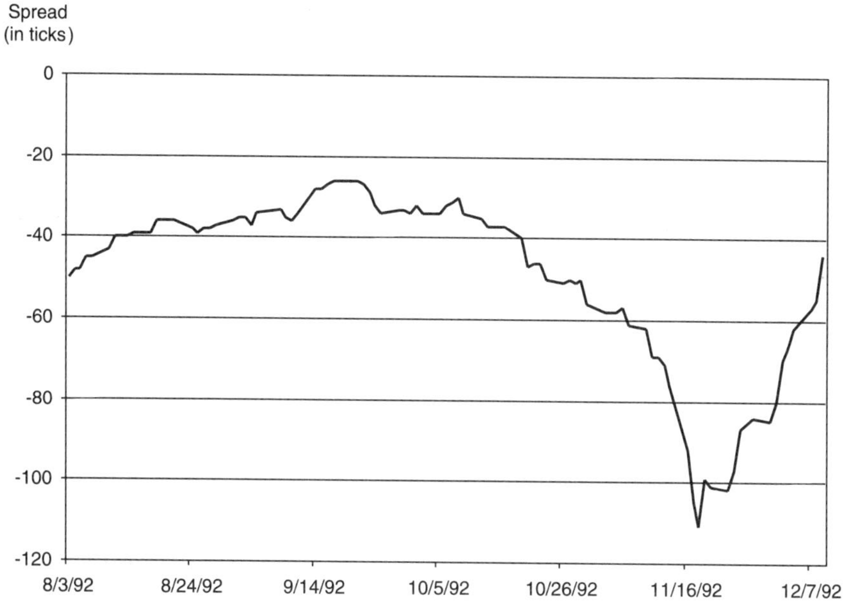

would without the turn. Thus, we know that about 15 ticks of the current December TED spread can be attributed to the turn.

By the same token, the December/March Eurodollar calendar spread is 15 ticks lower than it would be without the turn.

EFFECT OF THE TURN ON LIBOR AND EURODOLLAR VOLATILITIES

Uncertainty about financing rates over the turn is an additional source of volatility for the 1-month and 3-month deposit rates to which the December LIBOR and Eurodollar futures contracts will settle. The focus of this section is on how best to determine the effect of turn-rate volatility on the volatilities for options on December LIBOR and Eurodollar futures.

The biggest hurdle to reckoning the effect of turn-rate volatility on LIBOR and Eurodollar volatilities is the problem of how to represent turn-rate volatility. The few observations that we have

EXHIBIT 16.8

LIBOR Futures Calendar Spread
December 1993/January 1994

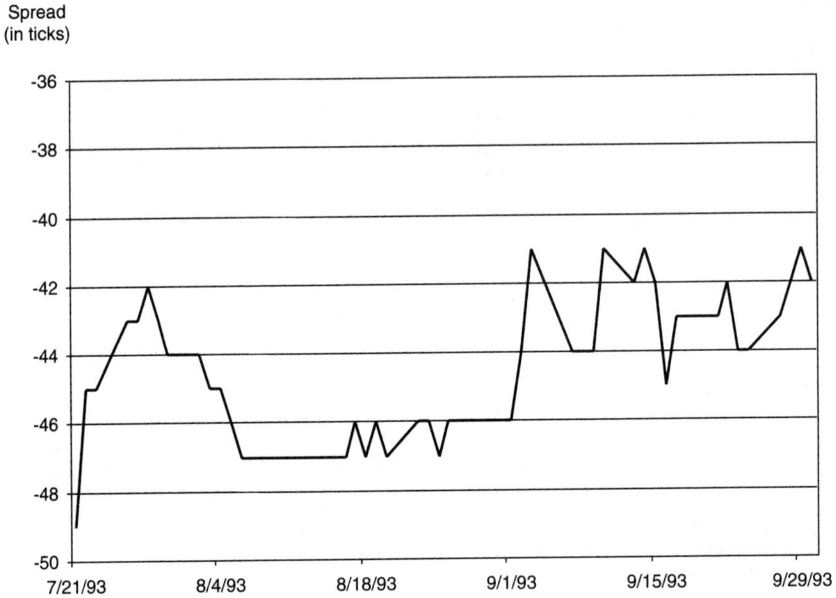

on the turn, which are shown in Exhibit 16.3, suggest fairly strongly that turn rates are not lognormally distributed. With so few observations, however, we only have what we think are two reasonable guides to choosing an alternative distribution. The first is that the size of the turn rate premium should be related to the level of interest rates. The second is that the chance of getting a huge turn premium should be fairly large even though most turn premiums will be close to zero.

One way to satisfy the first reasonableness check is to allow the ratio of the turn rate to the non-turn rate to be the random variable so that the turn premium is directly proportional to the level of rates. For example, a turn/non-turn ratio of 1.5 would produce a turn rate of 9 percent if base rates were 6 percent. If the base rate were 3 percent, the turn rate would be 4.5 percent. The turn premium in the first case would be 3 percent, while the turn premium in the second case would be 1.5 percent.

We can satisfy the second reasonableness check by allowing the behavior of the ratio of turn to non-turn rates to be described by the gamma distribution, which has fat enough tails to allow for a comparatively high number of very large outcomes.

Using this approach, we can simulate the distribution of the 1-month and 3-month deposit rates that span the turn using various levels of volatility for non-turn rates and for the turn/non-turn ratio. From these simulated distributions, we can determine the effect that turn-rate volatility should have on the volatility of the December 1-month LIBOR and 3-month Eurodollar futures contracts. The results of these simulations are shown in Exhibits 16.9 and 16.10.

EXHIBIT 16.9

Add-on Turn Volatility Premium
3 Percent Forward Rate

	Base Rate Volatility							
	1-Month LIBOR				***3-Month Eurodollars***			
Volatility of the Turn Ratio	***2-Day Turn***		***4-Day Turn***		***2-Day Turn***		***4-Day Turn***	
	15%	**25%**	**15%**	**25%**	**15%**	**25%**	**15%**	**25%**
25%	0.40	0.56	0.86	1.10	0.33	0.53	0.68	1.04
35%	0.48	0.60	1.12	1.25	0.35	0.54	0.76	1.08
45%	0.62	0.68	1.51	1.49	0.39	0.56	0.90	1.17

EXHIBIT 16.10

Add-On Turn Volatility Premium
6 Percent Forward Rate

	Base Rate Volatility							
	1-Month LIBOR				***3-Month Eurodollars***			
Volatility of the Turn Ratio	***2-Day Turn***		***4-Day Turn***		***2-Day Turn***		***4-Day Turn***	
	15%	**25%**	**15%**	**25%**	**15%**	**25%**	**15%**	**25%**
25%	0.72	1.05	1.46	2.00	0.65	1.04	1.30	1.99
35%	0.83	1.11	1.81	2.20	0.69	1.05	1.51	2.07
45%	1.02	1.23	2.33	2.52	0.76	1.10	1.69	2.21

Theoretical Turn Volatility Premiums

How much is turn-rate volatility worth for options on December LIBOR and Eurodollar futures? The results shown in Exhibits 16.9 and 16.10 suggest that it should be fairly small. Consider the case in which

- The volatility (i.e., standard deviation) of the turn/non-turn ratio is 45 percent
- Forward deposit rates are around 3 percent
- The base rate volatilities of 1-month LIBOR and 3-month Eurodollar rates are 25 percent
- The turn period lasts 4 days

As shown in Exhibit 16.9, the contribution of volatility in the turn rate would add 1.49 percent to the volatility of the December LIBOR futures contract, and 1.17 percent to the volatility of the December Eurodollar futures contract. The contribution is smaller for lower levels of volatility. And, at any given set of volatilities, the contribution is smaller for a 2-day turn than for a 4-day turn.

The effect of turn-rate volatility is higher if the level of non-turn interest rates is higher. This is shown in Exhibit 16.10, where everything is the same as in Exhibit 16.9 except that the level of non-turn rates is 6 percent rather than 3 percent. At this level of rates, we reckon that the effect of 45 percent volatility in the turn/non-turn ratio combined with 25 percent base rate volatility is an increase of 2.52 percent in December LIBOR and 2.21 percent in December Eurodollar volatility for a 4-day turn.

SO WHAT?

These results may not seem very exciting at first glance because they cannot shed much light on whether December LIBOR or Eurodollar options are rich or cheap. They can be a powerful tool, however, in evaluating spread trades between December LIBOR and Eurodollar options.

For instance, even in the extreme case with rates at 6 percent, turn ratio volatility at 45 percent, base rate volatility at 25 percent, and a 4-day turn, the effect of turn-rate volatility on the difference between LIBOR and Eurodollar volatilities would only be about

0.3 percent (the difference between 2.52 and 2.21 as shown in Exhibit 16.10). In less extreme cases, and with a 3-day turn, the effect would be smaller.

Also, we find that the spread between the historical volatilities of the December LIBOR and Eurodollar contracts over the past 2 years has actually been around zero to slightly negative. The dotted lines in Exhibits 16.11 and 16.12 show historical volatility spreads for 1991 and 1992. Exhibit 16.13 shows that the historical LED volatility spread has been below zero for the December 1993 contracts as well.

Now contrast the theory and the evidence, both of which point to a small volatility spread, with the spread between the implied volatilities for LIBOR and Eurodollar options. In 1991 and 1992, and again in 1993, the options market has paid a hefty premium for the LED volatility spread. The average implied volatility spread in 1992, for example, was about 4.5 percent. At this writing,

EXHIBIT 16.11

LED Volatility Spreads
December 1991 Contracts

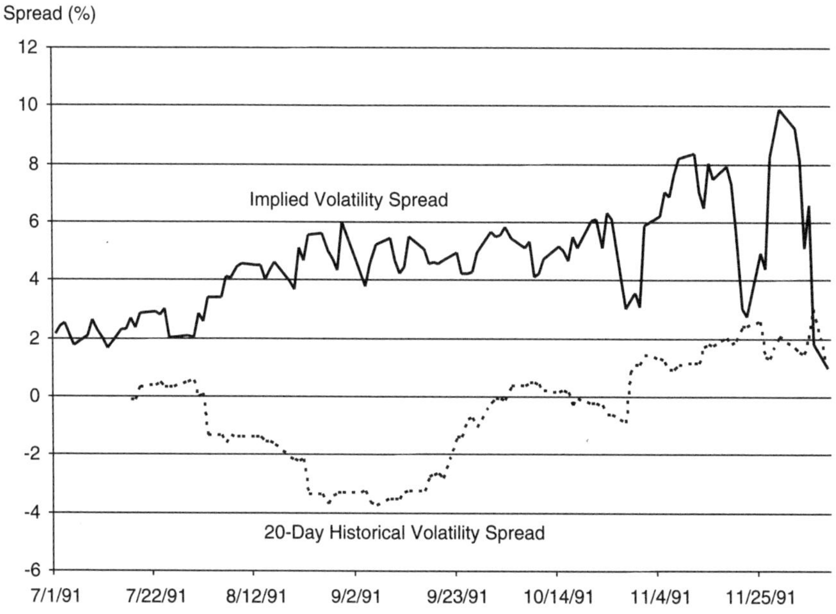

EXHIBIT 16.12

LED Volatility Spreads
December 1992 Contracts

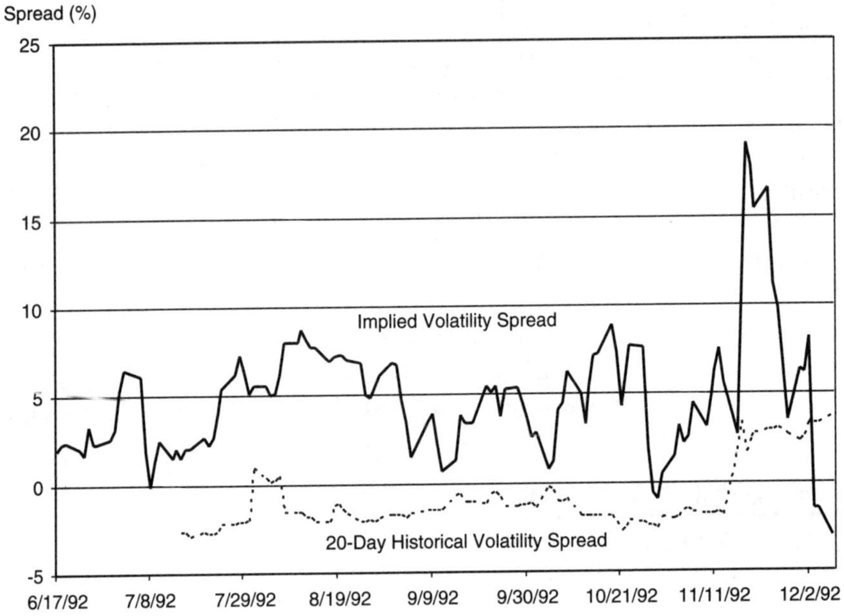

the LED volatility spread for the December 1993 contracts is trading around 7 percent, which is far more than is warranted by either the theory or the evidence.

We view this as an opportunity to take advantage of an apparent mispricing. For example, to sell December 1993 LIBOR volatility and buy December 1993 Eurodollar volatility, on September 20, 1993, one could have:

- Sold 100 December 96.25 LIBOR straddles at 37 ticks per straddle, and sold 3 December LIBOR futures to make the position delta neutral.
- Bought 106 December 96.50 Eurodollar straddles at 25 ticks per straddle, and bought 4 December Eurodollar futures to make the position delta neutral.

Thus, the spread position could have been established for a net credit of about 12 ticks per straddle or 1,050 ticks for the position.

EXHIBIT 16.13

LED Volatility Spreads
December 1993 Contracts

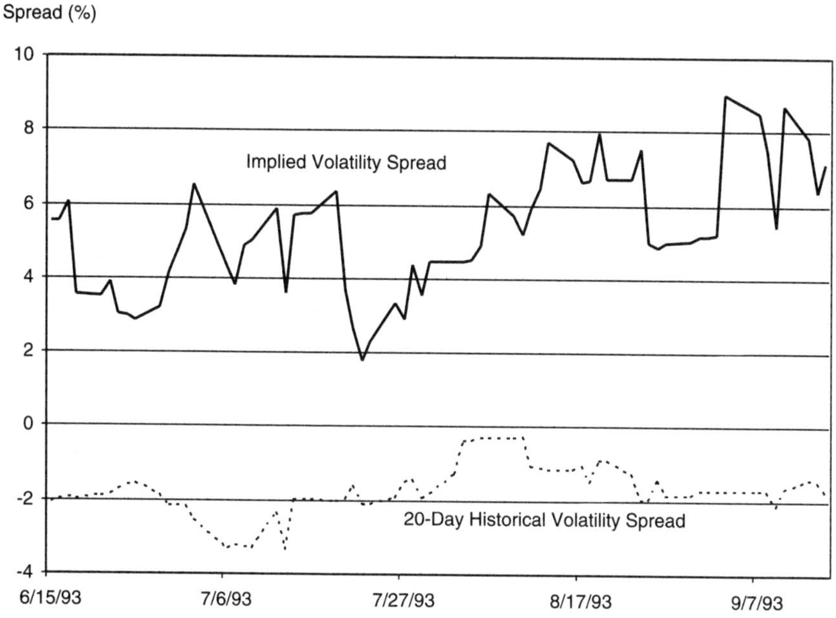

A position like this would have some interesting and desirable characteristics. First, because the spread is long the low-volatility options and short the high-volatility options, the net position provides a rare opportunity to be long gamma and to have time decay work in your favor at the same time.

The Risks in the Trade

As shown in both Exhibits 16.11 and 16.12, the implied LED volatility spread is highly variable. Thus, even though the additional premium paid for LIBOR volatility seems not to be justified by either the theory or the evidence, a position that is short LIBOR volatility and long Eurodollar volatility can produce large swings in a trader's P/L from day to day. Also, a sharp increase in the turn rate can be costly for anyone who is short LIBOR volatility. In late November 1990, for example, such a spike in the turn rate increased the 20-day historical volatility spread to around 14 percent.

Even so, there are two ways the trader can make money on the trade. The first is a collapse in the implied volatility spread so that it accords more closely with what it should be. This is far and away the most satisfactory outcome because it avoids the need to actually work for a living by managing the position until the December expiration of the options.

If the implied volatility spread does not collapse, the trader can still make money if the realized difference between December LIBOR and Eurodollar volatilities proves to be less than 7 percent. In this case, if the position is properly managed, the trader can profit from the relatively higher time decay that would be taken in on the LIBOR options than would be paid out on the Eurodollar options.

CHAPTER 17

The Turn: An Update

Chapter 16 reproduces the research note:

- Trading the Turn (1993)

To help traders keep an eye on the market's view about the turn, we created the "Eurodollar and LIBOR Turn Report," shown in Exhibit 17.1. This report shows by year how much the December contract is out of line, how many days there are in each year's turn, and what the distortion implied for a turn premium in the year-end Fed funds rate.

In the particular example shown here, the turn distortions are comparatively small by historical standards, and so are the turn premiums. For that matter, on September 10, 2002, the distortion for the Dec '02 contract appeared to be negative. For the rest of the December contracts, the futures rate distortions are all 2+ basis points, implying Fed funds premiums of anywhere from 44 basis points (Dec '06) to 116 basis points (Dec '07).

HEDGING THE STUB

The period between today and the first available futures contract's expiration has become known as the stub, and the term financing rate that covers this period is called the stub rate. Any trade or hedge that combines spot commodities with futures is exposed to

EXHIBIT 17.1

Eurodollar and LIBOR Turn Report

Carr Futures Eurodollar and LIBOR Turn Report

As of close 10-Sep-02 Target Funds = 1.75%

Month	Eurodollar Futures Rate	turn days	turn distortion (bps)	turn premium (bps)	implied year end FF rate	bps of turn prem for 1bp of distort	turn butterfly (ticks)	fly p/l (ticks) for 100 bps of turn prem
Sep-02	1.813%							
Dec-02	1.775%	2	-8.62	-391	-2.16%	45.50	-17.2	4.40
Mar-03	1.910%							
Jun-03	2.180%							
Sep-03	2.545%							
Dec-03	2.895%	2	2.00	88	2.63%	45.50	4.0	4.40
Mar-04	3.205%							
Jun-04	3.455%							
Sep-04	3.670%							
Dec-04	3.880%	3	2.00	56	2.31%	30.33	4.0	6.59
Mar-05	4.050%							
Jun-05	4.210%							
Sep-05	4.355%							
Dec-05	4.530%	3	2.00	51	2.26%	28.00	4.0	7.14
Mar-06	4.665%							
Jun-06	4.805%							
Sep-06	4.920%							
Dec-06	5.075%	4	2.25	44	2.19%	22.75	4.5	8.79
Mar-07	5.185%							
Jun-07	5.300%							
Sep-07	5.405%							
Dec-07	5.540%	2	2.75	116	2.91%	45.50	5.5	4.40
Mar-08	5.620%							
Jun-08	5.710%							
Sep-08	5.780%							
Dec-08	5.880%	2	2.25	93	2.68%	45.50	4.5	4.40
Mar-09	5.935%							
Jun-09	6.015%							
Sep-09	6.080%							
Dec-09	6.160%	4	2.50	47	2.22%	22.75	5.0	8.79
Mar-10	6.190%							
Jun-10	6.255%							
Sep-10	6.310%							
Dec-10	6.370%	3	2.25	58	2.33%	30.33	4.5	6.59
Mar-11	6.385%							
Jun-11	6.440%							
Sep-11	6.490%							
Dec-11	6.555%	3	2.75	70	2.45%	29.67	5.5	6.74
Mar-12	6.565%							
Jun-12	6.605%							

Month	LIBOR Futures Rate	turn days	turn distortion (bps)	turn premium (bps)	year end rate	bps of turn prem for 1bp of distort	turn butterfly (ticks)	fly p/l (ticks) for 100 bps of turn prem
Sep-02	1.82%							
Oct-02	1.79%							
Nov-02	1.76%							
Dec-02	1.79%	2	4.50	74	2.49%	16.5	9.0	12.12
Jan-03	1.72%							
Feb-03	1.76%							
Mar-03	1.82%							
Apr-03	1.86%							
May-03	1.96%							
Jun-03	2.04%							
Jul-03	2.12%							
Aug-03	2.25%							

The information contained herein is based upon sources that we believe to be reliable, but we do not represent that it is complete or accurate. Nothing contained herein should be considered as an offer to sell or a solicitation of an offer to buy any financial instruments discussed herein. Any opinions expressed herein are solely those of the author. As such, they may differ in material respects from those of, or expressed or published by or on behalf of Carr Futures, its officers, directors or employees.

EXHIBIT 17.1

Continued

Carr Futures Eurodollar and LIBOR Turn Report

As of close 10-Sep-02

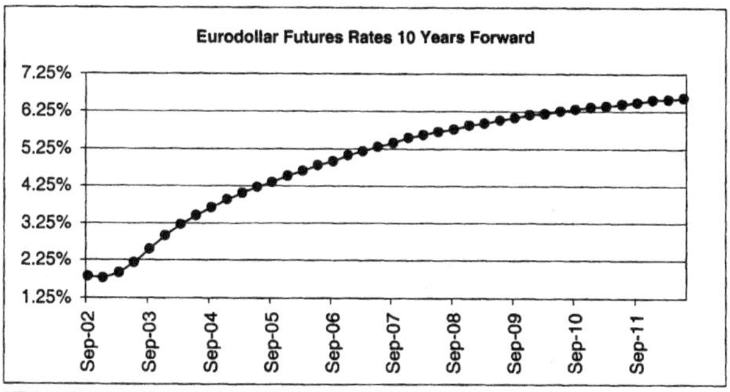

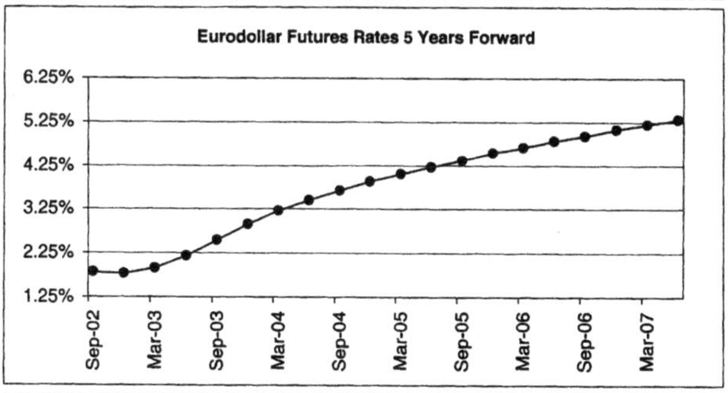

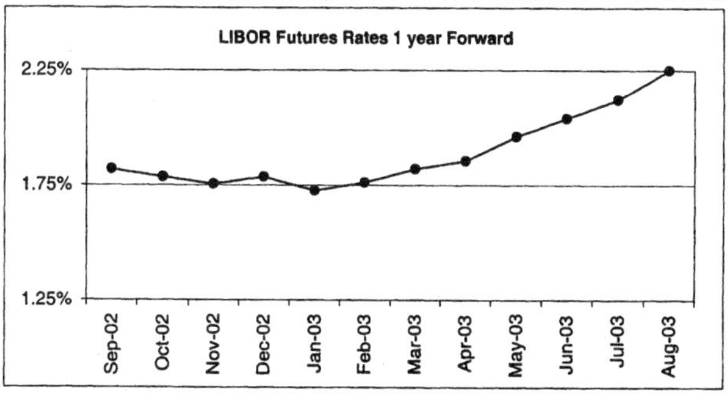

stub rate risk. One way to offset this risk is to borrow or lend in the term money market to create offsetting interest rate exposure. The best available futures solution employs the Fed funds futures that are traded at the Chicago Board of Trade. These contracts are especially well suited to hedging very short-term money market risk—first, because Fed funds rates track term repo rates well, and second, because the contracts settle to averages of realized Fed funds rates, so there is very little slippage.

The "Stub Hedges" report, shown in Exhibit 17.2, was designed for clients who want to use futures rather than term repo to hedge their stub rate exposure. In the example provided here for the close of business on September 10, 2002 (trade date of September 11, 2002), you can see examples of various spot commodities traded against different futures. For example, the stub for a Treasury bond or note hedged with Eurodollar futures was 6 days, and the appropriate hedge for this risk would be 6 Sep '02 Fed funds futures. For a spot equity position hedged with S&P equity futures, the stub period was 99 days, and the stub hedge would comprise 20 Sep '02 contracts, 21 Oct '02 contracts, 20 Nov '02 contracts, and 12 Dec '02 contracts.

EXHIBIT 17.2

Stub Hedges
Using CBOT Fed Funds Futures

CARR FUTURES
Chicago

Stub Hedges
CBOT Fed Funds Futures

Trade Date: Wednesday, September 11, 2002

CBOT FED FUNDS FUTURES HEDGE

Cash	Futures hedge		Stub period dates: Actual		Stub period dates: Phase-shifted		Total	CBOT contracts per $100,000,000 market value of cash instrument				
	Type	Code	Cash settle	Futures value	Start	End	stub days	Sep-02	Oct-02	Nov-02	Dec-02	<-- contract
								9/1/02	10/1/02	11/1/02	12/1/02	<-- first rate date
								9/30/02	10/31/02	11/30/02	12/31/02	<-- last rate date
Tsy	Eurodollar	ED	9/12/02	9/18/02	9/11/02	9/17/02	6	6	0	0	0	<-- stub hedge
Equity	S&P 500	SP	9/16/02	12/24/02	9/11/02	12/19/02	99	20	21	20	12	<-- stub hedge
Gold	Gold	GC	9/13/02	12/2/02	9/11/02	11/30/02	80	20	21	19	0	<-- stub hedge
Tsy	30 Yr Tsy 10 Yr Tsy 5 Yr Tsy	US TY FV	9/12/02	12/2/02 First delivery	9/11/02	12/1/02	81	20	21	20	0	<-- stub hedge
Tsy	30 Yr Tsy 10 Yr Tsy 5 Yr Tsy	US TY FV	9/12/02	9/30/02 Last delivery	9/11/02	9/29/02	18	18	0	0	0	<-- stub hedge
Tsy	2 Yr Tsy	TU	9/12/02	12/2/02 First delivery	9/11/02	12/1/02	81	20	21	20	0	<-- stub hedge
Tsy	2 Yr Tsy	TU	9/12/02	10/3/02 Last delivery	9/11/02	10/2/02	21	20	1	0	0	<-- stub hedge

PART FOUR

Building Blocks: Eurodollar Options

Calls and puts on Eurodollar futures have provided highly effective tools for trading the yield curve and hedging interest rate and interest rate volatility risk. The Chicago Mercantile Exchange began offering options on Eurodollar futures in 1985. The first options listed for trading were structured so that they expired when their underlying futures contracts expired. They were, as a result, designed to behave like the individual legs of interest rate caps and floors.

Over the years, the CME has filled in the menu of options that can be traded by listing options that expire months or years before their underlying futures contracts expire. One can, for example, trade serial options on a September futures contract that expire in July or August as well as the quarterly option that expires in September. Thus, one can trade 1-month, 2-month, and 3-month options on a rate that is 3 months forward.

Also, one can trade mid-curve options. For example, one can trade options on the Sep '04 futures contract that expire in September 2002 and September 2003 in addition to the option that expires in September 2004. These mid-curve options have proven especially useful for those who want to take limited risk positions on the level and shape of the forward rate curve and for those who want to hedge convexity exposure and over-the-counter Treasury options.

The material in part 4 is intended for those who know something already about options in general but who want to know about Eurodollar options in particular.[1] With this in mind, we will cover:

- Option contract specifications and grid of available options
- Price, volatility, and risk parameter conventions
- Caps, floors, and Eurodollar options
- Structure and patterns of Eurodollar rate volatilities
- Practical considerations

The section on Eurodollar rate volatilities is especially important for Eurodollar option traders because it provides useful insights into the term and maturity structures of volatility and the shapes of distributions of Eurodollar rate changes.

1. The chapters in parts 4 and 5 presuppose a basic familiarity with option concepts and the use of option pricing models. For those who wish to learn more about option pricing and risk characteristics, we recommend John C. Hull's *Options, Futures, and Other Derivatives*, 5th ed. (Upper Saddle River, N.J.: Prentice Hall, 2003).

CHAPTER 18

The Eurodollar Option Contract

Eurodollar option contracts were listed by the Chicago Mercantile Exchange in March 1985. The first options had quarterly expirations and expired on the same date as their underlying futures contract. Over time, the CME has added serial options, mid-curve options, and options on the 5-year bundle. Eurodollar options trade on the Exchange floor and electronically through GLOBEX.

The purpose of this chapter is to introduce Eurodollar options by covering the:

- Grid of available option expirations and underlyings
- Contract specifications

OPTION EXPIRATIONS AND UNDERLYING FUTURES

The owner of a Eurodollar call option has the right, but not the obligation, to buy the underlying Eurodollar futures contract at the option's strike price on or before option expiration. Similarly, the owner of a Eurodollar put option has the right, but not the obligation, to sell the underlying Eurodollar futures contract at the option's strike price on or before option expiration. Because Eurodollar options can be exercised prior to or at expiration, they are American-style options.

We further distinguish Eurodollar options based on their underlying futures contract. This provides us with four types of options:

- Standard quarterly options
- Serial options
- Mid-curve options
- Five-year bundle options

Standard Quarterly Options

Eight standard quarterly options are available for trading at any given time. These options expire in the March, June, September, and December cycle. The underlying futures contract has the same expiration date as the option. So, for example, the standard Sep '02 option is on the Sep '02 futures contract.

Exhibit 18.1 shows a grid of available options along with their underlying futures contracts as of the close on June 17, 2002. The standard quarterly options are shown on the diagonal from the Sep '02/Sep '02 box to the Jun '04/Jun '04 box.

Serial Options

Two standard serial options are listed, also. Serial contract months are those that fall outside of the March, June, September, and December cycle. Serial options have expirations in January, February, April, May, July, August, October, and November. The underlying futures for these options are the following quarterly futures contract. For example, Exhibit 18.1 shows that the Jul '02 and Aug '02 serial options are on the Sep '02 futures contract.

Mid-Curve Options

Traders use mid-curve options to trade short-dated options on longer-dated futures. The four quarterly 1-year mid-curve options expire 1 year before their associated futures. For example, as shown in Exhibit 18.1, the 1-year mid-curve option that expires in Dec '02 is on the Dec '03 futures contract.

There are two serial 1-year mid-curve options. The underlying futures contract for each option is 1 year away from the quar-

EXHIBIT 18.1

Grid of Available Options
June 17, 2002, Close of Trading

Futures Expiration	Option Expiration									
	Jul '02	Aug '02	Sep '02	Dec '02	Mar '03	Jun '03	Sep '03	Dec '03	Mar '04	Jun '04
Sep '02 White	serial	serial	standard Sep							
Dec '02 White				standard Dec						
Mar '03 White					standard Mar					
Jun '03 White						standard Jun				
Sep '03 Red	serial 1-yr mid-curve Short Jul	serial 1-yr mid-curve Short Aug	1-yr mid-curve Short Sep				standard Red Sep			
Dec '03 Red				1-yr mid-curve Short Dec				standard Red Dec		
Mar '04 Red					1-yr mid-curve Short Mar				standard Red Mar	

EXHIBIT 18.1

Continued

Futures Expiration	Option Expiration									
	Jul '02	Aug '02	Sep '02	Dec '02	Mar '03	Jun '03	Sep '03	Dec '03	Mar '04	Jun '04
Jun '04 Red						1-yr mid-curve Short Jun				standard Red Jun
Sep '04 Green			2-yr mid-curve Green Sep							
Dec '04 Green				2-yr mid-curve Green Dec						
Mar '05 Green					2-yr mid-curve Green Mar					
Jun '05 Green						2-yr mid-curve Green Jun				

Note: Excludes options on 5-year bundles.

terly futures contract that follows the option expiration. So, the Aug '02 1-year mid-curve option is on the Sep '03 futures contract (see Exhibit 18.1).

Two-year mid-curve options also allow traders to trade short-term options on longer-term futures. There are four quarterly 2-year mid-curve options. The associated futures contract expires 2 years after the option expiration.

Five-Year Bundle Options

There are two quarterly and two serial 5-year bundle options. These options give their owners the right to buy, if a call, or sell, if a put, the 5-year futures bundle beginning with the first available quarterly futures contract. Five-year bundle options trade only on the Exchange floor, not electronically.

OPTION CONTRACT SPECIFICATIONS[1]

The Eurodollar option contract specifications are described below and summarized in Exhibit 18.2.

Contract Unit

An option to buy, in the case of a call, or an option to sell, in the case of a put,

- One Eurodollar futures contract—for standard, serial, and mid-curve options
- One 5-year futures bundle—for 5-year bundle options

Price Quote

Bids and offers are quoted in IMM (International Monetary Market) index points. For example, a quote of 0.35 represents an option price of $875 [= 35 basis points × $25/basis point].

1. The contract specifications were taken from the CME Rulebook as of June 4, 2002. Please visit the CME's website at www.cme.com for the most recent information.

EXHIBIT 18.2

Eurodollar Option Contract Specifications

Contract unit		One Eurodollar futures contract. For options on the 5-year bundle, the contract unit is one 5-year Eurodollar futures bundle, or 20 futures contracts.
Price quote		IMM Index points
Tick size		0.01 (1 basis point)
Tick value		$25 $500 for options on the 5-year bundle
Minimum fluctuation		1. Contract month whose underlying futures contract is the nearest expiring futures contract month—0.0025 (one-quarter tick) 2. First 4 contract months in quarterly cycle and first 2 months not in quarterly cycle (excluding contract month whose underlying futures contract month is nearest expiring)—0.005 (one-half tick) 3. Second 4 contract months in quarterly cycle—0.01 (one tick) 4. All other contract months—0.01 (one tick) 5. 5-year bundle options—0.01 (one tick = $500) 6. Mid-curve options—For first 2 contract months in quarterly cycle and first 2 months not in quarterly cycle—0.005 (one-half tick). For other mid-curves—0.01 (one tick)
Strike price increments		0.25, with special listings of 0.125
Price limits	CME Floor	None
	CME GLOBEX	Trading halts when primary futures contract is locked limit.
Listed contract month		• 8 quarterly standard options; 2 serial standard options • 4 quarterly 1-year mid-curve options; 2 serial 1-year mid-curve options • 4 quarterly 2-year mid-curve options • 2 quarterly 5-year bundle options; 2 serial 5-year bundle options

EXHIBIT 18.2

Continued

Trading hours	CME Floor	Monday through Friday: 7:20 a.m.–2:00 p.m. CST
	CME GLOBEX	Monday through Thursday: 2:13 p.m.–7:04 a.m. CST the following day Sunday: 5:30 p.m.–7:04 a.m. CST the following day
Last trading day		1. Options in quarterly cycle (except mid-curve and 5-year bundle options)—option trading terminates at same date and time as underlying futures contract 2. Options not in quarterly cycle, mid-curve options, and 5-year bundle options—close of trading on the Friday preceding the third Wednesday of the contract month
Exercise of option		Buyer may exercise option on any business day option is traded

Tick Size

The basic tick size is 0.01 (or 1 basis point, often represented by bp). The dollar value of a tick is \$25. The dollar value of a tick on the 5-year bundle option is \$500 [= \$25 × 20 contracts].

Minimum Fluctuation

The minimum fluctuation for an option depends on its type (standard, 1-year mid-curve, 2-year mid-curve, or 5-year bundle); on whether it is a quarterly or serial option; and on where the option falls in the quarterly or serial cycle. The minimum fluctuation varies from 0.0025 (one-quarter tick) to 0.01 (one tick) based on these factors. See Exhibit 18.2 for details.

Strike Price Increments

Option strike or exercise prices are usually in increments of 0.25, although strikes of 0.125 are possible for options that are near expiration. For the nearest options in the March quarterly cycle and the two nearest options not in the March quarterly cycle having the same underlying futures contract, 0.125 strikes shall be listed beginning on the Exchange business day following the expiration of the spot month options in the March quarterly cycle. For the nearest options in the March quarterly cycle and the two nearest options not in the quarterly cycle 1-year mid-curve options, and the nearest options in the March quarterly cycle 2-year mid-curve options, 0.125 strike prices shall be listed beginning on the Exchange business day following the expiration of the last contract month in the same listing cycle.

When an option begins to trade, the Exchange establishes the strike range of available options. The Exchange adds additional exercise prices up or down as the futures market rises or falls. For options on 5-year bundles, the strike prices are based on the average price of the futures contracts in the bundle.

Listed Contract Months

All option types, with the exception of the 2-year mid-curve option, trade both quarterly and serial expirations. Two-year mid-curves have quarterly expirations only. The breakdown is shown in Exhibit 18.3.

EXHIBIT 18.3

Number of Standard, Serial, Mid-Curve, and Bundle Option Contracts

Option	Contracts Listed
Standard quarterly	8
Serial	2
1-year mid-curve quarterly	4
1-year mid-curve serial	2
2-year mid-curve quarterly	4
2-year mid-curve serial	0
5-year bundle quarterly	2
5-year bundle serial	2
Total	24

Contract Type and Month Symbols

Each Eurodollar option contract is identified by type and by the month and year of expiration. Exhibit 18.4 shows the symbols used by the CME for each option type and Exhibit 18.5 shows the symbols for each contract month. For example, the 2-year mid-curve option that expires in December 2002 would be designated by E2Z2. The 1-year serial mid-curve option that expires in August 2002 would be designated by E0Q2.

EXHIBIT 18.4

Option Type Symbols

Type	Symbol
Standard	ED
1-year mid-curve	E0
2-year mid-curve	E2
5-year bundle	Y5

EXHIBIT 18.5

Contract Month Symbols

Month	Symbol
January	F
February	G
March	H
April	J
May	K
June	M
July	N
August	Q
September	U
October	V
November	X
December	Z

Sample Option Quotes

Bloomberg makes use of the contract month symbols in its option quote screen. For example, in Exhibit 18.6, October 2002 call and put prices are displayed next to the symbols 0EV2C and 0EV2P. Note that Bloomberg uses 0E, rather than E0, to designate the 1-year mid-curve contract. Bloomberg also uses 2E, rather than E2, to designate the 2-year mid-curve.

Trading Hours

Eurodollar options trade on the floor of the CME from 7:00 a.m. to 2:00 p.m. Chicago time. Standard and mid-curve options trade on GLOBEX Monday through Thursday, 2:13 p.m. to 7:04 a.m. the following day and Sunday from 5:30 p.m. to 7:04 a.m. the following day. Five-year bundle options do not trade on GLOBEX.

Last Trading Day

Standard quarterly options terminate trading at the same date and time as their underlying futures contracts. This means that the options stop trading at 11:00 a.m. London time on the second London bank business day immediately preceding the third Wednesday of the contract month. This is 5:00 a.m. Chicago time, except when daylight savings time is in effect in either, but not both, London or Chicago.

Serial options, mid-curve options, and 5-year bundle options all terminate at the close of trading on the Friday preceding the third Wednesday of the contract month.

Exercise of Option

The owner of a call or put may exercise the option on any business day that the option is traded. An option that is in the money at the termination of trading, and has not been liquidated or exercised prior to the termination of trading, is exercised automatically at 7:00 p.m., unless the Clearing House receives instructions to the contrary.

EXHIBIT 18.6

October '02 1-Year Mid-Curve Option Prices

GRAB — Comdty **OMON**

At 13:35 Vol 51,450y Op 97.630 Hi 97.650 Lo 97.560 OpInt 352,407

Template List | Edit | Contract Months | Security List | 0EZ3 Comdty

Option Monitor: EURO$ 1YR MID-CRV Dec03

Center 97.61 Number of Strikes 18 -or- % from Center Exchange C (Composite)

CALLS

Ticker	Strike	Bid	Ask	Last	Volume
0EZ3 OCT 02 (Contract Size: 1000000.00)					
1) 0EV2C	96.250			1.3400 y	
2) 0EV2C	96.375			1.2150 y	
3) 0EV2C	96.500			1.0900 y	
4) 0EV2C	96.625			.9650 y	
5) 0EV2C	96.750			.8400 y	
6) 0EV2C	96.875			.7150 y	
7) 0EV2C	97.000			.5900 y	
8) 0EV2C	97.125			.4700 y	
9) 0EV2C	97.250			.3500 y	
10) 0EV2C	97.375	.2150		.2600	
11) 0EV2C	97.500			.1550 y	
12) 0EV2C	97.625	.0800	.0900	.0900 y	
13) 0EV2C	97.750	.0400	.0450	.0450	
14) 0EV2C	97.875	.0200	.0250	.0200	
15) 0EV2C	98.000	.0050	.0100	.0100 y	

PUTS

Ticker	Strike	Bid	Ask	Last	Volume
0EZ3 OCT 02 (Contract Size: 1000000.00)					
19) 0EV2P	96.250			.0025 y	
20) 0EV2P	96.375			.0050 y	
21) 0EV2P	96.500			.0050 y	
22) 0EV2P	96.625			.0050 y	
23) 0EV2P	96.750			.0050 y	
24) 0EV2P	96.875			.0050 y	
25) 0EV2P	97.000			.0050 y	
26) 0EV2P	97.125			.0050 y	
27) 0EV2P	97.250	.0100	.0150	.0100	
28) 0EV2P	97.375	.0250	.0300	.0250	
29) 0EV2P	97.500	.0500	.0550	.0550	
30) 0EV2P	97.625	.0950	.1050	.0950	
31) 0EV2P	97.750			.2050 y	
32) 0EV2P	97.875				
33) 0EV2P	98.000				

Australia 61 2 9777 8600 Brazil 5511 3048 4500 Europe 44 20 7330 7500 Germany 49 69 920410
Hong Kong 852 2977 6000 Japan 81 3 3201 8900 Singapore 65 212 1000 U.S. 1 212 318 2000 Copyright 2002 Bloomberg L.P.
G641-86-0 03-Oct-02 13:40:20

Assignment

After long options have been exercised, parties who are short the options are "assigned." This assignment is done by random selection of clearing members with short positions in the appropriate options. The clearing member assigned an exercise notice shall be assigned a short futures position, in the case of a call, and a long futures position, in the case of a put. Assignment of the futures position is done at the option's strike price; the futures position is then marked to market.

CHAPTER 19

Price, Volatility, and Risk Parameter Conventions

Early on in the life of options on Eurodollar futures, the market gravitated to the idea of thinking about the volatility of the underlying futures rate but quoting the options in terms of price. Thus, the price of a Eurodollar option depends on the distribution of the underlying rate, and the volatilities are quoted as relative rate volatilities. But an option's strike or exercise price refers to the underlying futures price.

PRICING OPTIONS ON FUTURES

The list of inputs or assumptions required to price an option on a futures contract is shorter than it is for options on spot commodities. With options on spot commodities, one typically needs three pieces of information for the model to calculate the forward price—the spot price, a financing interest rate, and a convenience yield of some sort (e.g., coupon, dividend, deposit rate, etc.). With options on futures, the futures price is the underlying price and is used in lieu of the forward price. Thus, when pricing options on futures, the list of inputs includes:

- Strike price
- Underlying futures price
- Volatility

- Time to expiration
- Discounting interest rate

where the discounting interest rate is used only to calculate present values.

Consider an example of pricing Sep '02 Eurodollar calls and puts on the Sep '02 futures contract on June 17, 2002. The futures price settled at 97.895 on that day, so we will use the 98.00 strike calls and puts in this example, with the calls slightly out of the money and the puts slightly in the money. The discounting interest rate used was 1.879 percent for all of the theoretical calculations. Price and risk information for these options is provided in Exhibit 19.1.

EXHIBIT 19.1

Pricing Sep '02 Eurodollar Options
Closing Values, June 17, 2002
Futures = 97.895; Discounting Interest Rate = 1.879%

	Call	Put
Description		
Strike	98.00	98.00
Underlying futures	Sep '02	Sep '02
Expiration	9/16/2002	9/16/2002
Days to expiration	91	91
Market and Risk		
Option price (market)	0.0625	0.1675
Implied volatility	26.238%	26.337%
Delta	0.324	−0.673
Gamma	1.297	1.296
Vega	0.00378	0.00379
Theta	−0.000542	−0.000541
Rho	−0.00000157	−0.00000421
Time value	0.0625	0.0625

Data source: Bloomberg. Visit www.Bloomberg.com.

OPTION PRICE (MARKET)

The 98.00 call settled at 0.0625, while the 98.00 put settled at 0.1675. In money, the price of the call would be \$156.25 [= 0.0625 × \$2500 = 6.25 ticks × \$25/tick], and the price of the put would be \$418.75 [= 0.1675 × \$2500 = 16.75 ticks × \$25/tick].

VOLATILITY

Volatility is used to characterize the variability of the underlying futures contract. It is one of the key inputs to an option pricing model, as shown in Exhibit 19.2. Without volatility in the underlying market, options would have no value apart from their intrinsic or exercise value.

Volatility usually describes the underlying instrument's relative price changes. In the Eurodollar futures market, however, volatility represents the variability of rate, rather than price, changes. The market quotes volatility on an annualized basis and typically as a percent. In mathematical terms, volatility is defined as the annualized standard deviation of relative rate changes, which are calculated as the natural log of the ratio of one day's

EXHIBIT 19.2

Option Pricing Model
Assumed Volatility → Theoretical Price

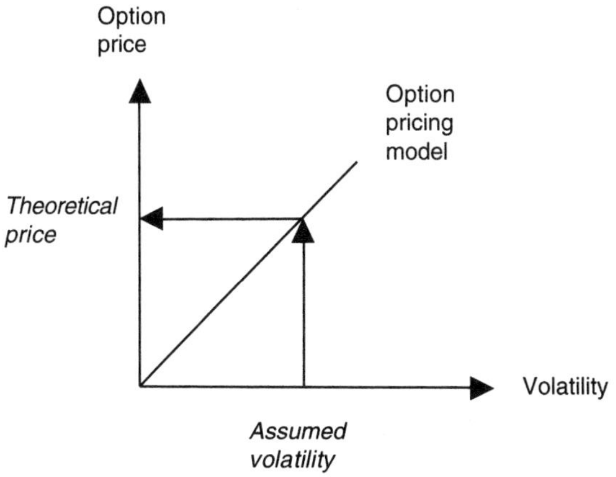

rate to the previous day's rate. Conventional option pricing models assume—correctly or not—that these relative rate changes are normally distributed and that rate changes are lognormally distributed. Exhibit 19.3 shows a normal distribution of rate changes plotted against a lognormal distribution. Notice that the lognormal curve is bunched on the left and skewed to the right.

Relative Rate Volatility

Estimates of Eurodollar rate volatilities are based on one-day relative rate changes. A one-day relative rate change is calculated as the natural log of the ratio of today's futures rate to yesterday's futures rate, which is approximately equal to the one-day change in rates divided by the starting rate. See Equation 19.1 for this approximation.

EXHIBIT 19.3

Distribution of Rate Changes

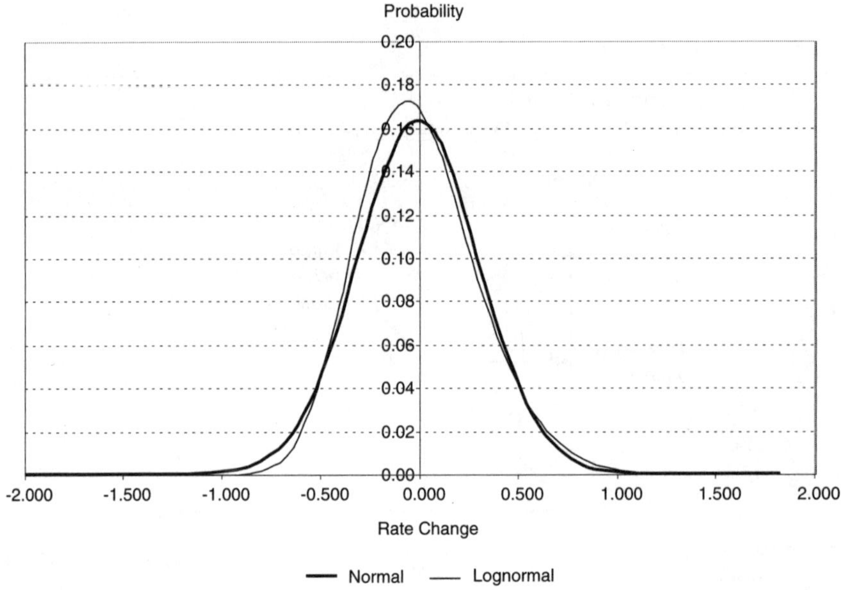

EQUATION 19.1

One-Day Relative Rate Change

$$1\text{-}day\ relative\ rate\ change = Ln\left(\frac{R_{t+1}}{R_t}\right) \approx \frac{R_{t+1} - R_t}{R_t}$$

where

R_t is the implied futures rate at time t
Ln is the natural log mathematical function

By convention, volatility represents an annualized standard deviation of daily price or rate changes. In the Eurodollar options market, volatility is quoted as the annualized standard deviation of daily relative rate changes. As shown in Equation 19.2, our practice is to assume that we know the theoretical mean of rate changes (we assume $\mu = 0$ without much worry) and so we divide by the total sample size n. The standard deviation of daily rate changes is then multiplied by the square root of the number of trading days in the trading year. We have some latitude in choosing this number because the number of trading days in a year is somewhat arbitrary. For the sake of writing out Equation 19.2, we have used 256 because it is between 250 (a 52-week working year with a couple of weeks off) and 260 (no time off) and because its square root is 16, which is easy to work with in numerical examples.

Given this approach to measuring Eurodollar volatility, a change in the futures rate from 2.105 percent to 2.205 percent would be 0.0464 [= $Ln(2.205/2.105)$, which is approximately equal to 0.10 percent/2.105 percent], or 4.64 percent. This would annualize to a number like 74.26 percent [= 4.64 percent $\times \sqrt{256}$].

EQUATION 19.2

Annualized Volatility

$$\sigma = \sqrt{\frac{\sum_{0}^{n}\left[Ln\left(\frac{R_{t+1}}{R_t}\right) - \mu\right]^2}{n}} \times \sqrt{256}, \quad t = 0, \ldots, n$$

where

σ is annualized volatility
R_t is the implied futures rate at time t
μ is the theoretical mean
Ln is the natural log mathematical function
n is the number of daily changes in the sample period
256 is the approximate number of trading days in a year

Rate (Basis Point) Volatility

Although it is more common to discuss Eurodollar volatility in terms of relative rate changes, there is a growing body of evidence that supports the idea of working with simple arithmetic rate changes. (See chapter 25, "What Happens to Eurodollar Volatility When Rates Fall?" for more on this point.) These arithmetic changes may be referred to as normalized rate changes or basis point rate changes. Either way, a 1-*day rate change* is simply the difference in two interest rates as shown in Equation 19.3. Equation 19.3 also shows the relationship between rate changes and relative rate changes.

EQUATION 19.3

One-Day Rate Change

$$1\text{-}day\ rate\ change = \underbrace{R_{t+1} - R_t}_{\substack{Rate \\ volatility}} \approx \underbrace{Ln\left(\frac{R_{t+1}}{R_t}\right)}_{\substack{Relative \\ rate \\ volatility}} \underbrace{R_t}_{Rate}$$

Period Volatility

Because volatility is expressed as an annualized standard deviation, it is often useful to be able to scale it down to suit shorter trading horizons. For one thing, most traders have to mark their books to market at least once a day, so an annualized volatility means nothing. For another, most traded options expire in less than a year, so an annualized standard deviation is really beside the point.

To transform an annualized volatility into a shorter period standard deviation is easy. For example, we can convert an annualized volatility into a 1-day standard deviation by simply undoing the annualizing that was done in the first place. Equation 19.4 shows how this is done. For example, if annualized Eurodollar rate volatility is quoted as 24 percent, the 1-business-day standard deviation or volatility will be 1.5 percent [= 24 percent $\times (1/\sqrt{256})$ = 24 percent/16]. This 1-day volatility or standard deviation is especially useful when evaluating an option trade's profits and losses. As shown in chapter 21, "Structure and Patterns of Eurodollar Rate Volatility," a 1-standard deviation change in the underlying rate is just enough for the effects of gamma to offset the effects of theta.

EQUATION 19.4

Calculate Period Standard Deviations from Annualized Volatility

$$1\text{-}day\ \sigma = \sigma_1 = \frac{\sigma}{\sqrt{256}} = \frac{\sigma}{16}$$

$$t\text{-}day\ \sigma = \sigma_t = \frac{\sigma}{\sqrt{\dfrac{256}{Days_t}}}$$

where

σ is annualized volatility
$Days_t$ is the number of trading days in the period
256 is the approximate number of trading days in a year

We can use the same approach to calculate a longer period volatility. The only difference is that we divide the annualized standard deviation by the square root of the number of periods of that length in the trading year. For example, if we wanted to calculate the 1-week value of 24 percent volatility, we would get something like 3.35 percent [= 24 percent/$\sqrt{256/5}$], which is roughly the equivalent of dividing 24 percent by the square root of the number of weeks in the year.

Once we know how to calculate a standard deviation for any time period, it is easy to find basis point volatility over the same period. We can get to basis point volatility by multiplying period volatility times the futures rate, as shown in Equation 19.5.

EQUATION 19.5

Basis Point Volatility over Time Period *t*

$$Basis\ point\ volatility_t = \sigma_t \times R_t$$

where

σ_t is the standard deviation for time period t
R_t is the futures rate at time t

IMPLIED VOLATILITY

Implied volatility is the level of volatility that sets the theoretical option price equal to the market option price. It is a measure of how volatile the futures rate is expected to be over the remaining life of the option. If we input a market option price to the option pricing model, the model returns an implied volatility, as illustrated in Exhibit 19.4.

EXHIBIT 19.4

Option Pricing Model
Market Price → Implied Volatility

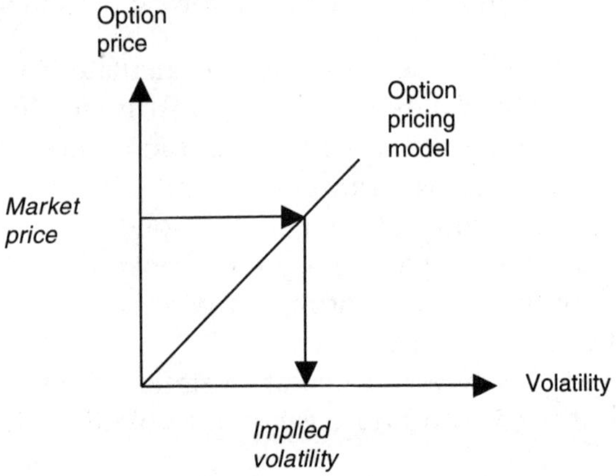

We will now interpret the implied volatilities for our 98.00 strike call and put options. The implied volatilities were 26.238 percent and 26.337 percent, respectively, which are the results of finding theoretical call and put prices that would equal their market prices. These volatilities are relative interest rate volatilities rather than the relative price volatilities. With an implied futures rate of 2.105 [= 100.000 − 97.895], a relative rate volatility of 26.238 percent would correspond to an annualized rate volatility of 0.552 [= 0.26238 × 2.105], or 55.2 basis points.

RISK PARAMETERS

Risk parameters are used to describe an option's sensitivity to market or time changes. The risk parameters delta, gamma, vega, theta, and rho are summarized in Exhibit 19.5 and described in detail below.

EXHIBIT 19.5

Summary of Risk Parameters

Risk Parameter	The Change In. . .	Given a Change In. . .
Delta	Option price	Futures price
Gamma	Delta	Futures price
Vega	Option price	Volatility
Theta	Option price	Time
Rho	Option price	Discounting interest rate

Application of Risk Parameters
For Small Changes in Market Conditions

Risk Parameter	Application
Delta	$\text{Option price}_{\text{New}} = \text{Option price}_{\text{Old}} + \text{Delta} \times \partial\text{Futures}$
Gamma	$\text{Delta}_{\text{New}} = \text{Delta}_{\text{Old}} + \text{Gamma} \times \partial\text{Futures}$
Vega	$\text{Option price}_{\text{New}} = \text{Option price}_{\text{Old}} + \text{Vega} \times \partial\text{Volatility}$
Theta	$\text{Option price}_{\text{New}} = \text{Option Price}_{\text{Old}} + \text{Theta} \times \partial\text{Time}$
Rho	$\text{Option price}_{\text{New}} = \text{Option price}_{\text{Old}} + \text{Rho} \times \partial\text{Interest rates}$

Delta

An option's delta is the approximate change in the option's price given a small increase in the underlying price. The delta of the 98.00 call, which is slightly out of the money with futures at 97.895, is 0.324 and is shown in Exhibit 19.1 as positive. With this delta, if the underlying futures price were to increase 10 ticks, the call price would increase approximately 3.24 ticks [$= 0.324 \times 10$ futures ticks]. The 98.00 put's delta is shown as -0.673, which indicates that if the underlying futures price were to increase 10 ticks, the put price would fall approximately 6.73 ticks [$= -0.673 \times 10$ futures ticks].

Notice that even though the driving force behind the options is the variability of interest rates, the option is still on the future's price rather than the rate, and the options' deltas are defined in terms of changes in the underlying Eurodollar futures price.

Gamma

Gamma is the change in the option's delta given a change in the underlying futures price. It is always positive for a long option. The 98.00 call has a gamma of 1.297. With a 10-tick increase in the futures price from 97.895 to 97.995, the call's delta increases from 0.324 to 0.4537 [$= 0.324 + 0.10 \times 1.297$]. This makes sense because the call is closer to the money at the higher futures price. The 98.00 put has a gamma of 1.296. With a 10-tick increase in the futures price, the put's delta becomes less negative as it changes from -0.673 to -0.5434 [$= -0.673 + 0.10 \times 1.296$]. The higher futures price makes the put less in the money.

Vega

Vega is the increase in the option's price given a 1-percentage-point increase in volatility. In this case, if volatility were to increase from 26.238 percent to 27.238 percent, the call's price would increase by 0.00378. The put's sensitivity to a change in implied volatility is almost exactly the same. The units of vega are price points.

Theta

Theta measures the rate at which the option's price falls with the passing of time. With a theta of −0.000542, a 5-day passage of time would cause the call option's price to fall by about 0.00271 [= 0.000542 × 5]. The units of theta are price points.

Notice that the theta of the put is ever so slightly smaller (in absolute value) than it is for the call. This is because the passing of time has two effects on the price of an option. One is a fall in the value of the option because the passing of time reduces the range of things that can happen to the underlying rate by the time the option expires. The other is an increase in the present value of the option because the discounting horizon is growing shorter. This is a comparatively small effect in most cases, but because the put's price is larger than the call's price, the present value effect is larger. As a result, the net rate of time decay for the put is slightly smaller than it is for the call.

Rho

Rho measures the effect of a change in the financing or discounting interest rate on the price of the option. With options on spot commodities, a change in this rate affects the option's price for two reasons. First, if one is holding the spot price of the commodity fixed, an increase in the financing rate will increase the commodity's forward price and will, as a result, increase the price of a call and decrease the price of a put. Second, an increase in the interest rate decreases all present values. As a result, if the option is priced to be paid in cash, then an increase in the discounting interest rate will reduce the option's price.

With options on futures, you increase this rate while assuming that the futures price is fixed. Thus, the only thing that can happen is that the present value of the option, and hence its price, falls. This is true both for the call and for the put. As shown in Exhibit 19.1, the call option's rho is −0.00000157, while the put option's rho is −0.00000421. The put's rho is, in absolute terms, larger than the call's rho because the put's price is higher than the call's and so, as a result, are any present value effects.

Generally, in our own risk reports, we omit values for rho because they tend to be very small relative to those for delta, gamma, vega, and theta.

Intrinsic and Time Value

The option's time value is its price net of any exercise or "intrinsic" value. The call option is out of the money so its entire price of 0.0625 is time value. The put is 0.105 points in the money, so its time value is also 0.0625 [= 0.1675 − 0.1050].

CHAPTER 20

Caps, Floors, and Eurodollar Options

Eurodollar options are the exchange-traded counterparts to interest rate caps and floors, which are traded over the counter. An interest rate cap, which pays the holder if *LIBOR* is above the cap rate at the rate setting date, is akin to a Eurodollar put, and an interest rate floor, which pays if the reference rate is below the floor rate, is like a Eurodollar call. Exhibit 20.1 shows the comparison between the exchange-traded and over-the-counter products.

The usual cap or floor comprises a sequence of "caplets" or "floorlets." That is, a cap is a sequence of single options whose payoff cover periods shorter than the life of the cap. For example, a 2-year cap with quarterly resets would comprise a sequence of 7 options, each of which depends on the value of 3-month *LIBOR* on the day the option expires. Thus, the first caplet in a 2-year cap traded in June 2002 would expire in September and would pay off or not depending on whether 3-month *LIBOR* on the rate setting date was greater than the cap rate. The seventh caplet would expire in March 2004 and would depend on the value of 3-month *LIBOR* then. Exhibit 20.2 illustrates this 2-year cap.

From a pricing standpoint, there are three main differences between over-the-counter caps and floors and exchange-traded Eurodollar options. First, caps and floors tend to be European-style options, while Eurodollar futures options are American-style

EXHIBIT 20.1

Cap and Eurodollar Put; Floor and Eurodollar Call

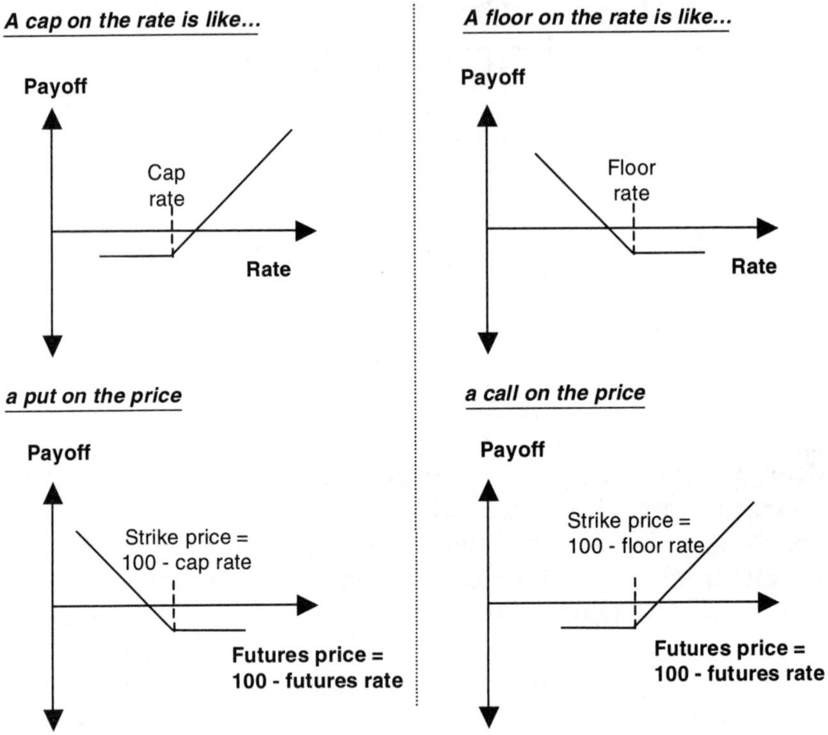

EXHIBIT 20.2

Rate Setting on a 2-Year Cap

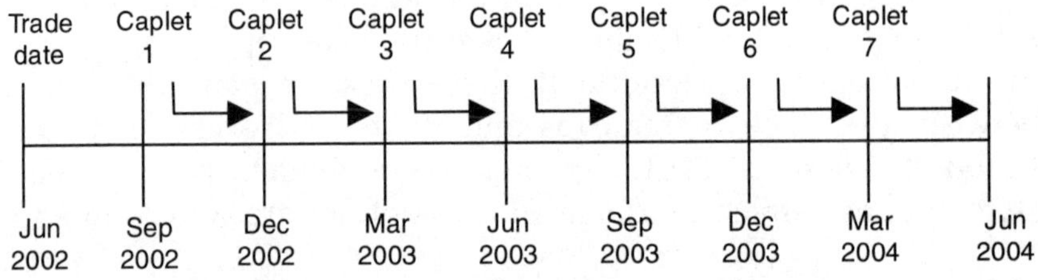

options. Second, the nominal payoff to a cap or floor depends on the days in the interest calculation period, while the nominal payoff to a Eurodollar futures option is a fixed $25 per basis point. Third, the holder of a cap or floor usually is paid in arrears—that is, at the end of the interest calculation period—while the holder of a Eurodollar option collects at option expiration.

The differences and similarities in payoffs for a cap and a Eurodollar put are illustrated in Exhibit 20.3. The conditions under which the two pay off are identical as long as the strike price on the Eurodollar put is set equal to 100 less the cap rate and as long as the reference rate for the cap is 3-month *LIBOR*. If *LIBOR* is less than or equal to the cap rate at expiration, the futures price will be greater than or equal to its strike price, and both instruments will pay nothing.

On the other hand, if *LIBOR* exceeds the cap rate at expiration, the holder of the cap collects an amount equal to

$$\textit{Notional amount} \times [\textit{LIBOR} - \textit{Cap rate}] \times \frac{\textit{Days}}{360}$$

at the end of the interest calculation period. The holder of the Eurodollar put would receive

$$\$2500[\textit{Exercise price} - \textit{Futures price}]$$

on the day the option expires.

EXHIBIT 20.3

An Interest Rate Cap is Like a Eurodollar Put
Put Strike Price = 100 − Cap Rate

3-Month *LIBOR* at Expiration	Value to Put Holder at Expiration	Payment to Cap Holder in Arrears
LIBOR < cap rate, or futures > strike price	0	0
LIBOR = cap rate, or futures = strike price	0	0
LIBOR > cap rate, or futures < strike price	Number of puts held × (exercise price − futures price) × $2500	Notional amount × (*LIBOR* − cap rate) × (days/360)

Exhibit 20.4 provides a comparison of the prices of Eurodollar puts and the component legs of a 2-year interest rate cap struck on June 17, 2002. The futures rates used in this exhibit were the implied Eurodollar futures rates at the close of business on June 17, and the implied volatilities (not shown) were market implieds. The cap rate was set at 3.50, which was roughly in the middle of the futures rate curve, and the Eurodollar put strike was set at 96.50 [= 100.00 − 3.50]. For simplicity, the caplets have been arranged so that their rate-setting dates fall on Eurodollar futures expiration dates, and all caplet periods in this example contain 91 days. All option prices are expressed in Eurodollar option terms. To find the dollar value of any one option, simply multiply its value by $2,500.

The Eurodollar put prices are shown under the column labeled "American." We also have valued the options as European style. For the full strip of puts, the value of early exercise that goes with the American-style options was 0.10637 [= 4.30934 − 4.20297]. The cap prices are simply the European put prices scaled by (91/90)/(1 + *Rate* (91/360)), which increases the payoff to reflect the 91 days in the caplet periods and decreases the payoff to reflect the fact that the cap holder gets the money at the end of the 91 days rather than on the expiration or rate setting date. A

EXHIBIT 20.4

Comparing Eurodollar Puts to an Interest Rate Cap
June 17, 2002

Expiration	Futures Rate	*96.50 Put Price* American	*96.50 Put Price* European	3.50 Cap Price
9/16/2002	2.105	0.00257	0.00256	0.00258
12/16/2002	2.495	0.03238	0.03226	0.03242
3/17/2003	3.055	0.22779	0.22655	0.22731
6/16/2003	3.635	0.55759	0.55188	0.55293
9/15/2003	4.120	0.89915	0.88323	0.88383
12/15/2003	4.495	1.19036	1.15788	1.15759
3/15/2004	4.720	1.39950	1.34861	1.34752
	Total =	4.30934	4.20297	4.20418

close comparison of the caplet prices with the European-style put prices shows that the day-count influence is greater for the shorter-dated caplets, while the discounting influence is greater for the longer-dated caplets.

The cap prices in Exhibit 20.4 are expressed in IMM, or Eurodollar futures options, terms for the sake of comparison. The convention for interest rate caps, however, is to quote the premium as a total dollar value or as a percentage of the notional amount if the structure is non-amortizing.

CHAPTER 21

Structure and Patterns of Eurodollar Rate Volatility

A large part of the challenge in trading Eurodollar options correctly is in understanding the way volatility is viewed and the way Eurodollar futures rate volatilities behave. We have noted already that the Eurodollar options market thinks about rate volatility rather than price volatility. And we have noted briefly the difference between relative rate volatility and basis point volatility. In this section, we fill in more of the volatility picture with discussions of:

- Historical, implied, realized, and break-even volatilities
- Term structure of Eurodollar rate volatility
- Maturity structure of volatility (volatility cones)
- Volatility skews and implied rate distributions

Some of these topics deal with peculiarities of the Eurodollar market, and some deal with options markets in general.

HISTORICAL, IMPLIED, REALIZED, AND BREAK-EVEN VOLATILITIES

The market looks at volatility in different ways to help it gain information about options and the underlying market. Here, we explain four different types of volatility—historical, implied, realized, and break-even—and show how they can be used to construct and interpret option trades. Exhibit 21.1 provides a summary description for each of the four volatilities.

Whether an option proves to be rich or cheap depends to a large extent on whether the volatility realized over the option's remaining life is less than or greater than the option's implied

EXHIBIT 21.1

Summary: Historical, Implied, Realized, and Break-even Volatilities

Historical volatility	Any statistical measure of futures rate (or price) variability based on historical data. Most commonly, volatility is stated as an annualized standard deviation of rate or price returns based on daily changes. Typically, the number of daily changes used in the calculation accompanies the measure. For example, a 1-month historical volatility would be a calculation based on 1 month's worth of daily changes.
Implied volatility	Implied volatility is calculated by finding a value for volatility that sets an option's theoretical price equal to its market price. It is equivalent to inverting the option pricing function so that one can use the option's market price as an input and solve for volatility rather than the other way around. Implied volatility is a measure of the market's expectations about the underlying's volatility over the remaining life of the option.
Realized volatility	Realized volatility is calculated the same way as historical volatility, but the rate or price changes are calculated using data gathered going forward through time rather than backward through history. The dividing line between the past and the future for this kind of calculation is the moment you buy or sell an option.
Break-even volatility	The amount of volatility that must be realized for the benefits of gamma (if you are long the option) to offset the costs of theta. If realized volatility equals implied volatility over any short horizon in the option's life, this condition is met. Strictly speaking, a long option position will pay the same as a delta equivalent position in the underlying if realized volatility equals implied volatility and if there is no change in implied volatility.

volatility at the time it is bought or sold. Our experience with interest rate volatility, as shown in Exhibit 21.2, is that it can vary widely over time. We have seen periods of very high volatility as the Eurodollar market responds to crises such as the stock market crash of 1987, the conflict with Iraq in the early 1990s, and the terrorist acts of September 11, 2001. We have also seen periods of comparative quiet. The 1990s, for the most part, were a period of generally low and falling interest rate volatilities.

As Exhibit 21.2 shows, implied rate volatilities tend to track historical volatilities fairly closely, although there are extended periods during which implied volatilities are either higher or lower than actual volatilities observed in the market. Such periods represent opportunities to buy cheap options or sell rich options, and the trader who has an aptitude for understanding and forecasting volatility will have an edge in this kind of trade.

As a rule, an option pays its way as an option if realized volatility equals an option's implied volatility. This rule applies to

EXHIBIT 21.2

Implied versus Historical Eurodollar Volatility
Lead Contract, 1984 through 2002

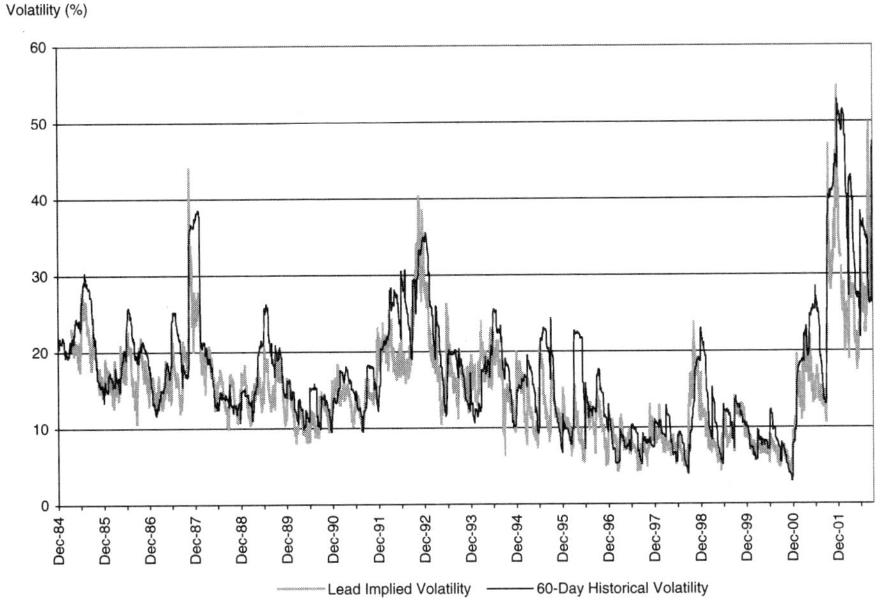

short trading horizons and is simply an extension of the theoretical work that went into the derivation of the original option pricing models. To apply this rule in practice, you need to be able to translate the annualized terms in which volatilities are measured and quoted into business-day terms. And to do this, you need use only the square of time rule. As an example, consider the Sep '02 option on the Sep '02 futures contract on June 17, 2002. At the close of trading, its implied volatility was 55 annualized basis points. If, as a rule, we suppose there are 256 business days in a trading year (an arbitrary but good assumption), this would translate into 3.4375 [$= 55/\sqrt{256} = 55/16$] basis points per trading day. The general rule for translating annualized volatilities into shorter period volatilities is shown in Equation 21.1.

EQUATION 21.1

Calculate Period Standard Deviations from Annualized Volatility

$$1\text{-}day\ \sigma = \sigma_1 = \frac{\sigma}{\sqrt{256}} = \frac{\sigma}{16}$$

$$t\text{-}day\ \sigma = \sigma_t = \frac{\sigma}{\sqrt{\dfrac{256}{Days_t}}}$$

where

σ is annualized volatility
$Days_t$ is the number of trading days in the period
256 is the approximate number of trading days in a year

The trader who buys this option will find that the benefits associated with the positive gamma will just offset the costs associated with the rate of time decay if the underlying rate changes 3.4375 basis points, either up or down. If the underlying futures rate changes more than this, the trader will earn more from gamma combined with realized volatility than he has paid through time decay. See Exhibit 21.3 for an illustration of the break-even volatility.

This break-even condition belongs in that small collection of things about finance that are amazing but true. It is surprising that textbook authors rarely make much out of this relationship,

EXHIBIT 21.3

Break-even Volatility

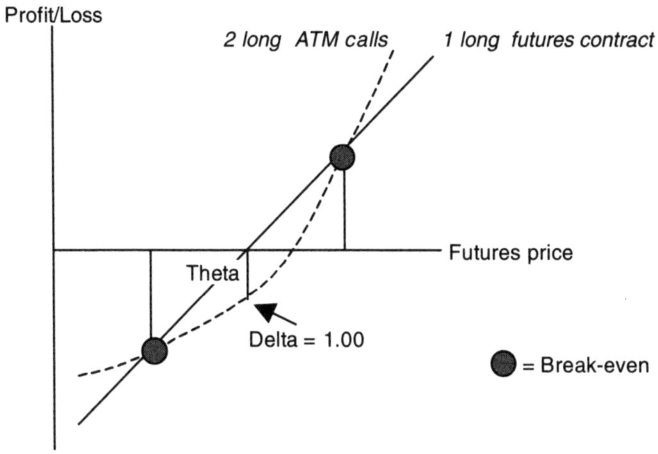

which is at the heart of option pricing theory and should be part of every option trader's tool kit. Gamma and theta are both functions of implied volatility, and their functional relationships are such that this break-even rule always works. You can satisfy yourself that the rule works by verifying Equation 21.2, which is simply the break-even or zero profit condition for a short trading horizon assuming no change in implied volatility. For help with the mathematics, see John C. Hull, *Options, Futures, and Other Derivatives*, 5th ed. (Upper Saddle River, N.J.: Prentice Hall, 2003).

As an aside, it is worth noting that this break-even rule is important for everyone who trades options, including those who use options to take directional positions. In Exhibit 21.3, the choice is between 2 long at-the-money call options (with an approximate delta of 1.00) and 1 long futures contract (with a delta of exactly 1.00 by definition). As the exhibit shows, the option trade will outperform the futures trade if the market delivers more volatility than the option market expected (as measured by implied volatility). The option trade will under perform the futures trade, however, if realized volatility is less than implied volatility. Thus, even directional traders who use options necessarily trade volatility at the same time.

EQUATION 21.2

The Relationship between Gamma, Theta, and Realized Volatility

$$Net\ profit = \left[\frac{\gamma}{2}(\partial R)^2 + \theta(\partial t)\right] = 0, \quad \text{if } \partial R_{Actual} = \partial R_{Implied}$$

where

γ is gamma, θ is theta, and both are functions of implied volatility
∂R is the change in the futures rate
∂t is the amount of time passed over the trading period
$\partial R_{Implied}$ is scaled to the length of the trading period

TERM STRUCTURE OF EURODOLLAR RATE VOLATILITY

One key feature of Eurodollar futures rate volatility is that it varies systematically with time to futures expiration. Exhibit 21.4 illustrates this relationship for both basis point volatility (upper panel) and relative rate volatility (lower panel). In both cases, the measure of volatility has been normalized so that the value for the 20th contract is 1.00. Thus, if annualized basis point volatility for the 20th contract were 95 basis points per year, we would set this value equal to 1.00. Having done this, if annualized basis point volatility for the 4th contract were 114 basis points per year, we would set this value equal to 1.20 [= 114/95].

These volatility structures provide three general lessons about futures (and forward) rate volatilities. First, futures rate volatility is greatest for contracts with 1 to 2 years to expiration. Second, futures rate volatility tends to be lowest for contracts that are about to expire. Third, from 3 years to 10 years to expiration, there is very little, if any, difference in rate volatilities. Basis point rate volatilities are nearly constant across the maturity spectrum from 3 years on out. And relative rate volatility appears to be lower only because the forward rate curve tends to be upward sloping.

We can see this pattern of rate volatilities in the structure of implied volatilities shown in Exhibit 21.5. Notice, in particular, the implied basis point volatilities at which options expiring in Sep '02 were trading at the close on June 17, 2002. All 3 options have

EXHIBIT 21.4

Normalized Historical Eurodollar Basis Point Volatility
1994 through 2002

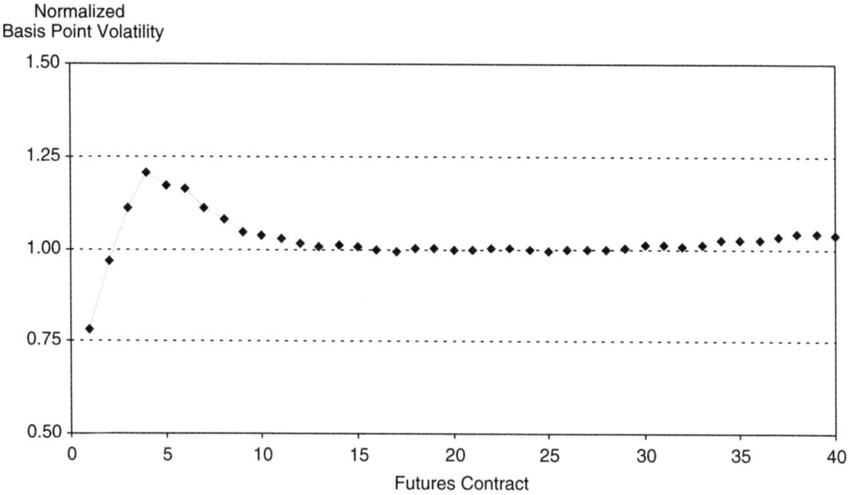

Normalized Historical Eurodollar Relative Rate Volatility
1994 through 2002

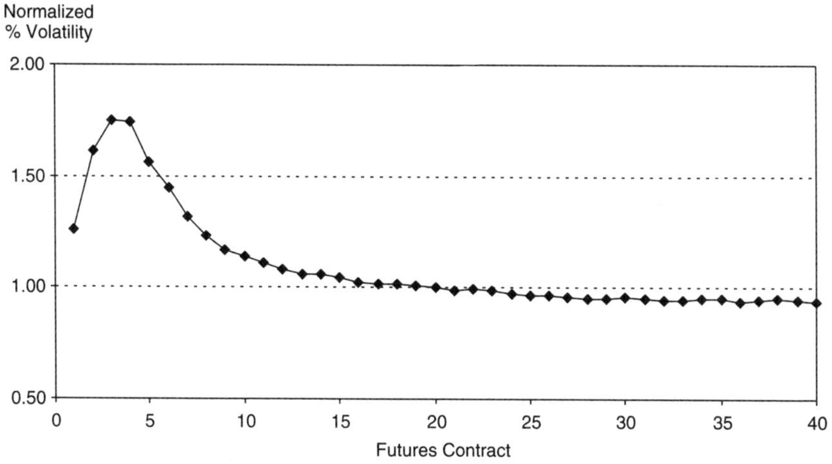

EXHIBIT 21.5

Basis Point Implied Volatilities for At-the-Money Call Options
June 17, 2002

Futures	Option Expirations									
Expirations	Jul '02	Aug '02	Sep '02	Dec '02	Mar '03	Jun '03	Sep '03	Dec '03	Mar '04	Jun '04
Sep '02	57.0	53.9	55.2							
Dec '02				93.0						
Mar '03					120.8					
Jun '03						133.3				
Sep '03	166.6	148.7	150.0				133.1			
Dec '03				152.6				133.6		
Mar '04					146.4				131.5	
Jun '04										n/a
Sep '04			129.4							
Dec '04				127.6						
Mar '05					129.0					
Jun '05										

3 months left to expiration and hence reflect the market's idea of how volatile their underlying rates will be over those 3 months. Their underlying rates reflect points on the futures rate curve that are a year apart. The Sep '02 futures contract expires in 3 months, the Sep '03 contract in 15 months, and the Sep '04 contract in 27 months. It makes sense, then, that these three options imply volatilities of 55 basis points, 150 basis points, and 129 basis points respectively.

Volatility Calendar Spread Trade

This time-varying feature of Eurodollar rate volatility opens up several possibilities for traders. A regular staple, for example, has been a volatility calendar spread trade in which one goes short options in one contract month and goes long options in the next contract month. For example, one might sell Jun '03 options on the Jun '03 futures contract at an implied basis point volatility of 133.3 and buy Sep '03 options on the Sep '03 futures contract at an implied basis point volatility of 133.1. Three months later, if the structure of implied volatilities remains unchanged, implied volatility in the Jun '03 options will have fallen to an implied volatility of 120.8 basis points, while implied volatility in the Sep '03 options will be more or less unchanged at 133 basis points. The volatility spread will have widened from 0 to 12 basis points. Carried another 3 months, the spread could widen out to almost 38 basis points [= 120.8 – 93.0].

Such a position if done on a vega-weighted basis[1] will tend to profit from the tendency of implied volatility in the nearby contract month to fall faster than implied volatility in the next longer-dated options.

Yield Curve Trade

The maturity structure of volatility also affords interesting possibilities for those who might use options for yield curve trades. For

1. Vega-weighted trades contain equal but offsetting amounts of vega from the long and short options. This way, a one percentage point increase in the volatility spread will deliver the same size profit (or loss), regardless of the way in which the spread increases.

example, Sep '02 options on the Sep '02 and Sep '03 futures contracts are trading at implied basis point volatilities of 55 and 150 basis points respectively. As a result, a trader could have sold options on the Sep '03 contract at nearly 3 times the cost of buying options on the Sep '02 contract. The difference in the two prices, even if warranted by the volatilities of the underlying rate, affords an opportunity for someone with a view on the slope of the curve between Sep '02 and Sep '03. For example, if you think the curve will steepen, you can get an edge by selling calls on the longer-dated contract and buying calls on the shorter-dated contract. On the other hand, if you think the curve will flatten, you can sell puts on the longer-dated contract and buy puts on the short-dated contract.

For a more complete discussion of these trading possibilities, see chapter 23, "Trading with Serial and Mid-Curve Eurodollar Options."

MATURITY STRUCTURE OF VOLATILITY (VOLATILITY CONES)

To get a sense of whether options are rich or cheap, option traders will compare the implied volatilities at which options are trading with historical volatilities. This is more easily done with over-the-counter options than it is with exchange-traded options because of the way the two markets handle expirations.

Exchange-traded options have fixed expiration dates (e.g., March, June, Sep, or Dec), while the over-the-counter option markets offer options with fixed times to expiration (e.g., 1 month, 3 month, etc.). Thus, it is easy to do a running comparison of implied and historical volatilities in the over-the-counter market because one can plot time series of 1-month implied and historical volatilities and know that like is being compared with like.

In the exchange-traded market, however, histories of implied volatilities reflect ever-decreasing forecasting horizons. For example, on June 17, 2002, options scheduled to expire in September had 3 months remaining to expiration. The volatility forecasting horizon for these options was the next 3 months, and the trader would want to compare these implieds with a distribution of 3-month historical volatilities. One month later, in July, the Sep '02 options had only 2 months left to expiration, so the trader would want to compare their implieds with a distribution of 2-month historical volatilities. And so on.

To handle this challenge, we devised what have become known generally as "volatility cones," which provide a graphic representation of the distribution of historical volatilities for different times to expiration. Against this backdrop, we can trace the history of implied volatilities as options age and see at a glance whether options appear to be rich or cheap in light of recent experience with actual historical volatilities.[2]

Examples of volatility cones for Eurodollar options are shown in Exhibit 21.6, which provides an analysis of the standard Sep '02

EXHIBIT 21.6

Volatility Cones and Histograms
Sep '02 and Dec '02 Quarterly Eurodollar Options
June 17, 2002

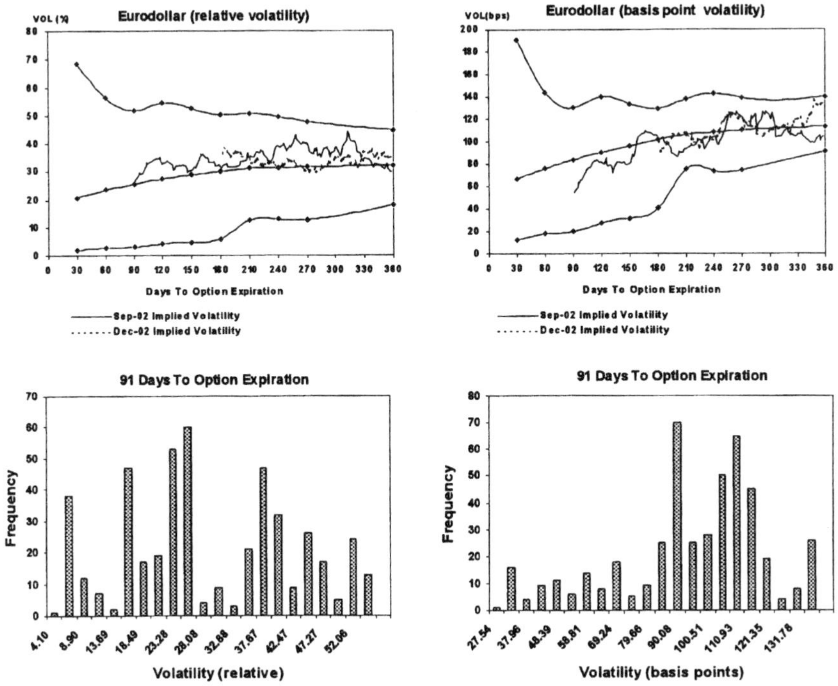

2. For a complete description of volatility cones, see Galen Burghardt and Morton Lane, "How to Tell if Options Are Cheap," *Journal of Portfolio Management*, Winter 1990, vol. 16, no. 2.

and Dec '02 quarterly Eurodollar options, and Exhibit 21.7, which provides an analysis of the Sep '02 and Dec '02 mid-curve options, for which the underlying futures were the Sep '03 and Dec '03 contracts.

In these exhibits, the cone-shaped figures represent the maximum and minimum historical volatilities estimated using data from the previous 2 years. The middle line represents the average. To construct these figures, we have estimated historical volatilities for every period ranging from 1 month to 1 year and posted the highest and lowest estimates for each set. We have then overlaid two at-the-money implied volatility histories—one for the option closest to expiration (the solid line) and one for the option next closest to expiration (the dashed line). Because time to expiration increases from left to right on the horizontal axis, time passes from right to left. The left-most value for each of the implied volatility

EXHIBIT 21.7

Volatility Cones and Histograms
Sep '02 and Dec '02 1-Year Mid-curve Eurodollar Options
June 17, 2002

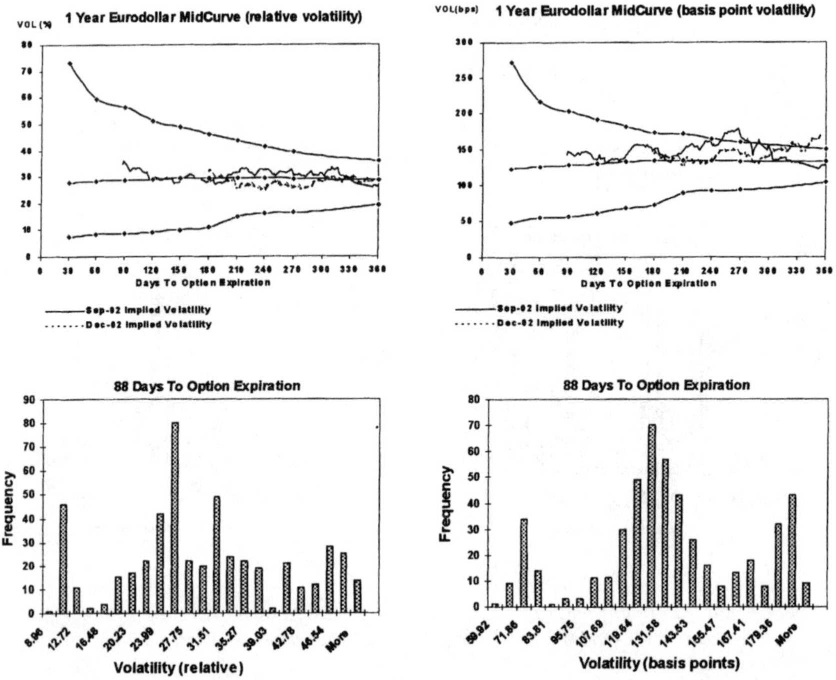

histories represents the at-the-money implied volatility for the two option contract months on the day the cone is drawn.

Thus, in both exhibits, the end of the solid line represents Sep '02 options, which had 3 months (shown as 90 days) to expiration on June 17, and the end of the dotted line represents Dec '02 options, which had 6 months to expiration on June 17. The left-hand panel provides the analysis in terms of relative rate volatilities, while the right-hand panel is shown in terms of basis point volatilities. Both cone diagrams have been augmented by a histogram that shows the actual distribution of historical volatilities for a horizon that matches the time to expiration of the shortest-dated option. In this example, the volatility histograms show the distribution of 91-day Eurodollar volatilities over the previous 2 years and make it easy to see how the current market value of implied volatility stacks up against its recent history.

These two exhibits provide examples of richness and cheapness that would be useful to traders and hedgers. For example, notice that both the Sep '02 quarterly and mid-curve options traded at volatilities that were either at the upper end of the cone, or even outside of the cone, when they had 9 months or so to expiration. Since these options now have 3 months left to expiration, the options would have been rich in December 2001. Also, notice that implied basis point volatility for the Sep '02 quarterly option is trading in the neighborhood of 50 annualized basis points. In the histogram, we can see that 50 basis points falls almost at the extreme left of the 91-day basis point histogram.

The shape of the cones reflects a reality about volatility that is obvious to every option trader: the range of volatilities that a market can deliver over short periods is far wider than is possible over longer periods. It is perfectly plausible that a market can be explosive for a few days or more, or completely dead for a few days or more, but it is less likely that a market can sustain a fever pitch of volatility for months on end or remain flat for months at a time. As designed, the cones provide the historical perspective on volatility that traders need to make decisions about buying and selling options with various times to expiration.

VOLATILITY SKEWS

The standard option pricing model assumes that volatility is constant and that price or rate changes are distributed according to some well-defined distribution—often a lognormal distribution. The options market, on the other hand, is more likely to price options according to the way it thinks volatility really behaves over time and the way changes are really distributed.

One result of plugging market option prices into a standard option pricing model is that options at different strike prices trade at different implied volatilities. Exhibits 21.8 and 21.9 provide examples of what is known broadly as "volatility skews." The options chosen for this example were the Sep '02 Eurodollar puts and calls at the close of June 17, 2002. On that day, the Sep '02 futures price closed at 97.895, so strike prices of 97.75 and 98.00 were right around the money. Implied volatility for the calls and puts trading at these strikes was about 25.75 percent. Options trading at strikes above or below these levels produced implied vol-

EXHIBIT 21.8

Implied Volatilities—Sep '02 Quarterly Eurodollar Options
June 17, 2002
Sep '02 Futures = 97.895

	Implied Volatility (%)	
Strike	**Call**	**Put**
96.00	65.928	53.652
96.25	59.247	49.106
96.50	52.123	44.155
96.75	44.491	38.719
97.00	38.983	36.407
97.25	32.196	31.377
97.50	26.407	26.574
97.75	25.823	25.618
98.00	25.715	25.864
98.25	29.401	29.088
98.50	42.828	43.561
98.75	54.061	na
99.00	66.891	76.561

Source: Carr Futures.

EXHIBIT 21.9

Implied Volatility Skew—Sep '02 Quarterly Eurodollar Options
June 17, 2002
Sep '02 Futures = 97.895

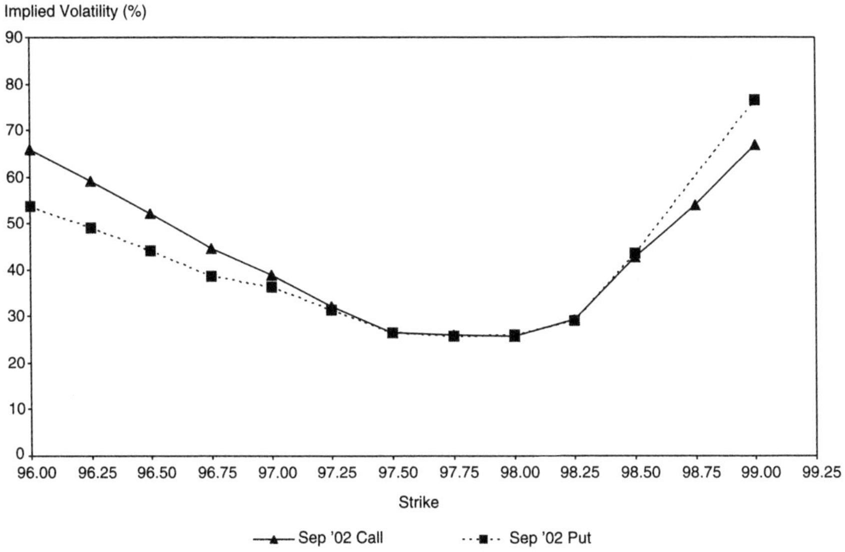

atilities that were all higher than the at-the-money implieds, and in some cases substantially higher.

It is worth noting that for options that are well away from the money, implied volatility calculations can be highly unreliable. For example, the 66 percent implied volatilities for the calls with strikes of 96.00 and 99.00 shed little if any light on the market's perceptions of yield volatility. Rather, the vegas of the options are very small because they are so far away from the money. And because the vega is very small, any small distortion in the price is amplified. In this case, the difference between 53.7 percent implied volatility for the 96.00 put and 65.9 percent implied volatility for the 96.00 call is probably worth less than a tick.

IMPLIED RATE DISTRIBUTIONS

Rather than calculating implied volatilities for options at different strikes, one can extract from the options' market prices a sense of

EXHIBIT 21.10

Implied Distribution of Futures Rates from Market Option Prices
Sep '02 Futures = 97.895
June 17, 2002

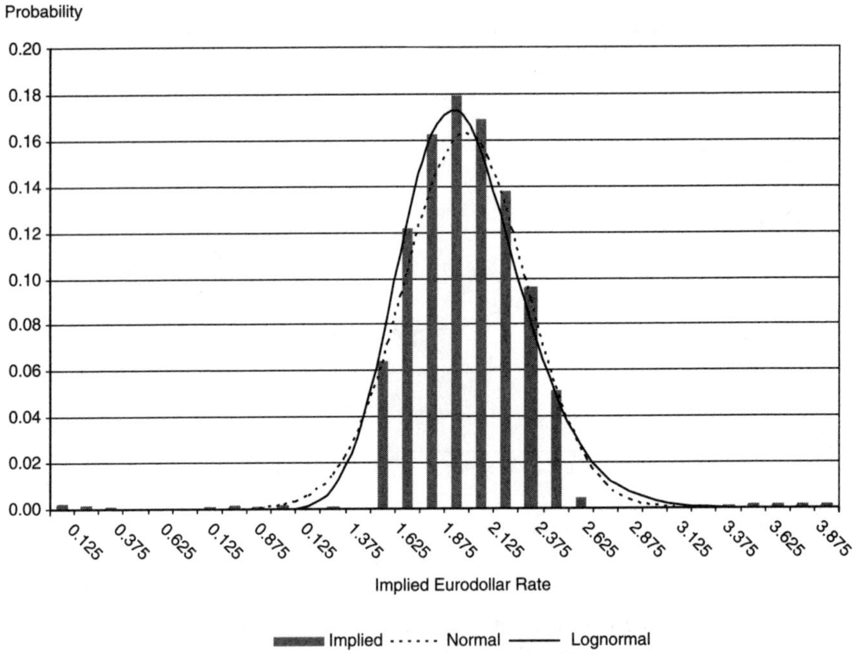

just what the market thinks the distribution of futures rates looks like. An option price can be thought of as the product of two things—the probability that an option will end its life in the money and what the option is worth if it ends up in the money. In a risk-neutral world, then, one can infer from an option's price the market's best guess about the likelihood or probability that the underlying futures rate will be above or below any given value.

If we construct the implied distribution for Sep '02 futures rates from the June 17 call and put option price data, the result is the histogram drawn in Exhibit 21.10. For purposes of comparison, we have overlaid two theoretical distributions on the implied histogram. One represents a lognormal distribution of rates, while the other represents a normal distribution of rates. Both have been drawn so that their means and standard deviations are the same as those of the implied distribution.

Visual inspection of the implied distribution suggests it has fatter tails than either of the theoretical distributions. It is also more tightly bunched toward the center. From that, one concludes that the implied distribution exhibits excess kurtosis.

CHAPTER 22

Practical Considerations

If you trade options on Eurodollar futures, there are two practical considerations that will help you avoid losing money. The first is the question of when to exercise an option on a futures contract early. The second is the problem of differences in expiration dates for the standard quarterly options on the one hand and serial and mid-curve options on the other.

EARLY EXERCISE

Eurodollar futures options are American-style options and can be exercised before they expire. The early-exercise principle for options on futures generally is simply this: once an option is trading at intrinsic value and has a delta of 1.00, the long should exercise the option. This rule is symmetrical and is true for both calls and puts.

The basic rationale for this rule is simple. The option ties up real cash while the underlying futures contract does not, because futures margin accounts earn interest. Thus, faced with two instruments that exhibit the same delta (1.00 or −1.00), the trader prefers the instrument that ties up the least cash. And this is the futures contract. Thus, the option holder exercises the option, takes the futures position, and frees up the cash.

Those who have learned about options by studying stock options (and this is nearly everyone, including my MBA students at the University of Chicago) sometimes have a hard time grappling with the early exercise rules in the futures. The early exercise rules for options on futures are very different from those for options on physical securities or commodities. With options on stocks, bonds, or foreign currencies, both the option and the underlying tie up cash. With options on futures, only the option ties up cash. Moreover, the underlying stock, bond, or currency spins off a dividend, coupon, or interest payment, while a futures contract does not. As a result, one can have asymmetrical early exercise rules under which one would never exercise a call on dividend paying stocks but might well exercise in-the-money puts.

CASH SETTLEMENT AND EXERCISE

Eurodollar options that expire on the same day as their underlying futures contracts are, for all practical purposes, cash settled. These are the standard quarterly options such as the Sep '02 option on the Sep '02 futures contract, both of which expire on September 16, 2002. The Chicago Mercantile Exchange's rules provide for the automatic exercise of all in-the-money options at 7 p.m. on the last day of trading. For example, if you are long a call option that is in the money, the exchange's clearing house automatically will assign you a long futures position at the call's strike price. But then the exchange will convert your long futures position into cash (since the futures contract expires that day, too) by crediting you with an amount equal to the difference between the futures final settlement price and the strike price (multiplied by $2500). Thus, although the options are exercised in principle, they are cash settled in practice.

Exchange rules also provide for the automatic exercise of in-the-money serial, mid-curve, and 5-year bundle options at expiration unless instructions are received to the contrary. These options expire on the Friday preceding the third Wednesday of the contract month. The practice of exercising options automatically places an interesting burden on the person with a long option position at expiration. The Exchange's understanding of whether an option is in the money at expiration depends on the value of the underlying futures price(s) at the close of trading Friday at

2:00 p.m. Chicago time. If a piece of news released after the 2:00 p.m. close causes interest rates to rise or fall, an option that was in the money at 2:00 p.m. may be out of the money later in the afternoon. To avoid exercising options that are now out of the money, the long option holder must issue instructions through his clearing member not to exercise options that had been in the money at the close of trading.

All of this means that you must have someone who can watch the market after futures trading closes on expiration Fridays and who has the authority to issue exercise (or non-exercise) instructions. You should keep in mind, too, that your deadline with your clearing broker will be earlier than the 7:00 p.m. deadline set by the Exchange.

PART FIVE

Eurodollar Option Applications

This section provides three research notes that deal with aspects of trading or hedging with Eurodollar options.

TRADING WITH SERIAL AND MID-CURVE EURODOLLAR OPTIONS (Chapters 23 and 24)

The first note, "Trading with Serial and Mid-Curve Eurodollar Options" (chapter 23), is a guide to the rich variety of trading opportunities that opened up when the Chicago Mercantile Exchange decided to list short-dated options on longer-dated Eurodollar contracts. Serial and mid-curve options are really the same thing but with different horizons. In both cases, the option expires before the underlying futures contract. Thus, it is possible to trade options that expire in 1, 2, or 3 months on futures that expire 1 or 2 years later. These options make it possible to hedge or spread against over-the-counter Treasury options. They also open up the possibility of using options to trade the slope and shape of the futures rate curve.

WHAT HAPPENS TO EURODOLLAR VOLATILITY WHEN RATES FALL? (Chapters 25 and 26)

The research note "What Happens to Eurodollar Volatility When Rates Fall?" (chapter 25) was the result of watching implied Eurodollar rate volatilities skyrocket when Eurodollar futures rates fell dramatically in 2000 and 2001. At issue here is the question of whether basis point volatility or relative rate volatility is more stable. One of the really interesting conclusions of this note is that there has been no obvious relationship between basis point volatility and the level of rates. That is, it seems as if the standard deviation of futures rate changes, when expressed in basis points, was just as high when rates were 2 percent as when rates were 8 percent. As a result, all of our ideas of the richness and cheapness of Eurodollar options, when based on implied relative rate volatilities, were useless. This led us to revise our volatility cones to show historical and implied basis point volatilities for Eurodollar options. An example of our new report is provided in "Eurodollar Volatility: An Update" (chapter 26), which compares volatility cones for relative and basis point rate volatility.

HEDGING CONVEXITY BIAS (Chapter 27)

The final chapter is "Hedging Convexity Bias" (chapter 27), whose purpose was to find a workable Eurodollar options hedge for the volatility exposure that swap dealers have when they hedge their swap book with Eurodollar futures. This challenge posed two problems. For one, swap traders with Eurodollar futures hedges are worried about rate volatilities for horizons up to 5 or 10 years, while most Eurodollar options expire within 2 years. For another, the "greeks" of the two positions respond differently to a change in the horizon. The gamma of a conventional option decreases with time to expiration while the "gamma" of a swap/futures position increases with the maturity of the swap. This note presents, however, a workable and inexpensive hedge solution that swap traders can use to protect themselves against losses when implied volatilities are high and are threatening to fall.

CHAPTER 23

Trading with Serial and Mid-curve Eurodollar Options

Galen Burghardt and Scott Lyden
Research note originally released June 22, 1998

SYNOPSIS

Serial and mid-curve Eurodollar options have been available at the Chicago Mercantile Exchange (CME) for a number of years. These options, which expire anywhere from 1 month to 2 years before their underlying futures contracts expire, open up whole new realms of trading opportunities, which, until recently, went largely unexploited owing to a lack of liquidity. Lately, however, trading volume and liquidity have picked up noticeably, as more and more traders have recognized that these options enable them to achieve exposures never before attainable with exchange-listed options. The main distinguishing feature of these options is that they provide high-gamma, high-theta vehicles for trading various segments of the futures or forward rate curve. This note explains some of the many uses for these products.

The array of options available for trading on March 25, 1998, is shown in Exhibit 23.1. Option expirations are displayed along the top with futures expirations along the side. The options are labeled using the names by which they are identified on the CME floor. March 25 closing bid and offered implied volatilities appear in parentheses below each option's name.

EXHIBIT 23.1

Quarterly, Serial, and Mid-curve Eurodollar Options

Underlying Futures Expiration	Option Expiration							
	Apr '98	May '98	Jun '98	Sep '98	Dec '98	Mar '99	Jun '99	Sep '99
15 Jun '98	Apr (6.5/7.2)	May (6.2/6.9)	June (6.4./6.9)					
14 Sep '98				Sep (9.4/9.6)		Volatility Curve Spread		
14 Dec '98			Yield Curve Spread		Dec (11.2/11.5)			
15 Mar '99						Mar (12.5/12.8)		
14 Jun '99	Short Apr (13.7/14.9)	Short May (13.6/14.8)	Short Jun (13.9/14.9)	Time Decay Spread			Red Jun (13.4/13.6)	
13 Sep '99				Short Sep (14.4/15.1)				Red Sep (14.2/14.4)
13 Dec '99					Short Dec (14.4/14.7)			
13 Mar '00						Short Mar (14.8/15.2)		
19 Jun '00			Green Jun (13.5/14.0)					
18 Sep '00				Green Sep (13.5/14.1)				

Eurodollar Strategy Triangle

The pivotal option for much of what professional traders are doing with these options is the "short June" option, an option that is based on the June '99 futures contract but that expires in June '98. This option creates a triangle of trading opportunities. You can, for example, use the June '98 and short June options to trade the slope of the yield curve and take advantage of the term structure of Eurodollar volatilities. Or you can use the short June and red June options to take advantage of different rates of time decay in the two options. In addition, you can use options along the hypotenuse of the triangle to ride the Eurodollar volatility curve.

FOMC and Other Volatility Trades

Short-term serial options such as April '98 and May '98, both of which are on the June '98 futures contract, provide excellent vehicles for trading short-term views on Federal Reserve policy. A number of traders are drawn to off-diagonal trades using short March (a March '99 option on a March '00 futures contract) and red September (a September '99 option on a September '99 futures contract) to produce long-term positions with an interesting mixture of gamma, vega, and theta.

Spreads against OTC Treasury Options

Mid-curves also make good spreading vehicles for OTC Treasury options. Changes in the underlying rates for the short June and green June mid-curves—the June '99 and June '00 futures rates, respectively—are highly correlated with changes in term Treasury yields on 2-year and 3-year notes. OTC Treasury options that expire in 1 to 3 months can be spread against corresponding mid-curves with comparable times to expiration.

LIFFE Joins the Crowd

The CME's success with serial and mid-curve options has prompted LIFFE to adopt a similar approach. On May 15, 1998, LIFFE has joined the crowd by listing serial and quarterly mid-curve options on their 3-month money market contracts including the Euro, Euromark, Eurolira, and Short Sterling.

THE FULL CONSTELLATION OF EURODOLLAR OPTIONS

The Chicago Mercantile Exchange has been filling in a matrix of options on Eurodollar futures that provides a wealth of option-trading opportunities at the short end of the curve. The full range of choices is illustrated in Exhibit 23.1, which shows the option expirations from left to right across the top and the underlying futures expirations from top to bottom at the left.

Notice just how rich the set of choices is. In addition to the standard quarterly options, you have serial options and mid-curve options as well.

Standard Quarterly Options

There are six standard quarterly contract months listed on any given day. Each quarterly option expiration corresponds to the expiration of the underlying futures contract, so you have June '98 options on the June '98 futures contract, September '98 options on the September '98 futures contract, and so on out to September '99.

Serial Options

Near-term gaps between quarterly options are filled by monthly serial options that expire before their underlying quarterly futures expire. Notice along the top row of Exhibit 23.1 that there are April '98 and May '98 options on the June '98 futures contract. Unlike the June '98 option on the June '98 futures contract, which expires on a Monday morning along with its underlying futures contract, the serial options expire on Fridays and require you to make or take delivery of the underlying futures contract if the option is exercised. These are not cash-settled options.

Mid-curve Options

Six quarterly mid-curve options are currently available for trading. The unique thing about these options is that they expire 1 or 2 years before their underlying futures expire. For example, you can trade a June '98 option for which the underlying is the June '99 futures contract. This particular option is identified in Exhibit 23.1 as "short Jun," the name by which it is known on the CME floor. Also notice that you can trade a June '98 option on the June '00 futures contract. This is a 2-year mid-curve option, identified in Exhibit 23.1 as "green Jun." Thus, you have three options that expire in June '98 with underlying futures contracts spread out at 1-year intervals along the futures rate curve. You also have short September and green September at this writing.

Serial 1-Year Mid-curve Options

The CME also lists hybrids of serial and mid-curve options. Notice, for example, that you can trade an April '98 option on the June '99 futures contract. This option is identified as "short Apr" in Exhibit 23.1. You also can trade the short May option, which is a May '98 option on the June '99 futures contract. Who knows? In time, the CME may list serial 2-year mid-curve options as well.

THE BEAUTY OF THIS DESIGN

In the old days (the 1980s), you were limited mainly to trading Eurodollar options that expired at the same time as their underlying futures contracts. Thus, if you wanted to use these options to trade the slope of the short end of the futures curve, the trade would have an unusual mix of gamma, theta, and vega. As shown in Exhibit 23.2, short-dated options that are at or near the money are relatively rich in gamma and theta while relatively poor in vega. Thus, with a yield curve trade, you would necessarily be long (or short) gamma and short (or long) vega.

EXHIBIT 23.2

Vega, Gamma, and Theta
At-the-Money Call

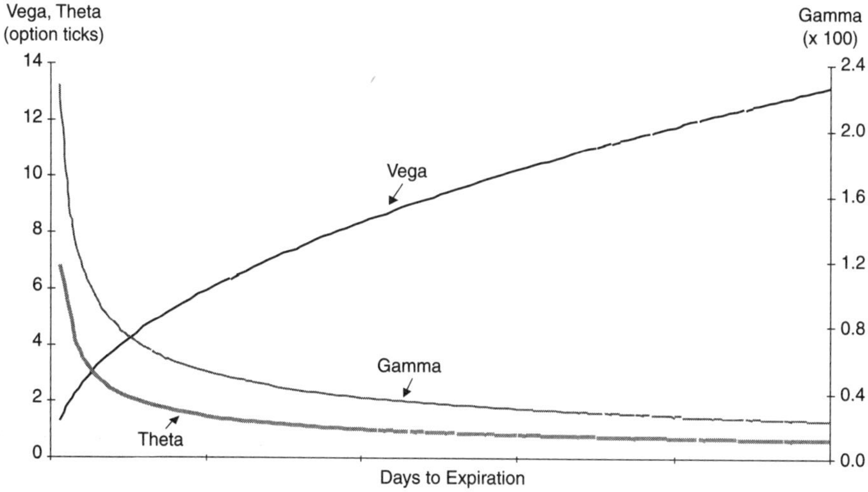

The enlarged menu of Eurodollar contracts enables you to trade options expiring at the same (or nearly the same) time on different parts of the curve. The great thing about this arrangement is that you can use options with very similar gamma, theta, and vega characteristics to trade the slope of the yield curve.

As a bonus, you can trade options with different expirations on the same underlying futures contract. Thus, you can do some interesting volatility calendar trades that were not possible before.

THE EURODOLLAR STRATEGY TRIANGLE

To get an idea of how these trades work, consider three possibilities that lie along the sides of the highlighted triangle in Exhibit 23.1. One possibility, captured by June/short June along the left leg of the triangle, uses options with the same or nearly the same expirations on Eurodollar futures representing different parts of the curve. This is a yield curve trade with an interesting volatility spin. A second possibility, captured by short June/red June along the bottom leg of the triangle, uses options with different expirations but the same underlying futures contract. This kind of trade captures differences in time decay. A third possibility, captured by March/red June along the hypotenuse of the triangle, uses different expirations on different underlying futures to ride the volatility curve.

June/Short June (A Yield Curve Spread)

Suppose you think the yield curve is going to steepen. The June '98 futures contract is trading at 94.33, which implies a rate of 5.67 percent. The June '99 futures contract is trading at 94.18, which implies a rate of 5.82. The calendar spread is only 15 basis points and is trading near the low end of the range for the spread between the lead and the first "red" futures.

Instead of simply buying June '98 futures and selling June '99 futures, you might buy the 94.375 June '98 call on the June '98 futures contract and sell the 94.25 June '98 call (known as "short June") on the June '99 futures contract.

One advantage of doing the trade with options is that you are usually buying a low-volatility option and selling a high-volatility option. This advantage appears in several forms. First, on March 25, you could do the trade at a 7-tick credit. For example, if you price the June '98 call at a mid-market volatility of 6.7 percent, the price you pay is only 5 ticks. At the same time, if you price the short June call at a mid-market volatility of 14.4 percent, you find you could sell it for about 12 ticks.

Second, as shown in Exhibit 23.3, you have a trade that gives you the appearance of positive gamma combined with positive theta. This highly peculiar situation is a direct result of the way volatility works on the options' risk parameters. For options that are at or near the money, higher implied volatility produces lower gamma and higher theta. Vega, in contrast, is largely unrelated to the level of implied volatility. Because you are long the low-volatility option (the June option at 6.7 percent) and short the high-volatility option (the short June option at 14.4 percent), you have a position that is net long gamma that produces positive time decay for you as well. The positive gamma is partly an illusion, of course, because it works only with parallel shifts in the two underlying futures rates. (The higher volatility for the short June option suggests that non-parallel yield curve shifts are very likely.)

Whatever your views on the position's net risk parameters, the higher volatility in the short June option gives you a nice cushion against a flattening of the curve and tips the odds in your favor overall. Exhibit 23.4 shows three futures rate curves—the current curve, the at-the-money curve, and the highest of the break-even curves. The current curve shows the 5.67 percent and

EXHIBIT 23.3

Risk Parameters of a Curve Steepener
Long 94.375 June '98 Call, Short 94.25 "Short June" '98 Call

	Option		
Parameter	**June**	**Short June**	**Net**
Delta	39.093	−41.13	−2.037
Gamma	211.959	−99.19	112.769
Vega	102.447	−104.57	−2.123
Theta	−0.041	0.09	0.049

EXHIBIT 23.4

A Curve-Steepening Trade with Eurodollar Options
Long 94.375 June '98 Call, Short 94.25 "Short June" '98 Call

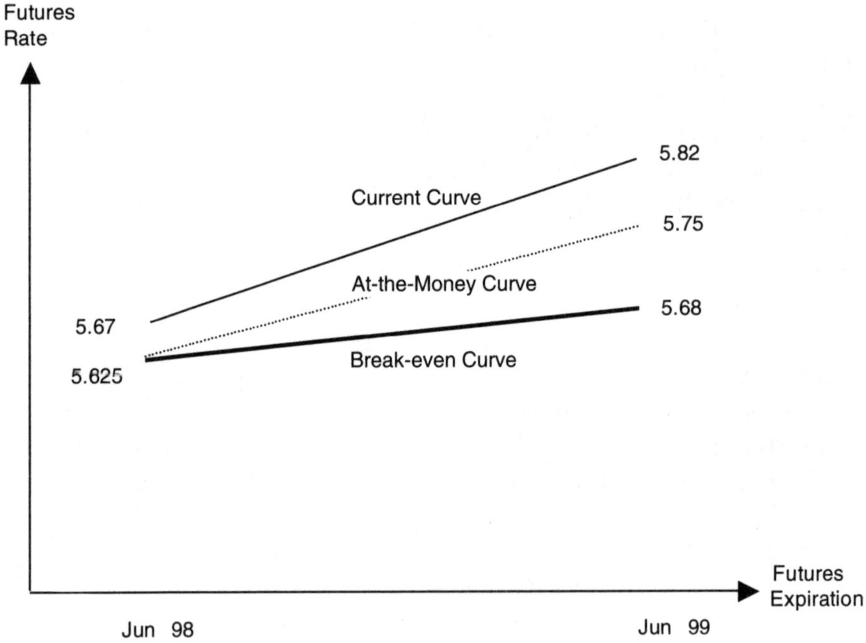

5.82 percent that correspond to market futures prices. The at-the-money curve shows the rates (5.625 percent and 5.75 percent) at which both options would expire exactly at the money. Notice that if the futures curve at expiration lies anywhere above the at-the-money curve, both options expire out of the money and you keep your 7-tick credit.

The break-even curve goes one step further and shows that the June '99 rate could fall an additional 7 ticks to 5.68 percent before the loss on the short June option would rob you of your gain on the trade. As a result, the curve can actually flatten from its current slope of 15 basis points to 5.5 basis points before you stand to lose any money on the trade. (This break-even curve, by the way, is only the highest of the possible break-even curves. Any parallel curve that lies below this one also represents a break-even outcome.)

Your edge in the trade is reflected in the profit/loss summary shown in Exhibit 23.5, where all curve-steepening outcomes are shown in the upper left-hand part of the table. With parallel shifts in the curve, which are shown along the diagonal from the lower left corner to the upper right corner, you make 7 ticks or a little bit more. If both rates rise, you make at least 7 ticks because both options expire out of the money. If the curve actually steepens, you stand to make considerably more. Even if the curve flattens slightly, you can make money. If you contrast the 33-tick gain associated with a 60-basis-point steepening of the curve with the 16-tick loss associated with a 60-basis point flattening of the curve, the odds are, in a crude sense, 2-to-1 in your favor.

Short June/Red June (A Time Decay Spread)

Another possibility is to trade a calendar volatility spread based on the June '99 futures contract. To do this, you have the June '98 option on the June '99 futures contract (known as short June), and the standard June '99 option on the June '99 futures contract (known as red June).

In this example, the implied volatilities at which the two options are trading are nearly the same, but the relative mixes of

EXHIBIT 23.5

P/L of a Curve-Steepening Trade at Expiration

Long 94.375 June '98 Call, Short 94.25 "Short June" '98 Call

June '98 Rate Change	*June '99 Rate Change*						
	30	**20**	**10**	**0**	**−10**	**−20**	**−30**
−30	32.52	32.52	32.52	32.52	29.52	19.52	9.52
−20	22.52	22.52	22.52	**22.52**	19.52	9.52	−0.48
−10	12.59	12.59	12.59	**12.59**	9.59	−0.41	−10.41
0	**7.17**	**7.17**	**7.17**	7.17	**4.17**	**−5.83**	**−15.83**
10	7.02	7.02	7.02	**7.02**	4.02	−5.98	−15.98
20	7.02	7.02	7.02	**7.02**	4.02	−5.98	−15.98
30	7.02	7.02	7.02	**7.02**	4.02	−5.98	−15.98

Steeper curve

gamma, theta, and vega for the two options are very different. Short June options, which have roughly 3 months left to expiration, will have relatively high gammas and rates of time decay, while the red June options, which have nearly 15 months left to expiration, will have relatively high vegas. As a result, you might consider a delta-neutral position in which you sell a straddle or strangle using the short June options and buy a straddle or strangle using the red June options.

There is no single right way to construct this trade because of the different relative mixes of gamma, theta, and vega. Consider the way things look, however, if you sell 100 delta-neutral short June 94.00/94.25 strangles at a price of about 20 ticks per strangle and buy 100 delta-neutral red June strangles struck at the same prices for a price of about 56 ticks per strangle. Your net debit would be 3600 ticks [= 100 strangles × 36 ticks per strangle], and you would find yourself with a position that has negative gamma and positive theta (because the short June options have relatively more gamma and theta) and that has positive vega (because the red June options have relatively more vega). You can think of this trade, then, as a time decay spread that will benefit from an increase in implied volatility but that is exposed to the risk of too much actual or realized volatility.

A look at Exhibit 23.6 shows that your break-even on this position as of the expiration of the short June options on June 12, which is the Friday before the standard futures expiration, is roughly 30 basis points up or down.[1] Thus, if you think that the

1. Finding your break-even for a trade with different option expirations provides an interesting insight into the relationship between volatility and break-even price or rate changes. Day to day, the break-even change in the underlying futures rate would be equal to [Futures rate × Implied volatility × $(1/\text{Days in the year})^{1/2}$], where days in the year is 365 if you work with a calendar year and is somewhere in the neighborhood of 250 if you work with a trading year. In this case, the futures rate is 5.82, implied volatility is approximately 14 percent, so that a 1-calendar-day break-even change in the rate would be plus or minus 4 basis points [$= 5.82 - 0.140 - (1/365)^{1/2}$]. If you take an option all the way to expiration, however, this rule of thumb is modified by taking 80 percent of [Futures rate × Implied volatility × $(\text{Days to expiration}/\text{Days in the year})^{1/2}$]. In this case, the break-even at expiration for the short June options would be plus or minus 30 basis points [$= 0.8 \times 5.82 \times 0.140 \times (79/365)^{1/2}$], which is about where the break-even lies in Exhibit 23.6. The 80 percent rule for the break-even rate or price change at expiration assumes that the position is delta-neutral on the trade date but is not rehedged thereafter.

EXHIBIT 23.6

P/L for a Delta-Neutral Time Decay Spread

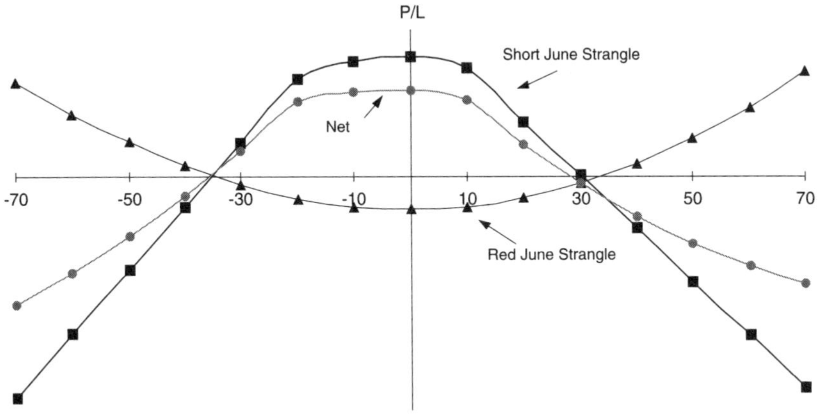

June '99 futures rate will change less than this, you will collect more time decay on the short June options than you pay on the red June options.

In the meantime, the position's positive net vega is a potential bonus because of the comparatively low implied volatility at which you are buying the red June options. The term volatility in the short June option, which has 79 days to expiration, is 14.4 percent. The term volatility in the red June option, which has 446 days to expiration, is 13.5 percent. Since the underlying futures is the same for both of these options, this trade allows you to buy 1-year volatility roughly 2-1/2 months forward at 13.3 percent.[2] If you view this as an exceptionally low level of implied volatility, you will welcome the positive vega that this trade affords.

March/Red June (A Volatility Curve Spread)

One well known feature of the Eurodollar volatility curve is that very short-dated futures rates exhibit quite a bit less volatility than do longer-dated futures rates. You can see this pattern in Exhibit

2. You can calculate the forward volatility in this example by finding the value of s^2 that gives you $[79 \times 14.4^2 + 367 \times s^2] = 446 \times 13.5^2$ where the squares of the volatilities are weighted by the number of days in their respective periods.

23.7, which shows the term structure of historical Eurodollar volatilities from the lead through the 6th contract. You can see the consequences of this pattern in Exhibit 23.8, which shows what the term structure of implied volatilities looked like on March 25 for the standard quarterly options on these futures contracts.

One way to profit from this pattern of volatilities is to "ride the Eurodollar volatility curve." Under the right circumstances, you can do this by selling near-dated Eurodollar options and buying further-dated Eurodollar options. One might, for example, sell the March '99 straddles on the March '99 futures contract at 12.6 percent volatility and buy vega-equivalent June '99 straddles on the June '99 futures contract (red June) at 13.5 percent volatility. For example, you might sell 111 delta-neutral 94.25 March '99 straddles for approximately 56 ticks per straddle and buy 100 of the red June 94.25 straddles at about 66 ticks per straddle for a net debit of 384 ticks [= 111 straddles × 56 ticks per straddle − 100 straddles × 66 ticks per straddle].

The resulting position would be vega-neutral, which sets you up to take advantage of a change in the implied volatility spread as the trade ages. In addition, you would earn net time decay on

EXHIBIT 23.7

90-Day Historical Eurodollar Volatility
A Cross-Sectional View

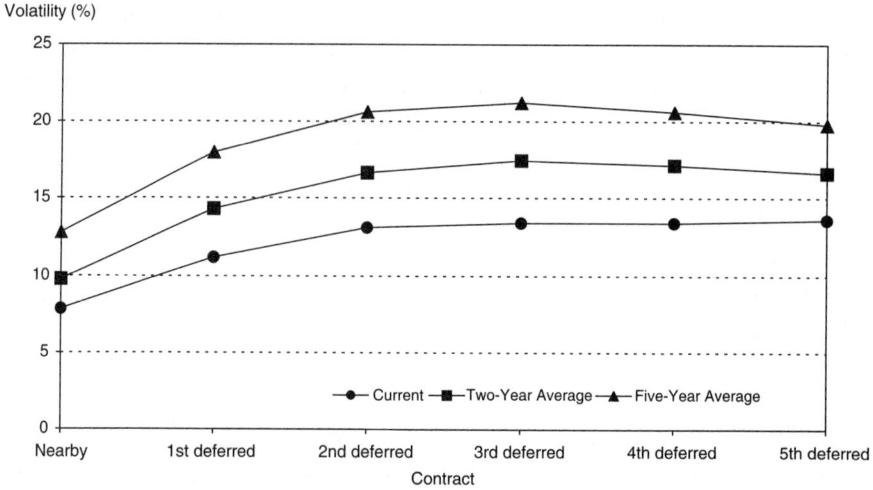

EXHIBIT 23.8

Term Structure of Implied Eurodollar Volatility

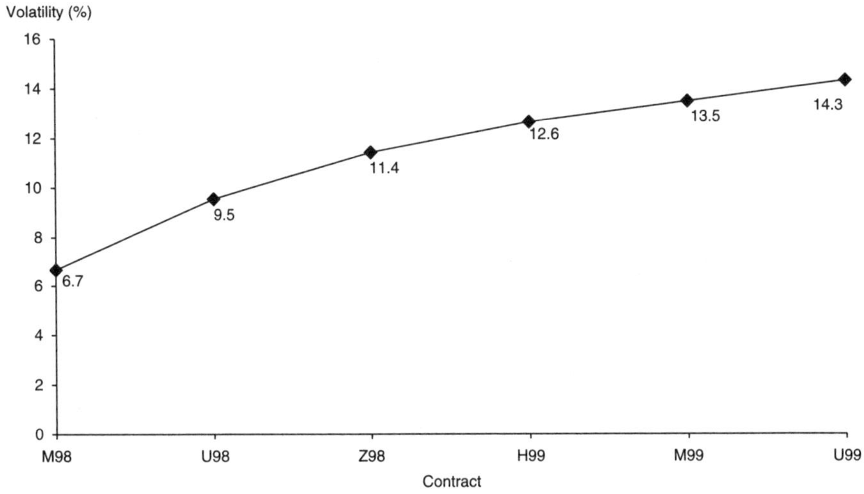

the position because you are short the higher theta option (and more of them). At the same time, you would be exposed to negative net gamma.

This is a trade that is put on for the comparatively long haul in the expectation that the implied volatility in the March options will fall faster than the implied volatility in the June options. For example, one might hold this position for 6 months to catch the steeper part of the volatility curve where the March '99 straddles might be trading at 9.5 percent, while the June '99 straddles (red June) might be trading at 11.4 percent. If so, you will have bought the spread at 0.9 percent [= 13.5 percent – 12.6 percent] and sold it at 1.9 percent [= 11.4 percent – 9.5 percent].

As long as there is no very great change in the March futures price, the trade can be expected to profit from a higher rate of time decay in the March options than would be paid on the long June options.

DIFFERENT VOLATILITY HORIZONS

For traders who study the calendar of economic events for sources of volatility, serial option expirations on the same underlying futures contract provide a tool for trading the economic calendar. Adding a month to the life of an option generally sweeps in one more release of key economic information such as non-farm payroll, NAPM, and the CPI. Also, an additional month might bring with it an FOMC meeting or some other key economic event.

Consider Exhibit 23.9, which shows the schedule of FOMC meetings as it appeared on March 25. We can see that the June '98 futures contract would be affected by any action the Fed takes on May 19 and by the market's expectations about what the Fed might do at its meetings in July and August. What is interesting about the schedule, though, is that the April '98 option on the June '98 futures contract expires well before the May FOMC meeting, while the May '98 option on the June '98 futures contract expires on the Friday just before the FOMC meeting. As a result, anyone who believes that nothing will be revealed about the Fed's intentions between March 25 and April 10 could sell April options and use the proceeds to buy May options and end up owning the May options cheap once the April options expire. Similarly, you might then sell May options and buy June options when you reach the high time decay part of the May option's life.

EXHIBIT 23.9

Timeline of FOMC Meetings

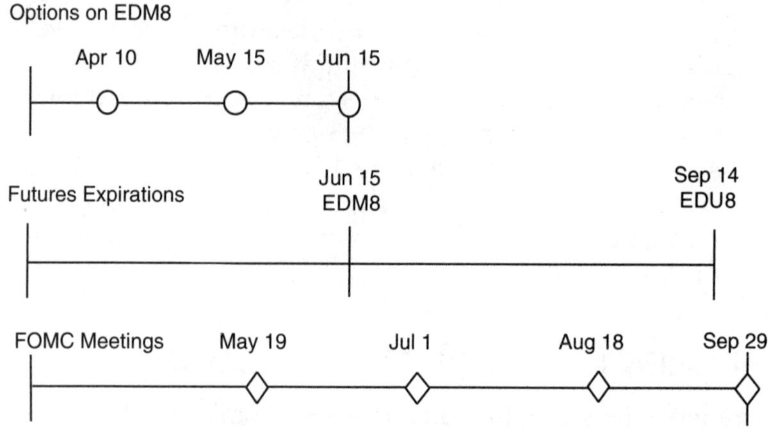

MID-CURVE OPTIONS VERSUS OTC TREASURY OPTIONS

The mid-curve options such as short June and short September make it possible to trade the spread between Treasury yield volatility and Eurodollar volatility. Before the introduction of mid-curve options, anyone who wanted to trade Eurodollar options against OTC Treasury options was stuck with one or another of two mismatches. First, if you matched the expirations of the options, the underlying rates were only loosely correlated. Second, if you matched the correlations of the two underlying rates, the option expirations could be a year or more apart.

For example, the June '98 option on the June '98 Eurodollar contract would have roughly the same mix of gamma, theta, and vega as a 3-month OTC option on a 2-year Treasury note. But the June '98 futures rate would be only loosely correlated with the spot or forward yield on a 2-year Treasury. Notice in Exhibit 23.10 that the lead Eurodollar rate changes only half a basis point for each basis point change in the on-the-run (OTR) Treasury yield and that the R^2 (explanatory power) of the regression is only 0.52.

A better match for the yield on a 2-year Treasury, as shown in Exhibit 23.11, would be provided by something like the 5th Eurodollar contract rate, which in this case would be the June '99 contract. This rate changes 1.17 basis points for each basis point change in the 2-year Treasury yield, and the R^2 is 0.94. But the June '99 option on the June '99 futures contract would have altogether the wrong mix of gamma, theta, and vega for a spread against a shorter-dated OTC Treasury option.

Now that we have the mid-curve options, though, we can have the best of both worlds. The April '98, May '98, and June '98 options on the June '99 Eurodollar contract provide good gamma, theta, and vega matches for OTC 2-year Treasury options with roughly 1, 2, and 3 months to expiration.

Eurodollar/Treasury Volatility Spread Trading

The volatility of any given Eurodollar futures rate such as that implied by red June (that is, the June '99 futures contract) can be thought of as comprising two parts: (1) the volatility of a corre-

EXHIBIT 23.10

First Eurodollar Rate (Dependent) against OTR 2-Year Treasury Yield (Independent)
April 26, 1996–March 25, 1998; $R^2 = 0.52$

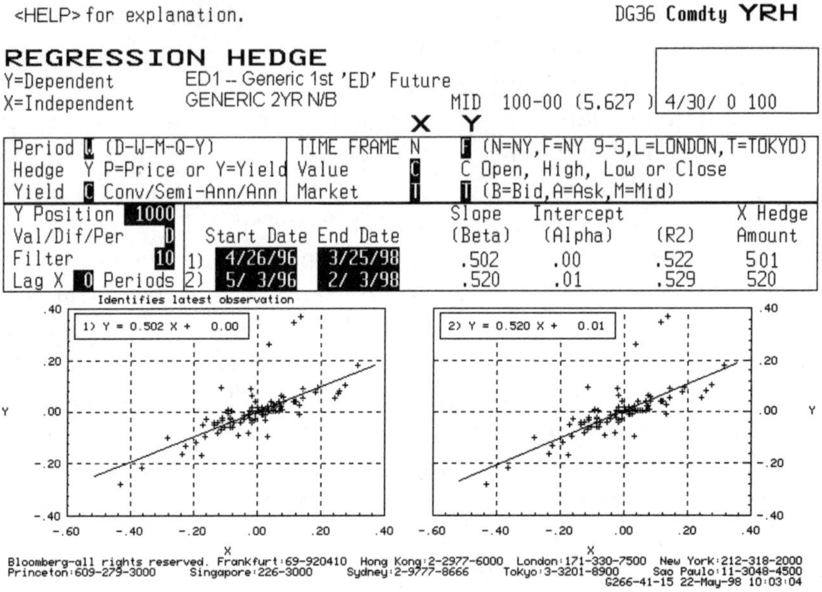

sponding forward Treasury rate, and (2) the volatility of the forward TED or swap spread. As such, the volatility of the Eurodollar rate will differ from that of a term Treasury yield for two reasons: (1) a less than perfect correlation between changes in the forward Treasury rate and the term Treasury yield, and (2) changes in the swap or TED spread.

Thus, if you can buy Eurodollar volatility at a level that is roughly equivalent to term Treasury yield volatility, you can benefit both from the lack of perfect correlation between forward and term rates and from changes in the swap or TED spread. An idea of the day-to-day variability of the TED spread is provided in Exhibit 23.12, which shows the recent history of the 1-year and 2-year term TEDs. A recent history of the spread between the 5th Eurodollar rate and the on-the-run 2-year Treasury yield is provided in Exhibits 23.13 and 23.14.

EXHIBIT 23.11

Fifth Eurodollar Rate (Dependent) against OTR 2-Year Treasury Yield (Independent)
April 26, 1996–March 25, 1998; $R^2 = 0.94$

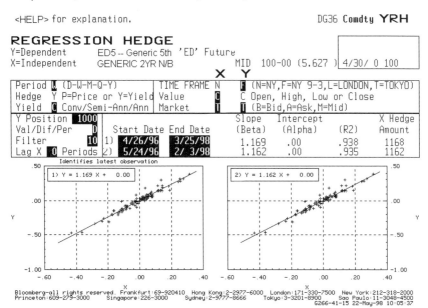

<HELP> for explanation. DG36 Comdty YRH

REGRESSION HEDGE

Y=Dependent ED5 -- Generic 5th 'ED' Future
X=Independent GENERIC 2YR N/B MID 100-00 (5.627) 4/30/ 0 100

X Y

Period W (D-W-M-Q-Y)	TIME FRAME N	F (N=NY,F=NY 9-3,L=LONDON,T=TOKYO)	
Hedge Y P=Price or Y=Yield	Value C	C Open, High, Low or Close	
Yield C Conv/Semi-Ann/Ann	Market T	T (B=Bid,A=Ask,M=Mid)	

		Start Date	End Date	Slope (Beta)	Intercept (Alpha)	(R2)	X Hedge Amount
Y Position 1000							
Val/Dif/Per D							
Filter 10	1)	4/26/96	3/25/98	1.169	.00	.938	1168
Lag X 0 Periods	2)	5/24/96	2/ 3/98	1.162	.00	.935	1162

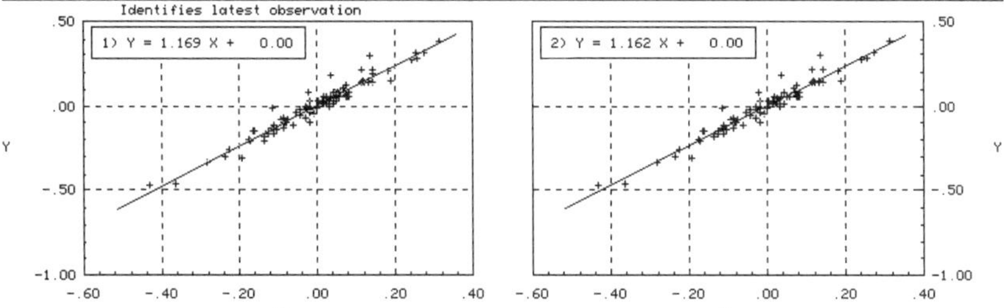

How Do You Compare the Volatilities?

Comparing implied volatilities in the two markets requires some care. First, the yield or rate levels are different. Second, the implied volatility quoted for an OTC Treasury option may be a forward yield volatility rather than a spot yield volatility.

Consider yield levels first. The June '99 Eurodollar rate on March 25 was 5.82 percent and the mid-market implied volatility for the short June option was 14.4 percent. At these levels, the normalized or basis point volatility of the Eurodollar rate would be 0.838 or 83.8 basis points annualized [= 0.144 × 5.82]. If we use the regression coefficient of 1.17 from Exhibit 23.11, we find that the corresponding change in the spot Treasury yield would be 71.6 basis points [= 83.8/1.17], which would in turn represent a spot yield volatility of 12.9 percent [= 0.716/5.571, where 5.571

EXHIBIT 23.12

TED Spread

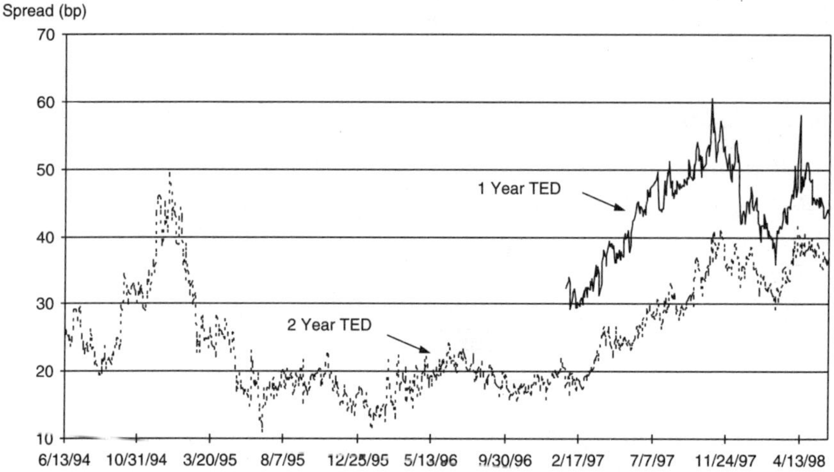

EXHIBIT 23.13

Yields of U.S. 5-Year Notes and 5th Eurodollar since June '94

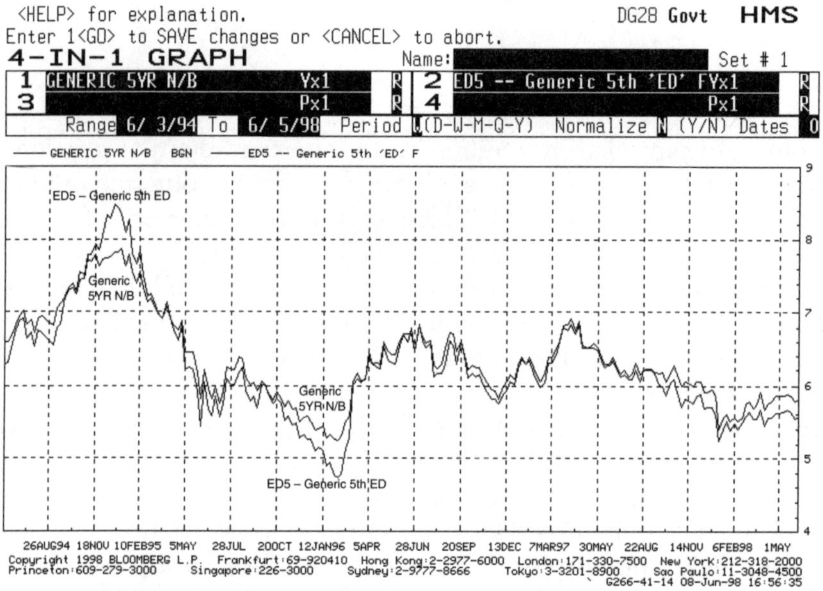

EXHIBIT 23.14

Yield Spread between 5-Year Notes and 5th Eurodollar since June '94
In Basis Points

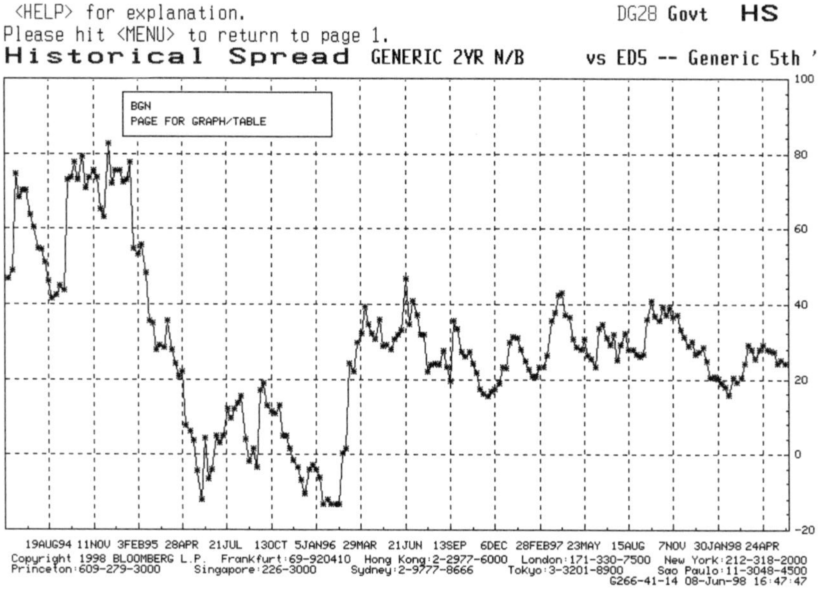

was the yield on the 5-1/2s of 3/00 on March 25]. As a result, any spot yield volatility above 12.9 percent would be rich relative to 14.4 percent Eurodollar volatility.

Forward yield volatilities tend to be higher than spot yield volatilities for two reasons. First, if repo rates do not change when Treasury note yields change, the change in the note's forward price will be nearly the same as the change in the note's spot price, but its forward DV01 is smaller than its spot DV01 so that the same price change translates into a larger yield change.

As a rule of thumb, you can convert a spot yield volatility into a forward yield volatility using the ratio of the note's spot and forward months to expiration. For example, on March 25, the on-the-run Treasury had just over 23 months to expiration. One month later, it would have 22 months to expiration. Thus, a spot yield volatility of 12.9 percent would translate into a 1-month forward yield volatility of approximately 13.5 [= 12.9 × (23/22)] percent. A 2-month forward yield volatility would be 14.1 [= 12.9 × (23/21)] percent, and so forth. In practice, you would take care to refine these volatilities, but the rule of thumb gives you a quick and fairly reliable comparison.

How Do You Construct the Trades?

One advantage of trading in the over-the-counter options market is that you can choose your strikes and expirations to fit your circumstances. Thus, you can force the Treasury option expirations to line up with the Eurodollar option expirations. Moreover, you can choose your strikes to correspond to equivalent strikes in the Eurodollar market. For example, with the June '99 Eurodollar rate at 5.82, you might trade strikes of 94.25 and 94.00, which correspond to rates of 5.75 and 6.00, which are 8 basis points below and 18 basis points above 5.82. If so, you could find appropriate strike prices for your Treasury options by finding the forward prices that correspond to yields that are about the same number of basis points above and below the current forward Treasury yield.

Once you have chosen your strikes, your last task is to find the appropriate amount of each option to do. Perhaps the easiest way to do this once one has lined up the expirations is to use the Eurodollar equivalent position of the Treasury note. If your OTC option were on $100 million of the on-the-run 2-year note and expires April 10, the Eurodollar hedge for the forward note exposure would be approximately 750 futures. Thus, the offsetting Eurodollar position would include 750 April '98 options on the June '99 futures contract. A May 15 option on the same note would require only 720 futures to hedge the forward note, and so you would do 720 of the May '98 option on the June '99 futures contract. A June option would require fewer still.

SOME THINGS TO KEEP IN MIND

Standard (non-mid-curve) serial options as well as serial and quarterly mid-curve options typically expire on the Friday before the expiration of standard quarterly options. For some strategies, such as the June-short June yield curve spread discussed above, this may entail slight expiration mismatches. Also, you must be prepared to make or take delivery of the underlying futures if these options are exercised, as they are not cash settled.

Strike prices for most Eurodollar options come in quarter point increments (e.g., 94.00, 94.25, . . .). In low-volatility environments this space between strikes can loom large. This is particularly true of options with relatively short times to expiration. Exhibit 23.8 showed that short-dated Eurodollar options can (and often do) have much lower implied volatilities than longer-lived contracts. Partly for this reason, the CME fills the spaces between some of the nearby contracts with so-called half-strikes, which come in 0.125 increments (e.g., 94.125, 94.25, 94.375, . . .). Every time a new quarterly option becomes the nearby option, half strikes are added for it and the subsequent two serial options. No additional contracts are given half strikes until the next quarterly contract becomes the nearby option, so the number of non-mid-curves with half strikes can range from one to three at any given time. The nearby 1-year mid-curve always has half strikes available.

LIFFE's OPTIONS

On May 15, LIFFE added 1-year mid-curves to its Euro, Eurolira, Euromark, and Short Sterling options offerings. Two quarterly and two serial expiration months are currently available. Much like the initially tepid reception that first greeted Eurodollar mid-curves, these contracts have gotten off to a slow start. With all the things that can be done with these products, it seems unlikely that they will remain underutilized for long.

CHAPTER 24

Serial and Mid-curve Options: An Update

The original research note on serial and mid-curve options (Trading with Serial and Mid-curve Options) was written in 1998. Since that time, the Chicago Mercantile Exchange has added to its array of Eurodollar options. It now lists 8 standard quarterly options rather than 6. Also, there are now 4 2-year mid-curve quarterly options, not just 2. As of this writing, serial 2-year mid-curve options have not been listed.

LIFFE, on the other hand, has revised its offerings of 3-month money market futures options. With the introduction of the Euro (€) and the death of the mark and lira, LIFFE no longer trades futures or options on EuroLira or EuroMark. Quarterly and serial options on Euribor and Short Sterling continue to have strong volume, but the 1-year mid-curve options remain underutilized.

CHAPTER 25

What Happens to Eurodollar Volatility when Rates Fall?

Galen Burghardt, George Panos, and Eric Zhang
Research note originally released October 18, 2001

We find that basis point volatility in the Eurodollar market has, for the past 10 years, been largely unrelated to the level of interest rates. As a result, we think that basis point volatility, as opposed to conventional relative rate volatility, is a better measure of volatility.

BACKGROUND

In the wake of the September 11 attack on the World Trade Center, implied Eurodollar rate volatility went through the roof. At the same time, Eurodollar rates fell a lot, raising questions about how one should interpret a volatility like 46.9 percent, which is the level at which implied relative rate volatility for at-the-money Dec '01 Eurodollar options peaked on September 19.

Exhibit 25.1 provides some help in answering these questions. On September 10, the day before the attack, implied relative rate volatility for Dec '01 options closed at 22.5 percent. Given an underlying futures rate of 3.29 percent for the Dec '01 contract, implied basis point volatility for the Dec '01 contract was 74 basis points [$= 0.225 \times 3.29$]. At the peak volatility of 46.9 percent, implied basis point volatility reached 116 basis points [$= 0.469 \times 2.48$]. By October 4, when things had begun to settle down, an

EXHIBIT 25.1

Key Rate Levels versus Dec '01 Implied Rate Volatility
September 10, 2001, to October 4, 2001

	Dec '01 Options			Mar '02 Options		
Close of Business	Implied Volatility	Futures Rate	bp Volatility	Implied Volatility	Futures Rate	bp Volatility
10 Sep '01	22.5	3.29	74	25.3	3.37	85
19 Sep '01	46.9	2.48	116	37.3	2.585	96
04 Oct '01	29.0	2.31	67	33.6	2.405	81

implied relative rate volatility of 29.0 percent produced an implied basis point volatility of only 67 basis points.

In other words, on September 19, implied relative rate volatility and implied basis point volatility were both higher than before the attack. By October 4, implied relative rate volatility was higher but implied basis point volatility was lower than before the attack.

WAS VOLATILITY RICH OR CHEAP?

Whether Eurodollar options were rich or cheap before and after the attack depends on whether you think relative rate volatility or basis point volatility is the better measure of volatility. We produce volatility cones for both measures, and it is apparent from Exhibit 25.2 that the two views are quite different. On September 19, implied relative rate volatility at 46.9 percent was outside of the cone and would be considered rich (see upper panel). On the same day, implied basis point volatility was certainly high, but was still within the range of historicals for the past 2 years (see lower panel). And by October 4, implied relative rate volatility still appeared somewhat rich, while implied basis point volatility was back to or somewhat below normal.

VOLATILITY AND RATE LEVELS

The main purpose of this note is to shed some light on the relationship between interest rate volatility and the level of interest rates.

EXHIBIT 25.2

Eurodollar Volatility Cones
2-Year History as of Close of Business October 4, 2001

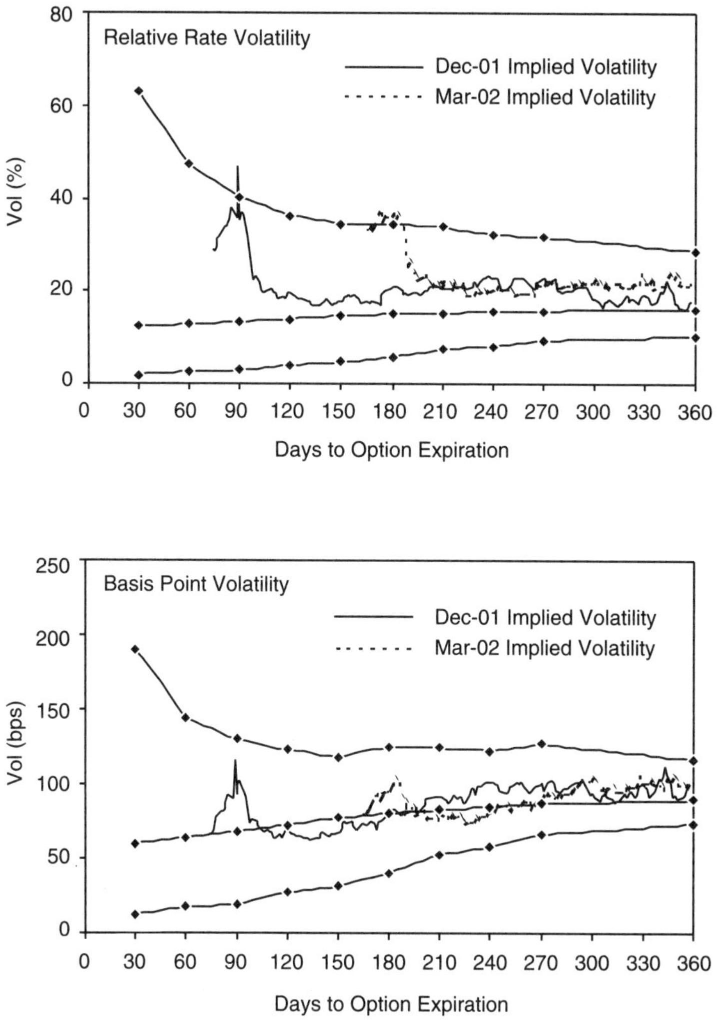

What we find is that while it is customary in the Eurodollar options market to quote rate volatility as a relative rate volatility—that is, as a change in the rate divided by the rate—the evidence suggests that basis point volatility provides a better measure of whether options are rich or cheap.

WHY RELATIVE RATE VOLATILITY?

The custom in the Eurodollar options market is to express or quote volatilities as relative rate volatilities. A 25-basis-point cut in rates from 6.00 percent to 5.75 percent would be expressed either as a decrease of 4.17 percent [$= -0.25/6.00$] or as a decrease of 4.26 percent [$=$ Ln (5.75/6.00)]. The same basis point cut in rates from 3.00 percent to 2.75 percent, though, would be 8.34 percent or 8.25 percent.

There are at least three reasons for thinking of Eurodollar rate volatility this way.

1. It makes sense. When rates are high, changes in rates should be high. And when rates are low, changes in rates should be low.
2. If rate changes are proportional to the level of rates, then interest rates can never be negative. Recent Japanese experience perhaps suggests that interest rates can be negative, but there must be some limit to how negative they can be.
3. Conventional option pricing models use relative changes as inputs. The standard closed form models rely heavily on the use of lognormal distributions. And so it is a matter of computational convenience to use relative rate volatilities when pricing Eurodollar options.

WHAT IS THE EVIDENCE?

The evidence is mixed. Consider Exhibit 25.3, for example, which shows the relationship between the annualized standard deviation of basis point changes in the lead Eurodollar rate and the level of the lead Eurodollar rate from 1983 to October 2001. Over this period, rates ranged from just over 2 percent (recently) to over 14 percent (in the early 1980s). The scatter has an upward sweep to it, and the regression line is positively sloped. The slope coefficient of 15.7 indicates that, on average over this period, the standard deviation of basis point changes rises 15.7 annualized basis points with each 1 percent increase in the level of rates. The R^2 of 0.37 suggests, however, that the relationship is weak and bears out what is evident to the eye in the loose scatter plot.

EXHIBIT 25.3

Eurodollar Rate Levels and Basis Point Volatilities
1983 to October 4, 2001

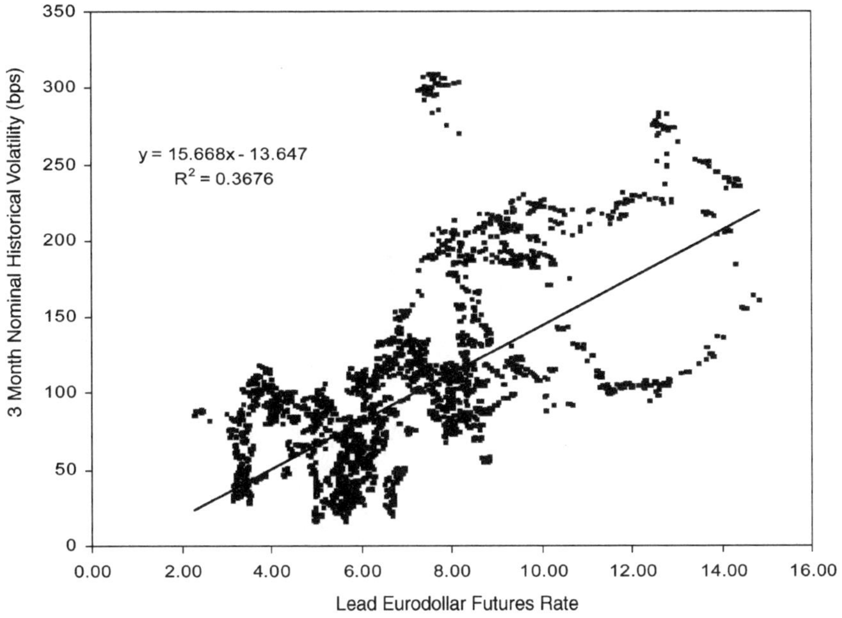

Now consider Exhibit 25.4, which shows what the relationship has looked like since December 6, 1990, when rates fell below 8 percent and stayed below 8 percent. Over this period, rates have traded between 2 percent and 7 percent, which is still a considerable range, and there seems to be no relationship at all between basis point volatility and the level of rates. The regression line even has a slight negative slope, which means nothing much given the R^2 of 0.05.

IS IT THE FED?

Probably. The tension between the relative and basis point views of rate volatility is due, at least in part, to the way the Federal Reserve changes rates. It would be one thing if the Fed's standard practice were to change rates, say, by 5 percent of the level of rates. If they did this, they would cut rates by 30 basis points if the level

EXHIBIT 25.4

Eurodollar Rate Levels and Basis Point Volatilities
December 6, 1990, to October 4, 2001

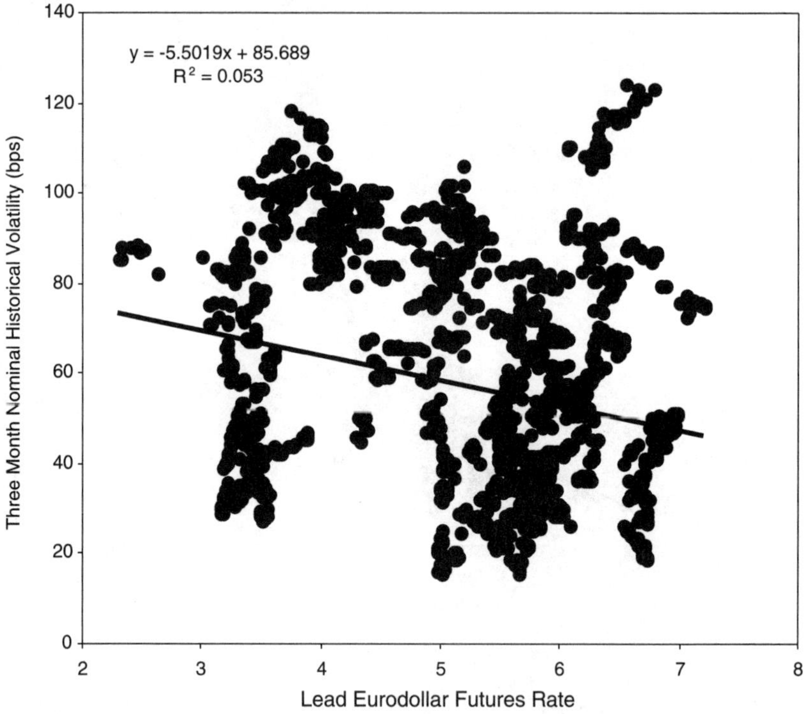

of rates were 6 percent and by 15 basis points if the level of rates were 3 percent. As it is, the Fed's practice has been to cut rates in multiples of 25 basis points no matter what the level of rates. Thus, it should be no surprise that the market looks at rate volatility in absolute or basis point terms rather than in relative terms.

PRACTICAL CONSEQUENCES

Just why the Fed does what it does may be rooted in its understanding about the way monetary policy translates into economic activity. If basis point volatility is unrelated to the level of interest rates, then relative rate volatility is inversely proportional to the level of rates. A halving of rates from 6 percent to 3 percent can be expected to double relative rate volatilities. This is borne out

EXHIBIT 25.5

Relative and Basis Point Rate Volatilities
January through October 2001

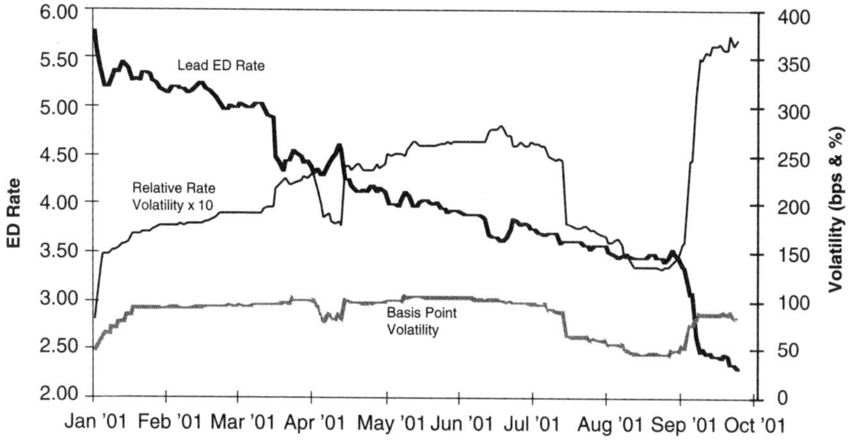

in Exhibit 25.5, which shows that basis point volatility has been fairly stable between 50 and 100 annualized basis points for most of 2001, while relative rate volatility has roughly doubled.

As a result, we cannot reasonably compare relative rate volatilities, either historical or implied, taken from a period when rates were around 6 percent and use them as a standard of richness or cheapness now that rates are trading around 3 percent and lower.

For this reason, we have produced a new set of volatility lines for money market contracts that compare implied basis point volatility [= Implied relative rate volatility × Rate level] with the historical distribution of historical basis point volatilities. (See lower panel of Exhibit 25.2.) We think these basis point volatility cones will be more reliable tools for gauging option richness or cheapness.

CHAPTER 26

Eurodollar Volatility: An Update

One of the striking lessons we learned about Eurodollar rate volatility when Eurodollar rates dropped below 2 percent in 2002 was that basis point volatility did not seem to be related to the level of interest rates. This insight prompted us to augment our volatility cone report to include basis point volatility cones in addition to the usual relative rate volatility cones.

The sample volatility cone report shown in Exhibit 26.1, using closing data from September 10, 2002, shows how important the distinction can be. Notice, for example, that on a relative volatility basis (the top left panel), options on the Dec '02 and Mar '03 contracts went through a period of appearing to be extremely expensive. At one point, implied relative rate volatility for the Dec '02 option reached 60 percent, while implied relative rate volatility for the Mar '03 option traded at 70 percent. Both of these implied volatilities were higher than any historical relative rate volatility for comparable times to these options' expirations over the previous 2 years. In basis point terms (see top right panel), however, both of these options appeared to be relatively inexpensive, trading in the lower end of the volatility cone. In fact, implied basis point volatility rose very slightly in the face of economic events of the time, but because interest rates had fallen so much, implied relative rate volatility rose dramatically.

EXHIBIT 26.1

Volatility Cones and Return Distributions
2-Year History as of September 10, 2002

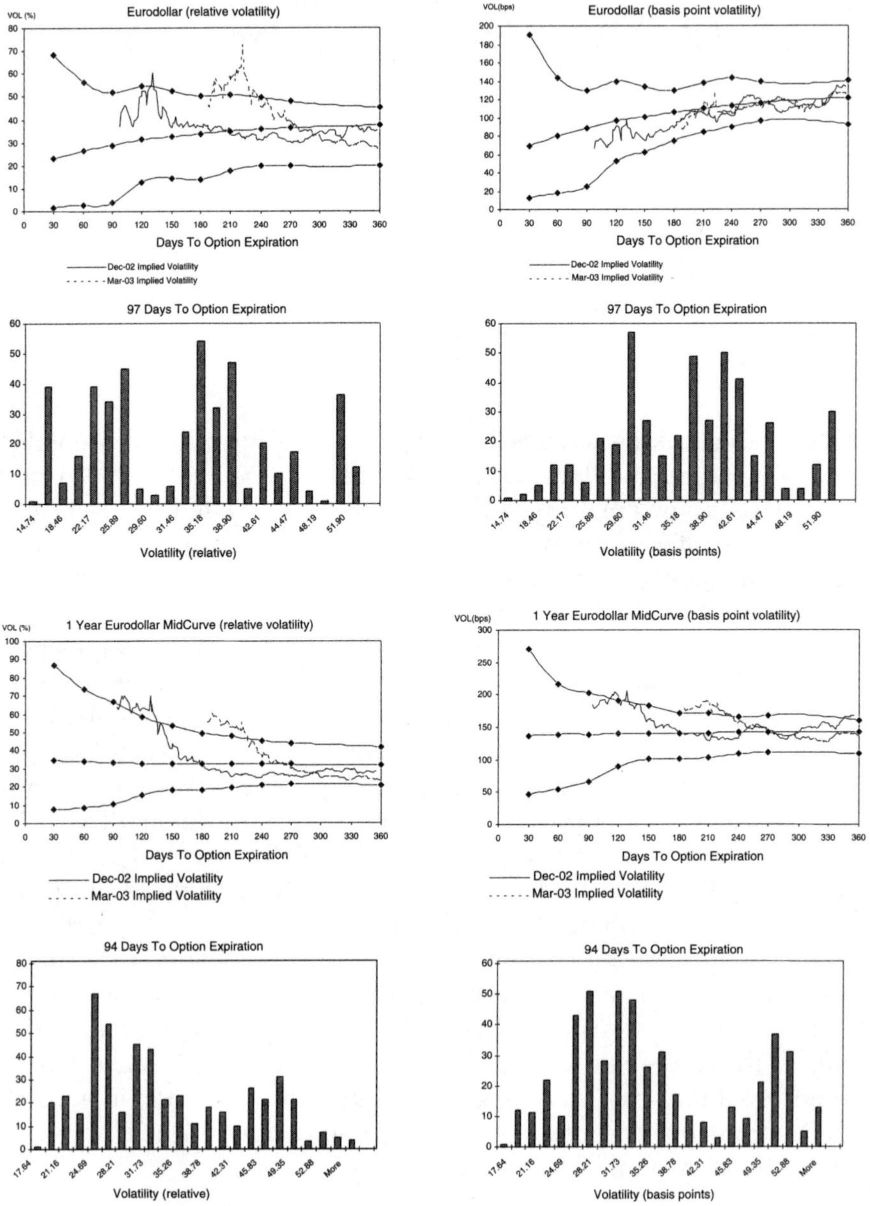

In light of our findings about the comparative stability of basis point volatility, the basis point volatility cone would seem to be the more reliable measure of richness or cheapness.

CHAPTER 27

Hedging Convexity Bias

Galen Burghardt and George Panos
Research note originally released August 2, 2001

SYNOPSIS

Anyone who receives fixed on a fixed/floating interest rate swap and hedges the directional exposure with Eurodollar futures is long volatility—both implied and realized. Increases in expected interest rate volatility will increase the value of the swap relative to Eurodollar futures, and large, realized swings in interest rates produce profitable opportunities to rebalance the hedge.

The risks in such a position, though, are that implied rate volatility might fall or that rates may prove to be less volatile than was expected when the swap was priced. In either case, the position loses money. The purpose of this note is to outline a plausible approach for hedging against these risks using exchange-traded options on Eurodollar futures.

In particular, we show that the longest-dated quarterly and mid-curve options have very useful characteristics for hedging swap/Eurodollar positions. As an example, we show that on August 1, 2001, both red Dec and short Jun options would have been good hedging vehicles for a 4-year swap.

The Challenges

Two major hurdles get in the way of hedging the volatility exposure in a swap/Eurodollar position. One is that the convexity/

gamma exposure in the swap position is more extreme in long-dated swaps than in short-dated swaps, while the opposite is true in conventional options on interest rates. The other is the mismatch in rate horizons. The swap/Eurodollar trader is concerned chiefly about the volatility of longer-term rates (e.g., 4- or 5-year swap rates), while options on Eurodollar futures are available on forward rates extending out no more than 3 years.

Overcoming the Challenges

Even with their shortcomings, the constellation of options on Eurodollar futures affords a possible solution. For one thing, changes in implied Eurodollar option volatilities can correlate well with changes in longer-term swap rate volatilities. For another, the effective gamma in a hedged swap is small relative to the vega exposure, so the gamma mismatch is not as great a hurdle as it might otherwise be.

Thus, as we show here, if it is possible to find a satisfactory cross-hedge for the implied volatility exposure, any residual exposure to unexpected changes in realized volatility should be fairly small.

HEDGING A 4-YEAR SWAP/ EURODOLLAR POSITION

In this note, we consider the problem of finding a suitable hedge for the volatility exposure in a 4-year swap hedged with Eurodollar futures. The first step is to express the gamma (convexity) and vega exposure of this position in Eurodollar futures terms.

Gamma

The upper panel of Exhibit 27.1 shows the P/L profile on August 1, 2001, for a position that receives fixed on $100 million notional amount of a 4-year swap and is short the appropriate number of Eurodollar futures. As yields rise, the position's net DV01 rises as well (from negative to positive). The lower panel of Exhibit 27.1 shows the change in the position's DV01 at different yield levels. In this exhibit, we use Eurodollar (i.e., quarterly, Actual/360 money market) basis points. As shown, the change in the DV01

EXHIBIT 27.1

Net Swap/Eurodollar P/L
$100MM 4-Year Receive Fixed Swap/Short Eurodollar Futures Strip

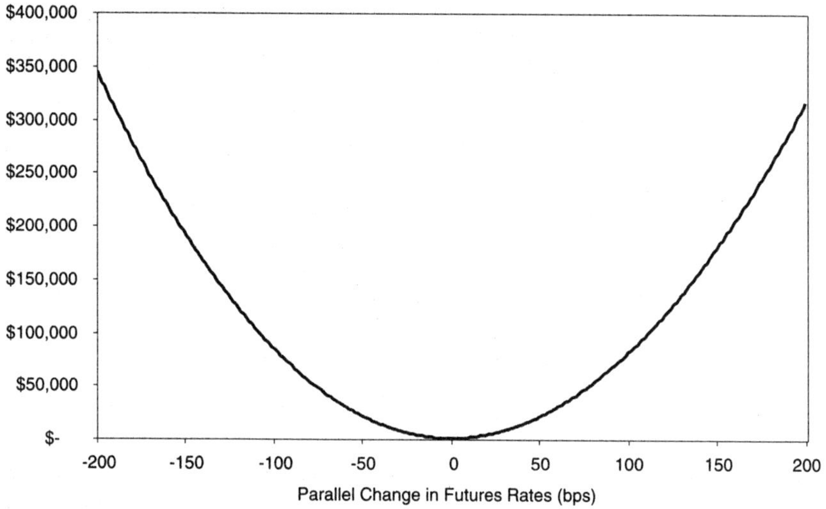

Change in Net DV01
With Respect to Changes in Eurodollar Futures Rates

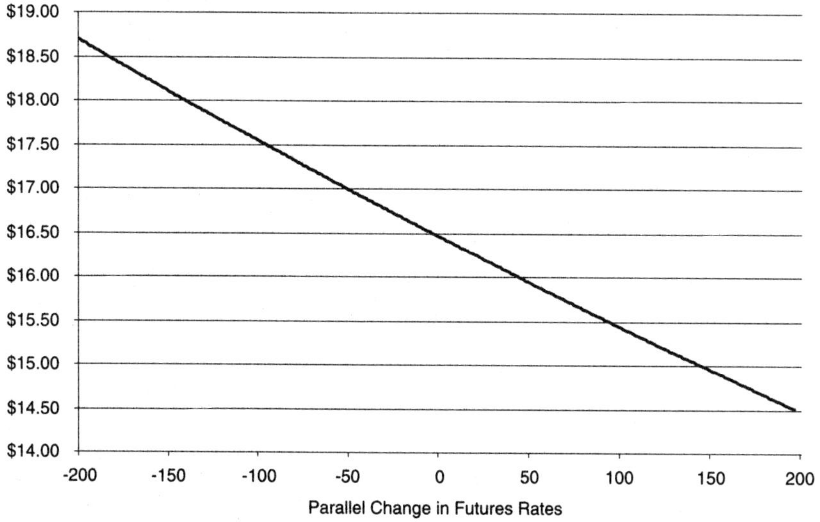

ranges between $18.68 when yields are low to $14.48 when yields are high, and is $16.45 at the current level of rates in the example. At $16.45, the convexity of the swap would be the equivalent of 0.658 Eurodollar contracts [= $16.45/$25].

Thus, to hedge the convexity in the position, we would need enough Eurodollar futures options to produce a gamma of 0.658 Eurodollar futures contracts per basis point.

Vega

Exhibit 27.2 shows how a 1-percentage-point change in all cap and swaption volatilities affects our estimate of the value of the convexity bias between swaps and Eurodollar futures. For an explanation of how we determine expected convexity bias and vega values, see chapters 7 and 8, "The Convexity Bias in Eurodollar Futures" and "Convexity Bias Report Card."

For a 4-year swap, the vega is 0.248 semiannual bond equivalent basis points. On $100 million of a 4-year swap, the value of a 1-basis-point change in the fixed coupon on August 1 would have been $36,135. Thus, a vega of 0.248 basis points would be worth $8,961 [= 0.248 × $36,135], which is the target amount required in the hedge.

From these calculations, it is apparent that exposure to changes in implied volatility is very much greater in the short term than exposure to changes in the level of realized volatility.

EXHIBIT 27.2

Convexity Bias Value and Vega

Swap Term (years)	Estimated Bias (bps)	Estimated Vega (bps)
2	0.5	0.054
3	1.2	0.131
4	2.3	0.248
5	3.6	0.399
7	7.3	0.822
10	14.1	1.679

Eurodollar Options

Exhibit 27.3 shows a partial menu of options that were available for trading on August 1, 2001. Option expirations are shown along the top of the table, while the underlying futures expirations are shown down the left-hand side. For the purposes of this exercise, we consider three possible options—two mid-curve options (i.e., green Dec and short Jun) and one standard quarterly option (i.e., red Dec). Exhibit 27.3 shows that within this set, the option expirations and the underlying futures expirations are inversely related. Green Dec has the longest-dated underlying (i.e., the Dec '03 futures contract) but expires first. Red Dec has the shortest-dated underlying (i.e., the Dec '02 futures contract) but expires last. Short Jun falls in between the two.

Which of these three options is likely to provide the best hedge hinges on four things: the relative mix of vega and gamma;

EXHIBIT 27.3

Options on Eurodollar Futures
August 1, 2001

Underlying Futures Contract	*Option Expirations**					
	Sep '01	**Dec '01**	**Mar '02**	**Jun '02**	**Sep '02**	**Dec '02**
Sep '01	Sep					
Dec '01		Dec				
Mar '02			Mar			
Jun '02				Jun		
Sep '02	Short Sep				Red Sep	
Dec '02		Short Dec				**Red Dec**
Mar '03			Short Mar			
Jun '03				**Short Jun**		
Sep '03	Green Sep					
Dec '03		**Green Dec**				

*Excludes serial and serial mid-curve options.

the relationship between the underlying futures rate and a 4-year term swap rate; the relationship between changes in the option's implied volatility and changes in term swaption volatility; and transactions costs.

Exhibit 27.4 provides a comparison of the gamma and vega values for the three Eurodollar options and for $100 million of the hedged 4-year swap. From the ratios shown in the right-hand column, it is apparent that short Jun most closely resembles the swap, while red Dec has somewhat too much vega per unit of gamma.

Exhibit 27.5 compares the relationships between changes in the three underlying futures rates and changes in a 4-year term rate. The topmost panel shows weekly changes in the second red Eurodollar rate (i.e., the rate underlying what is now the red Dec option) on the vertical axis against changes in a 4-year bundle rate on the horizontal axis. The middle panel does the same thing for the fourth "short" rate, which now would be the Eurodollar rate underlying the short Jun option.

The bottom panel shows the relationship for the second green rate, which now would be the rate underlying green Dec. At least for the period from January 1997 through June 2001, all three relationships look very much alike, although changes in the second green rate provided a very slightly better fit for changes in a 4-year bundle rate than did the other two.

Exhibit 27.6, which compares the level of implied volatility in second red Eurodollar options with the level of implied term swaption volatility, shows that implied volatility in Eurodollar options can track swaption volatilities fairly well. Although the

EXHIBIT 27.4

Option and Swap Characteristics
August 1, 2001

Option	Expiry	Strike	Gamma	Vega	Vega:Gamma Ratio
Green Dec	Dec '01	94.25	0.00573	34.50	6,021
Short Jun	Jun '02	94.75	0.00367	48.50	13,215
Red Dec	Dec '02	95.25	0.00321	53.50	16,667
Swap	na	na	0.65800	8961.00	13,619

EXHIBIT 27.5

Second Red, Fourth Short, and Second Green Eurodollar Rates As Proxies for a 4-Year Term Rate
Weekly Changes, 1/24/97–6/30/01

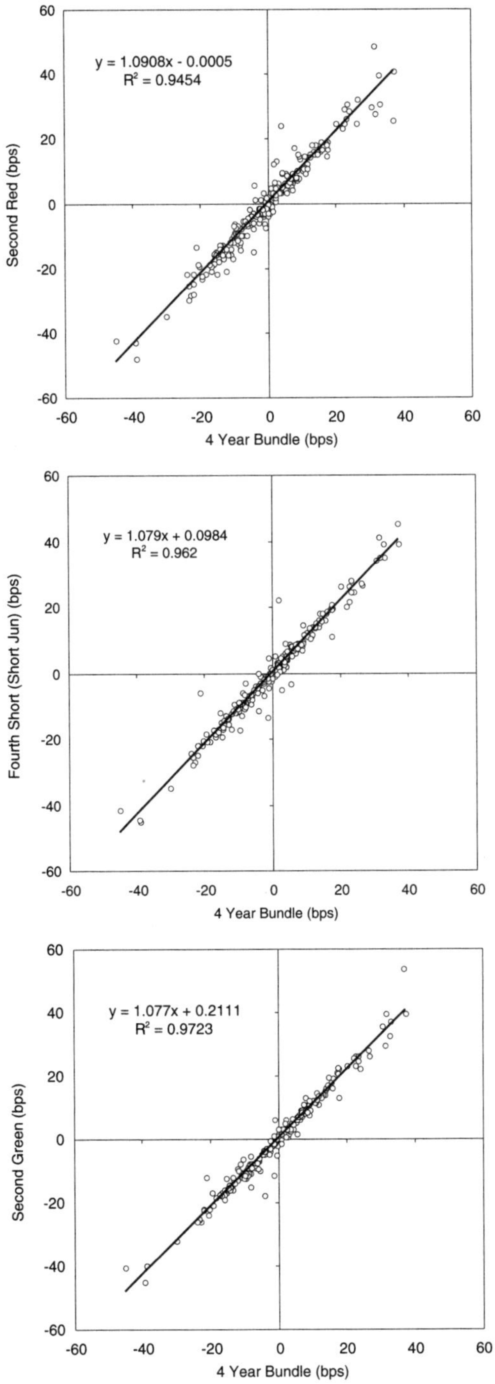

EXHIBIT 27.6

Second Red Eurodollar Implied Volatility As Proxy for Term Swaption Implied Volatility

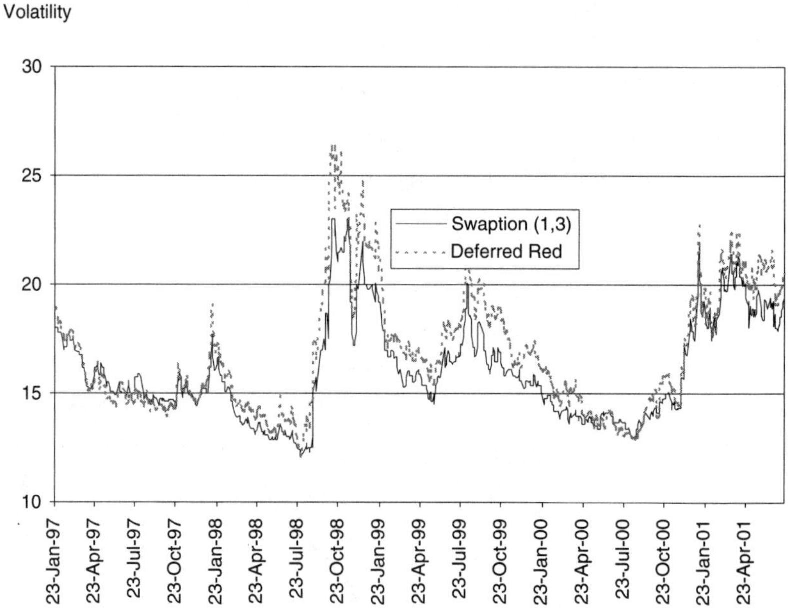

curve match is not perfect and the option horizons are not the same, the two volatilities do tend to rise and fall together.

From Exhibit 27.7 we can see that the relationship is best for the red Sep and short Jun options, represented in the upper and middle panels, which are labeled second red and fourth short respectively. Of these two, the fit is again very slightly better for short Jun than for red Dec. The fit for the second green option is, however, markedly worse than for either of the other two.

Given this evidence, the hedger would be nearly indifferent between using short Jun and red Dec as hedging vehicles. The differences in the two options' characteristics are inconsequential. The decision might turn, then, on transactions costs.

Transactions costs tend to favor red Dec in this exercise. Given its higher overall vega, we need fewer red Dec options to do the job than short Jun. In this example, we could sell 155 [= 8961/(1.08 × 53.50)] red Dec options struck at 95.25 or 171 [= 8961/(1.08 × 48.50)] short Jun options struck at 94.75. In these

EXHIBIT 27.7

Second Red, Fourth Short, and Second Green Eurodollar Implied Volatilities As Proxies for Term Swaption Implied Volatility

Weekly Changes, 9/25/98–7/13/01

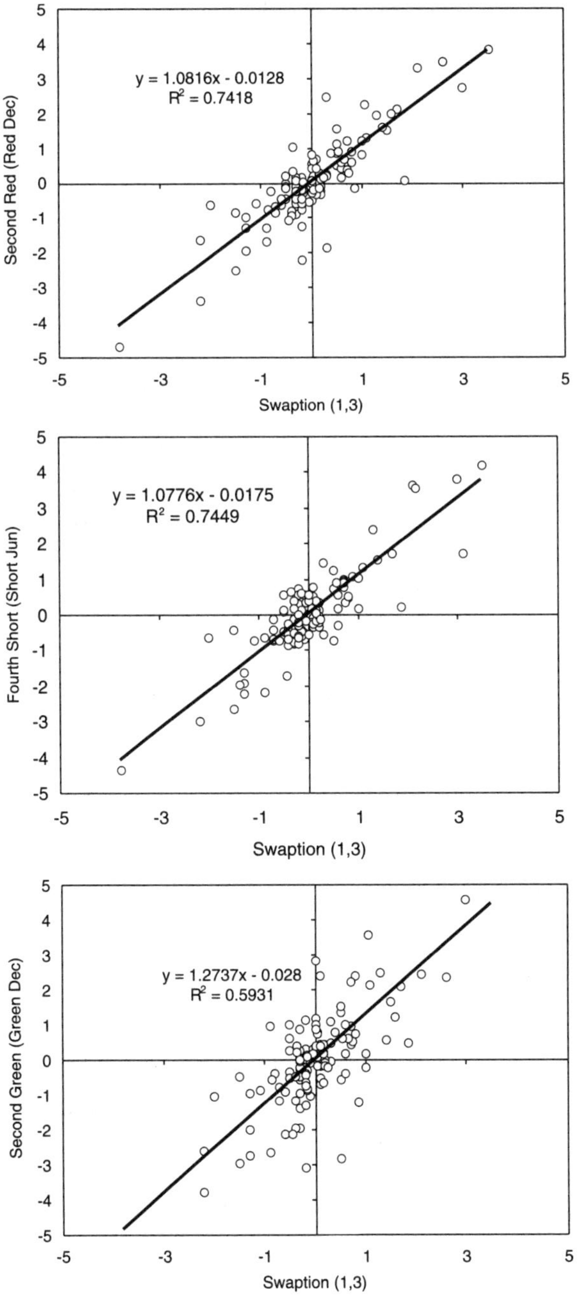

calculations, the options' vegas have been scaled up to reflect the estimated relationships between changes in their implied volatilities and changes in implied swaption volatilities. In both cases, implied volatility for the Eurodollar option tended to change 1.08 percentage points for each 1-percentage-point increase in our proxy swaption volatility (see Exhibit 27.7). The hedger's commission costs would be lower with red Dec than with short Jun. Whether market impact costs (those costs incurred because of bid/ask spreads) would be lower with red Dec would depend on the comparative liquidity of the two markets.

Gamma Mismatch?

Not much. The gamma in the swap/Eurodollar position is comparatively small to begin with, so the resulting mismatch in gamma between the swap and the 151 red Dec options is smaller still. The net gamma of the position would be only 0.173 [$= 0.658 - (151 \times 0.00321)$] if we assume parallel shifts in rates or as little as 0.129 [$= 0.658 - (151 \times 0.00321 \times 1.091)$] if we allow for the fact that changes in the second red futures rate will tend to be larger than changes in a 4-year term rate. In either case, the net gamma in the position would be nearly zero.

The Choice?

In this example, short Jun would nose out red Dec if not for the fact that the red Dec hedge likely would be cheaper to transact. Either option, though, would provide a serviceable hedge for the volatility exposure in the swap/Eurodollar position. And either of these options would be better than green Dec, which is inferior on all counts.

Robustness?

A simple hedge like this cannot be perfectly robust. It cannot capture changes in the slope of the yield curve, for example. Moreover, the vega and gamma of the swap/Eurodollar futures position depend less on the level of rates than do the vega and gamma of Eurodollar options at any given strike price.

To some extent, though, the vega and gamma mismatch would work to the advantage of a hedger who is long volatility in the swap/Eurodollar futures position (i.e., receiving fixed, short Euros) and who is short Eurodollar options as a hedge. If rates changed sharply, the hedger likely would have a position with both positive net vega and gamma and would likely profit as a result. On the other hand, the hedge should work fairly well if rates are stable.

GLOSSARY[1]

ATM At-the-money option. An option is at the money when its strike price is equal to the futures price.

BBA British Bankers' Association. The Chicago Mercantile Exchange uses the BBA's 11 a.m. 3-month LIBOR fixing as the final settlement rate for the Eurodollar futures contract. See BBAISR.

BBAISR British Bankers' Association Interest Settlement Rate.

BBA 3-month LIBOR is "fixed" daily at 11 a.m. London time. The BBA surveys 16 banks and asks them to quote the rate at which they would lend to major participants in the London Eurodollar market. The BBA eliminates the top and bottom quartiles from the survey and averages the remaining quotes. The fixing is rounded up to 5 decimal places when the sixth digit is 5 or greater.

For purposes of settling the Eurodollar futures contract, the British Bankers' Association Interest Settlement Rate (BBAISR) is taken on the second London bank business day immediately preceding the third Wednesday of the contract month. This value is rounded to the nearest 1/10,000 of a percentage point and subtracted from 100 to determine the Eurodollar futures contract final settlement price.

bey Bond Equivalent Yield.

bp Basis point, 0.01%, or 1/100 of a percentage point.

break-even volatility The value of realized volatility at which the cost of paying a long option's theta is just offset by the beneficial effects of gamma combined with the realized change in the option's underlying price or rate. See any good options textbook for a derivation of the "zero profit" condition, holding implied volatility constant.

bundles A 1-, 2-, 3-, 4-, 5-, 6-, 7-, 8-, 9-, or 10-year strip of quarterly cycle Eurodollar futures. A bundle usually begins with the first quarterly contract, but there is also a 5-year bundle 5 years forward.

cabinet trade A trade that allows the liquidation of deep-out-of-the-money options at the "cabinet" or "cab" price. The cabinet price for Eurodollar options is one-quarter tick, or $6.25.

---

1. Certain definitions are taken from the Chicago Mercantile Exchange's glossary and from the Chicago Mercantile Exchange Rulebook, both of which can be found in full at www.cme.com.

calendar spread A calendar spread comprises a long (or short) position in one contract month and a short (or long) position in a subsequent contract month. Eurodollar futures calendar spreads are used to trade the yield curve. Eurodollar option calendar spreads are used to trade the volatility curve or to take advantage of differences in the gamma, theta, and vega characteristics of options with different times to expiration.

CME Chicago Mercantile Exchange.

cones See volatility cones.

correlation A statistical measure of how two variables vary together. When squared, correlation is the fraction of the variance of one variable that can be explained using information about the value of one or more other variables. A negative correlation indicates that the variables change in opposite directions, while a positive correlation indicates that they change in the same direction. Correlations of -1 and 1 describe two variables that are perfectly correlated and for which, knowing the value of one of the variables, one can explain entirely the value of the other. A correlation of 0 indicates no relationship at all. A correlation of 0.5 indicates that 0.25 [$= 0.5^2$], or 25 percent, of the variance of one variable can be explained using the values of the other.

coupon yield curve A curve that plots the values of coupons at which coupon-bearing bonds would trade at par against their respective times to maturity.

CPI Consumer Price Index.

credit spread A measure of the basis point yield spread between a risk-free instrument (i.e., Treasury bills, notes, or bonds) and another instrument.

day-count convention The convention used to calculate the fraction of a year applied to an interest rate calculation. The money market convention is days/360 for the following currencies: U.S. dollar, Euros (€), Japanese yen, and Swiss franc. The money market convention is days/365 for the British pound and Canadian dollar. Other day-count conventions, used in swap interest rate calculations for example, include Act/Act, Act/365, Act/365 (fixed), 30/360, 360/360, Bond Basis, and 30E/360.

delta The change in an option's price given a small 1-unit change in the price of the underlying commodity or futures contract.

duration Duration is a weighted average of the times to a bond or note's cash flows. The weights used in calculating duration are the fraction of the bond's total present value represented by each cash flow.

Modified (or effective) duration typically is defined as the percent change in the full price (i.e., quoted price plus accrued interest) of a bond or note given a 1-percentage-point change in its yield. With a bond that bears regular coupons, the relationship between modified duration and duration is Modified duration $=$ Duration$/(1 + y/n)$, where y is the bond's yield and n is the number of times per year the coupon is paid.

For instruments without regular coupon or principal payments, or for instruments that contain embedded options, the instrument's "effective duration" refers to the percent change in its value given a 1-percentage-point change in its underlying yield. Effective duration makes more sense when discussing Eurodollar futures.

DV01 The dollar value of an "oh-one," or 1-basis-point change in any relevant interest rate. Also known as the DVBP, or dollar value of a basis point. DV01 can represent the change in the (present) value of a bond or swap position given a 1-basis-point change in its yield or some underlying rate. DV01 also can represent the change in any cash flow related to the underlying rate.

e Exponential. Commonly used to calculate future value (i.e., e^{rt}) and present value (i.e., e^{-rt}), where r is a continuously compounded annualized interest rate and t is the number of years in the period.

EBF European Bankers Federation.

ED The trading symbol for Eurodollar futures at the Chicago Mercantile Exchange.

edge The theoretical price of an option versus the market price of an option.

Euribor futures Three-month Euro (€) interest rate futures. This 3-month deposit contract is based on €1,000,000 and has a final settlement price that settles to 100 − 3-month Euribor.

Eurodollar time deposit A dollar deposit with a bank or bank branch outside of the United States or with an international banking facility located in the United States.

expiration date For Eurodollar futures and quarterly options, the second London business day immediately preceding the third Wednesday of the contract month. For serial options, mid-curve options, and 5-year bundle options, the Friday preceding the third Wednesday of the contract month.

expiring contract The futures contract that will expire next.

fair value The fair value of a Eurodollar futures contract is 100 less the fair value of forward 3-month LIBOR with a value date equal to the value date of the futures contract. The fair value of a contract is compared to its traded value to determine if the contract is rich or cheap.

FOMC Federal Open Market Committee.

forward deposit rate The rate associated with a deposit period that begins sometime in the future.

forward term deposit curve Same as a term deposit curve except that the terms begin at some date in the future.

forward yield curve Any yield curve for which time begins at some date in the future.

FRA Forward Rate Agreement. An over-the-counter instrument that is used to lock in a forward-starting short-term interest rate. For example, a 1 × 4 FRA represents a 3-month forward rate (i.e., 4 minus 1) that begins 1 month from now.

The difference between the FRA rate and the prevailing market rate at the start of the FRA determines the net cash flow to one of the counterparties.

front month contract The contract in the quarterly cycle that is nearest expiration.

gamma The change in an option's delta given a small 1-unit change in the price of the underlying commodity or futures contract.

GLOBEX The Chicago Mercantile Exchange's electronic trading platform.

historical volatility Any measure of volatility that has been estimated using historical prices or interest rates. Historical volatility typically is calculated as a standard deviation of price or rate changes and is a measure of how volatile the underlying price or rate has been in the past.

IMM swap A type of swap with reset dates that fall on Eurodollar futures expiration dates and with payment dates that fall approximately 3 months later on the following Eurodollar futures value dates.

implied volatility The value of volatility that sets an option's theoretical price equal to its market price. As such, implied volatility is implied both by the market price of the option and by the theoretical model used. Implied volatility can be thought of as a market forecast of how volatile the underlying price or rate will be over the remaining life of the option.

initial peformance bond The minimum performance bond deposit required from customers for each contract when a futures position is opened.

interest rate swap An agreement under which the two sides to the transaction agree to exchange cash based on hypothetical interest calculations. The most commonly traded swap is a fixed/floating swap under which one side agrees to pay a fixed rate on a specified notional principal amount, while the other side agrees to pay a floating rate on the same notional amount.

ITM In-the-money option. A call is in the money when its strike price is less than the futures price. A put is in the money when its strike price is greater than the futures price.

kurtosis One measure of the shape of the distribution relative to the normal distribution. The kurtosis of the normal distribution is 3.00. Positive excess kurtosis is the value of a distribution's kurtosis that exceeds 3.00 and describes a distribution with fat tails and a tightly bunched center.

lead contract The most active futures contract. The lead contract is designated by where it trades on the floor of the Chicago Mercantile Exchange. The lead contract may or may not be the same as the expiring contract.

LIBID London Interbank Bid Rate. The rate that the most creditworthy international banks dealing in Eurodollars pay for deposits.

LIBOR London Interbank Offered Rate. The rate that the most creditworthy international banks dealing in Eurodollars charge each other for large loans.

LIFFE London International Financial Futures and Options Exchange.

Ln The natural log mathematical function.

maintenance margin See maintenance performance bond.

maintenance performance bond A sum, usually smaller than the initial performance bond, which must remain on deposit in the customer's account for any position. Previously referred to as maintenance margin.

mark to market Marking a position to market requires valuing all positions, and hence all gains and losses, at market prices. Can also refer to the daily adjustment of the performance bond account to reflect gains and losses.

mid-curve options Quarterly 1-year mid-curve options expire 12 months before their underlying futures contract. For 1-year mid-curve options that expire in months other than those in the March quarterly cycle (i.e., January, February, April, May, July, August, October, and November), the underlying futures contract is the futures contract that expires 12 calendar months from the next March quarterly month that is nearest to the expiration of the option. For example, the underlying futures contract for the 1-year mid-curve option that expires in January or February is the March futures contract in the next calendar year.

For 2-year mid-curve options, the underlying futures contract is the contract that expires 24 calendar months after the month in which the option expires.

money market instrument Any of a number of short-term interest rate instruments, including bank deposits, commercial paper, and bankers acceptances.

MOS Mutual Offset System. The Eurodollar futures contracts traded at the Chicago Mercantile Exchange and the Singapore Exchange are considered fungible instruments. The two exchanges use the Mutual Offset System to allow Eurodollar futures contracts traded at one exchange to offset Eurodollar futures contracts traded at the other exchange. Also, open positions at one exchange can be transferred to the other exchange.

NAPM National Association of Purchasing Management.

Nominal value of an 01 See DV01. Usually refers to the actual change in a forward cash flow.

on the run See OTR.

open interest The total number of contracts outstanding that have not yet been offset or have not yet expired.

OTC Over the counter. An instrument that is traded directly between two counterparties rather than on an exchange.

OTM Out-of-the-money option. A call is out of the money when its strike price is greater than the futures price. A put is out of the money when its strike price is less than the futures price.

OTR On the run. The Treasury's most recently issued note/bond for a given maturity. The on-the-run issues tend to be the most liquid.

over the counter See OTC.

packs A series of 4 quarterly cycle Eurodollar futures contracts. The packs trade according to the color-coded grid developed by the Chicago Mercantile Exchange. The "whites" are the first pack to trade, followed by the "reds," "greens," "blues," and so on. Packs can begin with any specified contract month, e.g., 2nd red would refer to a 4-contract strip beginning with the 6th quarterly Eurodollar contract.

performance bond Funds that must be deposited by a customer with his or her broker; by a broker with a clearing member; or by a clearing member with the Clearing House. The performance bond helps to ensure the financial integrity of brokers, clearing members, and the Exchange as a whole. Previously referred to as margin.

PV01 The present (or price) value of a 1-basis-point change in rates. To convert the nominal value of a basis point to a PV01, multiply the change in cash flow by the price of a zero-coupon bond that matures on the forward cash flow date.

quarterly contracts Contract months with expirations in March, June, September, and December.

R^2 *R*-squared. In a regression of one variable (y) on one or more other variables (x), the R^2 of the regression is the fraction of the variance of y (the dependent variable) that can be explained using one or more x (independent) variables. R^2 values range from 0 to 1.

realized volatility Calculated the same way as historical volatility but with a starting date equal to an option's trade date. Realized volatility is a measure of how volatile the market proves to be during the time following an option trade and can be compared with the option's initial implied volatility to determine the potential *ex post* profitability of the trade.

Rulebook The Chicago Mercantile Exchange Rulebook is a complex document that covers all aspects of trading, settlement, performance bonds, etc. For the most recent version of the Rulebook, go to www.cme.com.

semiannual bond equivalent yield (SA BEY) The standard yield quote for U.S. Treasury bonds and notes.

serial contracts Contract months with expirations outside of the quarterly cycle. Serial futures and options contracts expire in January, February, April, May, July, August, October, and November.

serial options Option contract months with expirations outside of the quarterly cycle. Serial contract months expire in January, February, April, May, July, August, October, and November. Serial options are on the next following quarterly futures contract (e.g., the July option on the September futures).

settlement date In the Eurodollar time deposit market, the date on which interest begins accruing. The standard settlement period is two London business days for all terms except overnight (O/N) and tomorrow next (T/N), which settle same day and next day, respectively.

SGX Singapore Exchange (formerly the Singapore International Monetary Exchange, SIMEX).

spot deposit rate See term deposit rate.

stacks A technique used in the Eurodollar futures market where a single contract is executed in place of a series of contracts along the yield curve. The benefits of trading a stack are liquidity and ease of execution.

standard deviation A statistical measure of the spread of any distribution of a random variable. For the normal distribution, a range of 1 standard deviation above and below the mean includes about 68 percent of the outcomes; 2 standard deviations up and down captures about 95 percent of the outcomes; and 3 standard deviations includes about 99.7 percent of the outcomes.

In options markets, volatility is expressed as an annualized standard deviation of changes in the underlying price or rate.

straddles Long straddle: Long a call option and long a put option at the same strike price and with the same time to expiration. A long straddle is a volatility trade that profits, if delta neutral, when realized volatility exceeds implied or expected volatility. A short straddle tends to make money when the underlying market is less volatile than expected by option traders.

strangles Long strangle: Usually long an out-of-the money call and long an out-of the money put with the same time to expiration. Because the options are out of the money, the price of a strangle is less than the price of a straddle. Strangles often are used by traders who think that the underlying price will settle within the two strike prices (in which case they sell the strangles) or will settle outside of the two strike prices (those who are long the strangles).

stub rate The term deposit rate that runs from today until the first Eurodollar futures value date.

swaption An option on a fixed/floating interest rate swap with a specified fixed rate that begins on a specified forward date.

TED spread The spread between Treasury and Eurodollar rates. The TED spread is a measure of the credit spread between LIBOR (i.e., high-grade bank debt) and Treasury debt. The original TED was the price spread between 3-month

T-bill futures and Eurodollar futures, which would equal the difference between the implied Eurodollar and Treasury bill futures rates.

term deposit curve A curve that plots term deposit yields against time to maturity.

term deposit rate In the LIBOR market, deposit rates for terms that range from overnight to 10 years. With the exception of overnight (O/N) and tomorrow next (T/N), the value date for term deposits is 2 (London) business days from the transaction date. Also known as spot deposit rate.

term structure of deposit rates A graph or table of spot deposit rates versus maturity of deposit. The graph of this data produces a yield curve.

term structure of volatility A graph or table of volatilities versus maturity of instrument.

term TED spread The spread between the rates implied by a strip of Eurodollar futures and the yield on a Treasury note.

terminal wealth The value to which one dollar invested today, at a defined sequence of rates and with a complete reinvestment of periodic principal and interest, will grow as of a given date in the future. Terminal wealth can be calculated from a stub rate and consecutive Eurodollar futures rates. The inverse of terminal wealth is the zero-coupon price, or present value, of $1 to be received on the terminal wealth date.

theta The change in the option price given the passing of 1 day.

value date The value date for a Eurodollar futures contract is 2 London business days following its expiration date. In other words, the value date is the third Wednesday of the contract month.

variation margin Describes the cash that is paid into or out of an account to reflect changes in the market value of the position.

vega The change in the option price given a 1-percentage-point increase in the option's implied volatility.

vega-weighted spread trade An option volatility spread trade that is structured so that the long and short options provide equal but offsetting vegas. This ensures that the trade returns the same profit (or loss) if the volatility spread changes, regardless of whether volatilities rise or fall.

volatility A measurement of the variability, usually expressed as a standard deviation, of the underlying Eurodollar futures rate. Volatility is usually measured as a relative rate volatility (i.e., a change in the rate as a percent of the underlying rate), but can be measured in actual, or basis point, rate changes. Volatility can be historical, implied, or realized.

volatility cone A graphical representation of the maximum and minimum *n*-period historical volatilities estimated over any given history of prices or interest rates. Especially useful for gauging the richness or cheapness of options with different remaining times to expiration.

volume (of trading) The total number of contracts traded during any given trading period.

yield to maturity The internal rate of return that sets the present value of a bond's cash flows (i.e., coupon and principal payments) equal to its full price.

zero-coupon bond A bond that bears no coupons. Its price is less than 100 before maturity and 100 at maturity.

zero-coupon price The present value of one dollar for the stated term. A forward cash flow multiplied by the associated zero-coupon price gives the cash flow's present value.

zero-coupon yield curve A curve that plots yields from zero-coupon bonds versus time to maturity.

The shortest end of a dollar-based zero-coupon curve might be calculated from Eurodollar term deposit rates; the middle of the curve from Eurodollar futures rates; and the long end of the curve from interest rate swap rates. When properly constructed, zero-coupon yield curves can be used to calculate the present value of any cash flow on any date and to calculate forward interest rates between any two forward dates. Zero-coupon yield curves are the most basic building blocks for financial engineers.

INDEX

Assets:
fixed rate, 113

Bonds:
coupon-bearing, 4, 82
non-callable, 120
performance, 29, 37
U.S. Treasury, 4
zero-coupon, 4, 21, 72, 78, 80, 103, 177
Brazilian Mercantile & Futures Exchange (BM&F), 20
British Bankers' Association, 16, 35
British Bankers' Association Interest Settlement Rate (BBAISR), 34
Bundles, 8, 36, 133, 249–279
correlating value with Treasury notes, 264
decorrelation, 269
defined, 255
pricing, 260

Calendar spread, 313
behavior, 316
fair value, 314
implied financing rate, 314
value, 313
Callable agency notes, 133, 281–310
call protection, 281, 303–306
delta hedging, 287, 290, 299–301
hedging, 291
Eurodollar futures for hedging, 306–310
exposure, 284, 286
structuring a hedge, 286–291
synthetic forward notes, 288
value, 285
yield spread, 301–303
Cash flow method:
for hedging swaps, 106–111
for pricing swaps, 101–106
Cash settlement, 14
Certificate of deposit (CD) futures, 6–17
Chase Manhattan Bank, 8, 9, 16
Chicago Board of Trade (CBOT), 7, 12, 13, 14, 20
Chicago Mercantile Exchange (CME), 1, 7, 8, 11, 13, 14, 16, 20, 29, 34, 349, 405
GLOBEX, 8, 29, 36, 38, 356
Interest Rate Committee, 13
Citibank, 6, 7
Commercial paper
ninety-day, 12
thirty-day, 13
Compression risk:
hedging, 281–310
Continental Illinois, 8, 9, 16
Contract colors, 252
Contract specifications, 29–36, 355–362
assignment, 362
contract month symbols, 32
contract unit, 30, 355
exercise of option, 360
expiring contract, 33
last trading day, 35, 360
lead contract, 33
listed contract months, 30, 358
minimum fluctuation, 30, 357
mutual offset, 34
price limits, 356
price quote, 30, 355
settlement price, final, 34
strike price increments, 357
tick size, 30, 357
tick value, 356
trading hours, 34, 360
value dates, 36
Convexity bias, 117–125, 131, 135–178, 179–183, 404
bond equivalent yield, semiannual, 176
Carr Futures estimates, new series correcting, 185–188
"Daily Zero to Ten," Carr Futures report, 189–194
defined, 179
in Eurodollar futures (*see* Convexity bias in Eurodollar futures)

Convexity bias (*Cont.*):
greeks, 124, 132, 181–183
term TED spreads, 211
Convexity bias in Eurodollar futures, 135–178
continuously compounded yield, 177
correlation of rates, 148
drift, 159
Eurodollar futures, 137–147, 152–154
Eurodollar profit and loss, 174
Eurodollar strip rates, 175–178
forward swap rates, 168
hedge profit and loss, 174
hedge ratio, 173
hedging (*see* Hedging convexity bias in Eurodollar futures)
interest rate swaps, 137–147, 152–154
market's experience with, 169–170
mispricing, 170
money market strip yield, 176
pricing term swaps, 166–168
rule of thumb for calculating, 154–166, 172–175
semiannual bond equivalent yield, 176
swap book, 170
swap profit and loss, 173
swap rates, implied, 175, 177–178
swap value, 172–173
term TED spreads, 171
time to contract expiration, 158
value of, 147–152
volatility arbitrage, 171
zero-coupon bond price, 177
Coupon-bearing bonds, 4
hedging, 82
pricing, 82

Delta hedging, 287, 290, 299–301
costs, 299
risks, 299
Discount Corporation of New York Futures, 1
Drysdale, 8, 9

Eurodollar futures, 3, 11–20
calls and puts, 349
contract (*see* Eurodollar futures contracts)
convexity bias (*see* Convexity bias in Eurodollar futures)
Eurodollar futures (*Cont.*):
and Eurodollar time deposit (*see* Eurodollar time deposit)
hedging (*see* Hedging with Eurodollar futures)
hedging callable agency notes, 306–310
performance bonds, 29, 37
and term TED spreads, 197
volume and open interest, 29, 38
Eurodollar futures contracts, 29–41
contract specifications, 29–36 (*see also* Contract specifications)
volume and open interest, 38–41
Eurodollar market, 3–20
CD futures, 16–17
and Eurodollars, 9–11
Eurodollar futures, 11–16
finance revolution, 3–5
futures revolution, 5–6
interest rate derivatives, 17–20
money market developments, 6–9
Eurodollar options, 349–401, 403–451
caps, 375–379
cash settlement, 400–401
contract specifications, 355–362 (*see also* Contract specifications)
early exercise, 399–400
expirations, 351–355
five-year bundle options, 355
floors, 375–379
implied rate distributions, 395–397
implied volatility, 370, 381
mid-curve options, 352, 403, 405–427 (*see also* Trading with serial and mid-curve Eurodollar options)
pricing, 363–365
risk, 371–374 (*see also* Risk parameters)
serial 1-year mid-curve options, 409
serial options, 352, 403, 405–427 (*see also* Trading with serial and mid-curve Eurodollar options)
standard quarterly options, 352, 409
term structure of rate volatility, 386–389
underlying futures, 351–355
volatility, 365–370, 381–397, 404 (*see* Eurodollar volatility; Volatility)
volatility calendar spread trade, 389–390
volatility cones, 390–393
volatility skews, 393–395

Eurodollar time deposit, 21, 23–27
  interest calculations, 25–27
  LIBID, 23
  LIBOR, 23
  maturities and settlement, 23–25
  quotes, 23, 25
Eurodollar volatility, 365–370, 381–397, 404, 429–439
  basis point volatility, 429–439
  and Federal Reserve, 433–434
  measurement of, 430
  and rate levels, 430–431
  relative rate volatility, 429–439
  the turn, 335–338
  and World Trade Center attack, 429–430
Eurodollar yield:
  implied, 228
  unweighted, 199
  weighted, 199
Extension risk, 133
  hedging, 281–310
Exchange-traded market, 5, 18

Fair value, 54
Federal Reserve Board, 4, 6, 7, 8, 11
  and Eurodollar volatility, 433–434
  Regulation Q, 6
Forward interest rates, 43–53
  and convexity bias, 117, 168
  deriving, 44–52
Forward markets, distinguished from futures markets, 51–54
Forward notes
  pricing, 294
  synthetic, 288
Forward-starting term deposit curves, 65–67
Forward valuing, 75
Friedman, Milton, 7
Futures contracts:
  certificate of deposit (CD), 6–17
  Euribor, 39, 427
  EuroDM, 41
  EuroLira, 39, 427
  Euroyen, 41
  MIBOR, 41
  PIBOR, 39
  Short Sterling, 41, 427
Futures interest rates, 43, 53–67
  as break-even rates, 59–63
  convexity, 117
  deriving present and forward values from, 71
  forward-starting term deposit curves, 65
  futures contract, fair value of, 54–57
  richness and cheapness, 57–58
  yield curve trades, 63–65
Futures markets, distinguished from forward markets, 51–54

GLOBEX, 8, 29, 36, 38, 356
Greeks, convexity bias, 124, 132, 181–183

Hedge ratio, 70, 80, 109, 111, 113, 173
  calculating, 216–241
  forward term TED spreads, 240
  futures hedge ratios, 297
  managing, 85–87
  spot market hedge ratios, 297
  term TED spreads, 207, 211
  terminal wealth, 217
  unweighted strip spreads, 236
  weighted Eurodollar strip hedges, 237
Hedging:
  callable agency notes, 286–291
  compression risk in callable agency notes, 281–310
  convexity bias (*see* Hedging convexity bias)
  delta, 287, 290, 299–301
  with Eurodollar futures (*see* Hedging with Eurodollar futures)
  Eurodollar futures for hedging callable agency notes, 306–310
  extension risk in callable agency notes, 133, 281–310
  horizon, 268
  interest rate risk, 320
  interest rate swaps (*see* Interest rate swaps)
  scaling hedge, 271
  stacks, packs, and bundles, 133, 249–279
  stub period, 88, 343–346
Hedging convexity bias, 404, 441–451
  convexity/gamma exposure, 442
  Eurodollar options, 445

Hedging convexity bias (*Cont.*):
- four-year swap/Eurodollar position, 442–451
- gamma, 442, 450
- rate horizons, 442
- robustness, 450
- vega, 444

Hedging with Eurodollar futures, 69–94
- algebra, 70–71
- coupon bonds, 82
- credit spreads, 93
- date mismatches, 91
- deriving present and forward values, 71–74
- forward cash flows, 74–78
- forward valuing, 75
- hedge ratio, 70, 80, 85–87
- practical considerations, 87–94
- present values of cash flows, 78–85
- present valuing, 77, 78
- stub period, 88, 343–346
- term mismatches, 91
- whole contracts, 93
- zero-coupon bonds, 72, 78, 80, 81

Hong Kong Futures Exchange (HKEx), 20

Hypothetical securities method:
- for hedging swaps, 112–116
- for pricing swaps, 111–112

Interest rate derivatives, 4, 17–20
- exchange-traded money market futures, 18–20
- forward rates, 4, 19
- futures, 4, 19
- over-the-counter interest rate swaps, 18
- swaps, 19
- worldwide markets, 20

Interest rate risk, 143, 313, 320

Interest rate swaps, 95–129
- basis point, value of, 140
- cash flows, 97
- convexity, 117–125
- day-count conventions, 98
- and Eurodollar futures, 137–147
- fixed, 96–100, 105
- floating, 96–100, 105
- forward, 138
- forward-starting, 98
- global, 17, 18, 19
- hedging, 100–101, 106–111, 116–117, 442–451

Interest rate swaps (*Cont.*):
- implied rates, 177
- interest rate risk, 143
- notional principal amount, 97
- off-the-market, 116–117
- options on, 19
- over-the-counter, 18
- periodicity, 97
- pricing, 100–106, 111–112, 116–117
- spot, 98
- U.S., 17, 18, 19
- value of basis point, 140
- yield curves, 125–129 (*see also* Yield curves)
- yields, 98

Interest rates
- calculations, 23, 25
- forward, 43–53
- futures, 43, 53–67
- risk, 143, 313, 320
- short-term, 7
- swaps (*see* Interest rate swaps)
- term deposit, 44

International banking facility (IBF), 22

International Monetary Market (IMM), 30

Korea Futures Exchange (KOFEX), 20

Liability:
- fixed rate, 74
- floating, 74, 112

London Interbank Bid Rate (LIBID), 23, 25

London Interbank Offered Rate (LIBOR), 3, 23, 25
- calendar spread, 324, 333
- volatilities, effect of the turn on, 335–338

London International Financial Futures and Options Exchange (LIFFE), 20, 29
- serial and mid-curve options, 407, 425, 427

Markets:
- Eurodollar (*see* Eurodollar market)
- exchange-traded, 5, 18
- over-the-counter, 4, 18

Markowitz, Harry M., 4

Miller, Merton H., 4

Modigliani, Franco, 4

Money market deposit accounts, creation of, 6
Money markets:
  British pound, 26
  Canadian dollar, 26
  developments in, 6–11
  Euro, 26
  futures, 18–20
  rates, 127
  returns, 313
  strip yield, 176
  Swiss franc, 26
  U.S. dollar, 26
Montréal Exchange, 20

New York Futures Exchange (NYFE), 7, 12, 13, 14

Options:
  forward rates, 19
  futures, 19
  mid-curve, 352, 403, 405–427 (*see also* Trading with serial and mid-curve Eurodollar options)
  serial, 352, 403, 405–427 (*see also* Trading with serial and mid-curve Eurodollar options)
  swaps, 19
Over-the-counter market, 4, 18, 19
  caps, 19
  swaptions, 19
  Treasury options, 407, 419–424

Packs, 8, 36, 133, 249–279
  correlating value with Treasury notes, 264
  decorrelation, 269
  defined, 255
  pricing, 260
  proxies, 267
Positive carry trades, 59
Present valuing, 77, 78
Pricing, 82
  and convexity bias, 166–168
  Eurodollar options, 363–365
  interest rate swaps (*see* Interest rate swaps)
  mispricing, 170
  packs and bundles, 260

Quote practices:
  price level for individual contracts, 258–259
  pricing packs and bundles, 259–263
  ticks, 257–258

Regulation Q, 6
Replicating (*see* Hedging with Eurodollar futures)
Risk
  compression, 281–310
  extension, 133, 281–310
Risk parameters, 371–374
  delta, 372
  gamma, 372, 442, 450
  intrinsic and time value, 374
  rho, 373
  theta, 373
  vega, 372, 444

S&P 500 calendar roll, 134, 311–321
  calendar spread, 313–317
  cash management, 320–321
  interest rate exposure, 317–320
  interest rate risk, 313
  money market returns, 313
  portfolio replication, 320–321
Securities
  mortgage-backed, 4
Singapore Exchange (SGX), 20, 29, 34
Spreads:
  calendar, 313–317
  between callable notes and Treasury notes, 301–303
  credit, 93
  Eurodollar, 334
  LIBOR calendar, 324, 333
  against over-the-counter Treasury options, 407
  spread trades, evaluating, 338–342
  swap, 212–216
  term TED, 132, 171, 195–241, 243–247 (*see also* Term TED spreads)
  time decay, 413
  two-year note, 244
  unweighted strip, 236
  volatility calendar spread trade, 389–390
  volatility curve, 415

Spreads (*Cont.*):
  yield, 301–303
  yield curve, 410
Stacks, 133, 249–279
  correlating value with Treasury notes, 264
  decorrelation, 269
Stub rate, 209, 219, 343
Swap spreads, 212–216
Swaps (*see* Interest rate swaps)
Sydney Futures Exchange (SGX), 20

Term deposit rates, 44
Term TED spreads, 132, 171, 195–241, 243–247
  calculating, 199, 216–241
  carry and convergence, 210
  convexity, 171, 211
  curve-augmented, 251, 272–279
  date mismatches, 221
  directionality, 204–206
  discount factor, 222
  and Eurodollar futures prices, 197
  Eurodollar strip yields, 199, 224
  evaluation of, 211
  financing, 209
  fixed spread to Eurodollars (weighted), 230
  forward term, 211–212, 232–235, 240, 244
  hedge ratios, 207, 216–241
  history of, 197
  hybrid spread, 274
  as measure of credit spread, 195–196
  simple, 197
  stub rate, 209, 219
  swap spreads, 212–216
  terminal wealth, 217, 223
  trading, 206–211
  and Treasury bills, 197
  Treasury payment dates, 222
  Treasury yields, 199, 224
  two-year note spreads, 244
  value dates, 219
  zero-coupon note prices, 217–219
Terminal wealth, 72, 73, 89, 103, 217, 223
Ticks, 257–258
  contract specifications, 30, 357
  Eurodollar options, 357
Tokyo International Financial Futures Exchange (TIFFE), 20, 29

Trading:
  curve TEDs, 272–279
  with mid-curve Eurodollar options (*see* Trading with serial and mid-curve Eurodollar options)
  with serial Eurodollar options (*see* Trading with serial and mid-curve Eurodollar options)
  stacks, packs, and bundles, 133, 249–279
  the turn, 134, 323–342, 343–350
Trading with serial and mid-curve Eurodollar options, 405–427
  Eurodollar strategy triangle, 406, 410–417
  Eurodollar volatility spread trading, 419–424
  London International Financial Futures and Options Exchange (LIFFE), 427
  over-the-counter Treasury options, 407, 419–424
  serial 1-year mid-curve options, 409
  spreads against over-the-counter Treasury options, 407
  standard quarterly options, 408
  time decay spread, 413
  Treasury volatility spread trading, 419–424
  volatility curve spread, 415
  volatility horizons, 417–418
  volatility trades, 407
  yield curve spread, 410
Treasury yield, 199
  spread between callable agency notes and Treasury notes, 301–303
  unweighted, 224
  weighted, 228
Turn, the:
  defined, 323, 325
  effects on futures prices, 328–333
  effects on LIBOR and Eurodollar volatilities, 335–338
  "Eurodollar and LIBOR Turn Report," Carr Futures report, 343
  Eurodollar spread (December/March), 334
  four-day, 325
  hedging the stub, 343–347
  implications for futures spreads, 333–335

Turn, the (*Cont.*):
 implied turn rates, 332
 LED spread (December), 333
 LIBOR spread (December/January), 333
 monitoring, 343–346
 rate behavior, 326–328
 rules of thumb, 330–332
 spread trades, evaluating, 338–342
 TED spread (December), 334
 three-day, 325
 trading,134, 323–342, 343–350
 turn-rate volatility, value of, 338
 two-day, 325

Value dates, 217
Volatility, 365–370, 381–397, 404
 break-even, 381
 cones, 390–393, 430, 438
 curve spread, 415
 Eurodollar (*see* Eurodollar volatility)
 Eurodollar volatility spread trading, 419–424
 historical, 381
 horizons, 417–418
 implied, 370
 implied rate distributions, 395–397
 maturity structure, 390–393
 period, 368
 realized, 381
 relative rate, 366
 skews, 393–395
 term structure of Eurodollar rate volatility, 386–389
Volatility (*Cont.*):
 trades, 407
 Treasury volatility spread trading, 419–424
 turn-rate, value of, 338
 volatility calendar spread trade, 389–390
 yield curve trade, 389
Volcker, Paul, 4, 7, 13

Yield curves, 18, 21, 125–129
 coupon yield curve, 43
 forward rate curve, 43, 125
 inversion, 4
 par coupon curve, 125
 spread, 410
 trades, 63–65, 389
 zero-coupon curve, 43, 125
Yields
 bond, 127
 bond equivalent yield, semiannual, 176
 continuously compounded, 177
 Eurodollar, 199, 224
 money market rates, 127
 money market strip yield, 176
 spread, between callable notes and Treasury notes, 301–303
 Treasury, 199, 224

Zero-coupon bonds, 4, 21,103
 calculating price, 72, 78
 finding hedge, 80
 price, 177
Zero-coupon note prices, 217

ABOUT THE AUTHOR

Galen Burghardt, Ph.D., is senior vice president and director of research for Carr Futures. Formerly a senior vice president for Dean Witter Institutional Futures as well as vice president of financial research for the Chicago Mercantile Exchange, he has also served in the research division of the Federal Reserve Board. Dr. Burghardt is an adjunct professor of finance at the University of Chicago Graduate School of Business, where he teaches a popular MBA course on financial futures, swaps, and options.